Hearts of Darkness

Hearts of Darkness

JAMES TAYLOR, JACKSON BROWNE, CAT STEVENS, AND THE UNLIKELY RISE OF THE SINGER-SONGWRITER

DAVE THOMPSON

Backbeat Books

An Imprint of Hal Leonard Corporation

Published in 2012 by Backbeat Books
An Imprint of Hal Leonard Corporation
7777 West Bluemound Road
Milwaukee, WI 53213

Trade Book Division Editorial Offices
33 Plymouth St., Montclair, NJ 07042

Book design by Publishers' Design and Production Services, Inc.

Printed in the United States of America

Library of Congress Cataloging-in-Publication Data

Thompson, Dave, 1960 Jan. 3-
  Hearts of darkness : James Taylor, Jackson Browne, Cat Stevens, and the unlikely rise of the singer-songwriter / Dave Thompson.
      p. cm.
  Includes bibliographical references and index.
  ISBN 978-1-61713-031-1
  1. Taylor, James, 1948- 2. Browne, Jackson. 3. Stevens, Cat, 1948- 4. Popular music--
History and criticism. I. Title.
  ML3470.T53 2012
  781.64092'273--dc23

                          2011047484

www.backbeatbooks.com

CONTENTS

CONTENTS

INTRODUCTION

In October 1966, *Time* magazine published a one-page feature titled "The New Troubadours," celebrating the birth of literacy and sensitivity in the world of rock 'n' roll. Five years later, in winter 1971, *Who Put the Bomp* printed "James Taylor Marked for Death," which incorporated journalist Lester Bangs's carefully considered plea for literacy and sensitivity to be packed back into the classroom . . . or buried in a pit . . . or thrown off a cliff. Anything, as long as they were finally shut up.

"Hate to come on like a Nazi," the bellicose Bangs snarled. "But if I hear one more 'Jesus-walking-the-boys-and-girls-down-a-Carolina-path-while-the-dilemma-of-existence-crashes-like-a-slab-of-hod-on-J.T.'s-shoulders' song, I will drop everything . . . and hop the first Greyhound to Carolina for the signal satisfaction of breaking off a bottle of Ripple and twisting it into James Taylor's guts until he expires in a spasm of adenoidal poesy."

This book (which actually agrees with *Time*'s point of view, but has the Ripple on hand just in case) is the story of what happened in between those two extremes, which means that events later in the performers' lives, no matter how much retrospective light they may shed on the events retold here, are not a part of this tale. Jackson Browne's first wife has yet to commit suicide. James Taylor has yet to clean up. Cat Stevens has yet to convert to Islam and endorse the fatwah issued against Salman Rushdie.

Those are tales to be told another time, in another book, because this one is about something else entirely. This is the story of the music that ensured those later events would even be noticed; of the days of struggle, growth, and breakthrough that must take place before "fame" can be consolidated and "celebrity" developed; and the story, too, of the lives and lifestyles that contributed to those factors, as they in turn became a part of a wider tapestry, a musical story that for a couple of years at the dawn of the 1970s was set to completely rewire all predictions for the new decade.

Few people, and even fewer music historians, today truly bother to distance the singer-songwriter explosion of 1970–71 from the events and movements that either preceded or followed it, a state of affairs based largely on the continuity and longevity enjoyed by the best of its progenitors— among whom James Taylor, Cat Stevens, and Jackson Browne are irrefutably numbered. Yet the first two, Taylor and Stevens, shook away the trappings of the genre that they created at almost the first opportunity they were given; and the third, Browne, never saw himself slipping into their company in the first place.

True, not one of the three would so completely reinvent himself as did Elton John and Neil Young, two other performers who burst through on the same wave of introspective one-man balladeering, and from much the same launching pad, too. Neither, despite their longevity, have their personal legends attained the same peaks as that of Bob Dylan, whose own raison d'être, long before the term was coined, placed him in much the same vein of singer-songwriterdom as they.

Indeed, while those other performers could be said to have continued growing and developing throughout their careers, to the point where a new album from Neil Young or Bob Dylan remains as likely to excite controversy and comment as any older classic, it could be argued that Stevens, Taylor, and Browne have remained relatively static in the years since they unshackled themselves from their earliest burden. It is unlikely that there will ever be a *Modern Times* or *Le Noise* from these quarters.

But all have continued, albeit with some disruption and delay, to make music; all have retained and expanded upon their original musical following; and all have, once those adjustments were made, remained true to the notions that they started out with, to write and sing songs that speak straight to the soul of the listener. Baby James is *still* sweet, Jamaica *still* says she will, and the peace train is *still* on a straight track.

This book tells how they reached those points in the first place.

PROLOGUE

But Satisfaction Brought Him Back

Cat Stevens had suffered from writer's block before, but early in the New Year of 1973, he acknowledged that, finally, he had reached a stopping point. He was still writing songs; that faucet had never stopped dripping. But they were the same songs he'd always been writing, and he was sick of singing songs like that. He'd already made the decision to drop all his older numbers from his live show, but what was the sense in that if the new ones he was penning slipped seamlessly into their place?

He wanted to make a new album; his public demanded it, his record label suggested it, and his own work ethic insisted upon it. But it had to be something new, something different. He had now made six Cat Stevens albums. It was time to make a different one.

Three decades later, he looked back on that dilemma and laughed. "I realized it was all going terribly wrong, or a little bit out of control. So I did another whole 'let's do something different' thing. And I went to Jamaica and made *Foreigner*."

Foreigner is the album that banged the last nail into a musical coffin whose contents had been awaiting burial for a couple of years, but which—with the same tenacity that always attends the music industry's refusal to acknowledge the passing of its greatest cash cows—had been clinging to life regardless.

The cult of the singer-songwriter was a short-lived one but a powerful one as well. It was born of the folk scenes that devoured early-1960s America and late-1960s Britain, but eschewed the most common methodology of both (Arran sweaters, bushy beards, fingers in the ear, and a nearly nasal twang notwithstanding) in favor of a contemporary beat, a cosmopolitan sheen, and a lyrical thesaurus that was predicated almost exclusively around the word *I*. Or *me*.

"I've Got a Thing About Seeing My Grandson Grow Old."

"Let Me Ride."

"I Thought I Was a Child."

"I Want to Live in a Wigwam."

"Hey Mister, That's Me . . . ."

"Places in My Past."

"I've seen fire and I've seen rain . . . ."

These were not rock 'n' roll songs, although they would be filed in the "rock" section in the record store. But neither were they a part of any of the other musical genres that the music press of the day tried to file things into. They weren't pop, they weren't vaudeville, they weren't even (although they didn't always admit it) middle-of-the-road. They weren't country and they weren't folk. They were just *there*, a handful at first that drifted past your ears, a little laconic, a little bit sad, a touch of melancholy and a slice of psychiatry.

And the people who wrote the songs, well, they were a little laconic, a little bit sad, and a touch melancholic as well, and a few of them had been treated by psychiatrists too—which, said their supporters, was what gave them the right to psychoanalyze the rest of us; to question the standards by which we passed our lives and suggest alternate ways of living and giving.

None of which sounds like something—or anything—that could ever have set the world afire. But then you look at the charts for the first years of the seventies, and you realize that the world wasn't simply burning, it was consumed by an uncontrollable conflagration, a wildfire that swept in from so many different directions that even the firemen turned out to be arsonists, and the only thing that could stop the flames was the flames themselves.

By 1973, a lot of the fury had already been damped down, and the majority of the most egregious singer-songwriters had either faded away or not really flickered into life in the first place. There was the handful of names that everybody knew, who were the true kings of the musical heap, and they were still making records that sold. But beyond them there were dozens who never took off, or who scored a minor hit or two and then drifted away to a new life in plumbing or highway maintenance.

And then there was Cat Stevens, who had been in on the boom long before it was heard, and had been trying to claw his way out of it ever since. Six albums into a lifetime of almost painfully thoughtful lyricism, four albums into a career as the college campus bard whom everyone sang along with, Stevens was tired of his music, tired of his reputation, and tired especially of still being lumped in with the same sordid band of sad-sack sorry balladeers.

So it was time to do something about it. Something so raw, so radical, and, by his standards, so brutal that even if he'd recanted the next day and returned once more to his old benign self, the shock waves would still be reverberating.

It was during the U.S. leg of his 1972 world tour that he told *Stereo Review* magazine, "My next LP . . . is very different from the others. Some people will like it, and other people will not. I've got this sound people associate with me, and yet I want to move and change. What I want them to see in all my work is clarity. I can't stand music that's unclear." Or, as he told *Circus* magazine once the album was complete, "I don't want to go on playing predictable me. I've got to introduce an element of shock."

No specific incident stuck in his mind, no Rubicon was crossed as he crisscrossed the continent. Rather, he was haunted by the sheer grind of the outing, the repetition, and the nightly need to play exactly the same show to what increasingly felt like exactly the same people. "I wasn't really enjoying going onstage every night. I got very paranoid and started to think I was drying up. I said, 'What's wrong with me? This wasn't the reason I started.'"

There certainly was an element of predictability in his life. In early 1973, *Music Scene*'s Rosemary Horidee described Stevens as "now rank[ing] with James Taylor, Neil Diamond, and Neil Young as one of the world's greatest singer-songwriters." But *Star* caught a very different artist at work.

"I want the next album to really be something very special. I've got lots of songs at home which could be used for another album with a similar formula to [my last], *Catch Bull at Four*. But that wouldn't give me any real satisfaction. I want the next one to stand up on its own. . . . I want my next LP to be a real progression. This is my chance."

What he wanted, he determined, would be all new, all different. All alien, all foreign. So foreign that Stevens knew precisely what to call the new album. It would be *Foreigner*, and the man who had made his name on short songs of introspection would now be hanging his heart out on a side-long single sequence, a full-blown concept piece that he titled "The Foreigner Suite."

Everything changed. Out went the producer, Paul Samwell-Smith, with whom Stevens had spent the last three years and four albums; Stevens would be producing himself this time.

Out went the provincial London studios where he normally plied his trade. Cat Stevens was Jamaica-bound, heading for the same Dynamic Sound Studios in Kingston that Paul Simon and the Rolling Stones had utilized in the past, but pushing the studio to new heights as he did so.

Out went the cozy coterie of musicians who had performed on those same past discs. Drummer Gerry Conway survived the cull, and so did pianist Jean Roussel. But there was no room for his other old colleagues, not even for Alun Davies, the fingerpicking genius whose guitar sound, as much as Stevens's voice, had hallmarked each of those previous LPs.

In their stead, he called up a host of hit super-sessioners pulled from London and New York: Paul Martinez and Bernard Purdie, Herbie Flowers, and Phil Upchurch. Later still, invited by the NBC television network to premiere *Foreigner* on nationwide television, he cast the net even further.

Guitarist Danny Kortchmar, one of the kings of the Los Angeles session scene of the day, was among the musicians invited to partake. "There was a show on NBC called *In Concert*, and this thing was for that. He hired a big band to play the entire album, and so we all got together. I was completely over the moon, because the drummer was Bernard Purdie, and they tried to get David T. Walker, who was the principal R&B guitar player in Los Angeles at that time, a great musician. He was the man, but they couldn't get him, so they got me. I was over the moon to even be in the same sentence as David T., and absolutely thrilled to be playing with Bernard, and that's what I mainly remember about that gig."

In truth, that is all that many viewers remembered about the gig; the sight of some of America's greatest musicians playing their way through an album that . . . Well, put it this way: It's unlikely any of them would have actually wanted to own a copy if they'd not been asked to play on it.

That's how radical it was. That's how different it was. That's how un-Cat-like it was.

Stevens was thrilled. "This is a good album," he reassured the trickle of journalists who were airlifted to Kingston to catch the recordings in progress.

"In no way could I have made this album in London. There's no distraction whatsoever in this place. No phones or people wanting to meet you tomorrow for this, that, and a hundred and one other things. In this place, everything's done purely on a day-to-day work basis. You come in the studio feeling good and you get a good track down. This album is the quickest one I've ever recorded."

He laid out his intentions. "Those first three albums I did for Island were very nice and very chummy, but I don't want to come up with albums that are safe and predictable. I can only think of what's happening now. Before coming here to make this album, I made up my mind that from now on I'm not going to plan anything."

He talked of life becoming an "energy rush and storm," and looked to the future with such wide and bright eyes that it must have crucified him when *Foreigner* was almost unanimously slain in the press of the day. And years later, he remained puzzled by its reception, but not only by the bad reviews.

"Some people think it's my best album, which is strange," Stevens told *Mojo*. "But it just shows you that I had something more in me. I didn't want to become a parody of myself."

The key to the album was not, in fact, its title track, but a song that Stevens wrote back in September 1970, during his first ever visit to New York. "How Many Times," he told *Circus*, was born out of his preconceptions, and the ease with which the city destroyed them. "I had hoped the States would be different for me than England had been. I had a romantic, delightful image of New York, and suddenly I got there and couldn't believe the aggression that was going on."

It was that aggression that he wanted to funnel into *Foreigner*. "You see, I think just lately I've been listening to more black music than anything. I've found the rest rather insipid, really. Those guys, though, are not going round any corners. They're coming out with the facts as they are." No matter that music made under the influence of that immediacy might sound dated ten minutes later. Immediacy, spontaneity, the sudden shock of turning around and doing something that nobody expected; that is what Stevens wanted to deliver with *Foreigner*, because those are the things he had not been allowed to do from the day he first walked into a recording studio.

"I wanted an immediate feel to it," he told *Rolling Stone*. That was why he was producing himself. Paul Samwell-Smith, he said, "is a great producer, but he is very clean; if a note is wrong, he wants to fix it up. This time I wanted to do a certain part, I wanted to just play it, and let it be."

Later he would describe *Foreigner* as having been finished "completely subconsciously. It's an album that you can listen to without listening to it, if you see what I mean. I don't think *Foreigner* was a mistake, as some people have suggested.

"Before *Foreigner* I was planning ahead and living almost two months ahead of what I was doing in my head. So *Foreigner* brought me up to date and enabled me to start again; it was more or less a recycle."

And to *Melody Maker*: "This is the age of personal revolutions and that's when people and things change," he said firmly. "I want this album to be a shock. I want it to cause some kind of reaction. I don't just want people to say, 'Oh, the new Cat Stevens album is out this month. Have you got it?'"

In fact, he gave them something else, something very different indeed, to say about him, as *Rolling Stone* reported.

"A Stevens hit single played a part in a recent controversy in Britain. A music newspaper printed a picture of Stevens, and two readers who noticed he was wearing a swastika wrote the paper advising Stevens he could 'shove his "Peace Train" up his ass.'"

There was, of course, a flood of correspondence in the aftermath, with many of the letter writers knowledgeably defending Stevens by delving into the history of the swastika itself, and further venerating an ancient symbol whose hijacking by the Nazi party represented barely fifteen years out of over two thousand. Which, Stevens smiled, was a good thing.

"I'm glad it happened in that it showed the good behind a symbol that some might think represents evil. Of course, it was [also] an opportunity for someone to say that Cat Stevens is a cunt."

A cunt who had just released the most unexpected album of the year. And, ultimately, the most purging.

"Having a constant sound, like Glen Campbell or someone, bores me silly, so it's good to have changes. It's mysterious, and I like mysteries. I don't know where the hell *Foreigner* came from anyway. It was exactly what the title said, a foreign record for me. It didn't fit in with my usual pattern. I don't want people to judge me by my looks, my appearance or my image, or whatever I manage to get across, but by the music. Maybe that's why I put out *Foreigner*, to have a break from the predictable."

1

Where the
Children Play

The frail youth with the shoulder-length brown hair, the puppy-wide eyes, and the lips that looked like they could lacquer a lover hung in the shadows despite the glare of the stage lighting. His eyes were downcast as he concentrated on his instrument . . . but was that the only reason? Or was he masking his shyness as well?.

He didn't play as though he were uncertain. The chords that he picked out were rarely more than basic, even when they outlined one of his own compositions, but he handled them with a gentle effortlessness that—had anyone in the audience actually cared to pay attention—might have marked him out as a guitar player worth keeping an eye on.

Instead, most members of the crowd were too busy either waiting for their own opportunity to get up and play, or impatiently marking time while a friend prepared to do so. Yeah, the kid onstage could play his guitar. He could even write songs. What he couldn't do was sing. Or at least sing loud enough to be heard. Not for the first time that evening, a voice rose out of the crowd, louder than the hum of the rest of audience, louder than the sound of the guitar being strummed on the stage, and certainly louder than Jackson Browne's voice, and it told him what he should do.

"Sing louder!"

And Browne would raise his voice to what he thought was a shout, but which was still little more a meager whisper, and hope that this time, he was singing loud enough.

He never was.

There again, Jackson Browne never saw himself as a singer. Or a guitarist, for that matter. His goal was simply to write songs, and let other people suffer the torment of performing them. Seventeen years old, but already toting a portfolio that could make older songsmiths blanch, Browne had imagined the music industry to be a place whose denizens would flock to the words and music he wrote, and then treat them as sensitively as he himself did. Instead, he'd been reduced to this; to literally singing for his supper in a room full of singers, all of them convinced that they, too, had the lyrical skills to become the next Bob Dylan.

Maybe some of them did. But Browne's lyrics were better than most of theirs. Even if they still could not be heard.

Sometimes he wondered how he had ended up here, in this place at this time. Because that was a story in itself, and if anybody showed any interest in him, he might tell it.

He wasn't born in the United States, and he wasn't born Jackson Browne, either.

But some time after Clyde Browne III squawked his first screams in Heidelberg, Germany, on October 9, 1948, his American serviceman father, Clyde Browne II, and mother, Beatrice, abandoned his birth name and started calling him Jack instead. That was the name that Clyde II had been using for most of his life, after all, but just to make sure there'd be no confusion, they threw a pun into the renaming, too. The boy would be Jackson . . . Jack's Son.

Jackson Browne was just three when the family picked up and placed Europe behind them. They returned to the United States, to Abbey San Encino, the stone and adobe mansion that his grandpa, another Clyde, had built in Highland Park, on the northeastern fringe of Los Angeles.

There the boy grew to love art, threatened to become a talented painter; and there he followed his father's lead and listened to jazz. Back in Germany, Jack Browne had been a pianist for one of the bands that played around the army base where he was stationed, and had even jammed with a visiting Django Reinhardt one night. Now he was a jobbing player for whoever would have him, a printer by day and a musician by night. At home, his was the voice that convinced all three of his children to pick up a musical instrument.

Jackson gravitated toward the cornet, but he never truly took to it, was never able to transition from blowing the notes that he knew should be played to speaking the sounds that he heard in his heart; for it is that, he knew instinctively, that separates a musician from a simple player. Maybe he could ape a Louis Armstrong solo note for note. But that, he knew, was not the point. The point was to create solos of his own.

Instead, he found that receiving formal musical training—an endless succession of scales and hard graft—is essentially akin to learning any other subject at school. He struggled to find the fun in lessons and he never could. His father suggested he transfer his attentions from cornet to trumpet, but that was no better; and, as he grew older, it became a positive handicap. When his friends threw parties, one or two of them would always bring a guitar along and the other guests would sit in rapt attention as they strummed their simple songs. You could not capture a room with a trumpet. You were far more likely to empty it.

But music did become a motivating force regardless, particularly as Browne approached his teenage years and found himself confronted with the same kind of choices that all adolescent boys need to make; whether to devote his time to something constructive, or destructive? It wasn't quite a straight contest between the chess club and juvie, but a lot of young Browne's school friends seemed to have made their own decisions, and as he sat in class listening to the tales of the latest spate of vandalism or violence, he sensed his own heart making a similar choice.

In the end, it was his family who answered the question for him, as they abandoned Highland Park as refugees from the creeping urbanization of a neighborhood that had been ferociously suburban when they first chose it for their home. Low-income housing was drifting over the borders, and low-income lifestyles were chipping away at what had once been a world of fifties sitcom perfection. Highland Park remained a picturesque place, but the pictures that the older residents saw became less pleasing every day. Land prices dropped; the Spanish tongue blossomed. It was no longer a place where the senior Brownes felt that they could happily raise a family.

Now they lived in the aptly named Sunny Hills neighborhood of Fullerton, Orange County, where the biggest sign of rebellion seemed to be driving a GTO a few needle-shakes over the speed limit. For young Jackson Browne, however, even that revolution was out of reach. He really wasn't that deeply into cars.

In fact, he was a bit of an outsider all around. He didn't have the money to dress sharp like some of the kids, and although he was fair at wrestling, one of his high school's preferred sports, other physical activities left him lukewarm. There would be no spot on the football team for him, no endless hours at the baseball diamond.

He enjoyed surfing but, as in wrestling, his build let him down. He was so slim and frail that a decent-size wave could make mincemeat of him.

Music, however, fired him up, especially that memorable night when his elder sister Berbie came home with a couple of African-American folk musicians she knew, Joe and Eddie, and the entire family sat around singing and playing together, deep into the darkness. That might not have been *the* evening when Browne set the compass of his ambition to the true north of music. But it was certainly the one he would remember.

Joe Gilbert and Eddie Brown were southerners; Gilbert was born in Norfolk, Virginia, Brown in New Orleans. Their families moved to California in the fifties, and the boys met at high school when they both enrolled in the a cappella choir. Their first ever appearance as a duo saw them take first prize at the Berkeley High School talent show, and by the end of the decade they were regulars on the San Francisco–based television variety program *The Don Sherwood Show.*

They were also the young Jackson Browne's first hands-on exposure to the music that would come to dominate his teens, the folk sound that was gripping the teenage American imagination like nothing since the Hula-Hoop.

Folk music is the voice of the people, so it is ironic that the more people who actually hear it, the further it slips from their grasp. "Most folk songs today are written in Tin Pan Alley," the young Bob Dylan was prone to scoff as his own star rose in the early 1960s, and though the media was swift to rebrand his particular brand of politically reactionary strumming as protest music, that was what folk had always been, a querulous questioning of the status quo set to the simplest instrumentation and belted out with more conviction than actual singing ability.

Even the notion that "new" folk songs *could* be written seemed somehow anathema to the movement's purist heart, which was the other reason Dylan was so remarkable, even before most people had heard him. Adapting and adopting themes, tunes, and imagery that sprang from sources so traditional that they were lost in the mists of time, Dylan was fashioning an entire new folk repertoire, the first American since Woody Guthrie (who, with such ironic perfection, died just as Dylan commenced his ascent) to shake off the shackles of the past while remaining true to the blacksmiths who forged them.

Joe and Eddie did not protest. Their folk was strictly within the largely motiveless "sing along and clap your hands" vein that the likes of Dylan (with "Blowing in the Wind") and Tim Hardin ("If I Had a Hammer") would eventually be subverting. But that was all that the young Jackson Browne required, and all he would continue to require for some years to come.

Ironically, considering how deeply embroiled in political and environmental causes he would become later in life, Browne shrugged politics aside for the most part. He saw protest music as facile and vacuous, a vagary that had no significance for anybody beyond the journalists who coined the term and the idiots who perpetuated it. Certainly none of his friends ever spoke of "protest music" as anything they had any interest in; for them, again, the music observed and commented, as it had always done. Protest? It didn't mean anything.

Browne did throw his energies into the civil rights movement as that spread its tentacles into student life of the early 1960s, but he quickly became disillusioned, and not only by the sense that many of the causes that he heard espoused were doomed to failure because they simply weren't good causes to begin with. It was the movement's constant quest for easy solutions that bothered him; he felt they were being settled upon without any consideration of the wheels they might set in motion.

He recalled one such struggle, a local campaign that insisted blacks were being kept out of one particular neighborhood by racist whites. No, Browne argued back, they were out because they didn't want to move in. It wasn't neighborhoods people wanted, it was work, and if that particular area had no employment possibilities then why would anyone want to move there, black or white? That was the problem that needed to be addressed, the underlying roadblock that contributed to the cosmetic traffic jam. And until he came across a cause that made that distinction, he preferred to stay out of it.

Browne, then, did not intend to try to change the world with a song. For him, it was sufficient that folk music allowed him to play, to sing, to blend in with his friends. And maybe speak his mind.

Neither was he confining his ears to folk alone, to the likes of the self-styled Mayor of MacDougal Street Dave Van Ronk, or Woody Guthrie's young acolyte Ramblin' Jack Elliott. At the same time that the folk movement burst into the mainstream American consciousness, the tail end of the 1950s and into the pre-Beatles 1960s, there was likewise an explosive embracing of the nation's blues heritage, of veteran black musicians like Lightnin' Hopkins, Jimmy Reed, Sonny Terry, and Brownie McGhee. In later years, history would insist that it required the British Invasion of the Beatles, the Rolling Stones, the Animals and so many more to remind the United States of its roots in the blues. But where were the young Mick Jagger, John Lennon, and Eric Burdon importing their precious blues records from? The United States.

Browne was one of the myriad American teens who were well-versed in the blues long before the Stones rolled onto those shores; whose musical tastes had rejected the sweet pop and balladry that flooded in through the gates that early rock 'n' roll had opened and instead dug back into the past, to trace the new breed's heritage. Blues, folk, jazz, country—it was an open palette, and anybody with ears was digging deep into it.

Chip Taylor, destined to become one of the 1960s' most visionary writers and producers, but still a music-hungry teen at this time, recalled spending his nights with his ear pressed to the family's Motorola radio. Nightly, the young James Wesley Voight (as he was then known) would sit at the table in the hallway that divided the family kitchen from the bedroom he shared with two brothers, future vulcanologist Barrie Voight and aspiring actor Jon Voight, tuning into whatever sounds he could find, but hoping most of all to pick up the broadcasts from Wheeling, West Virginia—"the great country songs, the great blues songs. All the music that would come together in the 1990s under the banner of Americana, but at the time, that was our folk music."

For Chip Taylor, the music would take him to New York with a country band that played around the Irish pubs before. When Taylor was just sixteen, they landed a deal with one of the biggest black labels in the city, King Records, the home of James Brown. For Jackson Browne, it brought him out of himself. At home, he would sit back listening to the records that either he or sister Berbie stacked up around the gramophone, and if he could lay his hands on brother Severin's guitar, he would strum along until he'd taught himself the tune. Then, evenings and weekends it would be down to the beach, where everybody played, and everybody listened. Indeed, there were so many guitarists sitting on the sands that Browne wasn't merely able to teach himself to play on a succession of borrowed instruments; it would be a couple more years before he even needed one to call his own. Before that, he would just borrow from whoever wasn't playing theirs at the time.

Brother Severin was, naturally, the guitar owner Browne turned most frequently toward, and finally his persistence paid off. Severin was buying an electric guitar and rather than sell his now redundant acoustic, he promptly handed it to Jackson instead.

Sister Berbie, meanwhile, was doing her own bit to encourage their youngest brother's musical inclinations. Active within her high school's folk milieu, she was one of the team of students who organized hootenannies, the open mike song and strumming shows that had suddenly become the center of American teenage life. There she came into contact with every would-be singing, strumming, songwriting student in the school, and was in fact dating one of the most able of them all, an angular-faced young man named Steve Noonan—whose father was the owner of the Aware, a downtown coffeehouse that was one of *the* focal points of Berbie"s high school's folk explosion.

As she became more aware of her brother's enthusiasm, Berbie permitted Jackson to accompany her on a few of these sojourns and, long after she and Noonan broke up, Jackson and the songwriter had become solid friends.

It was impressive company for Jackson to be keeping, all the more so once he was introduced to Noonan's early-sixties songwriting partner, Greg Copeland, an enthusiast who, with Noonan by his side, thought nothing of raiding the school's music department for whatever instruments they required (the bass fiddle was a favorite) and staging impromptu bluegrass concerts before class.

It was friends such as Copeland and Noonan who nurtured the musical seeds that Joe and Eddie had first planted in the young Browne; they who persuaded Browne to go to see Joan Baez at the open-air Hollywood Bowl on October 12, 1963. It was a concert that would literally change his entire perspective on music.

The twenty-two-year-old Baez was enormous in 1963; indeed, it is a sign of just how all-consumingly huge the protest music scene had become that she was the first singer to sell out the 17,000-seat Hollywood Bowl since Frank Sinatra, at the height of his bobby-socksing singing career, nineteen years previously.

For three years now, Baez had been *the* face of American folk, a dark beauty with a voice of crystalline purity and an ear that could draw unmitigated diamonds from the rust of the hoariest folk song. A denizen of the Boston coffeehouse circuit, but a complete unknown in the wider world, she exploded out of the annual Newport Song Festival in 1959 and since then had placed three albums on the U.S. Top 20, an unprecedented feat for a performer so young and, in marketing terms, so specialized.

Baez's repertoire was largely traditional and largely English. She performed folk standards like the murder ballad "Mattie Groves," the supernatural "The House Carpenter," the allegorically rousing "The Trees They Do Grow High." But she would dip into the American canon too, teasing heartbreak afresh from the murder ballad "Banks of the Ohio," walking the "Lonesome Road" to "East Virginia"; she sang Guthrie and Leadbelly. She listened for new voices too: those of her sister Mimi and *her* boyfriend Richard Farina, for instance; Carolyn Hester, Eric Von Schmidt . . . and Bob Dylan. Baez was singing Dylan's praises before most people even heard him sing, and as she toured the United States through 1963, the nasal little hobo look-alike was an integral part of her entourage, her lover when she was offstage, her special guest when she was on.

He was onstage alongside her in Hollywood too, a scruffy ragamuffin who had long ago perfected the "gee, shucks, great to be here" stance that Baez's audience expected of even the queen's most favored courtier. But then he opened his mouth to sing, usually a song of his own creation, and even Baez sometimes looked on with awe-struck amazement.

Old hands in the audience knew what to expect. They'd seen Baez pull Dylan from her hat so many times before. For fifteen-year-old Jackson Browne, however, the tousle-haired Midwesterner who sang through his nose wasn't simply a surprise. He was a revelation.

"The first music that I heard that I really went crazy for was Bob Dylan's," Browne enthused. "Songs like 'Talking World War Three Blues' or 'The Lonesome Death of Hattie Carroll' and 'Blowin' in the Wind.'"

Of course he'd heard Dylan's antecedents aplenty; Pete Seeger and the Weavers, Woody Guthrie, Joe and Eddie. But those singers had spoken to the world. Dylan spoke to him, first from the stage of the Hollywood Bowl, where the singer introduced a brand-new song, "Lay Down Your Weary Tune," and laughed as Joan Baez stumbled her way through it because even she had not had time to learn it yet; and then at home, where young Jackson sat alone with his record player, listening to the Bob Dylan record he'd bought the next day, the singer's self-titled debut.

By the time Dylan's second LP, *The Freewheelin' Bob Dylan*, was released the following month, Browne had absorbed its predecessor into his very DNA and was now ready to do the same thing with this new one. "I would get the [new] Bob Dylan album and I would breathe it . . . until he put out the next one," Browne laughed. "If, when I die, they open my brain and do a cross section, like the rings of a tree or something, they will find several years in there when there's nothing but Bob Dylan."

Browne's epiphany was not his alone. Across the country, in the wilds of southern New Jersey, the young (two years Browne's senior) Patti Smith experienced a similar awakening when she caught Dylan onstage with Joan Baez; in Chapel Hill, North Carolina, James Taylor heard the same magic for himself. And in every town and city in between, countless other young teens made their own discovery: that the simplest of all musical equations—a guitarist who wrote, sang, and performed his or her own songs—was capable of taking music to a whole new plateau. One where a successful performer did not need to sing about girls and boys and cars and sex in order to be accepted. He needed to simply sing about himself.

That was what Browne and Smith and Taylor and everybody else who was bitten by the Dylan bug found exciting, and not only because it was within their reach in musical terms. Browne was excited because Dylan's example connected with another of his ambitions; the drive to literally speak to people one-on-one, to move them and make them either think or react.

He had no interest in "making it," in making records or playing the Hollywood Bowl; and even when he catalogued his own teenage idols, Dylan and Baez and Richard Farina, he saw no need, felt no urge, to emulate their material successes. All he wanted, he said, was "to speak to people as Richard Farina had spoken to me."

He just needed to find a voice of his own.

Dylan was the first in a succession of body blows that were to reshape the American music scene in the early 1960s, and do so in astoundingly rapid succession. Discover Dylan in late 1963, and you would still be absorbing the shock waves when, scant weeks later, you would experience another epiphany as the Beatles made their television debut on *The Ed Sullivan Show*. Process them into your musical DNA and a few weeks later, you'd have the Rolling Stones. And it's hard to say, today, who made the biggest difference.

Browne saw the Stones for the first time almost exactly a year after he first caught sight of Dylan, sitting in a seething crowd watching in amazement as row upon row of teenage girls removed their panties, wrapped them around anything that would give them some weight, and then hurled them toward the stage. Musically and lyrically, the Stones were the antithesis of what Dylan had become; scarcely writing their own songs yet, they were still largely reliant on the blues for their repertoire. But they too spoke to audiences; they too connected with something deep inside the people who saw them. They became something else for Browne to think about.

The British Invasion crashed into his psyche. It is no coincidence at all that one of the biggest hits the older Browne would enjoy should be with a cover of a song he first heard performed by the Hollies in 1964, the buoyant "Stay." Nor was it by accident that he repaid the Kinks for a teenage decade full of favorite songs by guesting on front man Ray Davies's 2011 album *See My Friends*, and demanding the Kinks reprise "Waterloo Sunset."

"It wasn't my idea," Davies admitted. "He wanted to do 'Waterloo Sunset' and I really wasn't sure how it would work, because he's a singer from Southern California, and that's such an evocatively London song. But he came in with his guitar, he sat down and played it, and the point of the collaborations was to let people slide into the way they wanted to do it, and he changed the key, which allowed me to find new expression with my voice. We just cobbled it together on the spot and it was a great experience."

Born from essentially an Anglified version of the experiences that shaped Browne's own youth, the dislocation of once leafy suburbs being consumed by the creeping morass of urbanization, the British Invasion's breed of rude suburban R&B supplanted folk in Browne's musical mind around the same time as Dylan's growing desire to shake the shit from his shoes saw him begin distancing himself from the squawking babe he had birthed.

Within six months of Browne's first Stones show, Dylan was plugging his guitar in at the 1965 Newport festival and topping the chart with "Like a Rolling Stone," and Browne himself was growing his hair and spending his summers in San Francisco with sister Berbie. Now a shoulder-length-haired brunette who had just discovered LSD and allowed its imagery to populate his lyrics, he was writing more songs. One of his compositions from this time was titled "Lavender Windows." The title says it all.

In fall 1965, Browne entered his senior year at high school. He would not mourn its passage; as it is for so many people, school was simply something that he endured because he had to, and whose pretensions and problems he saw through every time he asked a question that a teacher could not (or would not) answer. American youth were becoming more and more politicized, but still the highest points on the campus agenda would be the length of a girl's skirt or a boy's hair, all those apparently crucial elements that adulthood regard as symbols of teenage rebellion, but which actually matter naught in the face of the subjects that go undiscussed. He lost himself even more in his guitar, to the point where later in life he'd admit that his instrument was his most lasting memory of school. Everything else had simply gone in one ear and out the other.

Still, he stuck it out, a halfway confident kid with an acoustic guitar, a way with the ladies, and now, a newly hatched love for the Byrds, the Los Angeles band that blended the poetry of Dylan with the drive of the Stones into an all-California cocktail of sound. In fact, they were on his mind the night he finally tired of one of his friends, a fourteen-year-old named Janet, telling him that she wanted to be a singer, without ever actually getting around to prove that she could sing. So Browne pushed her into it.

"Sing."

Every Thursday night at the Paradox, a folk club fifteen miles away in Tustin, would-be performers were invited to show up for open mike nights. Browne was a regular visitor to these events, but he never got up on the stage himself. Standing in front of an audience and singing the songs he was writing simply wasn't a part of his plan. But he handed Janet the lyrics to "She's a Flying Thing," taught her how to sing it and somebody else how to play it, and then sat back in fury as the pair reduced his song to rubble, a country-tinged monstrosity that he barely even recognized.

"So sing it yourself," someone else told him and, although Browne went through the fires of hell in the hours before he took the stage for the first time, that's what he did. But he never truly became comfortable with standing up there—and it showed in the barely audible whisper with which he would torment the audience as they stood staring at him. More than once he would cringe as a shout from the crowd demanded that he sing louder, and even his friends admitted that his voice was little more than faint background noise. He could already write songs, everyone agreed. But he needed someone else to sing them. He needed his own Byrds.

2

Sweet Baby James

For somebody whose background seems so goddamned privileged, James Vernon Taylor had managed to get himself seriously fucked up.

Born in Boston on March 12, 1948, he was the second of five children (his older brother, Alex, was born two years earlier, sister Kate and brothers Livingston and Hugh across the next four years). His boyhood was—well, from the outside, it sounds idyllic. Summer vacations on Martha's Vineyard, that luxurious hidey-hole on the Massachusetts coast where the would-be rich go to burn away their pasty complexions; the rest of the year in Chapel Hill, where home was an eleven-room pile set in twenty-eight acres of North Carolina woodland and pasture.

His father, Ike, was working toward the deanship of the University of North Carolina Medical School, and the old man believed resolutely in allowing his children all the freedoms they could grasp. They would think for themselves, speak for themselves, act for themselves. Nothing was impossible, nothing was forbidden. Life was for living, and that was how the Taylor brood was raised. To live.

Music, mother Gertrude (usually shortened to the less intrusive Trudy) believed, was one direction in which those instincts could be channeled, while the differing environments in which the children found themselves were ideal for instilling a profound love and understanding of the natural world around them. The family played together, sang together, lived together, laughed together, and they could probably have sold washing powder together.

Later in life, James Taylor would recall the things that marked out life in the piedmont. The distinctive bottles of Nehi soda pop, "your favorite drink in your favorite flavor," as the ads used to proclaim.

Locusts, descending upon the region like a biblical plague in miniature to shatter the natural silence of the hills with their insistent dry-winged chirrup.

The distinctive red soil, and the way it smelled whether the air was wet or dry.

Kudzu vine, the mile-a-minute growth that seemingly manifested itself overnight without warning, then proceeded to devour everything in its path. The so-called vine that ate the South first entered the United States in 1876, when the Japanese brought it over to show at the Centennial Expo in Philadelphia. Since then it has been spreading at a rate of some 150,000 acres a year, and every summer, the Taylors would watch as the local landscapers battled to tear the vine down from every foothold it gained. Even in a family as large as the Taylors', James felt as though it was his environment that shaped him, not people and possessions.

Yet he was not withdrawn. Childhood was a constant struggle for attention, first among his brothers and sister, fighting to be noticed or heard above the general hubbub, and then at school, where he pushed himself forward in every lesson, his heart set on the highest grades, and set to break when he didn't achieve them. He volunteered for every job that parents or teachers could set him; he was an achiever, and sometimes an *over*-achiever. Some people, he realized later in life, move forward in this way, and some don't. And some, like James, slowly go mad.

The signs were probably there all along, in his bouts of moodiness, his inability to settle, and, yes, that manic sense of accomplishment. *I must, I must, I must*. But lots of kids go through phases like that and, besides, it wasn't as if the boy was a hermit. In fact, he was completely the opposite. With a frame that grew tall before it ever appeared gangly, hair that grew lush before it grew long, and a voice that some people admit they could listen to forever, Taylor might not have made friends easily, but those he did make became allies for life.

Friends like Danny Kortchmar, whom he met on the Vineyard when he was twelve or so, and from whom he might well have become inseparable had Chapel Hill not kept calling him home. Taylor had just been given his first guitar, a gift from his adoring parents, and he'd taken his first lessons, too, strumming through folk, blues, and some rudimentary jazz under the highly attuned ear of a blind music teacher at the University of North Carolina.

They were valuable lessons, too. In Carolina, he listened to Hank Williams, the king of American country music, but he also heard a lot of blues and gospel. For a time, he fancied himself the white Ray Charles, but he was also sharp enough to realize that there was no way his voice, already what could politely be described as mellow, was going to swing in that direction. So he paid attention instead to what he heard on those visits to the Vineyard. No matter that he would later write off the local folk scene as little more than the musings of the white-collar, Harvard-and-afterwards crowd; it was what he could play, and it was that which drew him close to Kortchmar—or Kootch, as the boy was already being called.

Kootch was shorter than Taylor, but so were most people. But he was more extroverted and gregarious, too. They made a good team, and the moment Kootch discovered that Taylor, apparently unique among the Vineyard vacationers, shared his love of blues and R&B, the pair were conspiring their musical future.

"We grew up together on the Vineyard," Kootch reflected. "We met when we were little kids and taught each [other] to play guitar." Kootch did most of the teaching, though. First he showed Taylor some loose chord changes, then he ran through his own repertoire of Lightnin' Hopkins, John Lee Hooker, Muddy Waters, and the rest of the blues crew.

"We both played and we both influenced one another tremendously; we both had a great love of music." The first time he realized Taylor could sing, he laughed, was while they were hitchhiking together one day. Taylor burst into song and Kootch was astonished. He'd never met someone who could really sing before.

Touring the local coffeehouses under the name of Jamie and Kootch, the two teens slipped easily onto a scene that not only nurtured its own local heroes, but was also a magnet for performers better known for working the circuit of clubs that comprised the Cambridge and Boston folk scene, at that time as formidable and elitist a company as any in the country.

The scene itself rose out of the legendary Club 47, a progressive jazz club until the day in 1958 that the teenage Joan Baez took the stage for a one-off performance, and wound up winning a Sunday afternoon residence that she packed with her own friends and family. Soon Baez's sister Mimi, years before she found fame alongside her husband Richard Farina; Harvard alumni and Weavers monolith Pete Seeger; the Springfield, Massachusetts–

born bluesman Taj Mahal, and native American UMass grad Buffy Sainte Marie were headlining the Club 47 stage to sellout crowds, and other venues were opening to accommodate their followers.

Now, it was hard to throw a rock in Cambridge without hitting either a folk club or a folk musician, and one did so at one's own peril, because they were an aggressive bunch of peaceniks when riled, and they took their music seriously.

Singer Tom Rush was one of the wide-eyed folkies who arrived in Cambridge with his ears full of the hits of the day: the black radical Josh White; San Francisco's Kingston Trio, whose very first album topped the *Billboard* chart four years before Bob Dylan was heard of; Connecticut's clean-cut Highwaymen; and so forth. "And I had to be totally reeducated. It was like being sent to a camp by the Communist Party, to cleanse your aberrant belief. I was told that Josh White was commercial and that was bad. What they wanted was ethnic, and the ethnic guys were of course the old actual sharecroppers, coal miners, chain gang [convicts], etc. Incredible music.

"So I was reeducated and I did my best to be ethnic, although it was difficult for all of us because we were a bunch of Harvard students singing about how tough it was in the coal mines and on the chain gang."

Somehow they muddled through, however, as the liners to the Elektra label's 1962 compilation *The Folk Scene* say of folkie Casey Anderson. He was "a college-bred singer who hails originally from Okmulgee, OK." But "despite his education and city upbringing," he grabbed the Southern chain gang chant "Grizzly Bear" and "presents [it] with a power and sincerity befitting the deep emotional drive which first produced it."

But the ability to perform was not the only prerequisite. An ear for the unknown, the ability to ferret out songs or arrangements that had not been heard before and present them in a unique light; that, too, was the key to authenticity, and upbringing be damned. It was hard work as well, so vacationing, weekending, or simply day-tripping, Rush and his contemporaries would descend upon the Vineyard to relax, recharge, and occasionally redesign their approach to their muse. It was amazing the new perspective on things that could be gleaned from a few nights on the shore.

For Taylor and Kootch, the opportunity to see the best of the Cambridge crowd on their home turf was one that they rarely passed by. Taylor certainly caught Tom Rush playing there, and Rush himself recalled years later, "We might possibly have met on Martha's Vineyard, because I spent a lot of summers there and he did too. But he was however many years younger than I and back then, five years' difference was huge."

"I . . . heard Tom Rush . . . and instantly became a big fan," James Taylor admitted. "I copied and learned a lot of his arrangements, so I guess it's fair to say that Tom was not only one of my early heroes, but also one of my main influences."

He chose wisely.

Tom Rush was the consummate East Coast folkie, the epitome of what the era still knew as "city folksingers." That is the term that writer Paul Nelson preferred, penning the sleeve notes to Rush's first, eponymous, album, and it is that imagery that clings most perniciously to the music that Rush was making close to a decade before any other term was applied to his muse.

His secret was simplistic, and it is easy to see the aspects of his craft that Taylor (and so many others) would borrow, or at least attempt to. "I always tried to find a little bit of a different take on things," Rush explained. "I remember being really impressed with a guy named Bobby Jones;—he specialized in Woody Guthrie songs—hearing him one night doing 'Pastures of Plenty.' It was like a religious experience. I'd heard the song a thousand times, but I'd never *heard* it. Bobby did it in such a way that it was a brand-new song, and I was so impressed that ever since then, I've tried not to just *sing* a song, but to find a way of doing it that would make the song fresh again. I'm working for the song."

The son of a math teacher, born in Portsmouth, New Hampshire, on February 8, 1941, reared in Concord, Massachusetts, and educated at Harvard, Rush was raised on the same musical diet as a lot of kids his age: Pete Seeger and the Weavers on the one hand, and the first flowering of rock 'n' roll on the other.

"When I was a little kid, I remember my parents giving me Pete Seeger 78s, and then 45s came along. . . . I remember hearing the Seeger stuff very early on. And then Tennessee Ernie Ford had a hit called '16 Tons,' and that Christmas [1955], eight different people gave me that record. I did like it, but I don't know that I needed eight copies!"

Childhood piano lessons supervised by "a very tough woman referred to as the Iron Lady; she was about the stature and shape of a fire hydrant," consumed his earliest musical musings; he hated every moment. It was a cousin bearing the memorable name of Beau Beales who taught him to love creating music. "He was more my dad's age, but he was a marvelous character, one of those guys I could imagine in a raccoon-skin coat. This guy could dive into a swimming pool, flip a cigarette into his mouth, and blow smoke bubbles from underwater, and when you're ten years old, that is big. And he played ukulele, and he taught me to play, and that was a lot of fun. So I liked the ukulele, but the ukulele turned into a baritone ukulele because it seemed more manly, and that became a guitar." And thus armed, Rush found himself forming his first band, at the New Hampshire State Mental Institute.

"My mother donated me to the hospital. She was always donating stuff to them, and one day somebody there said, 'You know, we've got a lot of patients in the inmate population who want to form a band. And the next thing I know, age sixteen, I'm heading down to the state hospital with my cardboard guitar case, to form a band with the inmates.

"It was a very strange experience, especially because all the musicians . . . and I'm sure this is coincidence, and had no hidden meaning . . . but all the musicians were in the forensics wing, the criminally insane.

"I had an axe murderer on lead guitar, an arsonist on drums, and nobody knew what the bassist was in for because he never spoke. He didn't often play the same song as the rest of us, either, so it really wasn't that different from other bands I've had, except they were always on time for rehearsals."

Later, at prep school in the town of Groton, Massachusetts, he formed a band with a few fellow pupils, again churning out hot teenage rock 'n' roll. But a cross-country trip with his parents that same year, 1957, reconnected Rush with folk music, after they stopped at some family friends' ranch in Jackson Hole, Wyoming. "They had some Josh White recordings and I was just blown away; I'd never heard a guitar played like that, or songs like that. It was magical, and I wanted to be just like Josh White."

Interviewed for the liner notes to his fourth album, in 1965, Rush described how he learned his musical trade by playing to the cows in a field near his home. The trick, he said, was to grow progressively wilder and wilder, because that kept the animals interested, but never to forget to feed them a handful of grass between songs, to keep them from stampeding.

It was an approach he learned to apply to his audiences, presenting them with ever more challenging material, but pulling back to play a familiar favorite before the crowd grew too restless. But his first ever concert in

Cambridge, following his arrival in town to study English at Harvard, taught him the downside to that maneuver.

"My first gig was a little club, a coffeehouse called the Salamander, in 1961. It lasted one night and I was fired for all the right reasons." Rush was booked to replace a flamenco guitarist friend of his, who had retired, he said, so he could move to Spain and live with the Gypsies. "Of course," Rush smiled, "when he got there, the Gypsies didn't want to have anything to do with him.

"But he asked me if I would like to take over this weekly gig and I showed up. It was a little coffeehouse with people playing checkers and drinking coffee and talking, and they propped me up in the corner and I played for thirty minutes, three thirty-minute sets, and at the end of the night the guy gave me my ten bucks and told me my services wouldn't be required again. I asked him why and he said, 'Well, the patrons were listening to you.' This was a problem, because they should have continued drinking coffee and playing checkers and conversing. I was supposed to be background music and I failed."

Other venues would prove more encouraging, however, and in 1962, playing a weekly residency at Byron Linardos's Unicorn Café, he was approached by "a gentleman named Dan Flickinger, who turned up and asked if I wanted to make an album? Well, I'd heard this a few times before, so I just said sure and he actually showed up the following week, dragging a tape recorder the size of an oven downstairs into the Unicorn.

"He recorded for two nights and he insisted on using complete takes. He said it was morally reprehensible to splice tape, to use the first half of song from night one, the second half from side two. Actually, it was probably because he didn't know how to splice tape. But we pressed up this LP, three hundred copies, and he took them around to the record stores in the back of his Studebaker. I don't know how many we sold, it couldn't have been more than a few hundred, and then the studio burned down and he disappeared."

Today, the prosaically titled *Tom Rush Live at the Unicorn* is regarded as one of the centerpieces of the early 1960s American folk movement as it grew up in the wake of Joan Baez and the slowly developing slipstream of Bob Dylan, whose own debut LP, *Bob Dylan*, had itself only appeared that same March. Certainly there was only one other act on the Cambridge scene, the Charles River Valley Boys, who could likewise point to an LP of their own, and whether or not Rush had intended it, he suddenly found himself regarded, if not as a regional elder statesman, then at least as a "serious" folkie.

Which made it all the more alarming when an aspiring young producer named Paul Rothchild descended upon the area, bearing with him a seemingly bottomless sheath of contracts to record for Bob Weinstock's New York–based Prestige label.

A primarily jazz-based concern, Prestige was just moving into folkier territory, and Rothchild had been recruited to ensure the move went smoothly. For some people, anyway. "Paul signed up a bunch of us, but not me," Rush laughed. "Pretty soon, everybody inside the 128 beltway had a record contract except me, which I guess was payback for jumping the queue with the *Unicorn* LP."

It was early 1963 before "Rothchild finally came to his senses and signed me up," and the Prestige Folklore label debuted later that same year with releases by Rush, Geoff Muldaur and Eric Von Schmidt (plus the lesser feted Mitch Greenhill, and Bill Keith and Jim Rooney). A second Rush album would arrive the following year, but by that time, both Rothchild and Rush had already departed, both bound for Jac Holzman's Elektra Records setup.

"I did my first Prestige LP and then Paul went to Elektra," Rush explained. "I wanted to go to Elektra too, he wanted me at Elektra, and so I went back to the Prestige folks and said, 'I want to get out of my contract.'"

Prestige refused, so Rush tried again. "I said, 'Okay, I'll do one more album for you,' and they still said no." It was time to play his trump card. Assuming the most serious expression he could, and hoping to God that nobody at the label realized just how ironic his words were, he declared his intention to quit show business altogether. "'I'm a Harvard grad and I have an English lit major. The possibilities are limitless.'"

"And they bought it! They said, 'Okay, one more,' so then I said, 'But I want Paul to produce,' and they said, 'Well, Jac Holzman will never allow that,' so I went to Jac and I said this is what I'd like to do, and to my surprise he said okay. So Paul and I went into the studio and in one week recorded the second LP for Prestige; then the following week we recorded the first LP for Elektra. Which actually came out before the Prestige album, because Elektra was racing and Prestige wasn't."

Label head Jac Holzman launched Elektra in 1950, inspired to form a label after attending a performance by soprano Georgiana Banister at St. John's College in Annapolis, Maryland, where he was a student. In late 1950, he recorded a fresh version of the same recital, issuing it as the LP *New Songs by John Gruen* (the composer) in March, 1951. Just five hundred copies were pressed, sold through the record store that Holzman had just opened, the Record Loft, in Greenwich Village, and it was there he met Elektra's next signing, folksinger Jean Ritchie.

Over the next four years, the infant Elektra issued twenty-four albums, including sets by folksingers Frank Warner, Shep Ginandes, Cynthia Gooding, Hally Wood, and Tom Paley; two titles by bluesmen Sonny Terry and Brownie McGhee; and field recordings from as far afield as Haiti and Nova Scotia. Actor Theodore Bikel cut a collection of Israeli folk songs for Elektra in 1955, while the arrival of Rush's beloved Josh White placed Elektra firmly on the outlaw fringe of the folk movement. Hitherto contracted to Decca, where he rose to become one of the best-loved African-American performers in the country, White joined Elektra after being blacklisted for alleged Communist sympathies during the McCarthy era. His first release, *The Story of John Henry and Ballads, Blues and Other Songs*, was the label's first double album.

Elektra's development through the late 1950s and early 1960s continued to be dictated by the mood of the folk community, as it underwent its own massive revival. Glenn Yarborough, Peggy Seeger, Oscar Brand, Shel Silverstein, Bob Gibson, and Paul Clayton recorded for the label; Elektra also dipped into the fertile Caribbean scene, with releases by the Original Trinidad Steel Band and Lord Foodoos and His Calypso Band; while an indication of Holzman's willingness to experiment further was offered by the 1960 release of English comedienne Joyce Grenfell's *Presenting*, a collection of extraordinary monologues about the life of a schoolteacher.

Elektra's biggest star of the early 1960s was Judy Collins, recruited in 1961 in response to Joan Baez (signed to the rival Vanguard label) but rapidly emerging as a diamond talent in her own right, both via such early LPs as *Maid of Constant Sorrow* and *Golden Apples of the Sun,* and a clutch of excellent hit singles. Tom Paxton, Phil Ochs, and the Ian Campbell Folk Group joined during 1964, while Elektra also handled two of the seminal folk compilations of the age, the three-LP boxed set of Woody Guthrie's

Library of Congress Recordings, and the British Topic label's *The Iron Muse* compilation of industrial revolutionary folk songs.

Other significant signings from this period included the Even Jug Band, a sprawling twelve-piece whose membership included John Sebastian, Maria Muldaur, Stefan Grossman, and Steve Katz. Their eponymous debut album appeared in 1964. Producer Paul Rothchild, very much Holzman's right-hand man, meanwhile, arrived in 1965, and he would be responsible for moving the label into the electric blues arena with the inspired signing, and subsequent commercial impact, of the Paul Butterfield Blues Band in 1965.

Nevertheless, signing Rush ranks among the smartest musical decisions that Rothchild and Holzman ever made, and the singer was thrilled in turn to be there. "It was the flagship folk label because Holzman spent a lot of time, money, and attention on the packaging and [on] the selection of the artists, [on] everything involved, [on] the presentation of a first-class product. I had many, many people tell me they bought those albums never having heard of me, but simply because they were on Elektra. They trusted the brand."

And they could trust Rush. He was boiling with such a vast and varied repertoire that his first two Elektra albums, *Tom Rush* and *Take a Little Walk with Me* were all but released back-to-back. Immediately he was hailed as a hero; Robert Shelton told *New York Times* readers, "Tom Rush is one of the most important of the city folksingers and white blues interpreters. He has achieved an unusual synthesis of sensitivity in statement and guts in feeling, in his music." And when observers remarked that the latter LP electrified his audience, they were not merely reaching for hyperbole. Drawing in Al Kooper, whose organ playing was such a feature of Dylan's still fresh *Highway 61 Revisited* noise fest, Rush abandoned his folkier side altogether and dedicated side one of the album to rock 'n' roll, in its most literal setting.

Rush was fifteen when rock 'n' roll hit, and he was an immediate convert. "Carl Perkins, Elvis Presley, Fats Domino, and on and on, and that was really quite a phenomenon. Suddenly there were all these artists who were completely different from one another, who were amazing and energetic and talented and outrageous. If your parents liked it, it couldn't be good."

Now was his opportunity to capture some of that energy and outrage for himself. Across three days of breakneck sessions, while the likes of Dylan and Judy Collins watched from the control booth, Rush and Kooper pounded through Willie Dixon's "You Can't Tell a Book by the Cover," Bo Diddley's

"Who Do You Love," Chuck Berry's "Too Much Monkey Business," and half a dozen classic rockers, topped by one of Rush's own occasional self-penned barnstormers, "On the Road Again," to create a virtual suite of songs that both reflected on the rock that most modern folkies had actually grown up with, and showed how they had all taken those ideas and fed them into their own modern muse. Or, as Kooper put it, "This was not to be an album of 'copies,' but a modern updated tribute to the heroes of our musical childhood. Now, however, they have all become unmistakably Tom Rush."

3

Before the Deluge

By the time he was fourteen, James Taylor was formidably armed with the Silvertone electric guitar in which he had invested $40. He was already writing songs as well; the first he remembers also came along when he was fourteen, and inevitably it leaned toward the folkier side of things. Occasionally he would throw a blues progression into one of his songs by dint of it sounding novel or distinctive, but for the most part his songs were designed as simplistically as they could be. The summer of 1963, at the same time that Jackson Browne was sitting on the beach, picking up girls with his few-chord wonders, Taylor and Kootch won a hootenanny contest on the Vineyard.

The following year, back in Chapel Hill, Taylor and brother Alex formed a band of their own, dubbed the Fabulous Corsairs. Together they gigged around the youth clubs of the area, playing the hits of the day, and they even cut a demo single at a little studio in Raleigh, coupling Alex's "You're Gonna Have to Change Your Ways" with James's "Cha Cha Blues."

Yet the freedom and excitement that Taylor enjoyed there and on the Vineyard were cut with a nightmare of increasingly terrifying proportions when high school term time rolled around again. His parents had packed thirteen-year-old James off to boarding school, Milton Academy, in Milton, Massachusetts, and he simply couldn't handle it.

Located just eight miles south of Boston, but light-years removed from any environment the barely teenage Taylor could have envisaged, Milton could trace its origins back to 1798, and had been educating with unflinching zeal since 1884. Since that time, the likes of T. S. Eliot, Buckminster

Fuller, and both Robert and Edward Kennedy had emerged from its halls, together with several administrations' worth of political figureheads. Harvard regarded Milton as one of its feeders, and Milton was proud to feed it—so proud that the system had little patience for any boy who was unable to keep up with the curriculum. And Moose, as Taylor's classmates nicknamed their towering colleague, was no exception.

He crashed. Big-time. His head was full of thoughts and ideas, but they were nothing that the Milton staff could get their own heads around. His attitude was frivolous, his sense of humor obtuse. And Milton was just too much for him; too high-powered, too bent on perfection. He quit once, returning to Chapel Hill for a big chunk of time, then returned to Milton for his junior year with the aim, simply, of getting through what remained of his education, and hoping college could provide a better future.

But even resignation didn't help. Depression swept in on unfathomable wings and with it an inability leave his bed. He should have been working; instead, he was sleeping twenty hours a day. His grades fell apart, and whatever friends he had were drifting away. And then, around Thanksgiving 1965, he began considering suicide.

That scared him. He sought out the advice of a psychiatrist, only to break down in the shrink's office. It almost came as a relief when he was told he was being sent for observation at a psychiatric hospital. In December 1965, seventeen years old, Taylor committed himself to the McLean Hospital in Belmont, Massachusetts. The largest of Harvard's psychiatric facilities, the $36,400-a-year McLean would be his home for the next nine months. The experience was intended to give him the opportunity to find his mental bearings, to understand *not* that he was in some ways "different" from his friends, but that that wasn't anything to be ashamed of. He had to find his own way through life, but while he searched, McLean would offer him safety and protection.

The doctors prescribed Thorazine to help him combat his depression, a heavy-duty neuroleptic that had been in everyday use in psychiatric care since 1954; at that time, the long-term effects that have since seen the drug condemned as a chemical lobotomizer were not yet known.

That said, even in development, Thorazine's usage (or at least its effect) was regarded as somewhat controversial, with its own creators, French psychiatrists Delay and Deniker, acknowledging that the small dosage rendered patients indifferent and lethargic, at the same time that they acknowledged that was a large part of the drug's purpose. If a patient couldn't be bothered to move, then he couldn't be bothered to kill himself, or do anything else that might cause harm. Effectively, Thorazine placed a patient's emotions into cold storage until psychiatry found a way of fixing whatever was wrong with him.

Details of Taylor's treatment, and his response to it are, understandably, a private matter. The facts of the matter, however, are conclusive. Slowly, the order and structure of the hospital day restored his equilibrium. Very slowly; certainly his psychological state ensured that he was in no fit state to serve when he received his military call-up papers, although he made certain that the induction officers would dismiss him outright by arranging for two white-suited hospital assistants to accompany him to the draft board.

But he completed his schooling at McLean, collecting his high school diploma from the hospital's Arlington School, and he reflected later that the establishment's greatest asset was its refusal to shovel students on through their term work. "We didn't have that jive nothingness that pushes most kids through high school. You can't tell a whole bunch of potential suicides that they must have a high school diploma."

Over the next year or so, two of Taylor's siblings would also attend McLean, brother Livingston and sister Kate—who became one of the first beneficiaries of the establishment's newly instituted music therapy program, even forming her own group, Sister Kate's Soul Stew Kitchen, with some of her fellow patients. James, however, was not there to see her. One day in the summer of 1966, he simply discharged himself from the hospital, hitching a ride with a southbound friend, headed straight for New York City. Kootch had called him to announce he was starting a new band. Did Taylor want to be a part of it?

He did. Kootch laughed, "James decided he'd had enough of McLean and jumped the wall, hitchhiked down to New York, stayed on my couch, and we started the Flying Machine."

With hindsight, it was inevitable that Taylor and Kootch would form their own band, a mature successor to the heady Vineyard days of Jamie and Kootch. At the time, however, Taylor had burned with impatience and, perhaps, envy, watching (or, more accurately, hearing) as Kootch had been swept into rock 'n' roll as easily, it seemed, as Taylor was swept into the hospital, and how (unlike Taylor) he was having the time of his life in the process.

The guitarist recalled, "As soon as I got out of high school, I realized . . . the Beatles had come out the year before [1964], and I realized I had to start a rock band. There was no way around it, no way that it wasn't going to happen. So I managed to find this diverse group of people. . . ." Among this diverse group was Joel Bishop (real name: O'Brien), a drummer but, more importantly, "a very influential fellow. He was extremely bright and well educated, into diverse areas. He knew an awful lot about music and film and literature and he was a huge influence on me."

Another discovery was vocalist John John McDuffy, "who we found when we came down to Harlem." Together they formed the King Bees, a white suburban band with a gritty taste for R&B. Digging back into the roots of the music he'd been playing on the Vineyard, "soul music and R&B," explained Kootch, "I really wanted to try that, and make it as good and as authentic as possible."

Multi-racial at a time when that was still considered a rarity, the King Bees' early days were understandably tentative. "We played discos, we played some joints in the Village like everybody did, then we played in Montreal for a couple of months, an army place where soldiers would go, and where beer would be ten cents, then it would go up to twenty cents when the band was playing."

Around and around the band went, but a booking in that part of upstate New York known as the Borscht Belt proved their making. Named and renowned for its popularity with the area's rich Jewish community, the summer resort area of the Catskill Mountains was littered with hotels, all of them calling out for fresh young talent to entertain the guests.

The King Bees landed a gig at the Royal Hotel. "We got to play up there as the kiddy band, playing dances for the teenagers." They were one of half a dozen groups that were on the hotel's books; another, to Kootch's eternal delight, was jazz pianist Eddie Palmieri's Conjunto la Perfecta . . . "the fantastic Eddie Palmieri Orchestra, one of the greatest Latin bands ever, and here I was at this young age, watching them every night. It was really an eye-opener, I had never heard music like that."

There, too, the King Bees met a young New York singer with her own growing reputation, Evie Sands. She had already cut a couple of singles and toured with the Shangri-Las, but right now she was on vacation with her parents. "She used to come and sit in with us for a couple of tunes and she was phenomenal," Kootch recalled. When Sands discovered that the King

Bees were planning to move back to New York, to take up residency at Arthur's discothèque, she promised to keep in touch.

Deep inside the East Forties, Arthur's was everything that the Borscht Belt was not. Heart-stoppingly hip, it was one of *the* centers of the Manhattan universe, "a very, very famous place," said Kootch, "a bit like Studio 54 became. You'd see all these movie stars there, everybody's frugging, everyone looks like Julie Christie. It was a great gig."

The King Bees were booked to play five sets a night, "half hour on, half hour off, and we were making $250 each, which was a fortune. They might as well have paid us $250,000 each. We all went out and bought a lot of clothes...."

Joel Bishop's disc jockey father, WMCA staple Joe O'Brien, pulled some strings and the King Bees landed an audition with RCA Records. They passed and a string of singles, beloved of modern garage enthusiasts and eBay bargain seekers, followed. Kootch still smiles at their memory. "It was a lot of fun, and when I listen back to them, we were pretty good."

Certainly good enough to attract the attention of Peter Asher and Gordon Waller, the studious-looking English duo who, riding their friendship with the Beatles in general (Asher's sister Jane was Paul McCartney's girlfriend), and the songwriting talents of Lennon and McCartney in particular, had scored a U.S. chart-topper with "World Without Love."

Further hits followed, some penned by McCartney, others drawn from the Buddy Holly, Del Shannon, and Phil Spector catalogs, and by early 1966, the simple duo of Peter and Gordon were as reliable hit makers as any bigger, louder, British Invader. Now the pair was planning a short tour of the American northeast, and they were searching for a band to accompany them. They chose the King Bees.

Kootch: "We were still playing Arthur's; they came and saw us, and for some unknown reason, they hired us to back them up—unknown, because we didn't play any of the kind of tunes they did. 'World Without Love' was the last thing we'd play; we were doing Otis Redding and James Brown. Plus, I never could learn to play the solo that's on the original record, I never could figure it out."

Bluesman John Hammond Jr. was another of the King Bees' most loyal cheerleaders, and would often drop by to sit in with them before retiring to the basement to light up a joint. One night, management caught them in the act. "That's when we got fired, that's what ended our tenure there," Kootch confessed. "So we went from there to a place called the Downtown Club in lower Manhattan, played there for a really long time, everybody came to see us, we saw everybody." Jimi Hendrix was a friend, months before he went to England to become a superstar; John John McDuffy knew him from the guitarist's stint with the Isley Brothers, "and he was completely unknown. But still obviously playing amazingly great guitar."

After a while, though, the excitement began to pale. "It got to be a dead end. We were playing every dump up and down the East Coast, playing gay bars, alcoholic bars, bars where they'd raise the price of beer when we played, every dump you could imagine, and we were getting tired of it because we weren't getting anywhere."

The King Bees split, but they had one more role to play. True to her word, their old friend from the Royal Hotel, Evie Sands, had remained in contact, and now she was delivering exciting news. Her manager and mentor Chip Taylor had just landed her a role in a new movie, *Step Out of Your Mind*.

Barely financed and never completed (although its putative theme song later became a minor hit for the American Breed), *Step Out of Your Mind* was envisioned primarily as a vehicle for Sands. But the movie needed a band, and Sands knew exactly who it should be. Kootch recalls, "Evie turned us onto Chip and his partner Al Gorgoni," and daily for however long the shoot required, the King Bees would turn up on the soundstage in the fluffy-sleeved purple getups that wardrobe supplied them with, and run through both musical and thespian paces.

All in vain. The plugs were pulled on *Step Out of Your Mind*, and nobody seems to remember why. "Maybe the backer got bored, or changed their mind, or ran out of money," Chip Taylor guessed. But he was not bothered. In an age when labels were throwing money at rock 'n' roll music, and all manner of other entrepreneurs, too, were throwing small fortunes at the pretty boys and girls they thought could be the next big thing, projects like *Step Out of Your Mind* came and went every day.

Particularly when you were the hottest kid on the songwriting block of the day. As the man who wrote "Wild Thing" for the Troggs, "I Can't Let Go" for the Hollies, and a string of hits in the Nashville world, Chip Taylor had recently been made associate professional manager of the leviathan CBS label's publishing wing, April-Blackwood. Now he and Gorgoni were ensconced in their own offices at 1650 Broadway, bang next door to the legendary Brill Building songwriting factory and, coincidentally, just three floors above the basement studio where Chip's first band, Wes Voight and the Town and Country Brothers, had once successfully auditioned for King Records.

The dynamic duo passed on the opportunity to work with the King Bees; the band was too close to self-destructing. But Chip was fascinated, regardless, by Kootch's stories about life on the Vineyard; and, in particular, by his tireless cheerleading for "his friend James, this guy from North Carolina, who he was going to be starting a group with, after *Step Out of Your Mind* was completed."

Kootch: "The thing is, back then it wasn't so much James's songwriting. He'd probably only written one or two songs back then. It was that he was such a phenomenal singer. That was interesting. We were very good friends and along with that he was a really good singer, and that's probably what I told Chip."

Chip Taylor remembered it slightly differently. "James did not have what you would call a good voice for the radio. But he did have songs." That was revealed the afternoon that Kootch walked into the office "and played us some songs that James had written. Danny brought me up a reel-to-reel tape and I listened to it, and 'holy shit!' I called up Al and said, 'We've got to stop everything. We've got to work with this guy!'"

Kootch knew exactly what he wanted for the new band. Joel Bishop wasn't going anyplace; he remained on drums. Another Massachusetts buddy, Zachary Wiesner (the son of MIT provost Jerome Wiesner) was lured down to play bass. Kootch would handle lead guitar, of course, and the newly liberated James Taylor was installed on vocals and guitar. Occasionally they would run into John John, the King Bees' old front man, and cast covetous eyes at his new gig, replacing Al Kooper in the Blues Project, but the new band had its own ace in the hole as well. They had Chip Taylor.

Plus, New York City was hopping. A few years earlier, the city in general and Greenwich Village in particular had blazed with the same folky intent as the rest of America, from the Vineyard of Taylor's summers to the Los Angeles of Jackson Browne's youth; a home away from home for a myriad of would-be troubadours and minstrels, all with their own personal take on the blending of pop with politics.

But things had changed; the city had changed. Out on the West Coast, you could still strum your way to stardom and the last year had seen the

Byrds take flight to prove that equation beyond reproach. Electrifying a Bob Dylan song was revolutionary enough; in fact, Dylan himself had only just taken that plunge. But electrifying one of the most boring songs he'd ever written, the interminably monotonous "Mr. Tambourine Man," and transforming it into something you actually looked forward to hearing again, that was a major accomplishment. Now all of California, it seemed, had set its sights on attaining the same musical heights at the Byrds, and the music its musicians made was as sun drenched as its beaches.

New York was grittier and its music moved likewise. There was the Lovin' Spoonful, John Sebastian's post–Even Jug Band vision of urban jug band blues that was many musical miles from the sun-soaked smiles that would become the group's Top 40 legacy. There were the Fugs, a snarling voice of poetic discontent woven not over melody, but over anger with a beat. There was the Velvet Underground, a band so far out on a musical limb that only artist Andy Warhol could truly fall in love with them. And so on. Brighter and more conventional sounds could still be found playing around, of course. But if your finger slipped anyplace close to the New York City pulse, it inevitably wound up falling into these darkest corners.

Blending fact-finding excursions with their own rehearsals, creating a sound that might blend into the cityscape without sinking into the teeming crowds, Kootch, Taylor, Bishop, and Wiesner had already worked up a rudimentary repertoire. By July 1966 they were ready for action.

First, a name. The Spencer Davis Group was hot on the charts at that time, a Birmingham, UK–based R&B act whose pounding, keyboard-driven sound was topping the charts all over the world. Inspired by the simplicity of the group's name (but maybe missing the point of it—the Spencers were christened after their bassist, Spencer Davis, not their front man, Steve Winwood), Kootch wanted to call the new band the James Taylor Group.

Taylor demurred. He was already nervous enough about stepping into the spotlight at the helm of the new group; even the Fabulous Corsairs, the group he'd led with brother Alex in Chapel Hill, had never played any venue much larger than a youth club or sock hop. The idea of thrusting his name into the spotlight was one headline attraction too many.

Instead, he suggested that they became the Flying Machine, inspired by one of the previous year's most electrifying cinematic phenomena, the movie *Those Magnificent Men in Their Flying Machines*. And maybe also by the whispers that they'd heard from across the other side of the country, about a hot new band in San Francisco called the Jefferson Airplane. From all the accounts of that group that had filtered into New York of the melodic folky gentility that was their stock-in-trade, the Airplane didn't sound that different from what the Flying Machine was preparing to unleash. It would just be a matter of who got airborne first.

The new venture didn't pay much at first. Twelve bucks a night, split four ways, was a good payday for a gig on the already brimful Manhattan scene. But at least clubs were willing to give new talent a trial, and there were enough venues crying out for cheap entertainment that almost any band could find work if its members set their sights low enough. Besides, even the poorest-paying gig in the lowest ranking nightclub counted as experience, and every time the Flying Machine set foot on stage, James Taylor's confidence, as both a performer and a songwriter, grew.

He had continued writing during his time at McLean, and although he later insisted that he only completed two songs there, he was happy enough to stick with them. Now, tapping into the same vein of creativity, he embarked upon a furious writing spree. He had an album's worth of songs written before the Flying Machine even found a regular gig, and a second album's worth by the time they started dreaming of recording.

He wrote from his own life experiences. Years later, writer Jules Siegel, in *Rolling Stone*, would seize upon the lyric to one of his McLean-era compositions, "Knocking 'Round the Zoo," and condemn it for sounding like "a sado-masochistic fantasy. Even in the mental hospital, James Taylor is still the aristocrat, still in control. The female attendant is paid to be his slave. And she'll hit him with a needle. I wonder what Bob Dylan would have thought of all this?"

Yet what else should he have written about? Stepping out of a teenage trauma that could not help but impact so hard on his psyche, Taylor found that the issues that had both consigned him to McLean and been addressed during his time there offered a more than fertile landscape upon which to base his music.

It was also unique. Four or five years later, English songwriters Kevin Coyne and Alan Hull (of the folk band Lindisfarne) would both draw upon their own experiences in mental hospitals to craft some of the most startling music of their era, with Hull's "Lady Eleanor" a truly eloquent evocation of the fine line that has always divided madness from beauty. But Coyne and Hull approached their art from the other side of the treatment table;

Coyne was an orderly; Hull was a nurse. Taylor was a patient, and the terrors that might have assailed his nights were very different, and far more personal, than those which even the most committed observer could ever experience.

Sober and reflective, darkly percolating around the Flying Machine's gathering grasp of minor key melodies and haunted harmonies, the words and music were just pouring from him: "Don't Talk Now," "The Blues Is Just a Bad Dream," "Something's Wrong," "Brighten Your Night with My Day."

The songs entered the group's repertoire slowly. "Back then we were doing mostly R&B covers," Kootch recalls. "There were a few other things, there were a few of his tunes. 'Brighten Your Night with My Day' was a very good song...."

Nightly through the early summer of 1966, Taylor would lead the Flying Machine through their dreams, playing to the ever-changing crowd of wannabe folkies, would-be hippies, and bemused out-of-towners who were claiming the Manhattan club scene for their own.

The band found a rehearsal space in the basement of the Albert Hotel on University Place, tucked between Tenth and Eleventh Streets in the Village; and a home, too. Fire had recently swept the top floor of the hotel, leaving just one room relatively unscathed. The hotel management could never rent it out to guests, but they offered it to the Flying Machine at the cheapest rate in town. Taylor had been crashing at Kootch's house for a time, and then with another friend way uptown on Eighty-Fourth Street. This new roost would keep him in the heart of the action. He and bassist Wiesner snapped it up.

They landed a regular gig, a short residency at the Café Bizarre, a radical hang-out three blocks below St. Mark's Place in the East Village. It was there that the Velvet Underground was playing when they were discovered by Andy Warhol. Now they had a record company (Verve) and a club (the Dom) of their own. Maybe the Bizarre would be that good to the Flying Machine?

It wasn't, but they didn't care.

The Night Owl Café at 118 West Third Street, between Sixth Avenue and MacDougal Street (the site is now occupied by Bleecker Bob's record store), came calling. The Lovin' Spoonful had just moved out, as they continued their transition from a Greenwich Village jug band to pure pop superstars, and the Flying Machine were seen as the ideal replacements.

Kootch recalled, "The Night Owl Café...had auditions every afternoon and bands from all over the tristate area would come in and try to get a job as one of the bands there. We went in there, auditioned, and we got the gig right away...because we had James Taylor. James back then was just a terrific singer...."

Ensconced in the Night Owl, the band members were living like kings. Three groups played four sets a night at the club: the Flying Machine, the Ragamuffins, and Lothar and the Hand People. But management was nothing if not egalitarian. Each band received $72 a night, plus a free meal.

That was enough to get Taylor out of the charred remains of the Albert Hotel and into a place of his own, a tiny room that he decorated as sparsely as he could get away with—a mattress on the floor and a radio—and then filled with the people he met on the streets, the runaways and junkies who he easily befriended, then allowed to crash in his pad.

The Night Owl was good to the group. It offered them exposure, experience and, most important of all, a sense that the band was airborne. Taylor repaid it with a song that would become the venue's theme for at least the time left on the Flying Machine's residency, "Night Owl." And the band's audience began to flower too.

Among the other local bands that Kootch and Taylor regularly tried to catch was the Myddle Class, whose bassist, Charlie Larkey, was dating Carole King, the doyenne of Brill Building songwriters, one half of the Goffin-King team that soundtracked the first half of the 1960s with their effortless encapsulations of teenage life. "The Locomotion," the dance craze that devoured 1962, was one of theirs; so were "It Might as Well Rain Until September," "Will You Love Me Tomorrow," "Up On the Roof," and "One Fine Day." Even more impressively, the duo's success was not thwarted by the rise of the Beatles, as was the case with so many other of their Brill Building buddies. British Invaders Herman's Hermits and the Animals both recorded Goffin-King songs, and the Monkees' "Pleasant Valley Sunday," among the biggest hits that summer of 1967, was a Goffin-King composition.

King was also coproducing the Myddle Class and one evening, as they looked out into the Night Owl audience, the Flying Machine were astonished to see the woman who cowrote an entire generation's worth of deathless pop hits standing there watching them. And she was applauding Taylor's own songs as loudly as he might have applauded hers.

Another night, Taylor and Kootch were laughing about how many groups on the scene seemed to have a blues song that declared their identity in the most dramatic terms possible. . . . "All these heavy songs," Taylor laughed to a London audience a few years later, "like 'I'm a Man' or 'I'm a Jackhammer' or 'I'm a Steamship' or whatever . . . 'I'm the *Queen Mary*.' We weren't to be left out of this, so I wrote . . . the heaviest blues tune I know. It's called 'I'm a Steamroller.'"

"We were sitting together talking and he was saying he wanted to write a heavy blues," laughed Kootch. "All the bands were blues bands, and he said, 'We've got to write a tune that's heavier than every other heavy blues,' and he came up with 'I'm a Steamroller' in about ten minutes."

Ten minutes. That, insists hindsight, is about how long the Flying Machine's relationship with Chip Taylor and Al Gorgoni would survive. But hindsight is wrong. In fact, the pair in general and Chip in particular would be a constant presence in the Flying Machine's life, as their instantaneous belief in Taylor's talent became an all but all-consuming passion.

"I could listen to James's songs and I would wonder what I was doing even trying to write songs of my own," Chip revealed. "But then I remember the first time James heard 'Angel of the Morning' [a Chip Taylor composition destined to become Evie Sands's next single] and he went mad over it."

A contract for Taylor's songwriting to be assigned to April-Blackwood was produced. In return, the band would receive a recording contract; Chip and Gorgoni were in the process of launching their own record label, Rainy Day Records, specifically for the Flying Machine's benefit; they even named it for one of Taylor's latest compositions, "Rainy Day Man." All Taylor had to do was sign on the dotted line, and the dreamer with the stars in his eyes didn't even consider not signing it. Or taking it for a thorough legal going-over. He made his mark and, years later, he would mourn that that one signature, inked when the band was desperate to record, passed the rights to some of his best-loved songs over to April-Blackwood. The company would come to own half of "Fire and Rain," "Something in the Way She Moves," "Don't Let Me Be Lonely Tonight," and more. All from what Taylor called a simple mistake. "I [just] wanted a sandwich," he said later. "I had no idea what I was signing."

Rainy Day Records was distributed by Jubilee Records, a label whose own most rainless days had occurred in the early 1950s, when it became the first black label to reach the white market (with the Orioles' "Crying in the

Chapel"). Since that time, the label had muddled by on a succession of R&B and novelty numbers, scarcely ever bothering the charts and maintaining equilibrium more through its parent company, the record wholesalers Cosnat Corporation, than through its musical endeavors. A bluesy white folk rock band like the Flying Machine was a whole new ball game for Jubilee, but Chip Taylor had only just started shaking the corporate cage.

"Like I said, James was special. So I thought we should launch him as a folk artist, or a jazz artist," Chip recalled. "Jubilee, like every other label in the country, were into singles. They would release three singles, and if they had some hits, then an artist would be allowed to make an album. You didn't put albums out until you got three hits. I came up with a different way to do it."

Chip's idea was simplicity itself. He wanted to circumvent the traditional pop machinery and simply push Taylor and the Flying Machine out on an album. All agreed that Taylor didn't have "a typical radio voice"; why shouldn't they "treat him like a jazz artist or a traditional folk artist"? Why shouldn't they bypass the mass marketing approach, and promote the band in a handful of select areas or even neighborhoods? "Have his records in the stores near where he plays. And try to develop two or three towns on the East Coast where he could play. We looked at cities like Boston and Washington, D.C. We wanted to create a vibe thing, where the people who went to his shows would want to buy the record. We would sell it in Greenwich Village, sell it where his shows were, Philadelphia, Washington, Boston."

The Flying Machine loved the idea and so, at first, did Jubilee Records. "And then they had a big meeting, and they decided not to. And that was a real big disappointment, to me and to Al and to James. They said we could cut as many tracks as we wanted to, but they wouldn't put it out as an album because back in those days that wasn't the way things were done."

Unfortunately, the clutch of demos that the Flying Machine cut under Chip Taylor's aegis were scarcely an album in themselves, even though they would later (1971) appear as one. Kootch condemned, "They took us into the studio for basically one day, and that is what you hear on that album. That album was not meant to be an album; those guys came up with no money, they came up with nothing, they didn't spend a nickel on us. They just put us in the studio for a day."

In fact, it was more like three hours, an in-and-out session at Select Sound Studios in New York City, during which the band laid down half a dozen songs, demo-shaped versions of five of James's compositions, and a Kootch number called "Danny's Song." From these fruits, Jubilee then authorized Rainy Day Records to proceed with a blink-and-you'll-miss-it release for a single of "Night Owl," the song Taylor wrote about the club of the same name.

There was a smattering of hope for the label's first release when local radio play allowed it to nudge a regional chart or two; and even more when it was leased to a Canadian label for release north of the border. But the record's performance was scarcely impressive enough to interest Jubilee any further. There would be no additional releases, at least during the Flying Machine's lifetime, and the group was clearly crumbling too.

Kootch continued, "We could never get management who respected us or understood what we were doing. I wish we could have got an Albert Grossman, someone like that, with half a fucking clue, to get interested in us. And I don't know why we didn't, because we had James Taylor."

But Taylor later admitted, and his bandmates backed him up on this, that even if the Flying Machine had defied the clichés and gotten airborne, he probably wouldn't have known much about it. He was already far too high.

4

Fire and Rain

Fire and rain. The flames of Jimi Hendrix's immolated guitar, and the tears of the Walker Brothers' heartbroken fan club. A tour that crisscrossed the British Isles like the spidery veins of an old man's ankle, and in the heart of it all, a young man, barely twenty years of age, sensitive enough to be hating almost every moment of the outing, but young enough to know that life did not get much better than this. This was the hottest tour of spring 1967, the Walker Brothers' farewell tour after two long years of teen stardom and Hendrix's hello to an eternity of fame, and Cat Stevens was a part of it. A big part.

"Cat Stevens," mused Noel Redding, the bassist with the Jimi Hendrix Experience. "To be truthful, we really didn't pay attention to any of the other acts on the tour, but I remember him on the bus, sitting quietly and reading, not really saying or doing much. He just seemed shy, but I know he says he talked with Jimi a lot. They used to hang out together after shows, go to discos and talk about girls...."

The shy boy agreed. They'd already met, the half-Greek singer from the West End of London, and the half-deified guitarist from the West Coast of America, a few weeks earlier, on *Top of the Pops*. British television's flagship pop show ruled the musical airwaves in those days, a happy hunting ground for every aspiring hit maker of the age, and Hendrix was riding his first hit that night in January 1967, a wired reinvention of the murder ballad "Hey Joe." Stevens, on the other hand, was an old hand at the game—"Matthew and Son" was his second smash in a row, and he did not expect his status to let him down on tour. Instead, everybody, even the headliners, wound up playing second fiddle to the Jimi Hendrix Experience, just as Hendrix had warned they would. "The Walker Brothers, Engelbert Humperdinck, and Cat Stevens, all the sweet people follow us on the bill, so we have to make it hot for them," he said in an interview on the eve of the tour, and he proved his intentions from the outset.

With ticket sales through the roof as a nation poured out to say good-bye to the Walkers, the tour opened at the Astoria in London's Finsbury Park on March 31, 1967. That was the night Hendrix set fire to his guitar, crouching onstage with a can of lighter fluid, squirting the liquid over his axe and then striking a match.

Stevens was backstage at the time, preparing for his appearance, when somebody shouted out a warning, something about a fire onstage. Everybody rushed to the wings to see Hendrix crouched over his blazing axe, his hands conjuring the flames higher, while the theater management fussed with the fire extinguishers. Stevens ran back to his dressing room and changed his shoes. His legs were trembling so badly that he did not trust himself to venture out in the Anello and Davide high heels that he'd bought for the occasion. He slipped on a pair of plimsolls instead.

The nature of the tour allowed each of the opening performers time to play just a handful of numbers. Clad in a green Edwardian frock coat, the retro-hip badge of the year's grooviest souls, Stevens performed four songs: "I Love My Dog" (his first hit), "Matthew and Son" (his second), "Here Comes My Baby" (which he wrote for someone else), and "I'm Gonna Get Me a Gun," his latest release. Some nights for variation, he would throw "If I Were a Carpenter" into the set, and the New Musical Express wasn't simply being kind when it described him as the surprise packet on the show. Gentle and reserved he may have seemed, but he threw a lot of energy into his performance.

The surprise packet was frequently in for a surprise of his own, however, particularly when he introduced "I'm Gonna Get Me a Gun." For that was the cue for Hendrix's mischievous rhythm section of Redding and drummer Mitch Mitchell to appear from behind the amplifiers on either side of the stage and squirt the boy with water pistols.

And the angrier Stevens became, the more his tormentors would try to provoke him, as one water pistol apiece became two and other props were introduced to the proceedings. Including, on the final night (at the Granada in Tooting, London, on April 29), a toy mechanical robot that rumbled nois-ily across the stage as a panel in its chest opened up and a bank of machine guns sprang into life. Stevens kicked out at the intruder, dealing it a number of hefty blows. "But that robot would not die," Redding chortled.

Six months earlier, of course, Stevens would never have believed that such a joke could even be played. Not on him, anyway.

He never saw himself as a cat. Steven Georgiou was born on July 21, 1948, in the Middlesex Hospital in London, the son of a café-owning Greek father, and a Swedish mother. An inner-city kid, he grew up in a world that revolved around the city's theatrical West End.

He went to school in Drury Lane in the heart of London's theater-land; he gravitated toward the stage doors and front doors of the tangled web of agencies, publishers, promoters and the like that comprised the showbiz scene of late 1950s London. He hung out in Covent Garden, where London's fruit and vegetables arrived from around the country; Denmark Street, where the music publishers and recording studios congregated; and Soho, where the late-night bars and coffeehouses flourished an area that, in the mid-1950s, was only just beginning to pick up the reputation that would eventually establish it as the red-lit heart of the London sex trade.

Right now, it was simply down-at-heel, as rapacious landlords preferred to allow the old brick buildings to simply crumble, rather than fix them up into something halfway habitable, as though they knew that soon, the only people who could stand it would be those whose customers wouldn't care about the damp stains on the walls, or the fuzz of mold round the window frames, because their attention would be focused upon more intimate sights and sensations than those. These were the playgrounds of Stevens's youth, and those were the theaters where his imagination flourished.

Vacations were usually spent in Sweden, where a sprawling family tree had planted an army of relatives, including a movie director, an artist, and even the man who designed the brass work for the royal palace. Stevens's parents had parted, and the only time he spent with the Greek side of the clan was at the café, where his mother continued to work. The boy spent the bulk of his own time on the streets, a raw, rough upbringing, but an inspiring one for everyone who shared in it, and the source of so many subsequent paeans to the birth of Swinging London.

The self-confessed weird kid who grew to be Cat Stevens allowed his surroundings full rein in his imagination. An avid artist, a boy who thought nothing of staying up till five in the morning drawing and sketching, he absorbed everything he saw on the streets and let it out in his artwork, and the more twisted and morbid it seemed, the happier he was. At school, he could always be relied upon to turn out a cruel, crooked caricature of another pupil or, more often, one of the masters, and when he showed one of his efforts to his Swedish uncle Hugh Wickham, himself a well-known Swedish artist, the older man was so full of praise for Stevens's little painting that he had it framed and hung on a wall in his home.

A few years later another admirer, Stevens boasted, was Gerald Scarfe, as he launched his cartooning career via the satirical magazine *Private Eye*. Stevens used to mail his work to Scarfe and could always bank on receiving a polite, even encouraging, letter in response. Nothing that the boy submitted, however, was ever published; in fact, most of the magazines and papers he contacted would promptly return the drawings to him with a note describing them as too grotesque.

A stoic boy who spent his time in his room drawing dark, wicked caricatures of his family and friends, Stevens later confessed that he frequently "nose-dive[d] into dark depressions, which are just a part of me," and found that solitude was his best friend in such situations. Yet such resilience in one so young did not mean that he was a happy youth. He wallowed in self-pity, imagining that nobody else could conceive of his suffering, and, again by his own standards, was forced to grow up quickly.

Yet it was Stevens's half-brother David, not his surroundings or upbringing, who turned his head toward music. Shortly before Stevens's tenth birthday, one of his elder sibling's school friends, thirteen-year-old Laurie London, scored a hit with a version of the gospel song "He's Got the Whole World in His Hands."

The first British child star of the pop era, London would prove the role model for a host of similarly youthful aspirants over the next couple of years, and brother David was adamant. If Laurie London could do it, anybody could. And Stevens realized he agreed with him. Weeks later, he bought his first ever 45, a copy of Buddy Holly's first British hit, "Peggy Sue."

It is difficult from this distance to imagine just what an impact records like "Peggy Sue," or any of the other rock 'n' roll hits that arrived between 1956 and 1958 had on the youth of their era. Even more so than in America, where R&B and other forms of what was then called race music were at least available, British entertainment was locked in a bubble of almost Victorian morality.

Looking back on his childhood, former Rolling Stone Bill Wyman spoke for an entire generation, the likes of Cat Stevens, and a host of other war and postwar babies too, when he recalled what passed for light entertainment. "Rock 'n' roll just wasn't around . . . there weren't bands. Rock 'n' roll hadn't been invented, skiffle wasn't even around. It was dance bands, dance music by Benny Goodman, Glenn Miller, and all that lot.

"There wasn't pop music; pop music was sung by very ordinary, horrible people in evening clothes, that copied American hits . . . and it was bloody awful."

Britain, in the years before rock 'n' roll came along, was often regarded as a wasteland, and anyone who lived through it seems more than happy to perpetuate that belief. The first record Wyman ever bought was Les Paul and Mary Ford's "The World Is Waiting for the Sunrise," and he still remembers rushing home to play it on the family's windup record player.

"Johnny Ray was the first singer I saw who had a bit of balls. I saw him at the London Palladium on my grandmother's television; the kids tore his trousers off, and that was the first time I ever saw fans attack someone on stage.

"But all the rest of it was dance bands, from my first memories of music, what I heard on my aunt's radio, or my gran's radio. There was no scene." What there was, was a sense of futility. For Wyman, and for the generation born immediately after him, life was simply something that was laid out before you, cold, gray, and immutable.

You accepted what you were offered because there was no alternative. Adolescence stretched out like a looming no-man's land, the final rite of passage before you stepped into your father's shoes and followed him to the office . . . to the shop . . . but first, two years serving in the armed forces.

National Service, the compulsory induction of every able-bodied school-leaver into one of Her Majesty's Armed Forces, was introduced in 1948, in part to halt a massive upsurge in juvenile crime in the immediate postwar period; in part to ensure that Britain, so unprepared for Hitler in 1939, would never be caught napping again.

When the United Nations waded into Korea in 1951, national servicemen supplied nearly 60 percent of Britain's infantry force; when Britain marched into Egypt in 1956, the conscripts were on the front lines again.

Everywhere that Britannia was perceived to be under threat, a fresh crop of eighteen-year-old boys was draped in green, and dispatched to duty, to serve their nation—with their blood, if they had to. And, like the rest of their impending adult existence, there was very little they could do to prevent or even postpone it.

Maybe that's why rock 'n' roll would become so important. Encountered fourteen, fifteen years into a life that had been mapped out before it had even begun, rock 'n' roll had an unpredictability that wasn't simply exciting, it was liberating. No one had ever heard anything like it—no one had ever sung anything like it; and how satisfying it was, after a hard day's obeisance to a crinkled adult world, to simply let rip with the feelings that you really felt meant something: "yes sir, no sir, three bags full sir, and awop-bop-a-loo-bop to the whole damned lot of you." But until that happened, it was a matter of just gritting your teeth and waiting.

The British *New Music Express* published its first pop chart on November 15, 1952—#1 was Al Martino's "Here in My Heart." Jo Stafford, Kay Starr, Eddie Fisher, Perry Como, Guy Mitchell, the Stargazers . . . over the next six months, and for the next three years, the best-selling 78s (there were very few 45s being released in Britain at that time) were show tunes, ballads, movie themes, and novelty numbers.

Occasionally, a local star rose to joust with the Americans and at least insert a hint of unpredictability into the brew. Emerging in 1954, the legendary Alma Cogan so shrugged off the drab austerity of the day that, at first glance you'd have sworn she was another Hollywood starlet. But her accent was pure London and her homegrown style so captivated the country that a decade later Paul McCartney was writing songs for her, and Andrew Loog Oldham was producing a projected next single. But she was an—maybe even *the*—exception.

Wyman again. "You had David Whitfield and Lita Roza and Dickie Valentine, doing all these songs like 'Green Door,' 'How Much Is That Doggy in the Window,' all the Doris Day songs, all the Connie Francis songs, they were all covered by these quite ordinary, middle-aged people."

But just because it looks like a wasteland and sounds like a wasteland, that doesn't necessarily mean it *was* a wasteland. The state-owned BBC held the monopoly on broadcasting in Britain; but, though the family wireless was perpetually tuned to the Beeb's brand of entertainment—light orchestral music and live dancing contests, prewar comedians and mind-broadening lectures—there were alternatives.

Radio Luxembourg, beaming out of the European principality of the same name, was powerful enough to be picked up across much of Britain and though the reception was invariably lousy, the R&B and blues records that filtered through the crackling ether at least hinted at a life beyond Sam Costa and Dorothy Carless.

Specialist record shops in the bigger city centers, too, splashed the edges of gray Britain with a dash of welcome color, namely the blues and folk that crept in on expensive imports to be treasured by the youths who would one day comprise the forces of the British Invasion.

And if you waited a few decades, one day you'd realize that the BBC itself wasn't so bad, as Deep Purple's Roger Glover explained. "Growing up in the fifties in England, the BBC . . . played every kind of music there was. And, though we complained about it, in retrospect that was a great education. Without the BBC we'd not have heard gospel music and classical music, folk, blues, and jazz. They'd dip into everything and it wasn't done with any style or anything. But in retrospect it wasn't so bad, because you look at kids growing up now, they get force-fed a particular subgenre of music, and that's it. They don't have the wide overview. They're very channeled. We heard everything, and we could take what we wanted.'

This was Stevens's musical background, then, and the sounds that would filter into his child mind were those that he would later be spitting out in his own songs and imagery.

He wrote his first song in his early teens. It was titled either "Darling Mary" or "Darling Nell," dedicated to the sister of one of his friends, whose name also was Mary (or Nell). They had enjoyed a short-lived but, in the way that is common to all young adolescents, intense relationship, and when it ended, Stevens was heartbroken. Mary (or Nell) had turned him away from her front door, and he raced home and, again, did what all heartbroken adolescents do. He wrote a song.

His first efforts fed from his other great love of the age, the musicals that sprang up all around his childhood home. He saw as many of them as he could, devoured the original cast albums that accompanied them, learned the lyrics to every song that appealed. *West Side Story* rarely left his turntable from the time it was released in 1960, when he was twelve, and he whiled away his nights reimagining its jagged New York grit in the heart of London, and conjuring scenarios that he could place in song, lyrical vignettes that he conjured from the same centers as his cartoons, the essence of a person caught in as few lines as possible.

During his first flood of fame at the end of his teens, Stevens regularly muddled through a litany of the other things that he would describe as influences. Few of them were singers; most of them were individual songs or their writers: Burt Bacharach, Jerry Lieber and Mike Stoller. He toyed with the notion of combining classical music and jazz. He dreamed of writing a theatrical play, and of conducting his own self-penned concerto. He worshipped Gershwin's *Porgy and Bess*, *My Fair Lady*, and *The Sound of Music*. And he admired simplicity, especially if it was arrived at from a starting point that was complex. That, he took to saying, was how he wrote his best songs, by starting them out at the most complex place they could be, and then slowly stripping everything back.

So a musical muddle, a hodgepodge that hopped between vaudeville and squares-ville; with lyrics and melodies that were pinned down by nothing so much as the fact that they could not be pinned. And yet his songs were also fiercely in tune with another movement that was percolating, the English folk scene that may or may not have been invigorated by the emergence of Bob Dylan in 1962–63, but which had certainly grasped its own destiny now.

No less than its American counterpart, all across London the folk movement was responsible for a massive insurgence of new venues, new dreams. Folk clubs sprang up in the bowels of any business that could accommodate them, from the lowliest pubs to the swankiest restaurants, and the young aspirant threw himself into that whirl, there to discover that the purer one's musical ideals, the more impure the fate that awaited.

Most of the places were holes in the wall, and most of the audience was there to get laid. Young men in the first flourish of "look ma, I can grow a beard," wearing clothes that gave them a studious air, with patches on their elbows and severe black-framed spectacles that flashed when they looked toward the stage; young women with spots, buck teeth, and stringy hair, dressed in strange, shapeless combos that could have been made from old potato sacks.

Not everybody was convinced by the earnest doings of these so-studious denizens. Like Tom Rush bemoaning the Harvard grad's search for the flavor of the chain gang, Karl Dallas, the doyen of British folk journalists, wrote wearily of the "bearded [men] in jeans [who] would bash out three chords on an acoustic guitar and sing a ballad about the Oklahoma dust bowl, oblivious to its lack of direct relevance to South Croydon."

But that was a bugbear that had haunted British music since the turn of the twentieth century; the manner in which songs about America and American life always sounded better than tales of hard times in old England. Perhaps it was the resonance of the very names; regardless of the fact that half of America's towns and cities were christened for places in the Old Country itself, a song about New York had a resonance that an ode to old York could never aspire to. Washington, D.C., sounded far more impressive than Washington, County Durham, and don't even think of comparing the A 36 to Route 128.

The first British blues bands, struggling out of the country's mid-1950s jazz boom, met the dichotomy head-on, by imbibing their musical journeys into the soul of Americana with the wide-open fascination of tourists visiting these places for the first time.

Bobby Troupe's original version of the rip-roaring "Route 66" is a sedate stroll down a highway that links one place to another. The Rolling Stones' journey down that same stretch of tarmac is delivered in a storm of delirious postcards—St. Louis! Oklahoma!! Amarillo!!! Gallup!!!! By the time they hit San Bernardino, the song is positively an orgasm of summer vacation memories, and that is why the blues translated so well—more than that, that is how the British Invasion was then able to sell the blues back to America. Because the Brits made the New World sound magical again.

Folk didn't work like that. In the mid-1950s, when a jocular banjo player named Lonnie Donegan first stepped out of the confines of Chris Barber's Jazz Band to regale the audience with a short set of folk songs, nobody saw anything more than humor and enthusiasm in his renditions of the Leadbelly songbook, and when his first LP was released in the United States, its title said everything you needed to know—*An Englishman Sings American Folk Songs*.

He sold the songs back to their country of origin, too. His rendition of "Rock Island Line" reached #8, one of the most successful British imports in pre-Beatles *Billboard* history, and earned Donegan the nickname "the Irish hillbilly" . . . which must have felt strange, considering he was Scottish.

The hillbilly tag stuck, however, and Donegan's first U.S. album over-flows with hillbilly anthems. "Wabash Cannonball," "The Wreck of the Old 97," and "Railroad Bill" all hailed from those parts, and if Donegan's native tones twisted the songs' expected sound into totally unexpected corners, the album's own liner notes have an answer for that. "Why can't a Britisher faithfully sing an American folk song with the same credentials that an American balladeer can sing 'Greensleeves' or 'Foggy Foggy Dew'?"

At home, of course, Donegan represented another musical force altogether, the father of what swiftly became known as skiffle. The dominant domestic musical form in Britain through the late 1950s, the simplistic vision of skiffle depicts a handful of reformed folkies bashing out borrowed dust bowl epics on an array of household implements—broomstick bass, washboard percussion, granny's elasticized corset, whatever.

But it went beyond that, then and now. In 1955, rock 'n' roll was still a distinctly American phenomenon, and one that the Brits simply couldn't compete with. Guitars were expensive; amps weren't cheap, and neither were drum kits. Like the protopunks of two decades later, young musicians took one look at the technological arsenals of their idols and then fled for the hills. The punks returned with used budget guitars and loudly buzzing amps; the skifflers came out with whatever they could find in the cupboard under the stairs. And though the means were different, the ends were very much the same: the creation, through muddle and mutation, of a uniquely British musical genre.

That, perhaps, is why the transatlantic traffic had slowed since Donegan's peak, as Britain returned to her insular musical ways. But the next wave of British Invaders, led by the Beatles, the Stones, and so forth, co-opted the blues by pushing even indigenous folksingers out of the American mainstream and back into the underground; while at home, the movement that skiffle had scoured for inspiration retired behind the young Donovan's collection of psychedelic cloaks and whimsy, to pursue its own peculiar vision. Bob Dylan experienced that vision when he popped over to make a TV show in 1962, and Paul Simon devoured it during the gap year he spent in the British capital on either side of Simon and Garfunkel's first album.

So much of the music Simon wrote at that time was influenced by the sights and sounds of the city, from the lonely musician waiting for a late-night train who laments his way through "Homeward Bound," to the idiosyncratic co-opting of the traditional "Scarborough Fayre," with its increasingly shrill and demanding requests for further gifts to satisfy the song's narrator's bloodlust for material wealth.

Simon cut an album in London too, one man with a single microphone and guitar, and a sixty-pound recording budget that was dwarfed by the magnitude of the songs that he recorded. Slip-sliding in and out of print during the 1960s and early 1970s, *The Paul Simon Songbook* was fated, equally slipperily, to fade in and out of favor too. Its maker himself has seldom been overkind about it, while the vast majority of listeners usually write it off as little more than a set of demos for songs that Simon and Garfunkel would soon be rerecording to far greater effect (and acclaim).

That may be true, but the sheer strength of the songwriting, and the vision that its (comparatively) unaccompanied rendering leaves intact, have both been dented by the songs' own subsequent popularity and arrangements. A stark "I Am a Rock" has a desolate urgency that the later revision could never re-create, while "The Sounds of Silence" packs a bare loneliness that is worth a new verse or two on its own. Indeed, it is remarkable just what a difference shedding Garfunkel's (admittedly much better) vocal in favor of the half-formed Simon's makes. "A Most Peculiar Man" boasts a dingy air that lines it up alongside any of the London scene's indigenous observations, while "Kathy's Song" (written by Paul in New York for Kathy in London) reminds us, perhaps, why love songs always sound better when sung by one of the lovers.

In fact, if any criticism can be leveled at the album, it is simply that it was recorded so quickly. But Simon was busy. He befriended guitarist Davy Graham, and included his instrumental "Anji" on the *Sounds of Silence* album; and made friends with another expat American, Jackson Frank, whose "Blues Run the Game" would also be recorded by Simon and Garfunkel.

He cowrote songs with Bruce Woodley of the Seekers, an Australian folk band that was topping the UK charts at the time; and by the time he left the city to resume Simon and Garfunkel's American career, both Simon and London knew they would never see the world in the same way again.

That was the world in which Stevens felt immediately comfortable. He discovered Dylan and Leadbelly and added them to his pantheon of heroes, admiring the discordance that was so often a crucial part of their delivery; Dylan's inability to "sing" correctly, Leadbelly's ham-fisted guitar and out-of-tune vocals. He started hanging out at folk clubs where he learned other people had adopted those same attributes for themselves, and another piece of the jigsaw fell into place. A bad singer is okay if he can write good songs and get the music's message across regardless. But most bad singers are just that: bad. There was a lot of bad going around the folk clubs.

Stevens was a student at Hammersmith Art School by now, and his love of folk music endured; he skipped class so he could hang out on the fire escape, strumming his guitar. Evenings were the time for his education: Bert Jansch, John Renbourn, Davy Graham, Paul Simon.

He even tried his hand at the circuit himself, forming a duo with his friend Peter James in 1963, and playing his own songs at a few none-too-memorable shows around whichever folk clubs would allow them the time. A year later, he tried again on his own, undertaking a handful of shows that kicked off at the Black Horse pub in Rathbone Street, but didn't travel much further afield than that. But he was a familiar sight at Bunjies Coffee Bar, alongside future legends like Roy Harper and Ralph McTell, but also a clutch of utter unknowns; Meg, the toothless old lady in plimsolls and headscarf, whose repertoire seemed to stretch no further than "Danny Boy"; an Armenian named Hrath Garabedian, who broke hearts with his version of Woody Guthrie's "Deportees"; and the visiting Americans Jackson Frank and Paul Simon.

Stevens made little impression on any of them. Cliff Wedgbury, an early friend and fan of Al Stewart, recalled "Sandy Denny . . . nursing Cat Stevens, whose dad owned an Italian [sic] restaurant around the corner," but any relationship the pair may have had was fleeting, and had ended by the time Stevens moved onto his next project, a trio formed with friends Andrew Koritsas and the singularly named (or at least recalled) Jimmy. The unit—the JAS Time—took its name from its membership's initials.

Stevens didn't fit. He could not get his head around the traditional songs that so many of his audiences demanded all performers be versed in; and his own compositions slipped far from that milieu, back into the theatrical streams that had ignited his pen in the first place. He loved folk, but the songs he was writing just didn't fit. They sounded, people complained, too commercial, but whereas other young aspirants might have taken that as an insult, for Stevens it was a compliment. Because commercial music was hit-record music, and that discovery came along at precisely the right time. He was studying to become a professional cartoonist, but he was losing faith in that dream. What if he became a musician instead?

His mother sighed; his father groaned. Nobody, it seemed, believed he could do it and that, Stevens later said, was the impetus he'd been searching for. The more people who doubted him, the greater his need to prove them wrong. In the past he had simply had an idea. Now he had ambition as well.

By early 1966, that ambition had pushed him back onto the circuit, this time under the name Steve Adams; and now it was pushing him through the office door of producer Mike Hurst.

It was late summer 1966 when the pair first met. Hurst was still trying to establish himself as something other than a former member of the Springfields, the band he'd formed with singer Dusty Springfield and who blazed brightly over a string of hit singles earlier in the decade. More recently, he had been performing with a new band, the Methods, but they, too, were on their way out, and Hurst recalled, "In 1965, when I finished with . . . the Methods because we couldn't get anywhere, I became a record producer and I went to work for a mad Californian called Jim Economides, who'd set up in London. He'd been a recording engineer at Capitol in Los Angeles, and came over. And Jim said he'd found this kid called Marc Bolan.

"Well, Jim the recording engineer was really not Jim the producer, so he asked if I would go into the studio with Marc and cut a couple of tracks. We went to Decca in Broadhurst Gardens, and we did [a song called] 'The Wizard.' And Marc was so spaced out. I asked him to explain what 'The Wizard' was all about, and he says, 'Man, he's there,' and I said, 'Where?' and he said, 'Outside the window in that tree.' I hadn't realized he'd read Tolkien, he loved it, whereas me, I hadn't read Tolkien, so I thought he was on another planet."

Stevens, on the other hand, was very much a part of a world that Hurst could understand. "I was working for Jim and there was a knock on the office door when there was nobody else in there one day, and there was a guy standing there with a guitar case and he asked could he play me some songs? I wasn't doing anything else; it was lunchtime, so I said, "Sure, play me some songs.' So he sat down and played me 'I Love My Dog' and I said, 'That's great. What's your name?'

"And he said, 'Well, it's Steven Georgiou, but I changed it to Steven Adams, and now I've changed it again but it's a really stupid name so I'm going to change it again.' I was now totally confused, so I asked, 'What is your stupid name. . . . He looked at me, he looked so shy, and he said, 'It's Cat Stevens,' and I said, 'Seriously, that's a great name. Keep the name.' And that's how we first met."

It could also have been the last time. Hurst continued, "I then introduced him to Jim because I thought he was great. And in typical fashion, Jim just said to me, 'The kid's crap.' I said, 'You gotta be joking, he's fantastic,' but Jim said, 'No, we don't wanna know, Boob' . . . he called everybody Boob. So that was that."

A second meeting with Economides went just as poorly. Invited over to Hurst's home in Kensington, Stevens was astonished to find both the American and Marc Bolan waiting for him, and listening politely through "I Love My Dog." They weren't impressed; according to Stevens, Economides was still barking Bolan's praise. They parted company soon after. At least for a short time.

Hurst: "Cat had a manager at that time called Bert Shalit, and Bert was a wallpaper manufacturer and very rich. Anyway, he came back to me and said he'd like to do a session with Cat, and would I produce it? And I thought, 'What the hell? Economides isn't interested in doing anything with it, so I will.'"

Booking into Pye Studios in Marble Arch, London, the pair cut four songs, including "I Love My Dog" and another song that Hurst "just knew" was a hit, "Here Comes My Baby"—"and I left it to Bert to hawk them round the place. And, as it turned out, nothing happened at all."

Visits to every record company in London, it seemed, were rewarded with nothing more than blank stares and a vehement shake of the head. Independent producers, the maverick breed that short-circuited the record companies by signing artists directly to their own companies and then leasing the tapes to the labels, proved equally disinterested. Daily, it seemed, the list of rejections piled up.

There was the occasional bright spot. Stevens had succeeded in landing himself a song publishing deal with Dick James Music, a company whose entire raison d'être appeared to be to sign up anybody who even looked like they might have song inside them, and then wait to see what happened. But he was not alone in that boat: Mark Wirtz, soon to find fame as the author of "Excerpt from a Teenaged Opera"; a young and completely unknown Elton John (still laboring under his given name of Reg Dwight); and American producer Kim Fowley were also on the company books, and, visiting the offices one afternoon, Stevens came face-to-face with the beanstalk maverick.

They fell into conversation and Fowley, as was his wont, handed Stevens a few sheets of paper. It was a lyric for a song that may or may not already have been called "Portobello Road," but that is what Stevens returned to him, a paean to the West London market whose secondhand-clothing stores and shops selling antique paraphernalia had established it as young London hipsters' most favored shopping destination.

Yet even topicality and a songwriting link to the man who discovered the Hollywood Argyles, Sandy Nelson and B. Bumble and the Stingers could not pull Stevens out of the doldrums. So time passed, and even Mike Hurst, the only industry player who had even showed an interest, had all but forgotten about Cat Stevens.

Hurst could be forgiven his forgetfulness, however. Despite his continued failure to get off the blocks as a producer in the UK, the Springfields' fame had not died with the band's demise. Indeed, in the United States they had ascended to something approaching legendary status as the first and only English folk act to even briefly impinge on the early-1960s scene.

"Silver Threads and Golden Needles," a song they had not even issued as a 45 at home, had been a Top 20 smash in America and was now a staple of so many homegrown folkies' acts. So when Vanguard Records (alongside Elektra, the royal family of the U.S. folk scene) found themselves seeking a new A&R man, it made sense to offer the job to someone who had already proven himself to have a keen set of ears.

Hurst accepted the job. "I was fed up with everything. I'd left Jim [Economides] and I was going to leave the country. I was going to immigrate to California with my family; I'd got the job with Vanguard Records. Literally my whole life was about to change. Then what happened was, the doorbell at my flat rang on a Saturday morning and there's Cat standing there with his guitar case, and he said, 'I've been to every record company in London and nobody wants me. Are you still interested?'

"So I said, 'Tell you what, the first song you ever played me, "I Love My Dog," I think it's a hit. There's only one thing missing, it needs a bridge.' And because I'd found out by that time that he was part Greek, I did that very Greek-restaurant-type thing: I suggested we put that in, that he 'na-na-na' it, which he did, and I said I'd take him into Decca Studios."

There was just one problem. Second only to EMI's Abbey Road mansions, Decca Records' West Hampstead studio was the best in Britain, with prices that matched its magnificence. With the best will in the world, Hurst could not afford to book the band on a whim. So he applied a little subterfuge, making an appointment to see Dick Rowe, the head of A&R at Decca Records, and laying it on the line. Or not.

"I told him a lie. I told him, 'I'm leaving the country to go to America, so for old times' sake, will you do me a favor?'"

He explained that he wanted to cut a farewell single, a Mike D'Abo composition called "Going Going Gone." All he needed was three hours in the studio. "Dick ummed and ahhed and eventually he said, 'For old times' sake, you've got three hours in [studio] number two.' So he gave me the time and I borrowed the rest of the money to pay for the musicians; then we went in to do 'I Love My Dog.'"

The next day, armed with an acetate he had cut at the studio, Hurst returned to Decca's massive headquarters on the Albert Embankment and prepared to tell Dick Rowe the truth. "He asked, 'How did it go?' and I said, 'I told you a lie. I didn't go into record my song, I went into record this new singer . . .' and he went absolutely apeshit. But I said, 'Before you say anything more, would you at least just listen to the record?'

"So he put the record on and it was like something from a bad Hollywood movie. He got halfway through the record, and he looked at me . . . . He didn't say a word, he just picked up the phone, and he went straight through to Sir Edward Lewis, the head of the whole company, who was upstairs in his eyrie at the top of the building, and he said, 'Sir Edward, would you come down here please?'"

Hurst froze. "I thought, 'Oh God, they're going to throw everything at me. It's a good job I'm leaving the country. . . .'" Neither did Sir Edward's arrival set his mind at rest. Slowly, almost sadistically, Rowe returned the needle to the revolving acetate and, in silence, he and Sir Edward listened to the record.

It finished and there was a moment's silence. Then Sir Edward turned to Hurst, "and he uttered the immortal words: 'My boy, you're a genius.' And I just stared at him and went, 'Mmmm.'"

Outside on the embankment, Cat Stevens sat impatiently in Hurst's car, too nervous to even venture inside the lion's den. Hurst could see him staring out of the window as he left the Decca offices, his eyes growing wider and more fearful as he tried to deduce the fate of his song from the look on Hurst's face.

Hurst, however, remained impassive. Finally, he got to the car and climbed inside, slumping down into the driver's seat.

"What happened?" Stevens's voice was as nervous as his expression.

"You're not going to believe it."

"Oh God, they hated it, didn't they? They don't want to know, either."

Finally Hurst could not hold his excitement in any longer. He repeated the final words Sir Edward had said to him before the meeting ended. "We're starting a new label, the Deram label. Would you like to launch it with this record?"

Forty-five years on, Hurst still laughs at the memory. "I was a mess. I just looked at Sir Edward and went, 'Yes, please.'"

5

Wild World

By early 1966, Jackson Browne was ready to abandon his attempts to make his voice heard, or even audible, and find a more reliable conduit for his songs. It was not an admission of defeat; rather, he knew that the experience would allow him to grow stronger, to refine his art without standing in the spotlight, and, best of all, he would not even have to take responsibility for the group's somewhat wacky name.

Who, after all, calls their band the Nitty Gritty Dirt Band?

Destined, within a decade, to become one of the biggest names on the West Coast rock scene, the Nitty Gritty Dirt Band grew out of the New Coast Two, a Long Beach jug band formed by, and comprising, singer-guitarist Jeff Hanna and singer-songwriter guitarist Bruce Kunkel.

Informal jam sessions at the legendary McCabe's Guitar Shop in Long Beach, a hangout for young players as diverse as Ry Cooder and Taj Mahal, developed into more regimented rehearsals, and slowly a lineup began to crystallize around a gang of like-minded players: Ralph Barr, Les Thompson, Jimmie Fadden, and, because the whole thing both looked and sounded like fun, Jackson Browne.

With a set that slipped from original compositions to such standards as "Gonna Sit Right Down and Write Myself a Letter" and "It's a Sin to Tell a Lie," the Nitty Gritty Dirt Band were a purist jug band catching a ride on the same revivalist coattails that had already ignited the Lovin' Spoonful. Observers laugh at the memory of the double-breasted pin-striped suits, whiteface, and cowboy boots that adorned the six musicians' frames; and the jugs and washboards that filled their van.

But an utterly unexpected victory in a battle of the bands competition at the Paradox landed them a gig at the Golden Bear in Huntington Beach, opening for Texas garage growlers the Sir Douglas Quintet as they rode the one-two punch of the hits "She's About a Mover" and "The Rains Came." And a few nights later, the Nitty Gritties were sharing a bill with the Lovin' Spoonful, as they ventured west for the first time.

The jug band's fame began to spread, and so did their musical horizons. But Browne never truly felt he belonged. He wrote one song that his bandmates adored, a ragtime novelty called "Melissa." But they passed over "These Days," which he wrote around the same time, and they looked askance at other numbers he brought along. If it couldn't be jugged, then it was of no use to them.

By summer 1966, shortly after the group played an utterly mismatched gig at the Glendale Ice House, opening for Captain Beefheart, Browne had quit the Nitty Gritty Dirt Band (another Paradox regular, their manager's brother John McEuen, replaced him); and by August, all of Browne's performing nerves were firmly placed behind him when Bob Sheffer and Hank Fisher, proprietors of the Paradox, persuaded him to play his first ever solo gig. And this time, not only could he be heard, he seemed to be enjoying himself, too. So much so that, when his girlfriend at the time, singer Pamela Polland, invited him to join her band, Gentle Soul, he made it clear that it was only a temporary measure. He wanted to get on with his own career.

An aptly named vocal duo, Gentle Soul originally comprised Polland and fellow vocalist Rick Stanley. But Stanley quit while the band still had some outstanding dates to play, so Browne stepped into the gulf. It was a short-lived venture; Stanley returned after no more than two weeks away, and Browne was free to return to his solo career.

But if Gentle Soul was just another passing fancy, Polland remained one of Browne's greatest local cheerleaders, singing his praises to all who listened, including Billy James, a publicist at Columbia Records. James and Jackson met at the Golden Bear one evening that fall, and days later, Browne was recording his first demo tape for Columbia. Before the label could act on it, however—possibly before they even heard it—James was jumping ship, taking on the plum assignment of opening Elektra Records' new Los Angeles office. And he wanted Jackson Browne to jump with him.

It was not an offer Browne could decline. The success of the first Paul Butterfield Blues Band album the previous year had seen Elektra begin moving closer to the pop mainstream they had hitherto kept at a deliberate arm's length. The label came close to resigning John Sebastian once he moved onto the Lovin' Spoonful, actually exchanging contracts before it was discovered that the group's publishing deal already bound them to the Kama Sutra label.

Elektra was more fortunate with Los Angeles band Love, which scored its first hit single in the spring of 1966 with "My Little Red Book." Love's debut album followed and, despite the general unpredictability of the band's music (sometimes brilliant, sometimes . . . not so brilliant), they remain one of the best-loved acts of the age, with their only serious competition coming from Elektra's next and, at the time of Browne's arrival, most recent venture into rock, the Doors.

This was the company that seventeen-year-old Jackson Browne was being invited to keep; this was the legacy that he would be expected to preserve; and in terms of painting his own private legend around his arrival in those halcyon corridors, his Elektra career got off to a flying start. On October 9, 1966, Browne signed up as a staff writer at Nina Music, the label's publishing wing. His entire $500 advance was spent buying his way out of a summertime pot bust.

Writer Joe Smith recorded Browne's recollections of his day in court. "There were two hundred black and Chicano kids in court that day and it was an inescapable fact that they were all going to the slammer, while the other three or four clean-cut kids like me, whose parents had paid a lawyer to stand up and say how 'upright' we were—well, you just knew we weren't going to jail. Whoever had the bread was gonna be all right."

And it looked like bread was not going to be a problem. Not now. Less than two weeks later after Browne signed with the publishing company, Nina repaid his loyalty by getting his lyrics in *Time* magazine.

≋

The New Troubadours.

It was a resonant term for what was, even if you acknowledged its innate tunefulness, a particularly unresonant turn of events.

Throughout its first decade of life, which we will say kicked off with "Heartbreak Hotel" in 1955, rock 'n' roll had been about tutti-fruttis and long tall Sallys, yeah yeah yeahs and a-lop-bam-booms. It was about Rolling Stones pissing on filling station walls, and rockers with locks that trailed so far down their backs that even their admirers confessed that a few looked like girls.

It was about kicking out the jams and getting down and with it; "Summertime Blues" and "My Generation." Articulating anger and fire-eating frustration. "Paint It Black" and "Like a Rolling Stone." Howling like Ginsberg and fucking like beasts.

It was not about sitting down and writing a poem to your heart.

It was not about speaking to your innermost child.

It was not a place to go if you wanted to talk about your *feelings*, and hands up everyone who felt a little bit betrayed when they learned that John Lennon wrote "Help!" for precisely those reasons? The last truly significant pop record that the Beatles ever made, transformed into a three-minute sob on the psychiatrist's couch; and, because the Beatles were never allowed to do anything without it immediately igniting a whole new trend—couldn't even break wind without a myriad imitators buying baked beans in their wake—suddenly thoughtfulness and analysis were the way to go. And, by the time the Beatles got around to "Eleanor Rigby," even *Time* magazine was paying attention.

The magazine's October 2, 1966, edition tells the tale, and christens the new movement, too. "The New Troubadours," screamed the article's headline, and that was foreboding enough. But it got worse.

The opening lines to the story set the stage. "'Zeeks!' gasped one teenybopper. 'You can't even dance to it!' She was referring to the Beatles' latest release, 'Eleanor Rigby,' in which the shaggy four sing to the accompaniment of a double string quartet."

Time applauded the Beatles' daring, for raising the barricades with which rebellious youth had hitherto ring-fenced its musical heroes, and it found echoes in the words of countless other commentators elsewhere in the media. Mature and stately, adult and accessible, "Eleanor Rigby" *was* the sound of "the familiar big beat of rock 'n' roll . . . receding."

But was it receding because it needed to recede? Or were there other forces at work here, forces that had less to do with rock 'n' roll needing to pause and take a quick breather than with the fact that the people who listened to the music had suddenly grown so goddamn old?

Fifteen in 1955, when Elvis ushered in the age of cool, and Eddie, Chuck, Gene, and Buddy were all banging on the door, you would be staring thirty in the face at the end of the sixties. Thirty! An hitherto unimaginable age that you would have spent the past two decades declaring tantamount to a death sentence.

And though you still felt much the same as you did half that age; still liked the same records, dug the same films, read the same books . . . well, that was the problem, wasn't it? They were the *same* records. In 1976, a twenty-eight-year-old Jackson Browne remarked, "most people [never stop] living the first twelve, or maybe fifteen, years of their life. When they're forty and talking about something, it could just as easily be about something that happened to them when they were ten." And he was right. Because youth is when you have time for those things, and a record or a movie or a television show is going to mean far more to you when you're in teens, and the most important thing in the world *is* that record (or movie or television show), than it will when life itself has taken over. Time to grow up, time to settle down, time to put away the air guitar and "could you turn that down a little? The kids are trying to sleep."

So first you turn it down and then you notice that the records you're playing have been turned down as well. That the Beatles are no longer screaming to be heard above a stadium full of keening schoolgirls, and are sitting around the campfire instead, singing songs about lonely people. That the Stones have stopped seeking satisfaction and Dylan now is sailing sad-eyed ladies across the lowlands.

It was nothing you could put your finger on. But there was a creeping literacy moving into the mid-1960s music scene. Songwriters were suddenly comfortable searching for words that rhymed with more meaningful terms than "baby," "yeah," and "like long hair." It was a dark sobriety, a sense of seriousness and, most chilling of all, a morbidity that may or may not have stepped from those hysterical early Beatles reviews that compared "I Want to Hold Your Hand" with the combined output of Shakespeare and Beethoven, and had been leaching into art's enfants terribles for a couple of years now. It's true, too. Have your work compared to that of a grand master long enough, and sooner or later you will start believing the hype. And, even more dangerously, you will start living up to it. Human nature does not permit otherwise.

Nobody was to blame, either. There is no single reason why rock was suddenly going soft on us, and no truly culpable party. Yes, the Beatles did their bit, of course, and so did Bob Dylan and the Band—expunge *Sgt. Pepper's Lonely Hearts Club Band*, *Blonde on Blonde* and *Music from the Big Pink* from the historical record of 1966–68, and an awful lot of grimness would have been averted too; a lot of hubris and po-faced panegyrics, and an entire school of "informed" rock writing that made a virtue of the fact that the writers themselves had been to college *and actually paid attention in class*!

That was a new development. Hitherto, rock reviewing had been the purview either of tired and bitter old newspaper staff men who'd seen youth fashions come and go, and traced a direct line of musical decay back to whatever had floated their boat when *they* were fifteen; *or* it was in the hands of the so-called teenybop press, who didn't care who the hell they wrote about so long as they were young, male, cute, and malleable.

But *Crawdaddy* crawled out in January 1966, a magazine that treated rock as though its words were engraved in stone; *Rolling Stone* rolled up on November 9, 1967; and almost smack-bang perched in between those two dates, *Time* magazine laid out the editorial brief for both, the first concerted nationwide attempt to transform rock music into something that could physically help shape the news, and not simply make it every time a passing pop star was caught looking happy while smoking a hand-rolled cigarette.

It is no coincidence, either, that the music that *Time* singled out as so special was essentially that to which *Crawdaddy* had handed its early accolades: Simon and Garfunkel, the Mamas and the Papas, and the Lovin' Spoonful were all profiled in the first four issues of Paul Williams's Brooklyn basement-based fanzine, and were all lionized anew in *Time*.

Twelve months later, in the first few *Rolling Stone*s, there they all were again, the grimly serious faces of rock music as more than a cure for the summertime blues, or the rest of the words that Roger Daltrey merely stuttered through: "Why don't you all just f-f-f-form an orderly line in the corridor and the doctor will see you shortly." This ain't rock 'n' roll, as David Bowie would later be paraphrased; this is mama's best chicken soup.

Lots of currents, lots of courses, lots of little pick-up sticks, and all of them pushing pop into directions it should never have looked in. A rock band with an orchestra, writing new concertos for guitar and cello; an album with an art libretto, emblazoned with the death threat "rock opera." And a singer with a conscience, with a soul-singing sadness, pouring out his heart with an inner-worldly wordiness and laying bare that same essentially teenage sense of personal angst that past generations had left locked in their journals, but which could now be set to a wistful melody and raised up as something somehow salable.

Misery loves company, after all, but even more than that it loves post-adolescent self-absorption, and "wow, if you think that last song was meaningful, wait until you hear the next one."

"In recent months," that *Time* feature continued, "the pop market has been penetrated by a new and impressive clutch of poet troubadours. They are mostly ex-folksingers who turn out their own numbers, are older than their forerunners and more musically sophisticated. They write songs with titles like 'A Single Desultory Philippic' [Simon and Garfunkel] and 'Sunshine Superman' [Donovan]. The recurring themes are loneliness, alienation, and lovers who walk 'on frosted fields of juniper and lamplight' [Paul Simon's 'For Emily, Wherever I May Find Her']."

To further illustrate the point, however, and perhaps to hammer it home with irrefutable finality, the magazine asked readers to consider another song, titled "Shadow Dream Song": "It's a crystal ringing way she has about her in the day, but she's a laughing, dappled shadow in my night . . . ."

The brief verse's author was not named or credited. But Jackson Browne's friends, family, and music publishers all knew his name. Which means that, with so much happening, or threatening to happen, in Los Angeles, it was pure teenage adrenaline that prompted Browne to place it all on hold and go to New York City instead. That and the fact that his sister Bernie's old boyfriend Steve Noonan had recently moved across the country, and Greg Copeland intended driving from coast to coast to visit him. In fact, Copeland and some other friends intended venturing even further afield, using New York simply as the starting point for a trip to Europe. Browne couldn't afford that, but New York was certainly doable.

They left early in the New Year of 1967, on a dead-of-winter journey that, with everyone taking turns to drive, took them just four days without stopping for anything more than gas and necessities. Of course Browne's memory of the trip wasn't all it could have been; he told writer Joe Smith that they left Los Angeles in January 1967 and listened to the Cassius Clay versus Sonny Liston prize fight on the radio as they crossed the Texas Panhandle. But that fight took place in 1965, and their journey was certainly too early in the year for the newly renamed Muhammad Ali's next fight, demolishing Ernie Terrell (the elder brother of the Supremes' Jean Terrell) on February 6, 1967—a match that was all the more memorable for the sheer brutality of the bout, but which would swiftly be absorbed into the background noise that surrounded Ali's loss of his championship title just two months later.

It doesn't matter. Whenever Browne arrived in New York, and whatever he listened to on the radio as they drove, he was immediately installed on the sofa in Steve Noonan's apartment, a few tiny rooms on the Lower East Side, at a time when that address alone conferred a certain bohemian gravity upon its occupant.

Certainly it was a world far removed from any Browne had seen before. Even Highland Park, which his family had evacuated when the neighborhood went downhill, could offer nothing to compare with the ragged slums of the *loisada*, the immigrant-packed and poverty-stricken warren of streets and tenements through which Browne and Noonan had to trudge every night, simply to get home.

Yet there was a status symbol of sorts in that address, not to mention easy access to most of the places where two teenage or thereabouts musicians might want to be; beginning with Greenwich Village and straggling out from there.

The East Village began almost literally at the bottom of their road, and David Peel, the epitome of New York street performers as the age of the hippie began to dawn, was quick to name his own band after the area he called home; David Peel and the Lower East Side Band would soon be joining Browne on the Elektra books, while another Elektra artist, singer Tim Buckley, was already a friend of Noonan's.

In fact, the two of them, Noonan and Buckley, had recently been booked to play a Sunday afternoon show at one of the State University of New York's smaller campuses, in Stony Brook, on January 13. Browne tagged along and, in the laissez-faire spirit of the day, was added to the bill. And, according to journalist Richard Meltzer, who met Browne for the first time at that show, Browne "just knocked everybody out," both in his own right and by association. "Seems like every song I'm doing is a Jackson song," Steve Noonan admitted during his opening set, and he was right.

Stony Brook was simply a one-off for Buckley; his main engagement in New York at that time was a residency at Andy Warhol's Dom, and that was an education for Browne as well, even before he entered the building. The term *hippie* was not yet in wide use in New York, but the first glimpses of its imminent preeminence were already making themselves noticed around the Village and St. Mark's Place.

Gone were the ragged jackets, checkered shirts, drab flat caps, and harmonica cases that had once stuffed the windows of the trendiest neighborhood boutiques, replaced by velvets and furs, fringes and tassels.

A military surplus store called Limbo opened up and did a roaring trade in army greens and camouflage, to kids who would never dream of donning such costumes in earnest; the military draft was creeping ever closer to a lot of them as the United States stepped up its suicidal intervention into Vietnamese politics, and cops were beginning to stop kids on the streets to check their identification papers.

Browne wasn't worried about the draft right now, because he knew officials wouldn't track him down to the couch in Steve Noonan's living room. Besides, you didn't go to the Dom to worry about things, much the same way as you didn't go to the Dom to listen to the music. You went because it was the Dom; and besides, a lot of the music was god-awful anyway, sound blasting from cheap amplifiers ricocheting from the walls of a building that had barely functioned as a Polish social club in the years before Andy Warhol took it over, and whose acoustics had only gotten worse once he moved his own apparatus in there. The scrawny albino with the hesitant handshake was an artist, after all, not a sound engineer, and not an acoustic technician either.

So when bands walked around complaining that the sound did strange things when they played at the Dom, Warhol took that as a compliment to his own genius. You could create art from anything.

Even from a discotheque on St. Mark's Place whose name, unbeknownst to everyone who read shorthand S&M terminology into it, translated from Polish as something far more domestic than that. The venue's full name was Polski Dom Narodowy, "Polish National Home," but "Dom" was "Mod" in reverse as well, and occasionally Warhol would tell somebody that was why he called the club that.

But no, the Dom was the Dom long before Warhol and his right-hand man Paul Morrissey cast eyes upon it; and long before they launched their own nitery in April 1966 with the Exploding Plastic Inevitable, a multimedia presentation that merged light, film, sound, and personality together into one seething, bubbling, beatific whole.

Lou Reed's Velvet Underground was the unrelenting soundtrack to the experience. The lights and slides of Daniel Williams and Jackie Cassen provided the visuals; the dancing of Gerard Malanga and Mary Woronov were the focal point, all whips and chains and writhing flesh, bloodied by gelatin slides and given fresh manic momentum by the merciless strobes. And though things had calmed down considerably in the ten months since the Warhol Dom's opening, the club retained at least a fission of the frenzy for which it once had been renowned.

Five movie projectors worked full-time, bathing the walls in Warhol's own cinematic vision. Five carousel projectors shot fresh images onto the stage every ten seconds. Colored gels and spotlights did crazy things to your eyeballs, and a huge revolving mirror ball, one of the first seen in a New York club since the golden age of the speakeasies, sent shards of light flashing across every darkened surface.

And all night long, the spotlight would seek out and then settle upon Nico, German model, Fellini actress, Andrew Oldham protégée and now Warhol superstar, ethereal beauty, and dazzling blonde, the New York underground's pick for the most stunning woman in the world.

Nobody could resist Nico. Warhol worshipped her, Lou Reed adored her, John Cale became her friend for life. Bob Dylan wrote a song for her, Iggy Pop carried a torch for her, Jim Morrison and Brian Jones were in love with her. Leonard Cohen started writing songs for her the same night he met her. Jackson Browne, then, was just the latest in the long line of men who had fallen beneath the former Christa Päffgen's intoxicating spell. "I had a gigantic crush on Nico. She was so fucking beautiful. I had seen these twenty-foot-high posters of her for the three weeks I'd been in New York and then I went down and saw her—it was even my first time in a bar, I think, because I'd just turned eighteen."

Nico was at the Dom with the Velvets when they opened the place; she was still at the Dom now that they had moved on, a solo artist who relied on whoever else was in the room with a guitar to back her up as she sang. Tim Buckley filled in a few times; so did her old Velvets bandmates Lou Reed and Sterling Morrison.

But she was in a weird position. Verve, the MGM subsidiary that picked up the Velvets on the strength of Warhol's reputation, clung onto Nico's contract after she and the band parted company, and now they were demanding an LP. The suits at the head office had never quite understood what she was doing with Lou Reed and his noisemakers anyway; saw Nico through the same starry eyes that any beautiful female pop singer ignited in the mid- to late 1960s, and Nico went along with their scheme because she accepted most offers that came her way. "It is better than saying no to them," she shrugged. "Because who knows what possibilities might then emerge?"

She was still establishing her repertoire. She sang three songs on the Velvets' first LP, and vocalized through a few more live. All the songs floated in and out of her own show, and Lou Reed had promised some to write her some more. But other songs came and went as the mood hit her.

Songwriter Tim Hardin, the junkie folk author of "If I Had a Hammer," had turned over a few of his songs to her. So would Leonard Cohen; so had Bob Dylan. But Nico was always looking for fresh material, so when her friend Danny Fields called her up one day to tell her about the young songwriting guitarist who he'd met at her show the previous evening, Nico wanted to know more. And when she realized that she had already spotted the young man herself, so preternaturally pretty and looking so hopelessly lost amid the Amazonian knights who normally haunted the Dom, she wanted to know more than that.

Fields reeled off all he had been able to glean. A teenage German-born army brat who was living on the Lower East Side, a friend of Tim Buckley, and a songwriter too.

Nico was intrigued. She placed a great deal of stock in the laws of coincidence, and playing alongside a fellow German, so far from her own birthplace, intrigued her. Besides, if there wasn't a synchronicity there, then there was another one in his family tree, a brother whose middle name was Severin, the central character in the Velvet Underground's "Venus in Furs."

Plus, laughed Fields, "He is *so* innocent!" He passed on what he had already determined was his favorite Jackson Browne anecdote; how, driving out from Los Angeles, he and Copeland stopped the car at a filling station in Missouri and Browne had asked for the key to the restroom. The old guy behind the desk handed it over, and it was only when Browne was inside the room that he realized he'd been handed the wrong key. He was in the ladies' room. And the old guy had *not* been making a political statement.

Fields introduced himself properly. He was an A&R man at Elektra Records. Browne flashed recognition; "I'm a contract songwriter for Nina Music." Fields called Nico's manager, Paul Morrissey, over; Morrissey asked Browne if he played electric guitar. Browne nodded. Then Morrissey asked if he'd play electric guitar behind Nico, and Browne melted.

Despite Nico's membership of the Velvet Underground, the New York media shared Verve Records' insistence that she was a folksinger, partly a consequence of a sweet little single she'd cut in London the previous year, a lightweight Gordon Lightfoot lullaby called "I'm Not Saying," but also because what else could a solo female singer do, if she wasn't performing out-and-out pop?

She wanted to step out of that image and all agreed that an electric guitar would be the easiest route they could take. Browne didn't have one of his own; he'd have to borrow one from a friend out on Long Island, he explained. But he had no hesitation, either. "I got a call, would I like to be her guitar player? I went over and got my brains fucked loose."

He could have had them fucked even looser. Installing Browne as her latest paramour, and a semipermanent houseguest at the West Village apartment where she raised her infant son, Ari, Nico was a demanding lover, as her most of her exes have testified at some point.

But she was also simply at the front of a long line of people who were apparently eyeing the young Jackson Browne with undisguised longing, and a cautionary voice for him to be careful who he sampled.

"Jackson was so pretty," Nico reminisced in 1981. "Jackson could have had anybody he chose, man or woman, boy or girl, but he was so young he did not realize. He used to tell me I was the only woman he wanted, and Lou would laugh at him for that, because he was the only boy that a lot of the men wanted."

Lou Reed, hanging at the Dom as one of Nico's occasional guest guitar players, befriended Browne quickly, setting himself up not precisely as a barricade against which Browne's admirers would crash, but at least as a purveyor of wry caution.

Richard Meltzer recalled there was "this famous publicist . . . and New York scene maker [who] was hanging around [Jackson] all the time, being nice to him and all for no apparent reason. Telling him stuff like he oughta have a TV show on which he could just be groovy, since he was such an oh-outa-site flower child."

Lou Reed tried to warn Browne to give his new friend a wide berth; Meltzer did too, and others as well. But Browne remained oblivious. "I really didn't know what was going on," he told Cameron Crowe. "I mean, I realized it later, just remembering scenes of what people said to me. But it was like candy or something. I knew what a fag was. . . . I knew that when this outrageous transvestite came up and said he was Nico's little sister, I knew what it was. It scared me. I kept my distance."

But his publicist friend took a little more figuring out. Lou Reed, Meltzer recalled, "tried to explain that this male person was after Jackson's ass, but Jackson missed the point until it finally turned out that what's-his-name unequivocally wanted to fuck him. Spooked the shit out of him."

There again, considering Jac Holzman once recalled that the first time Browne heard the word *hippie*, he thought it was an affectionate term for a small, hip person, that is no surprise. A lot of things spooked Browne at that time, including Nico.

When she wanted his favors, she was the best girlfriend in the world. She grabbed at Browne's songs as quickly as she grabbed at his soul, listening as he played through the best of the thirty or so that Nina Music had published and was now planning to press onto a demonstration disc, and inclining her head when she heard one she wanted to spend more time with. "Shadow Dream Song," the lyric that *Time* magazine had utilized to illustrate the literacy of the modern troubadour, fell into her live set; so did "It's Been Raining Here in Long Beach."

Steve Noonan recalled her performance. "I went to see Nico with Leonard Cohen, and we just sat there and watched Jackson play the electric guitar as an accompanist. This songwriter who would later eclipse everybody on that stage in terms of popularity, and yet he's playing backup guitar. It's kind of like hearing Jimi Hendrix as lead guitar for James Brown or something. [But] everybody starts somewhere, so Jackson's sitting there playing his electric guitar with Nico."

"These Days," already being cited as the most significant song Browne would ever write, was earmarked for the album that Nico was preparing to record; "The Fairest of the Seasons" and "Somewhere There's a Feather" followed it into the studio once the sessions began. She nodded, too, at "Holding," only to change her mind when he told her (so proudly, she recalled) that his old friends in the Nitty Gritty Dirt Band had already recorded it alongside "Melissa" for their self-titled debut album.

Nico shrugged. "Jackson had so many wonderful songs, and I could have my pick of them."

"This guy was a kid and he was writing these great songs," Browne's friend singer Warren Zevon mused. "I suppose I knew him before he wrote his masterpiece, but . . . he's always been great. When Jackson sets out to write a funny song, *fuck* it's funny. When he sets out to write a sensitive song, *fuck* it's sensitive."

Paul Williams's *Crawdaddy* threw its weight into the arena, its May 1967 issue presenting "an uncertified list of fine songwriters you may not know about (but should)." Browne's name was first on a registry that also included Pamela Polland and Rick Stanley, Greg Copeland and Steve Noonan, Tim Buckley, Leonard Cohen, Lou Reed, Ray Davies, and Neil Young. "These people have already written more beautiful songs than you could produce or sing in a lifetime, and they're all getting better. Go to them."

Nico agreed. Her debut album, *Chelsea Girl*, was titled for the Andy Warhol movie of almost the same name, and Browne's three songs were in sterling company: Tim Hardin, John Cale, Lou Reed, Bob Dylan. And in the studio, where producer Tom Wilson ensured that the entire LP was slammed down in just three days in April, his guitar playing chimed as distinctively as that of any of the more seasoned musicians who worked alongside them.

But the sessions were fast, and Browne's own parts were recorded in under a day, before Reed hustled him off to the RKO Theater to catch disc jockey Murray the K's *Music in the Fifth Dimension* supershow, a night in the thunderous company of Mitch Ryder, the Blues Project, the Who, and Cream. "What a day," Browne sighed, but he barely had time to process any of it before he headed out to California the following day, to try and mend a broken heart.

One night, as she and Browne played their show, Nico began telling the audience about a threatening phone call she had received a day or two before. Browne sat quietly, cradling his guitar as he always did, waiting until Nico had finished her rap. He was used to diversions like this, and so were the regulars in the audience. Suddenly, Nico whirled around to accuse Browne of being the caller.

He denied it, but Nico was hearing none of that. She had made up her mind, and that was something else about Nico. If she decided something was true, it didn't matter how much evidence was presented to the contrary. She would not budge.

So Browne budged instead, walking offstage with his guitar in hand. "I was stunned," he told Nico biographer Richard Witts. "I said, 'How could you think it was me, Nico? Fuck this, I'm going.'"

"Poor Jackson," mourned Richard Meltzer. "He was just so goddamn innocent."

6

Places in My Past

Penning the liner notes to Stevens's debut album in early spring 1967, Mike Hurst wrote of his belief in the unknown singer-songwriter. "When I first met Cat in July 1966 it took me precisely two minutes five seconds [the length of 'I Love My Dog'] to realize that short of an act of God, nothing would stop him being a success." Stevens, for his part, was simply grateful to have finally found such a dedicated supporter, although he would later admit that his decision to work with Hurst might well have been based more on fandom than on any musical instinct.

He told *Sounds* in 1971, "I was impressed by people who had been in the business, like Mike, my producer. He was with the Springfields and I used to like the Springfields when I was a kid, so I had this thing about him that he had to be right because he'd been around more than I had. Little did I know that he hadn't really succeeded up until then. He was an integral part of the group but that was all. He had never satisfied himself. So he tried to satisfy himself through me . . . ."

It was a charge that Hurst himself would later acknowledge. For now, however, nobody was investigating anyone else's motives. They were too busy getting ready for the release of "I Love My Dog."

Sir Edward Lewis's promise to allow Cat Stevens to launch Deram was not strictly true. Although "I Love My Dog" was indeed released on September 30, 1966, as part of the label's initial burst of 45s, in strict numerical terms it was the label's second single; DM 101 was the abruptly named Beverley's "Happy New Year."

"I Love My Dog" would, however, become the label's first and, for a time, sole hit, as a series of further Deram releases by such forgotten names as the Gibsons, the Truth, the Eyes of Blue, and Barry Mason fell unsold by the wayside, and other hopefuls (including Chim Kothari, the Pyramid, the West Coast Delegation, and a seemingly perennial underachiever named David Bowie) queued to join them in the sales dumper.

And why? Because they weren't Cat Stevens.

The music press of the day was utterly intrigued by Stevens. The Mediterranean good looks that he had inherited from his father; the rough-and-tumble childhood in the backstreets of theater land that he was so happy to talk about; the simple melodicism of his music, all of these things caught the editors' eye. And then there was his name, the stupid name that he'd been so keen to dispose of, but which Mike Hurst had persuaded him to keep.

Cat, declared the young man, was a name he'd been given by a girlfriend who thought his eyes looked feline, although other times have seen other stories told. He thought of it himself is one; he heard it in a dream is another. But the most imaginative is told, not by Cat or his friends, but by author Rodrigo Fresen, in his novel *Kensington Gardens*.

"Cat likes to write songs," writes the novel's protagonist. "He has one about his crazy love for his dog and another about his desperate need to buy a gun. They're good songs, but 'Steven Demetri Georgiou' is a bad name, and my father says, commands, renames him: 'From now on you'll be Cat Stevens.' My father gives him that name because Steven Demetri Georgiou has a Mickey Mouse face, and if there's anything my father likes, it's contradictions."

Contradictory or not, in October 1966, the newly christened teen sat down with *Disc and Music Echo* journalist Mike Ledgerwood to talk through his career so far. The resultant portrait of the artist as an arrogant kid appeared in the magazine's October 29 issue, and it still makes for revealing reading.

What, he was asked, was his favorite food? "Fruit—particularly watermelon. My ultimate dream is to be locked in a room with hundreds of peeled watermelons. I love slobbering into them."

His favorite drink? "It's silly, but it's water. Though I do like vodka and lime—probably because it looks like water."

He had a pet budgie named Pretty Boy, who was fifteen years old. He dreamed of a career in acting—serious stuff, though, no pop-star comedy. His greatest fear was that he might run out of songs. "Frightened of drying up as far as music is concerned. I've said that probably twenty times—then I find I've written a better song." And his greatest obsession was success. "I'm obsessed with success. If something means I'm successful I'll do it twenty-four hours a day. I love success."

So much, in fact, that he claimed to be quite willing to hold his seemingly preordained stardom at arm's length for just a little bit longer, to ensure that when it did arrive, it would be lasting. And so on and so forth, until it sometimes felt as though Stevens talked to the media simply because he loved hearing his own voice. He did not deliver quotes or sound bites. He simply opened the floodgates and gushed.

"It's funny because, although I was lonely, I always felt secure within myself until I came into the business. Now I'm frightened. I'm not mixed up, but when I try to sit down and work out what I am, it worries me because I don't know. All I know is I'm a liar. I lie all the time. And I find myself getting into violent arguments with myself through lying. And I'm very money conscious. Well, why not admit it? I have two worlds. The world of my music, which I love, and the world of money, which is great. But I like to know where my money is all the time and what's happening to it. It worries me. I like money."

On October 22, "I Love My Dog" entered the UK charts, and Stevens promptly found something to complain about. He hated the rain, he told visiting journalists, and it was raining the day he went Top 30. Forget the fact he had a hit record. He was brought down, he mourned, because it was raining.

Neither was the single to prove a major success. Although it raged to #6 on the prestigious pirate Radio London chart, where rankings were compiled from a random mixture of disc jockey tastes, ad revenue, and what Americans might call payola, "I Love My Dog" barely scraped into the official British Top 30 in November 1966, peaked at #28, and then slipped out again. Its entire chart life was over in just seven weeks. Later, Stevens mused that that was probably for the best, because of the pressures that would be brought to bear regarding trying to follow it up.

Nevertheless, the record focused enough attention on its young maker that he was able to grasp his dreams regardless. He had even picked out what car he was going to buy; and the fact that he couldn't drive didn't enter into his calculations. Right now, he was happy to ride about in Mike Hurst's Lotus Cortina. But a visit to the annual Earls Court Motor Show introduced him to one version of his future, as he drooled to passing newsmen about the black Jaguar 420G he had seen there. Black, with white windows. And why was that so appealing? Because everyone else had black windows.

Audiences were certainly intrigued by the newcomer. Voting in the then-prestigious readers' poll of *Disc and Music Echo* was already under way, with Stevens a barely fancied nominee in the Best New Act category. Nobody doubted that Cream, the thunderous power trio formed by Eric Clapton, Ginger Baker, and Jack Bruce that same summer, would walk away with the honors. Instead, Stevens took the title, and that despite the fact he was completely unknown when the voting actually started. But every time "I Love My Dog" was played on the radio, every time he gazed out from another magazine spread, another bag of votes was delivered to the newspaper offices.

His peers, too, seemed to accept his sudden preeminence. "I rather like that Cat Stevens thing," mused organist Georgie Fame of "I Love My Dog." "The words don't mean much," continued the man who had topped the UK chart earlier in the year with a song called "Yeah Yeah," "but it's good as a record. If this guy is handled carefully, he'll have a bigger hit still next time."

Fame and Stevens came face-to-face a few weeks later. On December 26, Stevens was booked as one of the opening acts (alongside folkie Julie Felix) at Georgie's two-week Fame in '67 show at London's Saville Theatre. It was the biggest gig Stevens had yet played, and Mike Hurst still recalls how excited he was when the initial booking was made. Brian Epstein, manager of the Beatles, owned the venue, and it was he who called up to personally invite Stevens to perform.

But the show did not go quite as Hurst intended. "I said to Cat beforehand, you can't just stand there in front of a mike. You've got to do something." The handful of live performances Stevens had made so far had been notable only for the singer's apparent inability to do any more than stand at the mike, apparently frozen to the spot.

"What didn't translate was the live performance part. If you're dealing with a big orchestra and everything, you've either got to be a consummate performer or you can't do it, and he was very uncomfortable. Hence, when he changed and just sat there with a guitar and another guitarist and a bass player, that's what he wanted to be. He could cope with that and he could do it bloody well. I should have seen it then, but I didn't."

"So I said, 'We've got to make you outrageous, you've got to be unusual.'" Hurst gestured toward the PA stacks that stood on either side of the stage. "'Let's open up the first number [so that] when the curtain opens, you're sitting on top of one of the PA stacks. Then you jump down and sing your song. At least it's an opener that's extraordinary.'

"So we went through this over and over again, and we get to the first gig. I'm sitting there, the curtains open and Cat's just standing there in front of the microphone! He was determined not to do anything, and of course it was quite boring, to be frank with you. . . ."

Stevens would learn, however. Fame's bassist, Mo Foster, recalled a show at the Mecca Ballroom in Glasgow where Cat was utterly intrigued by the venue's newly electrified rotating stage. "The old boy who operated it was confused by his three shiny new buttons. Cat had instructed him to rotate the stage so that, as the [opening] dance band went out of view, the stage would stop, Cat would leap on from the wings, the stage would carry on rotating and then stop for the gig.

"On the night, however, the guy became confused."

The show opened with the now relaxed and unprepared dance band completing a full circuit, and facing, once again, a roomful of screaming Glaswegians while Stevens and his band launched into "I Love My Dog" for the benefit of the brick wall behind the stage.

The focal point of these shows was Stevens's latest 45. In December 1966, Deram released Stevens's second single, "Matthew and Son." Titled for a furniture store that Stevens noticed as he was passing by South Kensington tube station one day, this plaintive lament for the lot of the workingman was an instant smash.

Radio London, bobbing about off the English coast, pushed "Matthew and Son" into the chart at #32 in the first week of January, from whence it leaped to numbers 6, 3, and 1 before the end of the month. On the BBC chart, meanwhile, it soared to #2 in the first week of February, sandwiched between the Monkees' "I'm a Believer" and the first ever hit for another Deram artist, "Night of Fear," by the Move.

Seven days later, Stevens held firm in second spot, halting the rise of the Rolling Stones' "Let's Spend the Night Together." And though "Matthew and Son" dropped to #5 on February 18, Stevens took solace in the knowledge that he now had two songs in the upper echelons of the British chart as the

Tremeloes' version of his "Here Comes My Baby" came in at #10. It would ultimately peak at #4.

"I've written about forty songs in all, and I understand that Lulu, and Paul and Barry Ryan are interested in some of my songs," Stevens mused, while adding that "[Here Comes My Baby] is one of my old numbers, written about eighteen months ago, and I was surprised when I heard [the Tremeloes' version]. It's not how I meant it to be done, but I really quite like it. I love other people doing my songs"

Less successful but equally applauded was that promised single by the Ryan twins. Regular hit makers for the past eighteen months, the singing sons of 1950s favorite Marion Ryan had fallen on hard times lately; after four successive Top 20 (or thereabouts) hits, their last two 45s had barely made the Top 50.

Released in February, Stevens's "Keep It Out of Sight" was, all assumed, the disc that would turn things around for them, all the more so after it was heralded in *Disc and Music Echo* with "utter bewilderment. . . . It sounds as though it was recorded at ten different sessions and then put together. Baffled I am. Then I notice the names of the talented Mr. Cat Stevens, who wrote it, and Messrs. Mike Hurst and Alan Tew, who put it together. Clarity. I now understand why the boys sound as though their voices are stretching and why they sound much deeper, why there are castanets, why violins hover, brass comes in and disappears and everything breaks up in a turmoil including my brain. This is the best record Paul and Barry have made."

Suddenly, a young man who had been completely unknown just six months earlier was being touted as one of the most important musical figures of the year. And he didn't bat an eyelid. Like so many other confident youngsters tasting the fame for which they now believed their entire life had been spent in preparation, he found it all completely natural.

Dawn James, a journalist with *Rave* magazine, caught Stevens at this most amazing time. "He walked along Carnaby Street, dark against the scarlet of Lord John, and the purple of Gear. His navy blue shirt and jeans hung limply on his slim body, his black hair curled toward matching eyes. He is called Cat Stevens, songwriter and singer, and really quite an ordinary eighteen-year-old. He likes cool, long-haired, short-skirted birds, he yearns for cups of coffee and plates of toast at ten in the morning. And he answers 'Yer' and 'No' to most questions because they seem, to him, adequate answers."

Yet she also pinpointed a melancholy that few of her contemporaries had ever drawn out of him, a seriousness that betrayed his status as a teenage idol. "I write my best songs when I am sad. If I am happy I cannot write well. Even if I write a happy song, I have to be sad."

What makes you sad? she asked, and Stevens shrugged again.

"Anything. It's not miserable sad, sort of [a] quiet, dreamy sad. I can get it looking at people, maybe shabby or ugly people or if it is a nice evening and I smell something in the air, spring or winter, something that moves me. It is hard to explain."

Then she asked him his ambition, and the depth of Stevens's ambition was apparent to all.

"All I really want is to build a temple on a hillside in Greece and live in it," he told her. "Just a cool, marble temple in Greece, where I can make music in peace. See, all I want to do is make music. I'd like to make real music that didn't need the human voice, something purely orchestral. And yet I like pop. It is an outlet for a certain music art. I don't sneer at it and want to leave it behind and do better things. But I do want real musicians and music critics to see something in my pop music."

In the meantime, Cat Stevens would remain a dandy. "I like clothes very much," he told *Mirabelle* magazine in March 1967, as he prepared to head out on the road with the Walker Brothers, Jimi Hendrix, and Engelbert Humperdinck. "A large variety of clothes, but I don't think I spend that much money on them. I'm certainly not extravagant over clothes."

Perhaps not, but promotional photographs from the era depict a youth who is still enjoying the first flush of fopdom, Carnaby Streeted to the gills. He recalled his first major appearance on television, performing "Matthew and Son" on *Top of the Pops* at the end of December 1966. He had decided he needed a white suit for the occasion and, for the close to one week before he was due into the television studios, he scoured London's boutiques for the cut of his dreams. He finally found it less than twenty-four hours before the show.

His third hit single funded further sartorial extravagances. Released in March with Stevens donning full western regalia for the accompanying snapshots, "I'm Gonna Get Me a Gun" was the least impressive of his hits so far, and certainly the least memorable. But past momentum would propel it to #7 on the UK chart (it reached #4 on Radio London), and that despite—or perhaps because—of the controversy that swirled around its title.

One of the most influential of all British music television programs, *Juke Box Jury*—a weekly show in which host David Jacobs and a panel of celebrity guests were invited to comment on the week's hottest new releases—set the ball rolling. Said panel was unanimous in its dislike of "I'm Gonna Get Me a Gun." But it was not the song that antagonized them. It was the gratuitously violent overtones of the title that raised the collective eyebrows, the notion that Stevens wasn't simply suffering from an itchy trigger finger of his own, but that he was advocating his fans go out and shoot someone too.

Watching the broadcast that Saturday night, Stevens was mortified. "I felt terribly hurt after *Juke Box Jury*," he told the *New Musical Express*. "In fact, I couldn't sleep all that night. I thought some of the things said were unnecessarily vitriolic and bitchy. . . . The trouble is, you don't think about those things when you put the record out—you're so wrapped up in it you can't see somebody else's side. I won't make the same mistake again, though. I've learnt from the experience. I don't want anybody to feel bad or brought down nor to entice kids to buy guns."

What he should have told people at the time of the song's release was that it was simply one distilled moment from his most extravagant conceit yet, a full western-themed musical. "And, in the context *of* the western musical, the sound wasn't bad—I liked it, but I see now that it was my fault for not explaining the context before it was released."

The western musical itself was one of a number of projects that Mike Hurst remembers percolating in Stevens's mind at this time; one of a number, in fact, that always seemed to be playing dodgem cars with one another inside his head. The prominence of "I'm Gonna Get Me a Gun," however, pushed this one to the fore, and Stevens hastened to detail it to the press. He predicted a major boom in western clothing and country music, and suggested his musical was an integral part of that. He spoke of taking the venture straight into London's West End, with himself cast as the a singing, dancing, acting lead character. He claimed such a musical would be autobiographical, a geographically flipped reimagining of the old dreams he'd had about *West Side Story*, when his childhood imagination restaged that in London. Now his London story was to be restaged in the west.

That was in March. By August, however, he no longer wanted to be a cowboy. Now he wanted to be a gaucho, the star of a musical titled *A Mexican Flower*. He told the *Record Mirror* in August 1967, "I really want to write a musical, and now I'm in the right frame of mind to do it—and because of this, I think I should be able to write some good songs for it. And it has to be about Mexico. I'm fanatically interested in that country at the moment—well, I always have been, ever since I was a kid. And this musical gives me a good excuse to actually go over there and absorb some of the atmosphere.

"I don't know what it is, but something's always drawn me to Mexico—perhaps it has to do with the music and the excitement of the place. I think I must have some Spanish blood in me or something. I dig anything to do with Mexico—but not modern Mexico."

He talked of visiting the country within the next year, but eschewing the cities and the hubbub that was likewise descending as the country prepared to host the Olympic Games. Rather, he would lodge with a Mexican peasant family, somewhere out in the wilds of the country. He would wear their clothes, ride their horses, adapt himself to their way of life. He would even eat their food. "Up to a certain point, anyway. You know, they make a sort of pasta over there that contains flies—I don't think I'll bother to eat any of that."

In the event, he visited the country briefly in August 1967, en route to his first trip to Australia. And he never mentioned it again.

7

Nothing but Time

As Jackson Browne and his teenage innocence departed New York City in a westerly direction, so another young man, another aspiring songwriting singer with a handful of name connections that ultimately took him nowhere, started running on a southward course.

He too was heading home; he too needed to heal from his experiences in the big bad city. Whereas Clyde Browne III made his farewells off his own bat, however, James Vernon Taylor had had no choice. It was either run or get run down.

He had learned a lot about music, but he had learned even more about drugs, he once said of his time in New York City, and he was probably correct. "Rainy Day Man," the song that had inspired Chip Taylor and Al Gorgoni when they were naming their own record label, was Taylor's vision of that particular slice of life, written from the inside and really not sounding too dreadful.

From the outside, however, he was losing everything he thought he deserved, both personally and professionally. As the bitter New York winter of 1966 began to wrap its talons around the city, Taylor took to hanging out in Washington Square, playing his guitar for the small change he could bum, and lengthening the list of dropouts and deadbeats who might call his apartment home.

The Flying Machine was crashing. Their Night Owl residency ended with the summertime tourist season, and they were thrown back onto the general circuit, playing whichever venues would take them, sometimes for even less than the twelve bucks they'd been happy to accept at the beginning.

One gig found them performing at a supermarket opening in Union, New Jersey, strumming "Knocking Round the Zoo" for the medicated housewives of bored suburbia. Another saw them booked to play a set at a United Jewish Appeal fashion show, although that one at least packed a memorable few moments, when they spied jazz man Charles Mingus in the audience. His daughter Carolyn was a model at the event, but he couldn't resist a few minutes on stage in his own right, joining the Flying Machine and pounding electric bass through a rendition of Little Richard's "Lucille."

The end for the Flying Machine, however, came in the sunniest climes imaginable. A booking came in from Freeport in the Bahamas, the Caribbean paradise that was just finding its feet in the tourist trade. The venue was called Jokers Wild and even the name seemed to breathe promise and renewal. But of course it didn't work out like that.

No matter that the band members' rooms overlooked the same placid blue waters where the likes of Frank Sinatra moored their personal yachts. No matter that the sun beat down on endless miles of sand and palm trees, while somber reptiles went about their lizardy business. No matter that the club had already hosted several dozen American and British bands in the past, and therefore knew exactly what luxuries would impress them the most. For three weeks, the Flying Machine endured hell on earth, a failing club in a run-down neighborhood with zero class and a not much larger crowd.

The food they were served was awful, the hours they were expected to play were regimental. Day slipped into interminable day, and yet another week in that hellhole loomed endlessly ahead of them. All the Flying Machine had to show for their time there were suntans, gut ache, and their return tickets home. So they packed all three together and fled. Then, safely back in New York City, they broke up.

"My memory is pretty spotty about this stuff, because I was getting high a lot back then," Taylor admitted to *Billboard* magazine in 1998. Dope had circulated freely on the circuit that Flying Machine plied, but when they fell off that circuit, Taylor found himself in a world that was even darker.

Chip Taylor saw him one day, just as the band was falling apart. Still disappointed by Jubilee's reluctance to take a chance on the Flying Machine, still convinced that, with the right handling, James Taylor had what it took to make a major splash, the older man listened wistfully as his protégé played through his latest composition, a melody and a few words that would one day become "Fire and Rain," then agreed to step back for a short time while

The Cat makes himself big. Scary!
AM Records/Photofest © AM Records

James Taylor reporting for duty.
Jack Robinson/Archive Photos/Getty Images

Jackson Browne . . . not yet late for anything.
Michael Ochs Archives/Getty Images

Cat Stevens's producer Mike Hurst (right) with Tom and Dusty Springfield in 1962.
GAB Archive/Redferns/Getty Images

James Taylor in London, 1968.
Photofest

The king of the city folksingers, Tom Rush, in Greenwich Village, 1966.
Michael Ochs Archives/Getty Images

Lawyers in love—Jackson Browne and Laura Nyro, 1970.
Michael Ochs Archives/Getty Images

Love me; love my Edwardian frills. The Cat goes Carnaby, 1967.
Photofest

James sorted himself out. "We made an appointment to meet up again in six months' time at a place called McGuinness's, where we used to enjoy hanging out," Chip Taylor recalled. And a door quietly closed in James Taylor's mind.

Bereft of a band, and with his one serious contact in the music industry no longer going full bore behind him, Taylor tried to keep things going alone. One afternoon he wandered into the Elektra Records office at 51 West Fifty-First Street, guitar in hand. He was looking, he said, for Paul Rothchild, and somebody called the great producer out to meet him.

Maybe Rothchild wasn't in the mood to audition new talent that day. Maybe he was on his way to lunch. Or maybe he'd already caught Taylor onstage with the Flying Machine and not been impressed. His job, after all, entailed attending live shows whenever he could, checking out talent before another label got in there. Either way, he made his excuses and slipped away, but not before he spotted somebody else to pass the young hopeful onto. A passing Tom Rush.

Ushered into an empty office, a room that had not even been furnished, the pair made themselves comfortable on the floor. They talked about their shared roots on the Massachusetts folk scene; about the Vineyard and Cambridge and the friends they had in common.

"The funny thing about James," Rush recalled, "was that Paul introduced me, but I should have met him earlier, because my roommate when I was still living in Cambridge was a guy named Zach Wiesner, who was a part of a band called the Flying Machine. And he kept saying, 'There's a guy in my band, you really got to hear his stuff,' and I'd be brushing him off, 'Zach, pick up the living room.' I'm not a neat freak, but this guy was spectacular. . . ."

Introductions now made, Rush decided to test Wiesner's recommendation. He asked (or maybe Taylor suggested) to hear a few of the young unknown's songs. A tape recorder was procured from somewhere and, moments into "Something in the Way She Moves," Rush knew he had struck songwriting gold.

Two years had passed since Rush's last album, *Take a Little Walk with Me*, and though he was not being rushed, Rush was nevertheless aware that Elektra's patience would not last forever. Two years over his contracted deadline to release his third album for the label, he admitted he was growing desperate. He was on the road a lot of the time, "and I was trying to find enough material to make another album and coming up empty-handed.

I just couldn't find enough traditional folk music that I felt I could bring anything to."

What became *The Circle Game* was birthed in Detroit in 1966. Barely into her twenties, a Canadian folksinger named Joni Mitchell had been gigging around the area, and when Rush arrived for a scheduled gig at the Chessmate, she was there awaiting him. "Joni asked if she could do a guest set, and I was blown away."

Already performing many of the songs—"The Dawntreader," "Sisotow-bell Lane," and "Song for a Seagull"—that would mark out her debut LP two years later, Mitchell held audience and headliner spellbound, so much so that she joined Rush on the road as his support at a number of shows, while he even arranged an introduction to Jac Holzman.

"Joni, I was trying to champion for a while," Rush remembered. "I was trying to get Jac to sign her, but he said no; 'she sounds too much like Judy Collins,' which she actually did at the outset. She was clearly very heavily influenced by Judy. 'Just listen to the songs,' I said, but it didn't work."

Instead, he decided to showcase her music himself. Three of Mitchell's compositions would be earmarked for Rush's next album: "The Urge for Going," which crept out as a single that fall, and was a massive hit in Boston; the title track; and the opening "Tin Angel." And with them came the notion of creating a thread that ran through the LP, tracing the rise and fall of a love affair. *The Circle Game* was, Rush modestly points out today, "one of the first concept albums"; in fact, ignoring the Beatles apologists who insist that *Sgt. Pepper* be given that tag, it was probably *the* first, although Rush never intended it as such.

"The writers came to me by divine design or something," Rush continued. Just two of his own compositions, "Rockport Town" and "No Regrets" (later to become a major hit for Cat Stevens's old touring buddies in the Walker Brothers) were scheduled for inclusion. Elsewhere, he relied upon friends and acquaintances to introduce him to material.

A song from country veteran Charlie Rich, and one holdover from his coffeehouse days, Billy Hill's "The Glory of Love," he told Taylor, were already set for inclusion alongside the Mitchell songs, while time spent with a Californian singer named Steve Noonan, newly signed to Elektra Records, had introduced him to another unknown, a teenage songwriter named Jackson Browne. His "Shadow Dream Song," familiar to so many readers of *Time*, was another strong contender for the new record.

Now, he was thinking, no fewer than two of James Taylor's songs, "Something in the Way She Moves" and "Sunshine Sunshine," seemed like ideal bedmates for the songs he'd collected.

Taylor's encounter with Rush was a rare bright spot in an increasingly dismal fall, however. Drugs provided the only other, especially after he was introduced to two gentlemen known only as Bobby and Smack. A mutual friend brought them into her life, simply telling Taylor that they needed a place to "hide out." Taylor agreed, and he swiftly discovered that Smack was aptly named.

Later, Taylor would reason that his own addiction to heroin was more of a psychological issue than a physical dependency, because he rarely used more than twice a week. But he also admitted that it could be very difficult to distinguish the two states of mind, particularly when his roommates, Smack and Bobby, were out robbing and mugging people in order to feed their own habits, then hightailing it back to Taylor's apartment to hide out from any pursuers.

Police arrest warrants were out for the pair of them and Taylor, somewhere within his opiate haze, knew that if things continued down this path, there might also soon be one out for him. "James just couldn't take it anymore," Kootch recalled. "He was living in this shitty little apartment that was just junkies and alcoholics." So he did what no teenage kid ever wants to do—he called his dad and begged for help. Twenty-four hours later, a rental car pulled up outside his apartment and the unflappable old Ike bundled Taylor and his last remaining possessions (those that were worth the trip downstairs, anyway) inside.

Hours later, Taylor was back in North Carolina and he might as well have never left. So, six months of rest and recuperation later, he set out on his travels once again. He spent Christmas 1967 with his family and then packed his guitar and suitcase. Only this time, he was going to London. The London of Cat Stevens.

Not that Stevens would have recognized it as his city. A year before, maybe. But now? People say that things can change quickly in the music industry, but the year or so that elapsed between the day he first met Mike Hurst, and that on which he walked out of their final session together, had seen Stevens fall faster than even fiction could dream possible.

≋

By the end of 1967, British rock was fully fractured.

The last few months in general, and those that had elapsed since the June 1 release of the Beatles' *Sgt. Pepper's Lonely Hearts Club Band* in particular, had completely realigned the landscape. No longer was it enough for a band simply to turn out a new single every couple of months and then round up the rest of their repertoire on LP. Now they were expected to make a statement, to offer a cohesive vision, to raise an art form that was still named from the days when it was considered "an album full of songs" to a plateau akin to that from which the classical composers gazed down.

It was a scenario that James Taylor would have recognized from Chip Taylor's abandoned dreams for the Flying Machine; it was one that Cat Stevens, too, had danced around with, his debut LP *Matthew and Son*. But Stevens was not interested in simply dancing. He wanted to bestride the art form like the colossuses elsewhere, and the only way he was going to get to do that was if he completely shattered the system under which he worked. And that meant wresting control of his own artistry.

As a songwriter, Stevens remained at the top of his game. Another hit loomed as American soul singer P. P. Arnold covered his "The First Cut Is the Deepest" for one of the year's most vibrant records. David Garrick was in the studio recording his "I've Found a Love." And *Matthew and Son*, was in the stores too, selling its way to a comfortable berth at #7.

It was, and remains, a remarkable album. Naturally the singles sucked you in; "Matthew and Son" and "I Love My Dog" were the opening brace; Stevens's own version of "Here Comes My Baby" came next. But they were simply the entrée into a world of baroque storytelling, short, sharp ballads that were more situation than song, layered in exquisite arrangements and instrumentation, with strings and woodwinds tossed on, and embroidered with such a sense of occasion that even the tinny crackle of a little mono record player (at that time, most record buyers' choice for hi-fi reproduction) could not help but astonish.

Mike Hurst: "I'll tell you how I heard him, I heard him like a James Bond soundtrack. To me, his songs were dramatic. If you listen, the first album, not the second one, I still think is a really great album. If you listen to 'Granny,' for example, it's so jazzy, it has some lovely influences. 'Bring Another Bottle' is another, it's so Latin. I just loved all those different influences, those theatrical styles of music. And he was actually writing those styles of music. All I was doing was amplifying and embellishing what he'd done in the first place."

Hurst's liner notes for the LP are as eloquent as the music itself, as he extolled the incredible rapport that the pair then enjoyed. "People write sleeve notes for various reasons: they're asked to, made to, or are just egotistical. I'm writing this for one reason: I know Cat Stevens better than most. Now, I could start off saying the usual, 'He's fantastic,' 'He's great,' 'He's a star.' Well, I've said it and I'll say one more thing that applies more than any other, he's original."

He outlined the team that worked behind the scenes: "Tony Hall, the best promotion man ever, Vic Smith, a really hip recording engineer, and his assistant, 'Lightning.' A great arranger, Alan Tew, our own promotion man and my partner, Cat's comanager, Chris Brough, and last and most of all Cat Stevens, for being the most original force on the music scene today."

Behind the scenes, Stevens had recruited a band to accompany him on stage, headlined by bassist Dave Ambrose and drummer Mickey Waller. It was a tight and concise team, and one that should have remained together for longer than it would.

Stevens, however, was balking—not at the success he was enjoying, or even at the records he was making, but at something less tangible: a gnawing sense that he could and should be doing so much more than he was being permitted to do. But even in adulthood, he found it difficult to vocalize this.

"Cat Stevens was never happy," Mickey Waller recalled. "Every time we rehearsed, every time we met up, he would always have something to complain about, whether it was the weather or his clothes or his record label or his money, it was a constant thing, and his mood really affected the band. We used to dread gigs because we knew that whatever happened, he would have found something to be upset about."

Right now, his greatest bugbear was Mike Hurst. In keeping with many of the industry practices of the day, Stevens had no say over what transpired in the studio. Arranger Tew, a gifted pianist whose eponymous orchestra were as familiar with pop music as film and TV scores, would bring in the players whom he considered were up to the standards that he and Hurst deemed appropriate for the occasions; players who could handle the host of esoteric instrumentation that the producer called upon. (Among them was bassist John Paul Jones, at the time one of Britain's most in-demand sidemen and later one-quarter of Led Zeppelin.)

Stevens himself could not play any of the instruments that Hurst called for. What rankled with him was the fact that he couldn't communicate with the people who could. From the outside looking into the smoky, boozy boys' club that was the world of the late-1960s session man, Stevens felt as though he was being tormented in a whole new language, a crazy code made up of the dots and lines on the pages of sheet music that he might never comprehend. He could explain until the cows came home how he wanted a song to sound, but unless he could write it down for the players, he might as well have been a mime artist performing for the blind.

Yet it might not have helped either way. What did he want the musicians to do? According to Hurst, he never said. It was only later, once Stevens began taking full responsibility for his musical output, that the young man's musical dreams became evident.

Hurst: "At the beginning what he did have, in his writing, when he played me a song, just him on his acoustic guitar, he'd always throw in bits that he'd either . . . He couldn't play them, so he sang them. And I'd hear these little bits, but I'd hear them as instrumentation and I'd think, 'Oh God, we've got to keep that in there, it's really, really good' . . . I thought, 'Yeah, that's such a nice little thing to hang the song on, I'll have something really weird play it. I'll have a harp play it.' Something totally bizarre, but it was 1967 and people could do that in 1967."

Not once did Stevens explain that what he sang on his demos, the "la-la-las" and "na-na-na"s that Hurst translated into instrumentation, was the exact sound that he wanted to hear on his records. That while Hurst threw in the musical kitchen sink, Stevens wanted to strip out all of the furniture and the wallpaper too. All Hurst knew was that Stevens was suddenly talking a lot more than he was writing, and dreaming a lot more than he was doing.

"He had dried up because he wanted to change. I think his dreams were real. The problem was, dreams aren't real."

"I used to dread recording sessions." Stevens confessed to *Crawdaddy* in 1971. One day, he recalled, he walked into the studio to find the session musicians sitting around drinking tea and reading the *Daily Mirror*. "For days before, I'd spend sleepless nights fearing having to walk into a studio and face a mass of blank uncomprehending and unsympathetic session men who would go mechanically through their chore, put down a technically perfect but totally antiseptic piece of recording of my music, and then drift off into the next session for the next guy."

It was a mark of Mike Hurst's studio genius that each of the records that he and Stevens made together was able to capture the songwriter's voice. But Stevens bridled regardless, silently stewing over the injustice of writing music that he was not permitted to arrange, and grumblingly reflecting in years to come that every day strengthened the conviction that he needed to take control.

He spoke of moving into business. He had recently taken to designing his own stage wear and pondered the launch of Cat Designs, catering to whoever else might want to dress according to his sartorial dictates. Half-brother David had been working in the fashion trade until recently, he said, and it was his expertise in the wholesale market that would power Cat Designs to the top.

It never happened.

He dreamed of hosting his own television series, and that did not seem so far-fetched. At a time when British TV did seem to be giving such things away like candy, Scott Walker, Cilla Black, and Lulu had all recently been signed up to host their own weekly shows, and each was geared to audiences far wider than the individual singer's traditional pop catchment area. Stevens's ambition was certainly premature (he had nowhere near the fame or name recognition of those other artists), but he nevertheless understood its value.

It never happened.

He planned a visit to San Francisco, too, the nexus of the burgeoning psychedelic scene of course, and the heartbeat of the peace and love movement that was consuming the Western world that summer. "I think it's a great scene—everything is really bubbling at the moment, and I'm inspired by the whole thing. It's like the music world is becoming one big happy family, and I think this San Francisco scene is bringing Britain and the States together—pop-wise, anyway—and making it so that one can be at home in both countries. It's a pity they can't have cheap excursions so that one could commute between the two places. . . ."

It never happened.

He even mused aloud on the possibility of shifting into movies, claiming to have received a few offers already, and this *might* have happened. But he turned down the proffered parts because they just didn't feel right, and while soundtrack work was coming his way, that wasn't to be either.

Lindsay Anderson, an enfant terrible of sorts in the world of British cinema, is best regarded today for the dystopian trilogy of *if. . .*, *O Lucky Man*, and *Britannia Hospital*. In 1968 he had yet to launch that series, and was known more for his theatrical work, and for 1963's *This Sporting Life*, when he was approached by producer Leon Clore to handle *All Neat in Black Stockings*, a comedy tracing the amorous antics of a central London window cleaner.

All Neat in Black Stockings would ultimately be helmed by director Christopher Morahan; Anderson pulled out after working with Clore and his crew on another project, a Kellogg's television commercial. But while the project was still alive, Anderson viewed it as his, which is why he was paying a visit to Mike Hurst.

"Lindsay Anderson came to my office and he asked me if Steve would write a song for a new movie he was going to do, *All Neat in Black Stockings*. He wanted this thing, so Steve wrote 'Twinkie' and we recorded it; then we went off to see a preview of the movie."

The pair were mortified. "As far as I was concerned, it was a soft porn movie," Hurst condemned. "These days, nobody would blink an eye but back then I thought it was very dodgy for Steve to get involved with it so we didn't. I think it's a lovely song, though, it's great. . . ." And, if he had only realized at the time, he smiled, "it turns out to be more like the stuff he'd do with Island a couple of years later."

Stevens acknowledged that his musical ideas were already shifting. He had learned a lot since "I Love My Dog," and, in conversation with the press, he expressed hopes that he would soon be allowed to demonstrate that learning. Sadly, his record company disagreed. When Stevens suggested his next single be "A Bad Night," a song that even he acknowledged was "a bit uncommercial," Deram promptly asked him to reconsider. Stevens, seizing upon the record as the battleground upon which he would make his stand, refused. His records were in danger of becoming formulaic, he argued; an artist needed to adapt to advance. He even threatened that his next record would be more of a turnaround still, a full-fledged classically themed offering.

But his confidence was swiftly shattered. "A Bad Night" not only proved to be a bad choice, but its failure ran hand in hand with the news that not a single West End theatrical promoter was interested in the Mexican musical. Defiant at first, Stevens initially insisted that he would raise the necessary money himself, but just weeks after one interview caught him buoyant and defiant, another—with the *New Musical Express*—found him despairing. "I'm at the crossroads now. I don't know how long I can continue as a pop singer. 'Bad Night' was an experiment. I'm not sure if it has worked out. I'm a little disappointed that it's not doing better, but I'm glad I took the chance."

Hurst: "When you're on a roll, when things are happening for you, it doesn't matter who you are, you always get the feeling that you're bullet-proof, and you can do anything. And it's not really true, because as soon as you do something that lacks what everyone thinks you've got, you've got a problem, because people love it when that happens. They love to start questioning you.

"One of the things I was always very sure about, which Cat didn't like at all: I always used to say to him, 'You are a big success now, so what you shouldn't do is go fall about in clubs and get pissed. Because all that's going to happen is people will end up writing about you, and they'll write things you don't like.' And of course he did exactly that."

Hurst would also counsel him against talking so freely to the press. With the shifting saga of the still nonstarting western/Mexican musical as ammunition, Hurst suggested that if Stevens had something to say, he should go through the official channels. "We had a press officer. I'd say, 'Go through Keith, use Keith Goodwin, but don't go and talk to the [press directly] because you'll make a mistake.' And every time he'd go to them and say, 'I'm going to do this, I'm going to do that,' and of course the press love that, because when it doesn't happen, they really enjoy it."

Stevens was tiring of being told what he could and couldn't do, though. That summer, reflecting upon the year since he first cut "I Love My Dog," he sighed exhaustedly, "Everything happened at once for us. I didn't have enough time to sit down and ask myself, 'What next?' I was just being carried along by it all, but now I must decide. I'm not going to do very much in the next month or so, except perhaps recording and writing. I also want to concentrate on record production, which has been taking up a lot of time recently."

He was in the studio with his old friend from his earliest folk club days, Peter James Hogan, recording what he insisted would be Hogan's debut single, a Cat Stevens composition, of course. He was talking with a Birmingham band called Yellow Rainbow, about possibly becoming their manager. And, in the midst of all this, he set about breaking with Mike Hurst.

Why? "Because I had music and ideas which hadn't been heard yet." In May 1971, Stevens told *Sounds*, "Every time I came up with an idea, they'd counteract it with their own idea and I'd never get what I wanted done. I realized that wasn't what I wanted things to sound like at the time, but I always went along with it.

"I was much too submissive. I agreed with them too much, but then it got to a point where I was so messed up, my whole feeling for music had gone. I was just writing songs to make singles, to be on television. These were the things I was led to believe were right to do. That it was a natural progression to go on having hits. Whereas the first thought I'd had was [that] I wanted to make music and be understood, and there's *no* way you can do that unless you really understand yourself, and I didn't understand myself."

Hurst takes a more prosaic view of the events that devoured that summer. "I have to say about the lawsuits, what exacerbated them, or the prequel, was really his brother David, because that's what really put the mockers on all. David wanted to manage him, and blood is thicker than water, as we all know."

The conflict began, as such things so frequently do, with nothing more venomous than a simple visit to Hurst's office, Stevens and brother David dropping by to apparently talk over the singer's career. In the midst of which, they let slip the true purpose of their visit. Hurst explains, "David didn't actually say, 'I want to manage him and I want him to leave you.' He looked at me and he looked at my business partner, Chris Brough, and he said, looking at Chris, 'I know where you get your money from,' because Chris had a lot of family money [his father, Archie, was a well-known television personality, and, in the days when such things were considered a ratings winner, a ventriloquist]. Then he looked at me and said, 'But where do you get your money from?'"

There was silence for a moment. "I looked at him and I said, 'David, I know exactly what you're saying to me. You're suggesting that I'm ripping Cat off and taking his money.' He goes, 'No no no,' but I said, 'Yes yes yes,' and he said, 'Well, I'd just like to see the accounts and everything.'"

Hurst fixed his interrogator with a steely gaze, then drew his attention to a guitar that was propped up in one corner of the office. "I said, 'Look, see that guitar over in the corner of the office there? If you're not out of here in five seconds, I'm going to take that guitar and I'm going to wrap it round your bloody head.' And he looked at me for a moment then he got up like a flash, pulled Cat to his feet, and went straight out through the door.

"And that was the beginning of the end, because I'd threatened his brother." A few days later, Hurst saw Stevens alone, and maybe he could have rebuilt a bridge. Instead, "I always put my bloody foot in it." Rather than apologizing after Stevens quietly told him, "You shouldn't have talked to my brother like that," Hurst changed the subject to the singer's new car.

"I said, 'I'll tell you something, Steve; you've got a new car, haven't you?'"

"Yeah."

"What is it?"

"It's a Merc 600. A big one."

Hurst smiled. "But you can't drive, can you?"

Stevens shrugged. "No. But David can."

≈≈≈

Sessions for what would become Cat Stevens's second album were already under way when singer and producer met in court. Hurst recalled, "Cat . . . or Cat and his brother . . . wanted out. I don't know what they wanted at the time—they just wanted out, like a lot of artists do. They want to move on, they want to do this, that, and the other, and the feeling at the time was ghastly. We did that second album *knowing* we were going to court." And knowing that the battle to extract Cat Stevens from the management contract he had signed with Hurst in September 1966 was going to be a hard-fought one.

The singer meant business. His lawyer, Oscar Beuselinck, was one of the country's best, or, as Hurst puts it, "one of the nastiest but hottest showbiz lawyers in London. Well, I had a bloody good lawyer too, not as good as Oscar, but mine was all right, so when we came to the first hearing, which was in the middle of doing the album, before we went into it my lawyer said, 'Whatever you do, just don't say anything.'

"I said, 'How can I go to a hearing and not say anything?' and he said, 'Because they'll say things you don't like. Don't rise to the bait, don't say anything.' So I said, 'Okay, fair enough,' and we went and sat in there with the judge, and the first thing Oscar says, after the judge asked what this was all about, what is the case, Oscar says, 'First and foremost, we are stating categorically that Mr. Hurst did not further the career of our artist, Cat Stevens.'"

Hurst leaped to his feet. "Are you kidding?" And brushing away his own lawyer's attempts to calm him down, sit him down, shut him up, he turned to the judge. "Please ask the plaintiff here how much he was earning three years ago?"

Beuselinck didn't blink. "That has nothing to do with it."

Hurst was furious now. "How can you say that has nothing to do with it? I'll tell you, three years ago he was earning four pounds a week in his father's restaurant. Now ask him how much he's earning today?"

Beuselinck remained calm. "That still has nothing to do with it."

"He's earning five, six thousand pounds a week! And you tell me I haven't—"

And that, Hurst laughed, is where the judge told him to sit down. "So I sat down and the next thing is, Oscar says, 'In any case, my client was a minor when the contract was signed, so his parents signed. They are foreign and unable to understand English.'

"Oh God, that did it for me. I was up again; I said, 'I know his father and mother, I speak to them in English all the time, their English is perfect.' And I blew it, I really blew it. Because that was that, it was virtually all over. We finished the album while the rest of it was going through, and the court found in his favor, and that was that."

Stevens and his brother celebrated their victory with the creation of Doric Management, and the immediate recruitment of Yellow Rainbow, both as a regular accompaniment for Stevens and an outfit in their own right. It was David who discovered the band, coming across them at a gig at the Holly Bush pub in Quinton, and then approaching them during the interval. Cat Stevens was looking for a backing band. Would they be interested?

Renamed Zeus, for the father of the Greek gods, the group promptly followed Stevens to London, to be installed in rooms above Shaftsbury Avenue's Moulin Rouge theater, and given free range of the Marquee Club, a few corners away, to rehearse. Zeus made their live debut as Stevens's band at the Palais de Sports in Paris on November 17, the first of two nights at a mini "Love In" festival which featured Soft Machine, Dantalion's Chariot, and the Spencer Davis Group alongside Cat. The band also took receipt of a cassette of his songs, from which Stevens suggested they pull a few favorites that he would then record with them.

As with the Peter James Hogan sessions, however, nothing came of the few recordings they did make, sequestered in Pye Studios with Stevens finding his way behind the desk. He seemed perfectly happy with how the tapes came out, too, but more and more of Zeus's time was spent waiting for him to do something . . . anything; sitting around their apartment wondering whether today was the day the phone would ring. It rarely did. But not because Stevens didn't know what to do with the band.

He didn't know what to do full stop.

8

Another Saturday Night

James Taylor arrived in London in January 1968, and he knew that he was scarcely walking virgin soil. For almost a decade, the London folk clubs had been, if not an irresistible magnet to his countrymen, at least a well-worn port of call, ever since the young Bob Dylan and the even younger Paul Simon had cut performing teeth on the streets of London earlier in the decade.

That was what James Taylor was searching for; the opportunity to expand his personal vision into a broader frame of both musical and creative expression. To anyone who saw him on the streets, Taylor was just another teen (albeit a remarkably tall one) who talked himself into and out of a variety of musical projects, wrote some songs, played some guitar, and who had doting parents who dipped into an inheritance to finance the boy's airfare to London. A friend from the family's regular vacations in Martha's Vineyard, Alby Scott, had agreed to put him up, so long as the guest didn't mind sharing living space with a newborn baby.

Taylor agreed.

On paper it was a big adventure. In reality, it was still a big adventure. Place names that were as unfamiliar to Taylor as the geography of American song was to English musicians soon became familiar. He knew how to get from Notting Hill Gate, the west London neighborhood where he stayed when he arrived, to the center of town, where the city still swung. He found the Carnaby Street of legend and the Portobello Road that Cat Stevens sang of. He decoded the intricacies of a street map that eschewed the traditional grids of America in favor of a medieval monkey puzzle, and a subway system that prided itself on its resemblance to a bowl of color-coded spaghetti.

Most important of all, however, was the ease with which he seemed to slip into the local musical consciousness.

The charts in the week that Taylor arrived in London were alive with their usual blend of rocking favorites, poppy ballads, and comical novelties. The Scaffold, a comedy trio whose number included Paul McCartney's brother Mike McGear, were in the Top 10 with "Thank U Very Much." Paul himself had two singles up there, the Beatles' "Hello Goodbye" and the *Magical Mystery Tour* EP. Georgie Fame was flying high with his recounting of "The Ballad of Bonnie and Clyde," Engelbert Humperdinck was celebrating "The Last Waltz," and Scott Walker was extolling the dissolution of a young man who wanted to be rechristened "Jackie." There were hits for TV funnyman Des O'Connor and TV funny group the Monkees.

There were no hits for Cat Stevens, though. A few weeks earlier, he told the *New Musical Express* that "at the moment, my songs are in great demand." However, he knew that might not be the case for long. "But . . . so were the songs of Mitch Murray and Chris Andrews, and they're both suffering a little right now because they stayed stagnant. I mustn't do that. I intend to grow with time, expand and change."

His second album, *New Masters*, showed little sign of that. Scarred by the legal battle that took place during its creation, and hamstrung by Stevens's seeming inability to come up with anything so memorable as the songs that his first album had groaned beneath, *New Masters* was released in December 1967, and it was scarcely even noticed.

Not even an appearance on one of the top-rated TV shows of the day could help Stevens: On December 9, 1967, he was the star on *Twice a Fortnight*, a show originally envisioned as a visual equivalent to the radio comedy *I'm Sorry I'll Read That Again*, and featuring many of the same cast. Future Monty Python heroes Eric Idle, Michael Palin, and Terry Jones, and *The Goodies'* Bill Oddie were among the regular cast, while the entire shebang was directed by the already near-legendary rockumentary pioneer Tony Palmer.

Yet *Twice a Fortnight's* ten-week run through late autumn 1967 is equally well remembered today for the musical interludes that, once a week (twice a fortnight, in fact), interrupted the comedy sketches and films. The Who, the Moody Blues, and Simon Dupree and the Big Sound all made memorable appearances on the show, although not, according to Palmer, without some complaint from the cast.

"Bill Oddie *always* objected to the rock groups, but I said . . . one time, I was telling him we had Cream coming on, and he replied, 'Cream what?' I'll always remember him saying, 'Cream what?' And I said, 'Well, actually, these guys are rather good.'"

Stevens appeared the week after Cream, gamely lip-synching his way through "Kitty." But "Kitty" was doomed to founder at #47, and when Deram rush-released "Lovely City" in the New Year, and it didn't even sniff the Top 50, it was clear that Stevens's career had at least hit a wall, if it hadn't stalled altogether.

Somebody pressed the panic button. Booking agent Harold Davidson called Stevens into his office and as good as declared the lad's pop career over. His only hope of maximizing the last few drops of his once formidable star power was to move into Christmas pantomime, that peculiarly British tradition of placing whichever celebrity was on hand into a two- or three-week theatrical season, re-creating a popular children's story.

It was not necessarily a career killer. Cliff Richard, for one, had been doing panto for a couple of years now, and even scoring hit records with the cast LPs. But Cliff was already an established superstar, a name known to every member of the family. He could command any venue he chose for his pantos, and he invariably wound up at the London Palladium.

Cat Stevens, on the other hand, was a mere three-hit wonder. Maybe, Davidson mused, he could find him a place in the provinces somewhere, get him a nice little earner in one of Britain's smaller cities. And because he had cut Mike Hurst out of his life, dissolved the contract that he was now discovering had kept so much industry idiocy at bay, all Stevens could do was shuffle his feet, look down at the carpet, and hope Davidson's hearing was good enough to hear his murmured "No, thank you."

Matters did not improve. It was just the Cat and his brother against the world, and the world didn't give a damn, abandoning him at precisely the time, it would seem from afar, when he should have been riding the biggest wave of his life.

Rock was relaxing, and it was doing so in a manner that seemed an exquisite fit for Stevens and his brand of gentle pop. While some of Stevens's peers, it is true, saw the unfettered ambition of *Sgt. Pepper* et al as an excuse for ever greater artistry, and that brand of absolute arrogance that soon would flower in the shape of the "rock opera," for others, it precipitated a wholly unexpected backlash and a return to basics; one man, one guitar, one song.

The folk clubs were still bustling and might, in fact, have been more lively than they ever were. Every pub that had a spare room to let seemed to be hosting some kind of regular song session; some of them even did well enough to raise the club's name higher than the hosting pub. But they all had one thing in common: a demand for original songwriters, people with voices and stories to tell.

In London, venues such as the Scots House, Les Cousins, and, out in the west London enclave of Earls Court, the Troubadour, were at their peak. In the suburbs and elsewhere, "arts labs" sprang up in any place that could house them, encouraging folkies, poets, painters, and mimes to express the freedom of unconfined creativity.

No matter that one denizen of these particular dens, Stevens's old friend Sandy Denny, later described her early career as time spent flitting round the country by herself, trying to find her way to one obscure pub after another. The circuit that these venues crowned was walked by each and every artist who even vaguely considered him- or herself a part of the English folk consciousness. Cat Stevens, with his own background in the scene, and his undeniable eye for the kind of melody that the mood of the moment was demanding, could have slipped right in.

So, as he found his way around this new and vibrant city, could James Taylor. The songs he brought with him, the gentle acoustics of "Something in the Way She Moves," "Knocking Round the Zoo," "Something's Wrong," and so on, all certainly fell into the requisite package. But there was an insularity to them as well, a sense that where folk spoke to the concerns of the everyman, Taylor sang only of his own personal struggles. And that was what his new friends responded to.

It was not a unique stance. On the same circuit at the same time, the young Al Stewart was chronicling the trials and tribulations of post-adolescence with his own startlingly accurate portraits of life in London's "bedsitterland," the street after street of rudely renovated houses in which anything even remotely resembling a room was converted into an all-in-one bedroom/living room/kitchenette, then rented out to the city's young singles.

Firmly seated in the shadow of Dylan and Paul Simon at the outset, Stewart cut a one-off single, "The Elf," in 1965, before signing with CBS in 1967 and releasing the still sublime *Bedsitter Images*.

Firmly a child of its times, it's an often naive collection, full of pertinent imagery, even if the lyrics do occasionally err on the side of contrivance. He was clearly seeking his own identity, too, and one song, the epic "Beleeka Doodle Day," lies so deep in thrall to "Desolation Boulevard" that you can almost hear Dylan banging on the walls. But it works despite that, while other highlights find him laying down the domestic soap-operatic blueprint that would serve him so well over the next few albums.

Indeed, Stewart's second album, *Love Chronicles*, was—and remains—dominated by its title track, an eighteen-minute outline of his own sexual escapades to date that caused a minor stir through the inclusion of an F-word in the lyric, but caused a major splash as it out-lowlanded Dylan's sad-eyed lady. Released almost simultaneously with James Taylor's introduction to the universe that Stewart extolled, *Love Chronicles* still stands as a virtual declaration of adolescent intent, the cares and concerns of a rising generation forever encapsulated in wax.

Taylor did not doubt that he belonged in this scene. A decade later he told *Stereo Review*, "It still doesn't seem to me that I was doing anything different from the other people around me. I was listening to folk music in Boston and Cambridge. It was really acts like Peter, Paul and Mary, Bob Dylan, Ian and Sylvia, the Kweskin Jug Band, Tom Rush, and the Kingston Trio that brought folk music to popularity."

Substitute those names for those that now touted folk music to the masses—Stewart, Fairport Convention, the Strawbs, Martin Carthy—and the line of descent was etched in stone.

At the same time, breaking into the London circuit was more difficult than Taylor had expected. He had assumed that he would simply be able to walk into the coffee bars, introduce himself as a singer, prove his words with a song or two, and at least play a few chords at an open mike night. Earn enough money to live, maybe make enough to journey farther afield, travel through Europe, see the world. But it wasn't as easy as he thought it would be. He was in England on a visitors' visa only; any attempt to work, even for tips, could see him deported without a leg to stand on.

Still, friends did their best. Judy Steele, a set designer for the BBC, introduced him to her own friends in the music industry and encouraged him to record a clutch of his songs alone with his guitar in whichever friend's flat would permit it, and begin taking them around the record companies. It was a short-lived conceit; then as now, it was difficult for anybody to get a foot through any label's door without knowing at least a handful of the "right" people, and Steele's network of contacts could not vouchsafe that.

Not with the quality of tape that Taylor was offering, anyway. So he scraped together the eight pounds that it would cost to hire a two-track recording studio for forty-five minutes, and, deep in the heart of Cat Stevens's old stomping ground, the now irrefutably red-lit Soho, he laid down forty-five minutes of music, the batch of songs that were destined for his first true demo tape: "Something in the Way She Moves," "Rainy Day Man," and "Circle Round the Sun" . . . the list went on.

The strange thing was, even with the resultant acetate sounding better than anything Taylor had recorded before—and that included the long-mothballed tapes he'd cut with Chip Taylor and the Flying Machine—his new London friends were still unable to help him. So, swallowing the sticker shock that was then attached to any transatlantic telephone call, not to mention the primitive technology that likewise attended such a venture, Taylor called up Kootch and asked for his advice.

The answer he received was swift and to the point.

Go see the Beatles.

≋

When history looks back upon the Beatles' Apple Records label, it tends to blame Paul McCartney for the entire debacle.

It was McCartney whose idea sprang to life in the first place, and who gave the company its name. It was McCartney who insisted that the enterprise move into music publishing, and who would subsequently play the greatest role in the label's recruitment of artists and the development of their talent. And it was McCartney who, having scored a monster hit first time out of the box (Mary Hopkin's international chart-topper "Those Were the Days"), proceeded to hurl an increasingly bewildering selection of soft rock favorites into a marketplace that was no longer so easily impressed as it once was by the mere coincidence of a Beatle's patronage.

Four years earlier, the Beatles name could (and did) sell almost any product you could imagine. By 1968, however, people were a little less susceptible to the old mop-top charm. It was McCartney who overlooked that. Him and a lot of other people.

When it was first announced that the Beatles intended to break away from the traditional power structure of the Anglo-American music industry and carve their own swathe through the outmoded debris, anticipation rocked the marketplace like an earthquake shaking a shantytown.

Indeed, the initial intentions were so grandiose that fiction could scarcely have conjured something so spectacular. In October 1967, long-time Beatles publicist Tony Barrow told *Record World* magazine that the Beatles *and* the Rolling Stones, the two biggest bands in the world, were considering joining forces as owners and operators of a recording studio, and maybe even a film production company, all geared toward helping to lamuch new groups and artists.

That was probably as far as the collaboration would go; there were no plans whatsoever to release any kind of "Rolling Beatles" record. But still, the combination of all nine musicians' talents and energies could not help but be a thrilling fusion, all the more so since both bands were effectively self-managed now; Beatles manager Brian Epstein was dead, Rolling Stones manager Andrew Loog Oldham had departed. For the moment, at least, the two bands were looking after themselves.

The Stones connection was a pipe dream. But the Beatles forged ahead, expanding their vision seemingly with every new idea that popped into their collective head.

On December 5, 1967, an Apple boutique was opened on Baker Street, under the aegis of three Dutch designers, collectively known as the Fool.

An electronics division was established, tasked with wowing the world with invention and technology. A Greek television repairman named Alex Mardas was given free rein there, and John Lennon quickly rechristened him Magic Alex.

The music publishing division was established, charged with gathering together every promising young songwriter that came its way, and quickly showing its intentions with the signing of George Alexander (of the band Grapefruit) and one of George Harrison's Liverpool buddies, Jackie Lomax.

A television department opened, and promptly devoured the British Christmas schedules with the broadcast of *Magical Mystery Tour*, the Fab Four's third movie. And maybe that was a portent to be paid stiff attention to, because it also became the band's first critical flop, so brutally savaged by the UK media that both ABC and NBC promptly abandoned their own plans to show (or even bid for the American rights to) the movie.

The boutique, too, was not long for this world. Its first six months of operation saw it hemorrhage a staggering half a million pounds sterling before Lennon finally slammed the door on the drain by throwing open the shop's portals one last time, on July 30, 1968, and giving away all the merchandise for free.

But the Beatles believed they were untouchable still, so now there was to be a record label too, devoted to every deserving young artist that the Beatles' eyes chanced upon. Ron Kass, the former head of Liberty Records' UK operation, was placed in charge of the outfit; Kootch's old buddy Peter Asher, whose pop career had folded with the dissolution of Peter and Gordon, was elected head of the A&R division and on May 14, 1968, appearing on NBC's *Tonight Show*, Lennon and McCartney outlined their goals.

"We've got this thing called Apple," Lennon explained, "which is going to be records, films, and electronics, which all tie up. And to make sort of an umbrella, so people who want to make films about . . . grass . . . don't have to go on their knees in an office, you know, begging for a break. We'll try and do it like that. That's the idea. . . . that's what we're trying to do."

"Big companies are so big that if you're little and good, it takes you like sixty years to make it," McCartney continued. "And so people miss out on these good little people."

On May 25, 1968, *Rolling Stone* magazine carried Apple's first solicitation for new talent, a full-page ad depicting Apple staffer Alistair Taylor togged up as a one-man band, beneath the banner headline "This Man Has Talent. . . ."

"One day," the ad continued, "he sang his songs to a tape recorder (borrowed from the man next door). In his neatest handwriting he wrote an explanatory note (giving his name and address) and, remembering to enclose a picture of himself, sent the letter, tape, and photograph to Apple music. . . .

"If you were thinking of doing the same thing yourself, do it now. This man now owns a Bentley."

Two weeks later, Asher and his staff were staring at a pile of more than four hundred tapes, and every day the postman delivered another sackful. Years later, remembering the first weeks of operation, Asher outlined a "typical" day at the office.

"I would arrive at a fairly normal time in the morning. I had an office on the top floor, where there were three or four and, at one point, five people working for me. As you probably know, Apple took out an ad saying 'Send us your tired and huddled tapes, and we will listen to them.' And that's what we did. We would go through them and listen and make notes and write people polite 'thank you' notes. Unfortunately, to be honest, out of all that stuff nothing really emerged. The people we actually signed came through connections with people we knew."

He is correct. Not one of the hundreds upon hundreds of demo tapes that were delivered to Apple ever unearthed a future Bentley-owning one-man band. It was the individual Beatles' own talent-spotting notions, and those of the people with whom they'd surrounded themselves, that filled the Apple orchard.

The first four Apple singles, released on the same day that summer of 1968, comprised the Beatles' own "Hey Jude," the debut single by Jackie Lomax, the aforementioned Mary Hopkin smash, and, possibly to emphasize the variety that label would encompass, the Black Dyke Mills Band, a brass band from the north of England that McCartney recruited to perform the theme tune to a TV series he was involved in, *Thingumybob*.

Others lined up behind them: Over the next twelve months, Apple would release singles by the Iveys, who would soon metamorphose into Badfinger and labor beneath the name of "the new Beatles" for a few under-achieving years; Trash, a band whose original name, White Trash, had been deemed too controversial to ever be uttered; American keyboard wizard Billy Preston; and the London branch of the Radha Krishna Temple. There was one other American on the roster—a Peter Asher discovery named James Taylor.

Inevitably, it was Kootch who put Taylor in touch with Asher, when they talked that day in early 1968. Taylor was getting nowhere in his search for someone with the right label connections in his new hometown, and originally called Kootch simply to get some moral support.

Kootch's advice was simple. "Call Peter and tell him I sent you." The friendship that Kootch and Asher had ignited back on that King Bees tour was still alive and well. If anybody would listen to Taylor's acetate, Kootch believed, it was his friend Peter Asher.

Taylor had nothing to lose. Calling the number Kootch gave him, Taylor introduced himself and asked if he could drop his tape by. Asher invited him to the apartment on Marylebone High Street that he shared with his girlfriend, Betsy, and, when he discovered that the young American was essentially homeless while he searched for his big break, offered him a berth on the family couch.

Asher recalled his first encounter with the quiet American. "I was at home in my flat and I got a phone call out of the blue from a rather nervous seeming American with a very pleasant speaking voice. I didn't know him but he told me his name was James Taylor."

Taylor had been in London for just two days, he said, and had cut his demo only the day before. Asher insists, "I still remember my utter astonishment and delight. These were not traditional rock 'n' roll songs. . . ."

It was Paul McCartney who rubber-stamped James Taylor's arrival as the first American on the Apple roster; he listened while Asher played him the acetate and asked for an introduction; watched while a nervous Taylor played a living room concert at McCartney's home; counted up the album's worth of songs that Taylor had already accrued, and gave the go-ahead.

An advertisement was placed in the back pages of *Melody Maker*, the first place that all out-of-work musicians looked when it came time to pay the rent each week, and the ensuing auditions on the top floor of the Apple building in Baker Street brought the rudiments of a backing band, keyboard player Don Schinn and bassist Louis Cennamo.

The Flying Machine's Joel Bishop was imported from the States to play drums and, in February 1968, the quartet began rehearsing and demoing together. (Two of these early takes, "Carolina in My Mind" and "Sunshine Sunshine," were included on the 2010 reissue of Taylor's debut album.)

Four months later, on June 1, Asher cc-ed an internal memo to Ron Kass and Neil Aspinall, Apple's managing director. "[James Taylor] is an American songwriter and singer who is extremely good. . . ."

Tom Rush's *The Circle Game* was out now, released in the U.S. in March 1968, and not only were both of Taylor's songs placed on it, but "Something in the Way She Moves" had been extracted as a single, too.

In years to come, Rush was understandably proud of his achievement, not only of putting James Taylor on plastic for the first time, but for bringing Jackson Browne and Joni Mitchell to prominence as well. "I think these three artists being represented on the same album got people's attention. People cared about who wrote the songs in those days, and the fact [that] there were these three unknown writers coming up with this brilliant stuff, all being represented for the first time on this project, that got people's attention. If they'd been on three separate albums, perhaps nobody would notice as much, but it seemed to indicate that something's going on here.

"Now this was not my intent; I was looking to make an album, and here were some songs I could use." Indeed, only Mitchell was on the critical radar at the time, and for a couple of years more, the presence of either Taylor or Browne on the disc was of most significance to the songwriters alone.

Crawdaddy's review singled out both Taylor's "Sunshine Sunshine" and Browne's "Shadow Dream Song" as occasions when Rush's vocal was swamped by arranger Paul Harris's ambitions, while *Rolling Stone*'s Barry Giffird sighed "It's not an exceptional album." He continued: " . . . [I]n fact, there are only two or three tracks worth hearing." But "foremost among these" was "Something in the Way She Moves," "which flows beautifully with Bruce Langhorne's fine country stylings pushing it through. Rush's brand of vocalizing fits perfectly . . . he can never get excited about anything."

The reviews were clipped and added to Asher's files on Taylor, and *The Circle Game* was added, albeit a shade misleadingly, to Aspinall's memo. "He wrote Tom Rush's last single and several tracks on Tom Rush's album. He and I have found a bass player and a pianist with whom he is currently rehearsing a dozen or so of his own songs. . . . [H]e knows exactly what he wants, and both the musicians with him are very competent. We intend to start recording him about [June 20] . . . [H]e is ready to discuss contracts and things as soon as you are."

They were ready too. Taylor was signed to a three-year contract.

Asher: "We had A&R meetings once a week, at which some kind of quorum of Beatles would turn up. We talked about works in progress, and who to sign. I had some overall influence, but none, for example, on John's projects. On *Two Virgins* [the first of Lennon and wife Yoko Ono's ultra-experimental indulgences] there was no input. And when George was off producing Jackie Lomax, he pretty much knew what he wanted to do. I didn't really have anything to do with it. But with some of them, I certainly helped. Paul with the Mary Hopkin album, I was very much hands-on. Paul was producing it, but I was certainly there and doing stuff. And obviously James was very much my baby, and I produced [his album] myself."

He was adamant on that point. "I brought [James] to the A&R meeting. Paul loved it; John didn't really care that much one way or the other. I said, 'Look, I'm signing this.' I think I probably would've quit if they'd said no.

But that wasn't even an issue. You make me the head of A&R and I find an act I love, I'm signing it. And they all went, 'Oh yeah.'

"To be honest, those meetings were always kind of woolly, so if you came in and said, 'I'm the head of A&R and I'm signing this act,' everyone would go, 'Right!' You could get away with a lot just by being decisive."

James Taylor recalled his own impressions of Apple and its owners. "Apple was open pickings for a long time there. Anybody who had an interesting-sounding idea would go up there and hit on the Beatles for bread, and an awful lot of money started going out. I think I was the first artist to sign, anyhow, so I was there near the beginning of it. It was a very high scene. It was as though finally here are some people who have a company and at the same time they're sympathetic to the artist's point of view. They're not just stock owners or chairmen of the boards. They're actually musicians and artists and it sort of had that feeling to it. It was a very exciting company to work for, but I guess there was really no one there who was looking out for the budget, and an awful lot of money went out, and they just about went broke and had to slow it down."

Taylor himself was about to benefit from Apple's profligacy, as he and Asher were booked into Trident Studios and left to their own devices for no fewer than three months. Asher, despite the fact that he had never taken on such a role before, elected himself the producer.

Asher explained, "I found James Taylor and I really believed in him. I didn't know who else we would trust to do it. So we decided that I should do it. I knew I had a lot of learning to do, hands-on learning on the way, but I knew some people I trusted in the business to ask, and I believed so strongly in James's ability and talent, it was actually not that hard. I think the trick is to admit when you don't know something and go to the trouble of finding out how to do it properly."

Independently owned at a time when many of the city's best studios were still controlled by the record companies, Trident was a new operation, perched in the seldom-frequented alleyway of St. Anne's Court, back in the heart of Soho. One of the first eight-track studios in London, it attracted the Beatles from the outset. George Harrison was already producing Jackie Lomax's Apple debut there; Paul McCartney was recording Mary Hopkin.

Taylor slipped into this company gratefully and unobtrusively. He was there for the Beatles' own shift to the studio; on July 31, the full group descended to record their next single, "Hey Jude." They would remain there for just four days, two of recording, two of mixing, cramming some thirty-six other instrumentalists into the long, narrow studio as McCartney's opus came together. And he was at a session for "Revolution" too, waiting for the Beatles to finish their business before he and Asher could get on with their own.

The twelve weeks that Taylor and Asher would spend in the studio were not wasted. For Asher, the entire affair was a learning experience that would teach him both the right things to do in the studio and some of the wrong ones; and for Taylor, it was a stint that would see him finally come to grips with the songs he had spent the last five years writing, and with the handful that was still pouring out.

Some of the songs he had on his mind dated back to the Flying Machine days; in fact, every one of his own songs that the band taped with Chip Taylor was earmarked for the new record: "Something's Wrong," "Knocking Round the Zoo," "Brighten Your Night with My Day," "Night Owl," and "Rainy Day Man." But others, like "Carolina in My Mind," were as fresh as his impressions of London, and destinations further afield too.

In late July, with the Beatles taking a brief break from recording, Trident Studios staff announced that they too needed a few days off. It was the ideal opportunity, Taylor decided, to shake London off his shoes for a weekend and take the hippie trail to Formantera, a Mediterranean hot spot in the Balearic Islands group.

There, the combination of utterly unspoiled vistas and exquisite archaeological treasures had conspired to fashion a countercultural beacon, one whose appeal was only amplified after artist Martin Sharp vacationed there in 1967, then returned home to write (with Eric Clapton) the Cream hit "Tales of Brave Ulysses." According to legend, it was on Formantera that the Greek warrior encountered the sirens, the sinister singing spirits who lure sailors to their deaths. A few years later, King Crimson lyricist Pete Sinfield would preserve his own island memories on wax with "Formantera Lady," recalling an encounter with one of the modern island's sexual mysteries.

Taylor was entranced, gazing out at the sunlit Mediterranean, meandering around the whitewashed stone cottages, and everywhere saying "hi" to the flower children who had taken root on the island, as if Formantera itself was the mythic garden to which they all dreamed mankind might some day return. Two idyllic days, he told *Rolling Stone*, were spent riding a bicycle and "drinking Romilar," a cough suppressant that, if consumed in large enough quantities, packed sufficient hallucinogenic qualities for most would-be cosmic voyagers. And he met a girl named Karin, with whom he took a boat out to Ibiza, the next island across, and spent one night under the stars, unromantically sleeping in the street because they had no money for a room. And there, while Karin slept, a song began to germinate.

Back home, the song struck an immediate chord with everyone who heard it, an aching ode to homesickness that he first performed publicly for Chris O'Dell, a fellow expatriate American who herself had recently fallen into the Apple Records orbit, a friend of Apple's Derek Taylor who was still trying to find her feet in the city.

O'Dell later admitted that she had no interest whatsoever in being introduced to an American when she'd only been in London for six days. But she allowed Derek Taylor to make the introduction and then found herself sorely regretting it as the young Bostonian installed himself in her hotel room for the evening, strumming the guitar that accompanied him everywhere and then, when she gently suggested it might be time for him to leave, telling her that he always stayed up late because that was when he did his best writing.

"I didn't want to be rude, so I sat on my bed for another half hour or so, listening to him strum his guitar and sing quietly under his breath," O'Dell wrote in her autobiography, *Miss O'Dell*. And when she went to sleep he was still there, working on a song that he hoped to finish before he crashed, and which he premiered for her the following morning, sitting in the bathroom while she readied herself for work. "Carolina in My Mind," she told him, was "truly beautiful."

It remains so. Well over a decade later, Taylor mused, "I think of that early time in London when I sing 'Carolina in My Mind.' The lyric dealt with being somewhere else, which has always made me feel real good, and it encouraged me that I could write a song that strong. I can always count on a goose pimple or two when I sing it."

Paul McCartney, too, was impressed. He was a more than occasional (but less than regular) visitor to the studio while the sessions went on, always ready to offer an opinion if he felt one was required; in fact, it was McCartney who suggested they scrap their first attempt at "Carolina in My Mind," and try it again, with McCartney on bass and George Harrison dropping by to add backing vocals to his bandmate's. Taylor repaid them with one of the lines in the song, the invocation to the "holy host of others standing around me" was a direct reference to his album's most special guests.

The Beatles' adoption of James Taylor is so much a part of his story today that it often passes without comment, by biographers and even by Taylor himself. At the time, however, it wasn't simply a big deal, it was one of the biggest deals any performer could imagine. Still the most enduringly popular band in the world, still the musical trailblazers to whom the rest of the industry looked for their next move, the Beatles were demigods and simply to be ushered into their presence was an honor that few people, musicians or otherwise, could ever dream of transpiring.

Now here was James Taylor, twenty years old and just two years out of a mental hospital, three thousand, three hundred miles from home, and with no more musical experience than could be gleaned from six months in a Greenwich Village bar and three hours in a cheap New York recording studio; here he was, the center of attention in the heart of London, with Paul McCartney and George Harrison buzzing around him.

Such an experience could turn anybody's head, but Taylor struggled to remain grounded. "It was great. It was *unbelievable*. I was a huge Beatles fan. I listened to them, as did millions, with absolute utter focus and attention to every note and every word. And just devoured everything that they came out with, and parsed it and learned it and reinterpreted it.

"So when it turned out that I got the opportunity . . . Just the fact that I was in this *pantheon*, really being present in Trident Studios in Soho, Leicester Square, where they were recording *The White Album*. It was just amazing."

Despite such star power, however, Taylor's album came together slowly, as producer Peter Asher literally learned his trade in the studio. "I was really anxious with this record to impress people, and I think as a consequence, I actually may have sort of overproduced the record a bit, in terms of over-decorating it with arrangements. I was really going, 'I've got to make people pay attention to this. This guy is so good, I *must* make them listen.'"

What he did not know, as he and Taylor have both since acknowledged, was *how* to make people listen. The notion of simply placing Taylor in front of a microphone with his guitar, and letting the tapes roll from there, was as far from their minds as it was from Mike Hurst's, as he sought to capture Cat Stevens on tape. Songs as idiosyncratic as Taylor's and Stevens', the feeling went, needed accompaniment that was just as idiosyncratic; the lone voice and guitar were the province of the folkie alone, and Hurst and Asher were not going to drop their protégés into that bag.

Hurst brought in one of London's most in-demand arrangers to beautify Stevens's vision; Asher did the same. Determining to pull out every musical stop he could find, he recruited ace arranger Richard Hewson to both orchestrate some songs, and to provide short linking passages between others.

Again, McCartney was instrumental in the decision, and he remained sufficiently entranced by the concept of linking melodies between individual songs that, the following year, he would be bringing a similar harmony to side two of the Beatles' *Abbey Road* swan song (and would return to it again on his *Wildlife* solo album).

Whereas the Beatles conspired to create one long continuous piece of music, however, and succeeded to the point where it is impossible to hear any of the suite's composite parts without your own ears bracketing it with its musical neighbors, here the concept was utterly misplaced. Or at least it was unusual enough to raise various critical eyebrows once the album was released, and it was difficult for even Taylor's friends to admit that many of the bridges worked very well. The opening segue from "Don't Talk Now" to "Something's Wrong," riding the theme of the traditional "Greensleeves," is one that always impresses. But others just seemed fussy and unnecessary, shoehorned in between songs that would have been far better served in splendid isolation.

Taylor, however, would not be around to witness any of this.

Back in New York the previous year, Taylor had fallen into drug abuse, he reasoned, because everything was going wrong. In London, everything was going right. And he still fell.

It was fun at first, but irresponsibility quickly took over. "I started to take a lot of codeine. I went to Europe and started to take opium and then I got into smack heavily for about nine months. I got into it real thick there."

Heroin was not an especially popular drug on the streets of London at that time, but it was growing increasingly prevalent. The law of the land had yet to criminalize the drug; rather, it tackled the problem by registering addicts and then working to wean them off the drug, while providing them with the fix they craved.

But the program was open to a lot of abuse; all you needed to do was buy a jack on the black market, shoot up, and then visit your local GP, declaring yourself an addict. The doc would do the rest.

Taylor was hooked again, and while he did check himself into a local rehab program, there to be prescribed the smack substitute visepdone, it had little effect. He returned to New York for a short stint of hospitalization and then went up to Stockbridge, Massachusetts, where he entered the then-revolutionary Austen Riggs Center, an institute that offered therapeutic, as opposed to chemical, treatment for a wide range of psychological problems.

Drug abuse was not one of the issues that the center acknowledged it dealt with, Taylor later explained. It was the underlying cause of drug abuse that it sought to remedy. "They're not equipped to deal with junkies, and I wasn't called a junkie. I wasn't admitted or dealt with as a junkie, but that was my problem. That was the manifestation of my problem. Junk, in itself, isn't the problem with me. It's a symptom of unexpressed and inexpressible anger, in a nutshell. It's a way of retreating from the world. It's a way of finding a comfort and a consistency in a chemical, and I guess I have an addictive personality."

Taylor would spend a total of five months at Austen Riggs. He was there when Apple released his self-titled debut album, in December 1968 in the UK and February 1969 in the U.S.; still there, too, when reviewer Jon Landau described it, in *Rolling Stone*, as "the coolest breath of fresh air I've inhaled in a good long while. It knocks me out."

Yet even that endorsement could not push it any higher than #118 in America, while the British chart remained wholly unbothered by the album, consequences both of Taylor's continued hospitalization and Apple's own internal disarray. And when he did finally get out of the hospital, it was to discover that his career had ground to a standstill.

So he did what everybody seemed to be doing at that time. He went to California.

9

You Love the Thunder

While James Taylor hung fire in North Carolina with his folks, or hung out in London with the Beatles, his old buddy Kootch was preparing to save the world. Or at least end the war.

Reflecting on his best friend's final days in New York, Kootch lamented, "It was breaking his heart. We were getting nowhere, it was destroying his health, and so he left finally and it was probably the best thing he could have done. And a week later I got a gig with the Fugs."

The Fugs were a looming presence on the New York City scene of the late 1960s, a loose union that poets Ed Sanders and Tuli Kupferberg, and drummer Ken Weaver first schemed in 1964, and which had been creating an unholy racket ever since. Ferociously political, but utilizing music and performance as the most potent means of pushing their message ahead, the Fugs were at the forefront of the civil rights movement as it bled into the antiwar protests, and though they were never likely to top the charts, the Warner Brothers label picked them up in 1967 and the band began preparing to record their major-label debut.

Kootch was introduced to the Fugs by Ken Pine and Charlie Larkey of the Myddle Class, "buddies . . . who were working for the Fugs as side Fugs. So I went over there and did the audition. I got the gig and for eight or nine months I played with the Fugs. I recorded one album with them, *Tenderness Junction*, which was their first for Warners, and amazingly enough, Richard Avedon took all our pictures, so somewhere there is a Richard Avedon portrait of me."

His membership also coincided with what would become the Fugs' most dramatic and audacious escapade yet—the exorcism of the Pentagon as the climax to the largest peace march yet to descend upon Washington, D.C. Up to 150,000 people, representing the combined might of some 150 different protest groups, then joined hands and encircled the building to stage an exorcism, while the cops and the national guard looked on in bewilderment.

Kootch details the day on his blog. "Abbie Hoffman was promoting the idea of getting enough freaks together to 'levitate the Pentagon'. . . . [T]he peace march ended at the Pentagon and the plan was to circle the building and raise it up in the air by sheer good vibes . . . yeah, we used to do stuff like that! Somehow, the Fugs had commandeered a flatbed truck that we [were] gonna use as a makeshift stage in the huge parking lot right next to the Pentagon."

There was some delay as the marchers made their way into position, and more as the crowd settled down to the sound of Ed Sanders's rabble rousing. Then, as Abbie Hoffman held back the national guard by waving around a water pistol filled with what he insisted was liquid LSD, the chant began.

"Out, demons out! Out, demons out. Out, demons, OUT!!" And then something happened.

Not according to official reports, of course. Official reports insist that the crowd simply stood around and made some noise, and then went its shiftless way.

But according to some of the march's more volatile organizers, the Pentagon rose thirty feet into the air, turned orange, and vibrated. And if that seems a little hard to believe, even Kootch is adamant that the building shifted and rose, just as Hoffman had predicted it would. "Amazingly, the Pentagon *did* levitate about a foot off the ground. Only for a short time. . . . [M]ost everyone missed it but me and few others. . . ." But it did move.

"So I played with the Fugs and we did all kinds of stuff; they were obviously politically active and it was a really fascinating time. At the time, everyone I knew, including me, was marching against the war, and so we were all politicized to some degree, but the Fugs more so."

Kootch quit the Fugs in early 1968. "The way I got out to California, I was really sick of playing with the Fugs, because the Fugs really weren't a musical endeavor. They were more of a freak show. It was a funny freak show, but I was serious and I wanted to play with a serious rock band.

"So this band called Clear Light came through town. They were signed to Elektra records, and they were supposed to be the new Doors. They did one album and then they fired their guitar payer and they were in New York auditioning guitarists, and the woman I ended up married to, Abigail Haness, introduced me to them.

"I auditioned, got the gig, and then flew out to Los Angeles with them."

Clear Light started life in 1966 as a Sunset Strip club band called the Brain Train, changing their name when they were signed to Elektra by producer Paul Rothchild (who also took over their management).

Lining up as vocalist Cliff De Young, lead guitarist Bob Seal, bassist Doug Lubahn and twin drummers Dallas Taylor and Michael Ney, the band had already dispensed with one guitarist, Robbie "the Werewolf" Robison, by the time they reached New York, replacing him with keyboard player Ralph Schuckett during the sessions for their debut album. Now it was founding member and principal songwriter Seal who was out, apparently after his own disagreement with Rothchild. De Young followed, and Kootch came in for the very last days of the band. But, like he said, it got him out to Los Angeles.

Clear Light was a shoestring operation. As a Fug, Kootch was earning $100 a week. As a Clear Lighter, he cleared just $30 a week plus $70 a month for rent, "which is kind of difficult to live on. But at that point I fell in with some people from Elektra. . . ." Including Barry Friedman, a promoter and producer who readily threw one of the spare rooms at his home on Ridpath and Laurel Canyon open to the new arrival.

Not quite the center for mythical hedonism that it would become over the next couple of years, Laurel Canyon was already established as a loose and not always friendly community into which a host of stars, star-fuckers, and would-be wannabes of all persuasion were thrown to learn, as one of their number, singer Linda Ronstadt, once put it, "about drugs, philosophy, and music."

A tangle of wooded roads and secluded homes that wound through the hills and valleys overlooking Los Angeles, Laurel Canyon was home to many in the music industry. A list of local residents certainly reads like a who's who of some description: Neil Young and Stephen Stills of the Buffalo Springfield, English bluesman John Mayall, "Happy Together" hit makers the Turtles, sundry Monkees, and Frank Zappa all lived within a partygoer's throw of one another.

Kootch: "On the block, Penny Nicholls lived down the road, and the engineer John Haeny. Paul Rothchild also shared the same house but he ended up moving out, and that was action central up there. Everyone was coming out there. Barry was producing everyone. He produced the Holy Modal Rounders [the seminal *The Moray Eels Eat the Holy Modal Rounders* album], he was producing Kaleidoscope, he was producing Nico, he was producing all these various acts. He'd come home with these acetates and we'd all sit around and go 'Wow.'"

One day David Crosby came by with Joni Mitchell, carrying the acetate for her first album. "He was telling everyone, 'You gotta hear this,' and Joni was very shy. . . . [S]he isn't really but she was that day. She went outside and Crosby played Barry and me this album, her first solo album that he'd produced, and it was brilliant. We all sat there and went, 'Oh God, she's got it.'"

Another day, he met Jackson Browne.

Browne had been back in Los Angeles for almost a year by now, returning to the city at the end of his New York adventure to discover his mother living in an apartment in Silver Lake, back in the Highland Park neighborhood, and his father in Japan, working for the U.S. forces' *Stars and Stripes* newspaper.

Silver Lake made a convenient base for him while he reacclimatized to California life, although that was not going to prove too great of a hardship. California was still the center of the universe. Back on the East Coast, the city had been thrilled by the lineup at Murray the K's Music in the Fifth Dimension show. Out west, an even more stellar gathering was being brought together for three soporific days and nights in the open air, the Monterey Pop Festival. Browne had a ticket for the show, of course, and Mark Bego, author of the Browne biography *His Life and Music*, credits Monterey with "strengthen[ing Browne's] drive to become a stage performer, as well as a songwriter, although circumstance as a whole was consolidating that ambition."

No matter that the Dom had turned sour in Browne's memory, his humiliation even prompting, five years later, a major and very public falling-out with his old friend Richard Meltzer, following the publication of the latter's memories in *Rolling Stone* in June 1972.

The fact was, his appearances there had afforded him the opportunity to debut his songs in front of one of the toughest audiences in America, at the same time as they found a home on one of the highest-profile LPs of the year. In certain circles, at least.

Nico's *Chelsea Girl* was released in October 1967, the putative sound-track to Warhol's smash movie of the same name. Nico herself hated it; the recording finished, producer Tom Wilson and string arranger Larry Fallon worked on, and then called Nico back to hear what they'd done.

"The first time I heard the album," she lamented, "I cried." They had destroyed it. "I still cannot listen to it, because everything I wanted for that record, they took it away. I asked for drums, they said no. I asked for more guitars, they said no. And I asked for simplicity, and they covered it in flutes! They added strings and—I didn't like them, but I could live with them. But the flute! I cried and it was all because of the flute."

In her eyes, everything about *Chelsea Girl* was shattered by that intrusive flute. But for other ears, the soft beautification of what might otherwise have been a very sparse listening experience only enhanced the songs that she had chosen. And just weeks after the album was released, Browne was contacted by a small music publication called *Cheetah*, for an interview that ran in the January 1968 edition.

Writer Tom Nolan caught Browne in expansive if occasionally cagey humor. "I've written a few good songs," Browne reflected, but "nothing really heavy yet"; in those days, the term had yet to be co-opted by the loud-guitars-and-grinding-vocals brigade, and still reflected upon a song's emotional content.

He was "headed that way," however, "just trying to be real. Trying to write what's around me, inside of me."

Something that was still inside him was the pain of his breakup with Nico. He told Nolan he had written a song for her following their breakup, "The Birds of St. Marks," "and that's all I'm prepared to say about that song." Twenty-some years later, however, he allowed Nico's biographer, Richard Witts, to reprint the lyric in *The Life and Lies of an Icon*, and almost every word that has ever been written about Nico, describing everything from the doomed beauty that she wore like a shroud, to the gothic splendor with which she paced her publicity, is present in Browne's evocations of "her throne of melancholy sighing" . . . "her dying midnight roses" . . . and his own "frozen words" and "weary secrets."

The *Cheetah* interview prefaced a period of considerable activity for the Jackson Browne songbook. A local band, Gregg and Duane Allman's

Hour Glass, included Browne's "Cast Off All My Fears" on their self-titled debut LP for Liberty Records. His old friends in the Nitty Gritty Dirt Band were preparing their second album and took "Shadow Dream Song" and "It's Been Raining Here in Long Beach" for their own.

And Elektra had two artists raiding his catalog in search of material. The Tom Rush album that Browne's "Shadow Dream Song" shared with James Taylor and Joni Mitchell was followed just weeks later by Browne's old friend Steve Noonan's debut LP for the same label.

No fewer than five Browne compositions made it onto Noonan's record: "The Painter" (written about the artist Steven Solberg), "She's a Flying Thing" (dedicated to Pamela Polland), "Tumble Down," the now-seemingly ubiquitous "Shadow Dream Song," and "Trusting Is a Harder Thing," a poem that Browne passed to Noonan one day with no intention of turning it into a song. The others, Noonan later reflected, were simply songs that Browne had abandoned in his own sporadic live performances. "I thought he might be leaving some nice ideas behind, so I kind of adopted them."

It was the success of a song Noonan contributed to the first Nitty Gritty Dirt Band album that brought him the Elektra deal, first alongside Browne as a songwriter with Nina, but then as a recording artist in his own right. "Buy for Me the Rain" reached #45 on the *Billboard* singles chart in the summer of 1967, seemingly confirming the old Orange County buzz that placed Noonan alongside Tim Buckley (and Jackson Browne) as the next surefire folk scene breakout. Noonan's demos were already circulating the office, in the form of one side of a two-LP set Nina had put together around their two Orange County prodigies, and it is an indication of just how prolific Browne was at this time that he spread no fewer than thirty of his own songs over the other three sides.

Noonan's ten (all but one of which was a Greg Copeland cowrite) were crammed onto the end. But it also indicates just how uncertain Elektra were of Browne's abilities that they viewed Noonan as the writer most likely to translate to the studio. Browne, in Elektra's eyes, was simply a songwriter.

And Noonan, it seems, was a troublemaker, unable to comprehend why the label wanted to cut an album with him and then load it down with a crew of rent-a-riff session men who simply played what they were told. No feel for the music, and not even much respect; he felt like a puppet, jerking to strings he had never known would be attached to him, and it was all the more shocking that the puppet masters were people he had been brought up to respect, the world-renowned kings of Elektra Records.

Instead, they were treating him like Cat Stevens, putting him into a studio and expecting him to do precisely what he was told. The difference is, Noonan fought back.

The final bust up came when Paul Rothchild saddled one song with an arrangement that Noonan could not stomach, but which the producer refused to budge on. They argued, Noonan rebelled, and Rothchild walked out, the album half finished and the singer's career seemingly in shreds. It would be six months before Noonan and producer Peter Siegel were able to complete the album, to be released with Rothchild's name completely whitewashed from the album credits.

The result was a subtly lovely album, but one that left nobody feeling especially happy, apart from a young New York photographer named Linda Eastman, whose cover shots of the singer rate among the most atmospheric pictures she would ever take, at least until she married Paul McCartney.

Browne was visiting New York City as these albums came out, opening for Judy Collins back in the familiar margins of Stony Brook College, and preparing, albeit briefly, to embrace a far more dramatic future than he had ever envisioned. Richard Meltzer had just introduced him to a local booking agent named Sandy Pearlman, at the same time as Pearlman was taking his first steps into rock management with a local band he had discovered, the Soft White Underbelly. The group had just one problem: They had yet to find a suitable vocalist. Perhaps Browne would like to try out?

Browne was keen to give it a go, taking up residence in the nearby house that the entire band (guitarist Allen Lanier, bassist Andy Winters, keyboard player John Wiesenthal, and drummer Albert Bouchard) shared, and where they could rehearse and jam twenty-four hours a day, and throwing himself into the proceedings.

"They were great musicians, they really were. . . . I'm afraid I was the least proficient musician among them," Browne told Joe Smith. He spent a week with Soft White Underbelly, rearranging his songs for their lineup, and "they played my songs really well."

But while jam sessions were trouble free, actually translating the songs to a style that both Browne and the band were happy with was another matter entirely. The new look group's projected live debut at Stony Brook was canceled, and the entire affair was abandoned. But the experience was not a waste, at least for Soft White Underbelly. Seven months later, on October 18, 1967, Soft White Underbelly accompanied Steve Noonan onstage at Stony Brook, on a bill shared with the Holy Modal Rounders and Phil Ochs, and so they got to play some Jackson Browne songs after all. It was Soft White Underbelly's first proper gig together, although it was only a few years later that anybody reflected what an odd beginning that was for the band that would (with manager Pearlman now their manager and producer) become Blue Öyster Cult.

For Browne, however, it was back to square one.

Kootch: "I met Jackson at Barry [Friedman]'s house. Everybody was falling by there all the time, probably because there was so much good weed there, and after I moved out of that house to another place in Holly Hill, Jackson used to hitchhike over to my place and we'd sit there and jam.

"He was a kid, he was like nineteen, and then I went to see him at a little club down in Hollywood and he was just performing solo. I sat there and listened and I said to myself, 'There's no question this guy is going to be huge, listen to these songs, listen to his voice.' It was the way he presented this stuff, it was irresistible, and he was playing 'Jamaica Say You Will' and songs like that, and he was obviously great. Everyone felt that way."

"You'd meet all sorts of great people at Barry's house," Browne recalled in Jac Holzman's *Follow the Music* memoir. "That's where I met Warren Zevon. I met David Crosby there. He and Stephen Stills and Graham Nash would come over and play their demo." It was host Barry Friedman, or Frazier Mohawk, as he preferred to call himself, who made the greatest impression on the young Browne, however, just as Browne made an impression on him. An evening spent listening to some of Jackson's songs ended with Friedman introducing Browne to one of his pet ideas.

In late 1966, Bob Dylan had taken himself off to the then utterly secluded hamlet of Woodstock, in the wilds of New York State, to hang out with a group of musicians he knew in the basement of a rental house, a band known prosaically as the Band. Recovering from the motorcycle accident that almost ended his career at age twenty-five, Dylan threw himself into recuperating around the music he had grown up with, writing that legendary body of songs that history would come to know as *The Basement Tapes*, but which are more properly viewed as the birthplace of modern pop Americana.

Dylan's *John Wesley Harding* LP and the Band's own *Music from the Big Pink* both resulted from the ensuing collaboration and, across the Western world, musicians were scrambling to try and replicate the natural, almost rural feel of the music that emerged from that basement.

For a star like Eric Clapton, this would entail breaking up the super-bombastic Cream and forming a new band, Blind Faith; for a star like Steve Winwood, it involved breaking up Traffic and joining forces with Clapton. At the other end of the scale, the budgets were less spectacular, but the mood remained the same. With Friedman molding the logistics, Browne and a handful of other local musicians were packed off to make the most of a newly acquired six-month lease on the Paxton Lodge in Paxton, California, a tiny spot on the map of the Pulmas National Forest. There, Friedman assured all and sundry, they would create music at least as organic and original as anything Dylan or Clapton was making.

Jac Holzman and Elektra bankrolled the deal to the tune of $50,000, the label head recalling that Friedman first voiced the notion some months before the Band album ever came out, on the final morning of the Monterey Festival in June 1967. "He proposed a music ranch. Take talented kids out of the struggles of trying to make it in the city, give them fresh air, good food, and the freedom to create whatever music came to them. It just struck me as a worthy notion and out of that enthusiasm came a 'yes.'"

The idea was simple. What the musicians viewed as a loose gathering of like-minded friends and associates, and Friedman called the foundation of his Los Angeles Fantasy Orchestra, would be installed to spark off one another; each working toward his own finished LP, but all throwing ideas into one another's pot.

Guitarist Ned Doheny, bassist Peter Hodgson, keyboard player Rolf Kempf, and banjo player Jack Wilce joined Jackson in the wilds, while Barry Friedman had only one regret. For reasons that he insisted were utterly self-evident, he had convinced himself that Jackson Browne's first album needed to be recorded in a cave.

A lodge-cum-resort-hotel built by Western Pacific Railroad in the early twentieth century, that had also served time as both a Prohibition-era speakeasy and a drying-out farm for alcoholics, was never going to match the grandeur of that initial scheme, as was soon proved.

As with every other utopian ideal—and the commune was certainly that—reality quickly got in the way of the dream. Girls were imported to brighten up the musicians' lonely nights and days. Friends. Drugs. Friends of drugs.

Five hundred miles from Laurel Canyon, Laurel Canyon was being recreated. There were joints for breakfast, joints for lunch, joints for dinner, joints for supper, and joints to chase away the munchies brought on by too many joints at mealtimes. In fact, the only thing that the band didn't seem to do much of was make music. They probably did, all concerned agree; it is difficult to leave a bunch of musicians alone in a house with a pile of musical instruments and not have them bash and bang around occasionally. But that was all they did, as eyewitnesses came away from Paxton with their memories apparently wiped clean. It wasn't the drugs, either. It was just the vibe. The ever-present haze of life in the lodge.

Elektra persevered. Minnesota bluesman Dave "Snaker" Ray was flown in to record his *Bamboo* LP with the Paxton Lodge band; and so were "Spider" John Korner and Willie Murphy, whose resultant *Running Jumping Standing Still* is rightfully regarded today as one of the all-time great roadhouse boogie LPs.

Such minor triumphs did little, however, to shake a growing belief that the entire project was not going anywhere, and probably never would. But before it all fell apart, one further conceit was placed into action, the recording of that long promised and, for Friedman and Browne at least, much anticipated Jackson Browne solo album.

Built around the best of the twenty songs that he had published with Nina, and titled for the name Browne found on a stillborn child's tomb in the local cemetery, *Baby Browning* was recorded in a matter of days, and then premiered for a visiting Jac Holzman. He closed down the enterprise within days. The music he heard, he insisted, was never going to make the cut; could never be packaged onto a disc and sold to unsuspecting members of the general public. It was time to end the experiment.

"I don't know quite what happened," Friedman mourned later. "Jackson wasn't ready and I was not at my best. It spun out of control. An incredible psychodrama was unfolding there, and I just escaped to my bedroom and hid under the pillow. Many musicians passed through Paxton. I run across them to this day and they say, 'I was there.' But I don't remember them."

Browne agreed. "I've never been able to collaborate with others. Another person with an idea is a problem for me. I'll be thinking of something and then another person will say, 'Hey, what about this?' And I won't even know what they're saying because I've been off in my head, thinking about something else."

Baby Browning, he sighed, "was badly played and badly realized. [Elektra] were a very image-minded company in those days and they wanted this to demonstrate what they were up to, but the people involved ought to have been able to make their own albums. As an album it was very unsuccessful, because we didn't have time to get to know each other, and, to be honest, I was terrible. Even if I'd made my own album, it would have been awful. It takes a long time to become a musician, and I hadn't been able to learn everything."

Elektra washed their hands of an expensive failure, paying off the $10,000 worth of damages that had been executed during the musicians' stay (several rooms had been repainted in a somewhat psychedelic style, while the hotel's pink neon sign had been demolished), moving out the studio that had been built into the place, paying for everyone involved to get as far from Paxton as they wanted to.

The label even surrendered the publishing contracts that had been built into the original arrangement, including Browne's two-year-old deal with Nina Music. Clyde Browne III was back to square one, back in Los Angeles, back on the street.

So he hung out with friends on Pico and Vermont. He goofed around with his old friends in the Nitty Gritty Dirt Band and, when they shot a short film for inclusion on television's *Rowan and Martin's Laugh-In* (on February 12, 1968), Browne was glimpsed within. Two weeks later, back at Stony Brook, he opened for Judy Collins.

He slept on people's floors and couches and wandered barefoot around Laurel Canyon. He gave up smoking dope, because he wanted to be taken seriously, and he found a new girlfriend, television model Janice Kenner. But most of all, he lived for Monday nights at a club on the far end of Sunset Boulevard, where Monday night was hootenanny night. The club was called the Troubadour and it was suddenly becoming a very hot spot.

10

Hey Mister, That's Me!

In late February 1968, Cat Stevens finally tired of the constant cough that had been aggravating him for a few months. He initially put it down to smoking too many cigarettes, and that might have had something to do with the weight loss that he had been noticing too. Didn't somebody tell him that smoking cuts the appetite? Yes, someone else said, but not this much. And although he was still convinced that there was nothing the matter, his friends became worrisome enough that he took his ailments to his doctor. A few tests and an x-ray later, and the prognosis came back, in the shape of a call that evening from the doctor. "I've booked you into a Harley Street nursing home this evening."

The initial diagnosis was pneumonia and, for the next week, that is what he was treated for. But when he failed to respond, more tests were ordered up and that is when the dread diagnosis was confirmed. Stevens was suffering from tuberculosis, a lung disease that, left untreated, kills more than half of its sufferers.

Virulent and staggeringly common (even today, it is estimated that one-third of the world's population is infected), TB was no longer the rampaging killer that it once was; prior to the development of the first vaccine in 1905, TB amounted to a near-death sentence for anybody who contracted it, and even after that, sufferers were more likely to be confined in sanitariums high up a mountain (where the cleaner, thinner air was regarded as beneficial) than to be allowed to remain even isolated within the general population.

Modern medicine had done much to lessen TB's terrors, but the disease remained startlingly easy to misdiagnose. A few years before Stevens came down with the illness, a professional soccer player named Roy Cheetham went to see his club physiotherapist to complain of his own bad cough. He was told to forget about it; it was a damp and chilly time, a lot of people were suffering from respiratory problems. He complained again a short while later, and this time he was told it was bronchitis. "Take these tablets and you'll be okay." Not until he was taken violently ill following a game in England's top division was he finally x-rayed and diagnosed.

If a professional athlete could be so easily misdiagnosed, what hope did a falling pop star have? Stevens was later informed that had he waited another three weeks before consulting his doctor, his chances of survival would have been negligible.

Very few people, initially, were privy to the exact nature of Stevens's ailment. Indeed, in the interest of keeping a bright face on for the media, it was reported that he'd be leaving the nursing home by the end of March, and visiting reporters had no cause for alarm. He was feeling a great deal better, he said, and he was writing new songs, as well as composing the score to an upcoming horror movie. As for when he would be discharged, he pointed to a date circled on the calendar, an upcoming London show by rock 'n' roll pioneer Bill Haley. Stevens would be there, he said, even if he had to go in a wheelchair.

He missed the show. Instead, he was moved into the country to continue a convalescence that was a lot more complicated than he had ever expected. He would remain there, in the rural surroundings of Midhurst, for the next three months.

Three months out of the city, three months out of the spotlight . . . three months that he spent going slowly out of his head. Although the nursing staff were as open as they could be about his condition, Stevens convinced himself that they were withholding the most vital information, and the most troubling. He saw no improvement in his condition and began to entertain dreams of a slow, lingering death.

"In the hospital I was really bored and fed up and I didn't know where to go, you know, or what to do. I was stuck in that bed for three months, so I said to myself, There's got to be something I could . . . that I could get something from the whole situation. This is ridiculous. I couldn't just come out of it and carry on—you know—'cause everything seemed so down. There was a gigantic cloud over my head at the time. I couldn't see through that and I really needed something to see me through."

One day, he laughed, he fled the hospital and hid out on a nearby farm, squatting in a tiny attic over a garage and living there for four days on pineapple chunks and apples. He returned to the hospital only after his food supplies—or his patience with them—were exhausted, and it was there that he began to seriously confront the issues that seemed to have been hanging by threads in front of his mind but were still too tenuous to reach out and grasp.

"Back in the hospital, I felt my music had been getting too complicated. I had a little record player and I played Bach again and again—he helped me out. Bach is like mathematics; it helps to clear your brain."

He turned to the pile of books that various well-wishers had sent him and picked up his copy of Paul Brunton's *The Secret Path*. Originally published in 1959, when its message of self-help was a fringe interest at best, former journalist Brunton's guide to awakening one's "Overself" through self-analysis, breathing, and mental quietude had been rediscovered by the late 1960s' own quest for spiritual enlightenment and rebirth, and Stevens reflected, "It was just what I needed. I read that book once and thought about it and I used it to meditate. There was nowhere that was quiet enough in the hospital. I had to creep out and there was this couch shed with a couch in it. I used to go in there and lock the door, then sit down and think. It was completely silent and that is where it came to me. It just happened. You reach that moment and you see it and say, 'Of course.' Then everything sprang from there like light."

It. A moment of self-realization. *The* moment of self-awareness. The knowledge that his career as a pop star was over. That it was time to begin again, afresh. As an artist.

Hindsight placed a brave face on the entire experience. Illness had given him the break that his career never could have; had provided him with the time, the space, and, most important of all, the solitude in which he could truly reflect upon what he had done so far, and where he wanted to go in the future. It was, he said years later, "an archetypal spiritual adventure. And I joined it."

He started to grow a beard, changing his appearance as he changed his outlook. He began to refer to himself, in his own mind if nowhere else, as a poet. His days as a pop singer, he determined, were behind him. Bored with the endless routine of his recuperation, he began studying art and taught himself to read music, to ensure that he would never again face the kind of humiliations he remembered suffering during his first days in the studio. He ordered in books on technical knowledge, electricity, and mathematics, and pipe-dreamed of combining algebra, sound waves, and vibrations into a whole new discipline.

The result, he declared, would be a new musical instrument, a machine that the performer would sing into, and which would then change the human voice into something else. Violins, perhaps. Or a guitar. Or even drums. He speculated on putting such a device into production, even though he had yet to actually confirm how, or even if, it would work. Years later, sampling technology and computers would allow any musician to create these sounds and many more besides. Right now, Stevens was thinking so far outside of the box that even he'd closed the lid on it long before he left the hospital.

It was July 1968 before Stevens was finally given the all-clear and allowed to say good-bye to the room that had been his world for twelve weeks. He immediately traveled to Venice, Italy, for a short vacation, but then it was back to London and back to work.

His break with Mike Hurst final, Deram suggested he get together with Mike Vickers, a former member of Manfred Mann, now carving his own dramatic path as a producer. Together, they would wade through the thirty-song stockpile Stevens had accumulated during his convalescence, and extract one single from the heap, while Stevens reserved another spin through the rest in search of material for his next album.

He mused gently of broaching conceptual territory; "I'd like to get some kind of story running through one side," he said, and perhaps the first seeds of his 1973 album *Foreigner*, with its side-long "Foreigner Suite," were planted there. What he did not expect was for the single "Here Comes My Wife" to come and go without any chart action whatsoever, although afterwards he agreed that it was just one more flop single in a career that was beginning to grow accustomed to the things.

"It's funny . . . because a review of 'Here Comes My Wife' in one of the pop papers said that it sounded a bit dated and so didn't stand much of a chance of being a hit. But if you look at a lot of records in the charts, they have a sort of dated feel about them. It's not that they're particularly old-fashioned—I think pop music is tending to get a bit simpler now than it has been for a few months, and perhaps on first hearing, a lot of it does sound a bit dated. But although they're less complicated, I think there's a lot more to a lot of the songs around now."

And simplicity was something he craved. Gone, he insisted, was the vast baroque bombast that had hallmarked his first two albums. The songs written during his convalescence, he insisted, were simpler than any he had penned in the past, and they were more personal as well. He had enjoyed being cut off from the pop business, enjoyed not having to deal with record company suits and booking agents with their panto dreams, and it was that, as much as any internal revelations he may have experienced, that would dictate his future course.

"As far as songwriting was concerned, I gained more scope. My whole outlook was widened. I know much more than I did before—it's just that everything doubled itself, so I had twice as much to do as I wanted. At the beginning, when I first started, I had a lot of energy, but I didn't have the direction. I wasn't sure. I wasn't sure how to cope with what I had. Because I knew that I could write music and I knew I was good. But I couldn't really express it that well."

What he could express was his belief that the Cat of 1968 was a very different beast to that of the previous year. "I think I've become more myself—it was the first time since I started that I'd been away from the pop scene and wasn't involved in the big hustle. I did a lot of writing and some painting and thoroughly enjoyed myself. In fact, I'm determined to start painting again seriously now—I've got a very good artist working at the moment redecorating my flat, and seeing him work has inspired me even more.

"It meant I could look at myself objectively—from outside of myself. In fact, I discovered a lot about Cat Stevens the pop singer. For example, I always thought I had a very different image to the one I actually had— apparently people thought of me as a manufactured 'star.' Whereas I was always under the impression that I'd made it on my own merits rather than because of any big publicity push or something. In fact, as far as I'm concerned, I did—but that's not the sort of image I have." And that was the image he needed to shake.

On February 23, 1969, Stevens made his return to the live arena, opening for the Who at the Chalk Farm Roundhouse. An eight-hour benefit for the London School of Economics, whose student body had been at the forefront of so many of the youth protests of the previous year or so, the concert also featured performances from Circus, Pete Brown's Battered Ornaments, the Third Ear Band, and the Occasional Word Ensemble, before the Who took to the stage for their last London concert before the release of *Tommy*.

It was a partisan rock audience that awaited the evening's entertainment, but any nerves that Stevens may have entertained regarding his reception by a crowd that probably didn't care much for his old pop image were swamped by a whole new set of concerns. No longer appearing with band and orchestra, Stevens opted to take the stage on his own, a lonely figure with just his guitar for company. And he won the day. In terms of volume, his short set was also the quietest of the entire show. But the audience listened, to his words and to his voice, and when it was over, they applauded warmly. Afterwards, he told everybody the same thing. In future, all he needed as backing was a guitar.

He was not going the "traditional" folk route, he insisted. Rather, he intended to create a contemporary course that was wholly personal—his own version of what he felt folk should and could be. He talked of the music he was now listening to—recent Dylan, Tom Rush, Van Morrison, Joni Mitchell and Tim Hardin. At Deram's insistence, he made one final grab for the golden ring of a comeback pop hit, even allowing the label to reunite him with Mike Hurst. But "Where Are You" would be his last release for Deram as well. He was cutting all ties with his past.

He laughed with *Rolling Stone* about those tempestuous last days with the label and the producer that launched him. "There were these clockwork players who just read the music, sat down and played it. We never went to do an LP; there was no original concept for it; they just tried to dilute everything you had into one standard, commercial tune. So I decided to freak out. I had this terrible song I brought in and said I wanted a hundred-piece orchestra and choir."

Hurst, too, laughs at the memory, not only at Stevens's demands for an orchestra, but also his insistence that it was a terrible song. "'Where Are You,'" Hurst argues, "was lovely.

"He had to come back to me," Hurst said of that final session. "Contractually he had to. Decca wouldn't let him go till he'd made that single and they insisted on me doing it. I think Steve thought it was the good-bye and he might as well just do it, and that was really the atmosphere. But the song is beautiful, it's a really nice song. It was ultimately the arrangement that let it down."

Hurst's arrangement.

"He came to me with this song and I could see that what he wanted to do from then on was . . . when I say it was a folkier style, it was an emptier style. It wasn't the big instrumentation and the kitchen sink that we'd had on a lot of tracks in the past. He didn't want that anymore and I could see that. What I couldn't see, to be absolutely fair . . . I didn't think it would work. And as it turned out I was wrong.

"It was such a change for Steve. I thought at the time, 'No you've made a mistake here,' and we did 'Where Are You' and I couldn't resist. I put strings on it because that's what I liked. But in retrospect, I've always looked back and thought to myself—'Yeah, Steve, you were right. You knew what you wanted to be. You were right.'"

A new musical raised its head. Encouraged by his recently acquired manager Barry Krost, Stevens began preparing *Revolussia*, a musical presentation of the last days of the Romanov dynasty, before the revolution of 1917 brought it crashing down. He already had a clutch of songs written for it—"The Day They Make Me Tzar," "Maybe You're Right, Maybe You're Wrong," and "Father and Son." Superficially, Stevens explained, the musical was about "change." But the strongest concepts, for Stevens himself, were idealism and adaptability. "Father and Son" may have been written about the relationship between Tzar Nicholas and his youngest boy. But within eighteen months, Stevens was able to tell a sold-out London Coliseum audience a very different tale about its origins.

"This is one of my favorite songs. It seems to say everything I want to say and I can't go on saying it, 'cause you can only say it once: It has to do with feeling frustrated, and it's to do with family and trying to get through to your family as well as trying to get through to society and school. My biggest hang-up was school.

"You know, 'cause I was never accepted in any way. Whatever I had to say was rubbish, and it was the same for everybody. Everybody goes through that, and it's so crazy, 'cause kids have so much more sense, and the teachers were out of it. [This brings a roar of applause.] Really, the teachers are the kids. There's a freaky kind of very funky strange people that teach. They do it for strange reasons. . . . They do it because they can't get to bed with anyone they want. So they take out their frustrations on these kids. I knew this guy, oh wow, he used to pay a penny to feel young boys. I mean, a penny! I charged two bob."

As an examination of a very particular relationship, voiced in terms that made its sentiments universal, the song became almost anthemic for a looming generation of listeners on both sides of the generational divide.

Stevens, however, never seemed certain which bank of that chasm he saw himself standing upon. He told *Rolling Stone*, "Some people think that I was taking the son's side, but how could I have sung the father's side if I couldn't have understood it, too? I was listening to that song recently and I heard one line and realized that that was my father's father's father's father's father's father's father speaking."

Revolussia was not his sole concern. Other songs were inspired by his own recent love affair with American actress Patti D'Arbanville; the couple split up after two years together, and Stevens wrote both the sweet "Lady D'Arbanville" and the deceptively misogynistic "Wild World" while deep in her shadow. And those were the songs, he said, that illustrated his intentions. Songs that might be cast in a light where everyman could understand them, but which had a deeper meaning that even he might never truly comprehend.

And he had just learned something else, he said. One of the greatest regrets of his career so far—one of his many "greatest regrets"—was that he had never been permitted to lock horns with America; had never been allowed to tour or even visit.

Now he was discovering a peculiar side effect of that prohibition, an audience that grew up around his LPs alone, with no exposure or even understanding of the pop star hue that tainted his European profile.

"Apparently," he mused as he contemplated his newfound freedom from Decca, "I'm considered to be a bit underground on the West Coast of America. A sort of Tim Hardin figure they've suddenly discovered."

And that really wasn't a bad thing to be.

11

Silent Sunlight

Like so many other of the musical events that took place during long hot summer of 1969, the annual Newport Folk Festival was to be utterly overshadowed by events taking place on a few fields of farmland in Woodstock, New York.

This was a blessing for the purists who still condemned Bob Dylan for dragging their comfortable little weekend getaway into the full glare of the international spotlight four years earlier, but a curse for the record labels who, year by year, weighted the festival dice toward their own commercial aspirations, and swamped the assorted hopeful minnows who had once regarded Newport as a stepping-stone to glory. Once, it was grumbled, "the next Joan Baez" could simply have piggybacked into a friend's performance and walked away with all the plaudits. Not any longer. Now she'd need a reputation and a record label before she could even get close to a newspaper story.

The Newport Folk Festival developed out of jazz impresario George Wein's Newport (Rhode Island) Jazz Festival, which itself was inaugurated in 1954. With tobacconist Louis Lorillard and entrepreneur Albert Grossman also on the team, Wein launched the new event in 1959 with a weekend-long (July 11–12) succession of folk-flavored performances and workshops at Freebody Park.

It was a successful event, conjuring some smart performances from the likes of Pete Seeger, Pat Clancy, Odetta, Earl Scruggs, and Martha Schlamme, as is readily demonstrated by the three volumes of live recordings released later in the year by the folk loving Maynard Solomon's Vanguard record label.

History, however, insists that the highlight of the weekend was the unscheduled arrival on the stage—and, from there, the folk scene itself—of the young Joan Baez, a special guest of singer Bob Gibson. Baez's performance comprised just two duets, "Virgin Mary Had One Son" and "Jordan River." But so pure was her voice, and so infectious her joy, that she not only stole the show, she made off with the festival itself. And when she returned just twelve months later, it was as a headliner in her own right.

Even her entrance to the festival grounds was an event. She was chauffeured in a Cadillac hearse, with her name emblazoned on the sides in silver tape.

Despite the success of the 1960 event, it would be 1963 before the Folk Festival returned to the calendar, by which time much had changed. Folk was in the public eye now, its progenitors were the new pop stars, its fans were hosting hootenannies, and the hootenanny itself had been co-opted by the man, to become the title of a weekly television show that was the very antithesis of the real thing.

The festival tutted at its commercial success and tried to draw a veil over such murky practices. But it was spread now over three days, July 26–28, and overseen by a nonprofit group of the most parochially minded figureheads on the scene, Pete Seeger, Pete Yarrow, Theodore Bikel, Jean Ritchie, and Erik Darling among them. And the two sides came together like white on rice. Some 47,000 tickets were sold for a weekend stuffed with seventy different performers, and the six live albums drawn from the event highlight the massive versatility and sheer adaptability of what its audience considered the "folk" genre should embrace.

Individual discs spotlighted blues, country and bluegrass, and old-time music; a fourth, *Newport Broadside*, was dedicated to so-called topical songs; two more, two volumes of *Evening Concerts*, wrapped up the event's main attractions—Baez, of course, Bob Dylan, the Freedom Singers, Jack Elliott, Dave Van Ronk, Judy Collins, and a new Canadian talent, discovered by television's *Bell Telephone Hour*, Ian Tyson and Sylvia Fricker. They already had a record deal, with Vanguard, and a debut album on the shelves. But it was Newport that made them stars. No less than Baez in 1959, the duo (accompanied by guitarist Eric Hord) was the incontestable highlight of the 1963 festival.

Approaching the American folk boom of the early 1960s from a date several decades after it peaked, one is astonished to find how deeply entrenched certain truths have become. Doomed poet tragedy marks the Farinas out as brilliant, association ensures Joan Baez will never be forgotten. Guthrie blood keeps the Arlo boy in motorsickles, and Dylan, of course, is self-perpetuating.

But Ian Tyson and Sylvia Fricker have never been granted much attention, and one doesn't have to look far to find out why. Too self-contained, too self-assured, they arrived in America with their proficiency already a fact of life, honed by years playing round the Canadian folk circuit. There was no chance to watch them learning to fly, no sense of seeing them grow with their audience. They simply were.

Were what? They *were* beautiful, they *were* brilliant, they looked great, and they dressed Mod with a capital M. Fricker had bangs to die for, and Tyson perfected the no-collar/skinny-tie/drainpipe-trousers look a full twenty years before the New Wave picked it up. But, as Fricker later reflected, "we never attracted the crazies like Dylan did. We had a romantic image with college couples, who identified with us." At one point, only Peter, Paul and Mary were selling more records than Ian and Sylvia, and that says it all.

But then you listen to those records, and theirs was a staggering repertoire. It's no secret that the strongest songs were those on which the two voices entwine—less well known is the fact that their taste in covers and traditional reinventions was equaled on every album by their own compositions. From *Ian and Sylvia*, "Rocks and Gravel" and "Old Blue" have both ascended to that rarified strata where they are all but folk staples regardless of authorship, while the later albums are equally rewardingly pocked with moments of staggering self-defined beauty. Tyson's "Four Strong Winds," the title cut from their sophomore album, is only the best known; Fricker's "You Were on My Mind" (from *Northern Journey*) is simply the best.

If 1963 saw the festival come of age, 1964 saw it defying the odds. It was staged at a time, as journalist Stacey Williams remarked, when sundry "self-appointed Cassandras [were] predicting the demise of the folk music movement, lamenting the plethora of indiscriminate 'hootenannies' and the British-made rock 'n' roll invasion."

The festival lineup, however, showed no signs of collapse, thrusting its customary array of new talent to the fore. Buffy Sainte Marie, Tom Paxton, and Phil Ochs all took their first steps toward household-name-dom at the 1964 show, while Judy Roderick emerged not only with a breathtaking performance, but with a broad enough repertoire to follow through with one of the finest albums of the age. Nineteen sixty-five's *Woman Blue* is one of those lovely, sparse folk albums that doesn't quite stay within folk's own parameters—Roderick grew up listening to blues and country, while a stint in San Francisco in the early 1960s saw her working the same blues-loving coffeehouse as the then unknown Janis Joplin. A luxuriously sensual version of "Rock Me Baby" is one early highlight of the album; an extraordinary revision of Sylvia Fricker's "You Were on My Mind" is another.

So much, then, for the death of folk. Or not. In fact, it would be the following year's event that sounded the death knell on the Newport Folk Festival as a living, breathing, and above all influential beast. Regardless of the true audience response to Bob Dylan's electric, eclectic set (tapes of the event really don't back up history's insistence that the entire crowd was up in arms), still that evening posited musical futures that had no time for linking arms and waving placards, and no further need for endless choruses of "We Shall Overcome."

Neither was Dylan the only drama. That was the weekend that Richard and Mimi Farina, too, arose from a place where the folkies felt comfortable, only to catapult them into a whole new arena, with their dulcimer-driven folk rock and proto-psychedelic imagery. Richard's ear for esoteric instrumentation left even the purists feeling strangely violated, while his lyrics painted portraits that the young Jackson Browne, for one, felt were painted directly onto his own heart.

For the occasion, the Farinas had worked up an extravagant act, scheduled to open with the two of them alone on stage, where they were joined, one by one, by additional musicians—bassist Fritz Richmond, guitarist Al Kooper and more—as the set progressed. By the time they hit the final song, the stomping "Hard Loving Loser," there would be a full electric band rocking out behind them, several hours before Bob Dylan took the stage backed by a similar hydra.

A sudden summer squall did not derail the Farinas. On a stage dangerously awash with water, with the audience soaked to its skin, the pair not only pulled off a remarkable performance, they also managed to persuade some 70,000 onlookers that it wasn't even raining.

Likewise, the two albums that Richard and Mimi Farina would record before Richard's death in a motorcycle accident on April 30, 1966, *Celebrations for a Grey Rainy Day* and *Reflections in a Crystal Wind*, rank among the most audacious, and certainly the most fascinatingly progressive, records of the entire folk boom, and NPR's Ed Ward, in the liner notes to the Farinas' 1999 collection *Pack Up Your Sorrows*, is convinced that had Richard lived, "these two would certainly . . . have given Bob Dylan a ride for his money."

Further evidence of this lofty prophecy would be served up by the third and final Farinas album, 1968's *Memories*. Compiled by Mimi Farina from a wealth of outtakes and other stray recordings, it's a piecemeal selection but an essential one, its dozen tracks spanning every dimension of her late husband's restless and, sometimes, ruthless ambition.

The majority of the songs were studio offcuts, including the semi-legendary "Morgan the Pirate," a six-minute epic that not only presages everything Fairport Convention would achieve on their early albums (another Farina song, "Reno, Nevada," was a regular in the English band's live set at this time), but was also intended as a farewell to Bob Dylan after his unceremonious breakup with Mimi's sister, Joan Baez.

Baez makes her own appearance on the album, with two of just three available tracks from the rock album she and Farina were recording at the time of his death. At the time of its abandonment, Baez described the project as an indefensible lapse in judgment, and an abrogation of her principles, and she was not alone. Dylan (of course) was extremely caustic when he first heard of the recordings, while Baez's fan mail bristled with horror. As she said, "'Don't go rock 'n' roll,' they tell me. It's dirty and sinful."

Dirty and sinful. As Pete Seeger raised the axe with which he intended cutting the electricity that supplied Bob Dylan's noise, and the audience howled its horror (and again, it doesn't matter whether they did or not; history and legend will not be denied), one thing was certain: Rock 'n' roll had indeed invaded, and folk music would soon be feeling the changes.

Buffy Sainte Marie, Eric Andersen, Joan Baez, Son House, and Donovan lit up the 1966 festival. Nineteen sixty-seven was conquered by Arlo Guthrie, and that gave the folk community a certain feeling of continuity; without Guthrie's father, Woody, it was likely there might never have even been a festival, so vast was the shadow he cast on American music. But 1968 was headlined by Janis Joplin, and 1969 saw the net cast even further and wider.

Irish rocker Van Morrison, country superstar Johnny Cash, and rock 'n' roll survivors the Everly Brothers were all packed into the billing, and so was a young Apple Records recording artist, James Taylor, graciously squeezed into the Sunday afternoon's young performers parade at more or less exactly the same time as astronaut Neil Armstrong was scheduled to place mankind's first foot on the surface of the moon.

So Taylor played in the knowledge that great swathes of the 2,500-strong audience before him had at least one ear glued to their transistor radios too. And that is precisely how it went down. Eight songs into his set, organizer George Wein appeared on the stage and Taylor was politely beckoned off. Mankind, Wein told the crowd, had walked on the moon, and that was why the music had stopped.

Backstage, Taylor was disconsolate. He had waited all weekend for his performance, and he was pulled off after fifteen minutes. But *Rolling Stone* put the smile back on his face with a review that insisted, "Those fifteen minutes set a standard for clarity, wit, and magnetism that was never equaled during the four days of the festival." That same organ of record would also insist that the five-minute ovation that rang out over the festival ground was aimed at Taylor, and maybe it was. But the moon landing was a big deal too, which is why Wein ended the afternoon's festivities there, and bade the audience celebrate history instead.

Besides, Taylor really had no reason to be glum, beyond the fact that despondency seemed to be his default status. Making his flesh-pressing way through the throng of admirers who came to commiserate with him on the curtailment of his performance, he ran into Joe Smith, the president of Warner Brothers Records, who not only congratulated him on the strength of his performance, but could talk knowledgeably about the Apple album, too.

And there was more. The pair fell to reminiscing about their Massachusetts backgrounds; Smith was a graduate of Yale and a former Boston disc jockey who only moved out to California because the late 1950s payola scandal had brought his career in Beantown radio to a premature end.

There, he landed a job in the promo department at Warner Brothers, a label that at that time was regarded as little more than a joke. Years later, Smith told Warners PR veteran Stan Cornyn, "I knew, as a disc jockey, that Warner Bros was a laugh. They made a lot of bad records, and when a label has that reputation you don't even open their envelopes." His new job was to stop people laughing, and he did it with such panache that his rise up the company hierarchy was as swift as it was inevitable. Because when Smith said an artist or a record was a hit, he was usually right.

ÅÅÅ

The day Smith met James Taylor, the likes of Black Sabbath, Jethro Tull, Doug Kershaw, Van Morrison, Fleetwood Mac, Deep Purple, Ry Cooder, the Faces and Alice Cooper had all joined (or were about to join) Warners, and that flurry of signings would more or less shape the course of the next few musical years on the sounds that were emanating from the label's Burbank lot. Now Smith saw how James Taylor, too, could play his part in the musical revolution that was to come.

Smith didn't go so far as to sign him on the spot; he was far too smart for that. The boy still needed to prove himself, and that was something that would take months of negotiation, both in the boardroom and in the legal department. But he let it be known that when Taylor was ready, he, president Joe Smith, would be waiting to listen to him.

Smith also introduced Taylor to the Everly Brothers, as they toured the festival grounds in the hours before their performance, and listened spellbound as the three of them, Phil, Don, and James, harmonized their way through Taylor's "Carolina in My Mind"—a song that coincidentally (or otherwise) was scheduled for the Everlys' own next single. On Warner Brothers.

Rolling Stone's enthusiasm for Taylor's performance was not surprising. Hot on the heels of writer Jon Landau's lauding of *James Taylor* back in April ("his reserve is a sign of his maturity. . . . [H]e sings with resonance and plays with grace"), Taylor then landed his own *Rolling Stone* inside-front cover, his features gazing intensely out over two columns of type that described first-hand his experiences of what was going on at Apple. The fact that most readers cared far more about what he was saying than about the guy who was saying it mattered naught.

Much of Taylor's conversation was old news, or at least old rumor. But seeing it laid out in his clear, calm, and matter-of-fact manner did bring home just how chaotic the Beatles' bacchanalia had become. Because Apple *was* in disarray, and even the Beatles (had they ever managed to gather together in one room long enough to issue a coherent sentence) would have admitted that.

The utopian dream had fallen apart with dystopian ease. Thieving employees, overambitious intentions, high hopes, and soaring costs had all conspired to rot the fruit, and now the band was battling over who would be the knight in armor who would gallop in to save the day.

Paul McCartney wanted his newly minted father-in-law, a New York lawyer named Lee Eastman, to pull Apple out of the fire; his bandmates went for an accountant named Allen Klein, impressed at that time by the amount of money he had apparently made for his other leading rock 'n' roll clients, the Rolling Stones. And while they sniped and squabbled, the roster of artists that had been gathered so proudly beneath the Apple banner was left to decay where it fell.

Klein became Apple's business manager on March 21, 1969, and immediately put Magic Alex, Ron Kass, and Alistair Taylor out on their ears. Two months later, Klein's ABKCo company assumed management of the Beatles as well as of Apple. Apple remained active, with no fewer than ten singles and eight albums being released throughout the first six months of Klein's stewardship, and no apparent slackening in the variety on display; the first days of Klein's watch included wildly experimental LPs by John Lennon and Yoko Ono and George Harrison, a second set by the Modern Jazz Quartet, and a live Plastic Ono Band album that devoted one entire side to Yoko Ono's yowling.

But Taylor was neither encouraged nor enthusiastic.

"I think the Beatles have discovered the business trip isn't fun," he told *Rolling Stone*. "You can't goof off. I get the feeling Apple is like a rich toy. I'm bitter, I guess. I feel they've let me down."

He had been back to England once since his hospitalization, intending to continue recording the new album that he'd started toying with during a flying visit to Los Angeles back in February 1969. Instead, he walked into Apple to find the offices in terminal meltdown.

There was nobody available to make a decision, nobody able to explain what was happening. Nobody to sign a check, nobody even to prepare the paperwork that would allow him back into a recording studio. Apple's publicity department had lined Taylor up a couple of television shows, a couple of club gigs, and a radio session, but they scarcely dented the national consciousness and really, what did it matter? Months had passed since the release of *James Taylor*, in an age when a week could make all the difference to a record's chances. With no likelihood of him releasing a follow-up any time soon, Taylor was at the end of his tether.

Apple was a disaster zone, he snarled. "Everybody's been fired or quit. Even some of the Beatles are getting confused." He, on the other hand, was just scared. Allen Klein, he told *Rolling Stone*, already had his record contract, "and now he's after my [publishing]. I know he is."

He was right, too. One of Klein's biggest beefs with the Apple setup, it seemed, was just how slapdash the company's organization had been, with one hand never knowing what the other was doing, until even the most promising avenues turned into lousy dead ends before long. Peter Asher was singled out for especial scorn.

"He's a wonderful kid," Klein told *Rolling Stone*. But he "never even signed James Taylor to Apple Publishing . . . [and now] we are under threat from CBS [April–Blackwood's parent company], which claims that it owns publishing on most of the songs on James Taylor's first LP."

Klein was demanding that Taylor be signed to Apple Music without delay, and was prepared to employ every trick in the book to make sure it happened. Including the holding back of Taylor's future career, beginning with any royalties he might be due. Klein, Taylor shivered, "[is] in charge of my money now. He's also responsible for my career. And it terrifies me."

It terrified others as well. As the long knives fell, almost everybody installed by the Beatles during those first few months of optimism was either shown the door or made their own way out of it. Peter Asher was one of those who took the latter option. When he joined Apple, he explained, it was because he believed in the company's founding principle, to help out artists in every way that it could. Remove that principle, twist it back to the industry norm of answering only to the fat cats who collected the biggest checks, and Apple was no different than any other label, and a lot worse than many of them. Because Apple had Allen Klein.

He was being polite—or at least diplomatic. Asher quit Apple and announced his intention to move to the United States and work there. Both Ron Kass, his old boss at the label side of Apple, and Ken Mansfield, head of the Apple's United States operation, were now ensconced at MGM; Kass, in fact, was running the company, and did not hesitate to offer Asher the position of head of A&R at what was still one of the largest and most successful record labels in America. Asher took the job and announced that he was thinking about taking on another one, too, one that would establish him as a manager in his own right. James Taylor would be his first client.

Garaging his newly purchased pride and joy, a 1968 Cortina GT, Taylor leaped at Asher's suggestion, and Apple, too, proved remarkably malleable.

Although Allen Klein was fiercely opposed to allowing Taylor to simply tear up his contract with Apple, this was one stance that all four Beatles agreed upon. The label had been established to help artists. Maybe it had failed in many of its aims, but that was no reason to change its approach. Taylor was released from his Apple contract and, as he set about establishing himself back in his American homeland, he did so knowing that Peter Asher was doing all he could to line up a new record deal.

"I didn't negotiate anything," Asher shrugged. "I just left and took the tapes with me.

Klein was furious. "Apple *made* James Taylor," he raged to *Playboy* the following November. "[Apple] gave him the exposure, the charisma of the Beatles' company. And then he just picks up and walks out on his contract. Didn't ask anybody, didn't talk to anybody, just went and signed a contract with Warners. Taylor didn't even make an attempt to work it out, so we're suing Taylor and Asher for $5 million damages, the money we would have made if he'd honored his contract."

It didn't happen. Asher continued, "The rumor is that they were gonna sue, and that Allen wanted to sue. One story is that George talked him out of it, but I don't know any of that for a fact. But I also know that no one could find any of the contracts, anyway. Allen Klein certainly said he was suing us. He did a *Playboy* interview and said that he had sued James and me each for $50 million [*sic*]. When in fact nothing had happened."

Klein, however, suggested that a settlement of some kind was reached. In 1994, he explained, "The problem with litigation is that, in America, you can fill out a complaint and the lawyer who signs it is not liable for anything. You are permitted to do that. You can say anything, but in trial, the ultimate outcome will obviate the mistakes that were made. But when you settle and you agree not to put anything out other than a one-paragraph thing saying we've all settled, and we're all happy, that's what happens. Nobody knows, and my lawyers always used to say, 'Forget it. To hell with them.'"

The other thing Klein did was to ensure that James Taylor's relations with Chip Taylor and Al Gorgoni would never be cordial again. Back when the Flying Machine broke up, Chip and James had agreed to meet up again in precisely six months' time at their favorite bar, McGuinness's. There they would see where their respective careers had led, and decide what to do with the Flying Machine's existing contract.

That meeting never took place. Chip Taylor recalled, "James called me a few days before the meeting and said, 'Look, I'm in London, I'm with Paul and George, and I'm about to sign to Apple.'"

So Chip Taylor and Al Gorgoni began negotiating with Apple instead, searching for a fitting settlement to their own still-valid contract with the singer . . . only to come up against the legal behemoth of Allen Klein, who effectively refused to negotiate anything.

Chip Taylor continued: "James asked if he could break the contract with Al and me, and we said yes. But the deal that was supposed to be worked out was never really worked out. Allen Klein didn't really do what he was supposed to do for Al and me, but we didn't want to sue James, so we just let it go."

Or not quite. Taylor and Gorgoni might have conceded defeat in terms of Apple, but if Klein was not going to pay them their fair share of James Taylor's broken contract, they would find other ways of recouping. They began preparing the release of the Flying Machine tapes themselves, through a new label, Euphoria.

≋

Taylor's appearance at the Newport Folk Festival, cruelly curtailed though it turned out to be, was one of the carrots with which Asher intended to woo Taylor's potential suitors. The other was no fewer than six July 1969 nights at the Troubadour in Los Angeles, wrapping up exactly one week before the festival.

There are, in the annals of rock history, a handful of concert venues whose names are at least as well known as those of the artists who filled them; and which, in many ways, are as much a part of these performers' stories, too. For punk rockers of a certain vintage, the names of CBGB in New York and the Roxy in London will live on long after the majority of acts who played there have been forgotten. On the New York folk scene, the Bitter End; in Cambridge, Massachusetts, Club 47; in London, Les Cousins. The British Invasion was born on the boards of the Marquee and the Cavern; the San Francisco psychedelic movement emerged from the Family Dogg and the Fillmore West.

The Troubadour slips effortlessly into this same company. The 300-seat club perched at 9081 Santa Monica Boulevard opened in 1957, on the very edge of the unspoken border that divides the madness of Hollywood from the money of Beverly Hills. It lived out its early years in a state of genial compliance, surviving on a diet of primarily folk and blues, rattling with the freight trains that made their ponderous way down the center of Santa Monica Boulevard, and really only making its presence felt when one of the giants of the scene turned up to play.

But the club's founder and owner, Doug Weston, had no qualms about the venue's success. "The people who play our club are sensitive artists who have something to say about our times," he was fond of saying. "They are modern-day troubadours."

The venue's existence was a parlous one all the same, and by 1961, Weston was on the verge of either closing the club altogether or transforming it into a jazz niterie. He borrowed money from his sister to keep the place afloat while he decided, and slowly business took off, aided in no small part by Weston's decision to book comedian Lenny Bruce into the venue in October 1962, an engagement that led to Bruce's first obscenity bust.

Notoriety did not follow, but the Troubadour's name was in the headlines at least, and as the folk boom flowered beyond the clubs and into the charts, so did the venue. Joan Baez, Odetta, and Peter, Paul and Mary were regulars, and the Troubadour's website features a story about the time that Bob Dylan led a late-night jam session there with only the club staff to witness his electric prowess, almost a year before he plugged in at Newport. The Byrds not only met at the Troubadour's regular Monday night open mike sessions, they also performed their genre-bending version of Dylan's "Mr. Tambourine Man" for the first time there.

Buffalo Springfield played their first ever show at the Troubadour, and when they broke up, Neil Young made his solo debut there. Fellow Canadian Gordon Lightfoot performed his first U.S. concert for Weston, and both Kris Kristofferson and Joni Mitchell introduced themselves to Los Angeles from that stage.

In fact, the Neil Young shows, in June 1969, were still fresh in the memory when Weston booked James Taylor into the club, largely on the strength of Peter Asher's enthusiasm.

"I knew Neil [Young] from the [Buffalo] Springfield, and it seemed to me that he had always been looking for a solo career," Weston recalled in 1992. "But that was the night when other people saw what the career ought to be, a solo songwriter singing songs about his own life, his own pain, his own thoughts. Before Neil, people wrote about the bigger issues, following Dylan's lead. Dylan rarely sang directly about his own life; he may have inserted it into his lyrics, but he did not openly discuss it.

"Neil went in the opposite direction, and I thought then that there was an avenue that other people would identify with. So when Peter [Asher] brought me James [Taylor], I listened to his Apple album and I could hear him moving in that same direction. People were sick of music that looked outwards all the time. They wanted to hear what was on the inside too."

"Those Troubadour shows . . . people look back on them and say that Doug was taking a chance, James was taking a chance, Peter was taking a chance," said Warren Zevon, himself a Troubadour regular. "An unknown artist playing six nights at a major Los Angeles nightclub. But that was what the Troubadour specialized in, showcasing artists that Doug believed in, or who people Doug believed in had faith in, and trusting the club's regulars to respect that belief. So an unknown playing six nights was nothing exceptional, because Doug knew that by the second or third night, the place would be packed and the lines outside would go on forever."

If James Taylor saw the Troubadour as the open door to a new stage in his career, however, for Jackson Browne, it was a final refuge, the one shining light in a landscape that had otherwise collapsed in upon itself, a landscape of unrelenting darkness and despair.

The Paxton debacle had been the final straw. Whether it was put into so many words or not, Jackson Browne had blown his chance at a career in the music business; blown it and then buried all the pieces. And the worst thing was, he was the last person to have realized that; remaining blissfully ignorant of his utter redundancy until the 1969 summer evening that he spent hanging out at Paul Rothchild's house in Laurel Canyon, talking with Rothchild and engineer John Haeny.

That was the night when he suddenly asked himself what on earth he was doing there.

His role in Haeny and Rothchild's world hit him like a landslide. He was nothing. A hanger-on at best, an amusement perhaps. Either way, he had no doubt. "I haven't done anything apart from sitting here getting loaded."

Not that there was anything wrong with getting loaded. It had gotten him out of the draft, after all. The day that Browne reported for selection, his bloodstream was so addled with chemicals that the military took one look at his blood test and sent him packing. But it left other people, the people who might have been in a position to help him in the music industry, looking very sideways in his direction.

The Elektra experience had soured him more than he realized. He had "botched it up," Browne told *Melody Maker* in 1976, "and I didn't know how not to botch it up again, I had a vague idea of what I wanted to do but I didn't have any idea how to do it, so I hung loose. I didn't want to get produced by a really good producer because I felt it would be out of my hands, I felt I'd be giving up part of what I wanted to do myself. So until I knew more about what I was doing and found people I felt I could grow with and give me room to solve some of the problems myself, I didn't take the offers."

His songwriting income had dried up. All the while he was on board at Elektra, he knew somebody would be pushing his songs out to other artists, even if they did tend to be his friends who recorded them, rather than absolute outsiders. Tom Rush, Nico, the Hour Glass, Steve Noonan, the Nitty Gritty Dirt Band, Hedge and Donna, Johnny Darrell—between them they had committed over an album's worth of Jackson Browne compositions to vinyl, and that was a remarkable achievement.

But how much more impressive would it have been if he had recorded those same fifteen songs himself; if it had been him who sang "Melissa" and "These Days," "There Came a Question" and "Shadow Dream Song"?

Now he was just another kid peddling his lyrics on the street, hoping against hope that somebody would hear him, or maybe hear about him, and want to cut one of his songs for a record. It was no way to live, and he was no longer certain whether he could. At one point, he even considered abandoning what minor foothold he still had in the music business and becoming a cop. Only the Troubadour held out hope for him.

He did not necessarily *like* the club. As James Taylor once observed, it was "one of the few places where the audience is actually treated worse than the act," and Browne did not disagree with that assessment, tongue in cheek though it was. He was a regular at the same open mike nights that had seen so many other artists get their start, but otherwise he rarely hung out there, and even more rarely threw himself into the whirl of changing allegiances that gave the club such a unique social flavor.

He recalled those Monday night sessions for writer Chris Charlesworth: "I'd go on sixth, which was the best time, before people left and after they'd been there a while, so they'd gotten into it. That's always been a strange audience because they tend to ignore you, but if you catch their attention or be outrageous or something, they'll cheer you on and go for it. I used to do it every week, five times in a row. After a while I started to get a positive reaction there, but it was tough."

Tough to watch as other artists used open mike nights as a stepping-stone to more regular, paid gigs. Tough to watch as the record company fat cats descended on the place, lining the streets outside with their flash cars, while they waited to see what favors their presence and possible approval might elicit tonight. Tough to watch as they all passed him by. And it was about to get tougher, too. The open mike nights became so popular that soon, Weston was demanding that would-be performers sign up for the shows in advance, forming an orderly line each afternoon, hoping they were there early enough to get a decent spot.

Andrew Gold, a local singer-songwriter who was making his own regular pilgrimages to the Troubadour, recalled "something Jim Croce once said, that there was no place in America that was more influential than the Troubadour if you were new on the block. Get a gig there and you really did have a chance to get signed. And he was right."

Not if you were Jackson Browne. Just like the Newport Folk Festival, more and more the Troubadour was being used to showcase already signed (or at least recognized) talent. And the pool of lucky hopefuls was scrabbling harder and harder for the available support slots. You needed a friend on your side all the time, and Browne sometimes felt as though he'd exhausted most of them.

Indeed, when Browne was asked about the artists he most frequently performed alongside, he usually demurred. Instead, he told stories about the characters who made certain that the place actually ran, owner Weston with the vile green suit that legend insisted he had not changed out of since he bought it, and whose own public persona was so larger-than-life that he even plastered his face on the Troubadour menus.

Then there were the doormen who knew who could and couldn't come in every night, and who enforced another of Weston's peculiar credos: that the Troubadour was in the business of supporting poor musicians, not rich ones. So don't bother asking if you can slip in for free, just because you've sold a million records. There were the guys in the kitchen, the people who cleaned the toilets. The bar staff. An entire solar system of unsung heroes. They were the people that Browne liked to talk about, not the people onstage.

There were exceptions, of course. The night Browne played his first show at the Troubadour was also the night that he met David Lindley, who was destined to become one of his longest-serving associates. Unbidden and unknown, Lindley walked into the dressing room as Browne was preparing to take the stage one evening. He listened to the song that Browne was strumming on his guitar, then took out his fiddle and played along. Browne later remarked that the song (whichever one it was, he seemed to have forgotten) never sounded the same again.

But most of his time was spent either considering the futility of even carrying on, or seeking out whatever thrills might assist him in blotting out the need to consider those things. So the news that James Taylor was coming to play was definitely a bright spot amidst Browne's summertime blues, if only because it let him know that there was at least a tiny niche out there for an artist who just wanted to sing his songs.

"We loved that James Taylor record," Browne's old Paxton coconspirator and friend Ned Doheny told author Barney Hoskyns. "[And] I know Jackson . . . really thought James was a force to be reckoned with. James broke the mold and made that whole scene acceptable in a way that it wasn't before."

12

Night Owl

The music that Doug Weston envisaged, the songs that spoke of "what was on the inside too," was not a new invention, of course. And neither was it exclusive to the Troubadour. Over the past two or three years an increasing number of "performer-composers," as the press then termed them, had arisen; some, like Tim Buckley and Elektra labelmates David Ackles, Tom Rapp, David Blue, Fred Neil, Tim Hardin, and Eric Andersen, destined for little more than cult greatness in their prime; others, like Young's fellow Canadians Leonard Cohen and Joni Mitchell, already bound for glory.

What separated James Taylor from these others, in a musical sense, was the sheer insularity of his muse. But that alone was not enough. He would also require marketing, which was something that the majority of those other names had never truly experienced. A full-page ad in the folk magazine *Sing Out!* was nice. But a full-page spread in *Rolling Stone* was a lot better. That was one of the pledges that Asher was searching for. Another was the guarantee that Taylor would not be regarded or referred to as one more in the long line of troubadours, and that was simply a matter of language.

He was not a composer-performer. He was a singer-songwriter.

With Taylor safely headquartered in the rental adobe they shared at 956 Longwood Avenue, and exploring Hollywood to his heart's content, Asher hit the record labels.

For a time, it looked like Vanguard might be his first choice, and there was considerable logic to that decision—logic and integrity. Even more than Elektra, label head Maynard Solomon had refused to allow blatant commercial considerations to shape Vanguard's destiny. From the outset, the label took as its motto "Music for connoisseurs"—and that's what it released.

The Vanguard label was launched in June 1950 by Solomon and his brother Seymour, built with a $10,000 advance from their father, Benjamin. The brothers' forte was jazz and classical music, and they established two labels to cater their tastes—Vanguard and the Bach Guild, an ambitious project intended to release recordings of all of its classical composer namesake's choral work. With such a modus operandi, it would take a decade, and the advent of Joan Baez, before Vanguard even sniffed a gold record.

Between 1953 and 1955, Vanguard released some twenty different jazz albums, including well-received and respected titles by Vic Dickenson, Sir Charles Thompson, Joe Newman, Buck Clayton, Don Elliott, and Ruby Braff—many produced by the legendary John Hammond Jr. However, a glimmer of the label's future came in the form of Brother John Sellers's *Sings Blues and Folk Songs* collection, released in 1954; and, two years later, in the release of the first album by Pete Seeger and the Weavers—a courageous move at a time when the group's political stance saw them all but boycotted by the rest of the industry. (Paul Robeson, another blacklisted performer, joined the Weavers at the label.)

Releases by Martha Schlamme and Cisco Houston followed, and by the end of the 1950s, Vanguard was essentially the biggest folk game in town. It became even bigger following the arrival of Baez, with her immediate preeminence immediately prompting Columbia (who actually rejected Baez) to sign their own female folksinger, Carolyn Hester.

That Hester's first husband, Richard Farina, would later marry Baez's sister Mimi (while Dylan, who guested on Hester's first Columbia album, soon became Baez's consort) is indicative of just how compact the folk scene was at that time; that the Farinas would then join Baez at Vanguard, on the other hand, proves the wisdom of the Solomons. What nobody could have imagined at the time was how time would bear out so many other of their signings.

Georgia-born singer-songwriter Patrick Sky, for example, was a dynamically contrary performer; indeed, if there is such a thing as the archetypal Vanguard artist, Sky might well be it. Even his peers were confounded by him; his gentle, reflective songs were, singer Dave Van Ronk memorably mused, "peopled by bits of verse, horrible puns, unprintable lyrics, japes, jibes, and a beer river flowing gently over your grandmother's paisley shawl."

But while today such a description conjures up visions of a Marilyn Manson–esque monster filling our children's ears with oaths and obscenities, *Patrick Sky*, this folky fiend's 1965 Vanguard LP, turns out to be nothing like that. Or maybe it is. You never heard "damn" on the radio back then, but Sky lets one slip (during the otherwise plaintive "Many a Mile") without even a guilty pause.

The proving ground for many of Vanguard's most adventurous (and far-sighted) signings was the *New Folks* series of various artists collections. Phil Ochs, Lisa Kindred, Bobby Jones, and Eric Andersen all made their debuts via these albums, with the latter rapidly emerging as among the label's most reliable performers as the early folk boom settled into its mid- to late-1960s reflective rock mode.

Andersen's influence was profound. According to legend, it was his "Come to My Bedside," a cut from 1965's *Today Is the Highway*, that persuaded Kris Kristofferson to start writing sultry love songs; and "Violets of Dawn" (from 1966's *'Bout Changes and Things*) that prompted Leonard Cohen to begin writing songs in the first place.

In fact, *'Bout Changes . . .* was a significant album all around, as Andersen escaped the Dylan-shaped shadows which haunted his debut and carved himself—and his entire genre—a new niche altogether. Andersen's thoughtful lyricism, stylistic versatility, and gifted storytelling fueled what, five years on, became the sensitive singer-songwriter boom of the early 1970s, peopled by the earnest young men (and women . . . they tended to be the ones without beards) whom history now politely recalls as, yes, those "new troubadours."

Whether or not he was aware of what he had created, Andersen himself refused to rest on his laurels. *'Bout Changes . . .* was still weaving its spell when its maker restlessly turned his back on all it portended, and rerecorded the entire album with a rock band! The liner notes to *'Bout Changes and Things Take Two* complete the tale and offer another vivid illustration of Vanguard's modus operandi of the time. "We asked Maynard Solomon . . . and he saw no reason why we couldn't make a new album with the songs from the last one. It hadn't been done before, but what did that matter?"

It didn't matter at all. It's impossible to play favorites between the two albums (although many people try); impossible to say which direction Andersen should have pursued next. Not that it would have mattered, as he promptly swung off on yet another different course. Andersen's next album,

1968's frustratingly lightweight *More Hits from Tin Can Alley*, was his last in either a folk or rock mode; the following year, he relocated to Nashville, seeing out his Vanguard contract with the aptly titled *A Country Dream*.

Which just goes to reinforce one fact: Vanguard was never simply a folk label.

As Asher saw it, the label's problem was that it was never particularly hit-oriented, either. Joan Baez remained Vanguard's biggest-selling act almost a decade after her breakthrough; only Country Joe and the Fish had truly come close to even equaling, let alone eclipsing, her, and their day was already passing. But Asher did not despair. He knew from other artists that the most obvious home was not always the most suitable one.

He marshaled his resources. The Apple album made a convincing calling card; so did a résumé compiled from the American and British reviews of the record, and the *Rolling Stone* commentaries too. A single of "Carolina in My Mind" had flopped, but that, Taylor joked, was not his fault. "One of the promo men told me it was because it had a hole in the middle." Actually, it was because Apple had a hole in the middle, and didn't actually promote it for more than the couple weeks it spent bubbling under the *Billboard* chart.

Still, Taylor was surprised, and naturally gratified, to discover that so many of his new friends were fans of his album; and when he reconnected with old friends, he really started feeling at home.

Kootch admits that when he first heard of his old bandmate's relocation to London, he felt a little left out, all the more so after Joel Bishop was flown out to join in the sessions. "Did I feel left out? Yeah, in a way I did. I recall at the time saying, 'Oh gee, London, glam London.'"

At the same time, however, "I had my hands full with what I was doing in Los Angeles, because it's not like nothing was going on; all hell was breaking loose. Los Angeles had taken over from London at that point." And the focal point of that outbreak was the Troubadour.

"When I moved to Los Angeles, we used to go down there every few nights and sit in the bar and try to act cool. There was always a bunch of things going on. . . . I missed the part where the Eagles and J. D. Souther and that crowd were all hanging out, but it was a magical place; it was the place where everyone went, and you had to play there. It was a gas to play there. Audiences were attentive; they came to listen. That's where you wanted to play."

Kootch had a new band now, and it was perhaps the one that he should have formed a couple of years earlier, when he first started hanging out with Carole King and Charlie Larkey. It was called the City and it was on course to record one of those strange little albums that is just so damned good it seems impossible to believe that it was ignored at the time.

"Clear Light broke up. They were a mess and I got blamed for the whole thing, and it was at that point that Carole decided to move to L.A." Still in demand as a songwriter, penning modern hits and future classics for anyone who would cover them, King had grown accustomed to hiring Kootch to play guitar on the demos of the songs she was writing while he was in New York, and he was among the first people she called once she arrived in L.A.

"Playing on her demos was a total education," Kootch enthuses. "I learned how to play on records from her, it was an extraordinary thing. And these demos were always coming out so great, and the artists who covered them, a lot of the time they were just imitating the demos. So Lou Adler convinced her to make an album of her own."

The City added drummer Jim Gordon to the core of King, Kootch, and Larkey, but while the unit's musicianship was not in question, King's image was. Unfairly or otherwise, she was still best associated with the string of Brill Building hits that had brought King and her then songwriting partner, Gerry Goffin, to prominence at the dawn of the decade, but which had fallen into such disfavor after the Beatles taught people to write their own material.

No matter, as Kootch explained, that "the Beatles learned from Goffin/King just like the rest of us; Carole had to find a new way to exist within this new paradigm, and she started writing songs that were more influenced by what was going on, the hippie movement, acts like Donovan and the Beatles. All these influences started appearing in her music, and so we made this album that highlighted them."

The sessions began loosely, with Kootch and Larkey sitting in King's Laurel Canyon living room, working up the tunes. "Even though we had a group name, this was Carole's record all the way. She would sing or play parts to Charlie and me, and once we got it right, we could hear how great this record was going to be."

By the time the team entered Sound Recorders in Hollywood, Kootch "was pumped. I was thrilled to be working with the people at the top of their game. I soaked it up like a sponge, and for me it was a learning experience of a lifetime."

The City never did gig. "Carole was too shy, too stage-frightened to play any gigs. We were supposed to do the Troubadour, and at the last minute she canceled because she was too nervous to do it. So obviously there wasn't much future to the City because we weren't gigging, so Charlie and I formed another band called Jo Mama, which had Abigail Haness [Kootch's wife] as the lead singer, and a couple of members of Clear Light, the ones that didn't blame me. We got a record deal [with Atlantic; Peter Asher would produce their debut album], we had management, and it goes on from there."

In a corner in the Troubadour, and deep into a long string of evenings spent elsewhere, Taylor and Kootch caught up with one another's activities, even smiling at memories of events that had simply been too harsh to even contemplate at the time they were taking place. The death of the Flying Machine, for example, "collapsing in flames, pieces on the ground," as Taylor would soon dramatically describe it.

"It was just horrible. James at that point had a nasty drug habit; Joel also had a nasty drug habit. I was the only guy who didn't. I was the big square. While everyone else was shooting dope I'd be going, 'Why are you guys so tired?'"

Other topics, however, were stickier. While so many other people, it seemed, fell over themselves to praise *James Taylor* to its maker's face, Kootch called it what it was: an overproduced mess.

"First of all, I had tremendous respect for Peter Asher's ability, and James I already knew was a genius who had the potential to be a huge star. I'd always thought that about him, from when he was a little teenager. He's just a charismatic character, he had a way about him, and he was also a phenomenal singer.

"But I didn't care for that album much. When I heard the album I was disappointed, because I didn't like the production of it at all. It was too produced; there was too much going on, and it covered up James's natural ability to communicate. If you listen to that Apple album, 'Night Owl' has about eight million horns on it, the whole song is a horn section. There's nothing but horns.

"The problem was, Peter wasn't sure how to present James, because there weren't too many James Taylors around at that time. It was a new kind of thing. He wasn't a soul singer, he wasn't a popster, he wasn't a glamour boy. He was this whole new thing, and it took a while to figure out the right context to put him in."

Asher was still figuring it out. Kootch continues, "When Peter and James came to Los Angeles after that album, we recorded 'Fire and Rain,' me and the members of Jo Mama, and it's not very good. It's very ordinary. Nobody knew how to play these songs, because they weren't rock 'n' roll, they weren't Brill Building pop, they weren't 'Strangers in the Night.' We all had to figure out a way to play them."

No matter. By late October 1969, Asher had landed Taylor a new publishing deal with Robbins Music, a part of Asher's own employer, MGM's, empire. Just days later, a record deal followed, as Joe Smith followed through on his Newport Festival promise. Warner Brothers was already home to Neil Young and Joni Mitchell. Any label that could understand and appreciate those artists, Asher felt, would understand Taylor as well.

What they did not understand, and what Taylor could not explain, was the apparent death wish that Taylor now nurtured; the need, it seemed, to respond to every step forward in his career by engineering a step backwards in his personal life. In London, it had been his return to drug use during the recording of his LP, and his hospitalization at the time of its release. Now, with a new record deal on the table and an album's worth of songs—those that had been destined for his second Apple LP—ready to go, he broke his hands and feet.

The accident happened in August, after Taylor returned to Martha's Vineyard following the Newport Folk Festival. Out in the woods one day, he came across a motorcycle that, unbeknownst to him, had been left there by the local police chief after it was reported stolen and then retrieved.

Neither did he realize that the vehicle was no longer roadworthy, because its brakes had gone. So he jumped on, revved up, and took off at fifty miles an hour down a fire lane, on a collision course with a tree.

It was his second crash in six months; last time, however, he merely suffered scrapes and bruises. There was also talk about another accident that Taylor was very fortunate to walk away from, an incident involving the lethal combination of a wood chipper and a chain saw. He had walked away from that unscathed, as well.

This time he wasn't so fortunate, not only in terms of the time it would take for the broken bones to heal, but also in that his injuries cut him off from the very tools of his trade. Unable to play guitar, or even hold a pen, the songwriter could not physically write songs.

He couldn't play Woodstock, either. Pulling strings that even he was not sure would lead anywhere, Peter Asher had landed Taylor a spot low down on the festival bill, and he was just about to book his airline ticket out to New York when he received the news.

Taylor's timing continued to be cataclysmic. Tom Rush had already transformed "Something in the Way She Moves" into something approaching a radio staple; now Beatle George Harrison had taken the same title and rejiggered it into a song of his own, as the opening line to the Beatles' haunting "Something." A key highlight of their newly released *Abbey Road* LP, "Something" was also poised for release as the Beatles' next single, and though even Taylor's friends may sometimes have seethed at the symmetry (while others boasted aloud of the honor), Taylor himself was simply happy to have received such a compliment.

"I never thought for a second that George intended to do that," he laughed to writer Paul Zollo in 2010. "I don't think he intentionally ripped anything off, and all music is borrowed from other music. So I just completely let it pass. I never gave it a second thought. I have stolen things much more blatantly than that. A *lot* of stuff. And I also steal from myself and just rework different things into songs."

He admitted that he "raised an eyebrow here and there," but he also acknowledged that what goes around comes around. "You know that song . . . 'I Feel Fine'? The end of 'Something in the Way She Moves' is 'I Feel Fine.' 'She's around me now almost all the time and I feel fine.' That was taken directly from a Beatles song."

Warners, like Asher, may have sighed at Taylor's incapacitation at a time when so much was swirling. But they were not disheartened. Taylor would not be in plaster forever. On October 15, the record contract was signed; two months later, Taylor and Asher would enter Sunset Sound Studios, once described by Paul Rothchild as the best in the country, to work at last on Taylor's second album. Which, to their minds, would really be his first. The debut was simply a dry run.

Playing back the Jo Mama take of "Fire and Rain," listening again and again to the performance and wondering why oh why it just didn't hit home, Asher decided to try and experiment. What would happen if he took away the band? Erased the guitars, erased the bass, erased the drums?

Kootch: "Peter in his wisdom said [that] what you need to do is take everything out of the way. All the musicians and strings and everything, and make a very spare album where all you really heard was James and the focus was on James. Not on the production, not on the band, not on anything that would draw away from James. And that was the right way to produce James Taylor."

Taylor himself was raring to go. Three months with his hands and feet in plaster had filled him with boundless energy. He knew the songs he would be recording by heart. Now he tore into them.

What became *Sweet Baby James* was recorded for $8,000 in just two weeks before Christmas 1969, and in fairness the songs that comprised it were barely superior to those that comprised his Apple album. What distinguished the new record from its predecessor, and what in turn ignited a whole new genre of introspective singer-songwriters around Taylor's example, was the sheer sparsity of its arrangements.

Reaching back to the two Tom Rush albums that had inspired him in his youth, and staring directly into the heart of *The Circle Game, Sweet Baby James* was an exquisite rendering of the folk moods that had swirled so dramatically earlier in the decade, but which had been ruthlessly updated too, to scrape away the rough instrumental edges that marked out an "authentic" folk record, and replace them with a more mannered and less charged soundscape.

Like the rock bands of the age that were turning their attention back to vintage rock 'n' roll and blues in an attempt to reconnect with their personal electric birthright, Taylor and Asher schemed a record that could almost have shared Al Kooper's thoughts on Rush's *Take a Little Walk with Me*: "a modern, updated tribute to the heroes of our musical youth." Only instead of turning his eye to existing standards, Taylor set about creating new ones

Kootch, inevitably, joined the proceedings. So, at the guitarist's invitation, did Carole King. Randy Meisner of Poco was the best known of several bassists passing through the studio as the sessions went on (John London and Robby West also guested); an all but unknown Pittsburgh teen named Russell Kunkel played drums—his wife, Leah, was Cass Elliot's sister, and he'd sessioned with David Crosby. Jack Bielan contributed brass, and Red Rhodes brought in the steel guitar. All would leave their mark on the recording, but all, too, grew swiftly accustomed to finding their contributions to each song left behind. Some singers employ musicians as background. Taylor and Asher thought of their band as a back*wash*, but far from being slighted, the musicians knew that it was the correct approach.

King, in particular, reveled in the sparsity, finding within it a freedom that more complicated arrangements would never have permitted. It was her keyboards, via which she was so adept at finding melodies that nobody else could dream of, that took Taylor's sometimes vague tunes and arrangements and boiled them down to their most essential components.

The key to both the album's musicality and to Taylor's own deeply personalized approach was the title track, "Sweet Baby James." Taylor's brother Alex became a father in May 1967, but it was some two years before James was able to finally meet the nephew that Alex had named after him. It was as he followed Route 95 south from Massachusetts to visit the boy in Chapel Hill that a new song came into his head, dedicated to the toddler.

He dug deep into his repertoire. "I'm a Steamroller" had lain dormant since the last days of the Flying Machine. Now he revisited it (as the abbreviated "Steamroller"), and it was still one of the heaviest blues around.

There was further lightheartedness in the song's closing cut, the pointedly titled "Song for 20G." Warners had contracted a ten-song album, and Taylor had just eight compositions that he was ready to record. He had already thrown in one cover, a brief and somewhat grisly rendering of the old standard "Oh Susanna"; now he needed to come up with one more number in order to collect the second half of his advance, a tidy $20,000. Cobbling together a collection of odd rhythms and riffs that he had lying around, Taylor simply unleashed the band in the studio, and let the song build itself from scratch.

The levity of that, and the sentimentality of the title track, however, were to be leavened by what instantly became the album's most dramatic and darkest moment, "Fire and Rain." First toyed with back in New York, when he premiered it for Chip Taylor, the bulk of the song was written in James's Chelsea, London, basement just as he was putting the finishing touches to the Apple album, the songwriter's response to the news, delivered six months after the fact, that one of his New York friends, Suzanne Schnerr, had committed suicide.

"When I was in New York with the Flying Machine for that year, I had a girlfriend. I was a country boy come to town and, you know, it was—Susie and I were really close. And, you know, I went to England. She committed suicide after. She was having terrible problems with her family. They had committed her, actually, because they wanted to control her. Really, it wasn't necessary. But they committed her in a state asylum and she eventually killed herself.

"But my friends . . . didn't want to burst my bubble. 'Let's wait until he's got the [LP] in the can and then we can let him know about it.' And so that's the way that first verse happened."

An already dour scenario, however, was swiftly furthered muddied by Taylor's own personal demons, as he pursued his heroin cure and reflected on the "sweet dreams and flying machines" that lay "in pieces on the ground."

"The second verse is about my arrival [back] in [the USA] with a monkey on my back, and . . . my desperation in trying to get through the time when my body was aching and the time was at hand when I had to do it. And the third verse of that song refers to my recuperation in Austen Riggs, which lasted about five months."

Taylor had already warned the world, via the pages of *Rolling Stone*, that he intended *Sweet Baby James* to be simpler than its orchestrated predecessor; "it has to be, because the music is simple, and a big production job just buries all my intentions." There were early fears, however, that perhaps it was too simple. "Sweet Baby James," culled as the album's first single, barely bothered radio programmers' conscience, and although the album broke into *Billboard*'s Hot 100 in March, it was at a lowly #90, and it scarcely looked as though it might climb higher.

But reviews were encouraging, and Taylor was soon basking in the glory of the album's critical reception.

"The songs that James Taylor sings . . . are born out of the torture that twice sent him to mental institutions," Al Aronowitz wrote in the *New York Post*. Taylor "speaks for his generation with the kind of cool authority that seems destined to elect him one of the spokesmen of his time." And, as if to underline Warner Brothers' own clear-cut ambition, Aronowitz concluded, "Is [he] going to be the next public phenomenon? It's a little early in the cycle for such an event, but that's the league James has applied for. May the Lord have mercy on him."

Right now he was still playing the Troubadour, and occasionally stepping out to other small clubs around the country, where he played to a mere couple of hundred curious faces. But even his detractors admitted that, with the right breaks and the right promotion, it might only be a matter of time before he was facing audiences ten times this size.

Those detractors could be cruel, however, for what is the point of being a detractor if you can't have a little dig once in a while? As the term *laid back* became common currency among fans and admirers searching for the secret to Taylor's musical style, so it also began to take on a pejorative tone, louder musicians remarking that their music was the antithesis of laid-back, making a virtue of the fact that they didn't simply sit on chairs, strumming their guitars and mumbling their misery.

"What caused glam rock?" asked Kim Fowley, Cat Stevens's long-ago cowriter, in his memoir. "Simple: James Taylor and saggy tits and granola. The food started looking very genteel, with leaves and tomatoes and grain, and then the music got all sensitive. Suddenly you have these castrated hippies with no skin tone making music with no rock 'n' roll stink to it. James Taylor sits on a stool and begets all kinds of men and women sitting on stools wearing overalls and flower-print dresses singing about Laurel Canyon dogshit. It was horrifying and it wasn't rock 'n' roll. . . ."

John Lennon, too, would weigh in, albeit a few years later. Working with Phil Spector on what would become the first draft of his *Rock 'n 'Roll* album, the Beatle and the producer got to discussing why such an album was even necessary; why, in 1973, they should find themselves restating the values that had once been taken for granted by a generation. The answer to that question would be delivered during the instrumental midsection of "Just Because."

"I want to take all the new singers, Carole and that other one, Nipples, I wanna take them and hold them tight, all them people that James Taylor had. . . . I wanna suck their nipples." And the only warning he gave Spector was an innocent request at the beginning of the take, "You don't mind if I change the lyrics, then?"

Fowley and Lennon were in the minority. American critics all but queued up to heap fresh panegyrics on Taylor's head, while across the ocean, the team behind a projected new music show on British television, the oddly titled *Old Grey Whistle Test*, seized upon *Sweet Baby James* as the very blueprint for the program. "It was the atmosphere of [the] record, the tone and feel of the music, that set the agenda," host Bob Harris explained. *Old Grey Whistle Test* would remain on British television for much of the next twenty years, while its first years so successfully adhered to the Taylor template that modern appreciations of the show can still be delivered with one shorthand image, a lone guitarist on a stool, eyes closed, brow furrowed, and lips drawn in introspection.

Which, as Taylor was discovering, was precisely what his audience required.

On March 7, 1970, Taylor appeared for the first time at the Gaslight in New York, to find a city that was still in shock.

The previous day, an anonymous ten-room brownstone, 18 West Eleventh Street, next door to actor Dustin Hoffman's home, had simply exploded. Right now, the authorities were still blaming a gas leak; it would be a couple of days more before they would discover the furnace still intact beneath several tons of charred rubble. But a whisper on the street was already pointing in other directions, toward any one of the many underground guerilla organizations that called New York City home, who had flourished within the same febrile environment as Kootch's old buddies in the Fugs, but who had taken armed, rather than musical, resistance as their chosen approach.

And so it would transpire: The building was rented to members of the Weathermen, a counterculture body whose very name spoke of their cultural lineage; they'd borrowed it from Dylan's "Subterranean Homesick Blues." And the dead—Terry Robbins, Theodore Gold, and Diana Oughton—were known members of the group. According to the authorities, Robbins was in the process of building a bomb when the explosion took place. His fellow conspirators, meanwhile, were studying maps of the tunnels that ran between the buildings of Columbia University.

Taylor was almost brutally apolitical, but he knew that his music touched upon the same deep emotions that the revolution's goals also scraped: the knowledge that life had grown too complicated, too plastic and too fake; that society was no longer run by the people who comprised it, but by the handful of men who had appointed themselves its leaders, most of whom had never even been elected.

Daily in the newspapers, tales of politicians being nurtured in the pockets of big business did the rounds; nightly in the bars, people spoke of how the industrial concerns that built bullets and bombs had more influence on the course of the Vietnam War than the soldiers who were actually using them, of how the top dogs of business and industry had more influence over the running of the country than any mere politician or president.

Taylor did not address those concerns. The likes of Country Joe McDonald, the Jefferson Airplane, the Fugs, and David Peel had been ramming those beliefs down their listeners' throats for years now.

Instead, he took a leaf from Tom Rush's book. Rush, too, had eschewed political protest, even at a time when such outrage had been all the rage. "I never did get into the protest side, first of all because a lot of the protest singers were preaching to the choir, but also because I felt that a lot of the songs weren't very good. There were exceptions. Dylan wrote some very good topical songs, but in general I think it was pretty boring. So although I got involved in various causes, I never took it on stage. My job was to give the audience a little bit of a vacation from being reminded how terrible things were."

Taylor agreed. What people needed now was the chance to cool off, to step away from the flames of righteous rage that burned in the heart of every would-be freedom fighter, and maybe contemplate them from a position of calm and consideration. And every gig on his spring tour, as he danced from the folk clubs to the university campuses, clutching the newly purchased luggage that his mother had sent him for the occasion, and crashing on whichever floor or dorm would take him, he pressed himself gently into his audience's souls, by becoming their soul.

Disc jockey Kathy Dorritie was one of the New Yorkers awaiting his Gaslight performance. She was already what you could call a charter member of his fan club. She had discovered him not with the success of *Sweet Baby James*, but with the Apple album, "the one where he's looking so sexy, lying on the ground in his beigey Sunday best, like a bad boy daring to mess up his clothes. I'd never heard his voice or anything about him. I bought that LP on the strength of that photo alone. Then I fell in groupie-love with him, once I played the record. But the first time I got close to him, touched him, was when *Sweet Baby James* was being released."

From its first advance copies, Dorritie recalled, *Sweet Baby James* had taken off with New York's FM-radio DJs, and Taylor's local star was rising fast. "He probably could have sold out Carnegie Hall at that point. Instead, his management put him in that tiny Greenwich Village café, a tiny venue for such an obviously emerging star. But it was perfect, because there were throngs of people lined up in the street to see him . . . way too many to ever be able to get inside. And it made quite an impression on the public and the press. The electricity in the air was palpable. The whole of Greenwich

Village seemed abuzz. It was one of those nights when I felt like I was in exactly the right spot at exactly the right moment in time. And it seemed as if everyone else there felt like that too.

"Much of the crowd that made it inside for the show/s (there might have been two sets; I forget) was made up of music industry execs and the media, so I knew how blessed I was to be among them, although my DJ status at Aux Puces and the unofficial PR I had been doing for James—gifting the albums, along with a few tabs of acid to the most influential people I knew—probably counted for something."

Much to Taylor's, and everybody else's surprise, Carole King had agreed to accompany him on the road, to add bare piano to his acoustic whispering, but also as an integral part of a mutual admiration society than cannot help but have boosted both Taylor's confidence and her own. They were never lovers; King still laughs incredulously when she is asked that question. But they did deeply love one another, and those long days and nights spent traveling between concerts were spent talking not only about music, but their own loves, lives, and aspirations.

It was their friendship, and their abiding respect for one another as human beings, that gave Taylor the strength he needed to push on through the miasma of his slowly burgeoning fame; and, ultimately, it would give King the strength to become a concert performer in her own right. To this day she credits Taylor alone with providing her with the confidence to step out on stage. For now, however, she was content to remain in the shadows, a barely noticeable presence behind the piano on the stage, while Taylor sat out front, alternating selections from the two albums with favorite covers.

His brother Livingston's "In My Reply" was often in his set; so was Joni Mitchell's "For Free," a song that he may or may not have settled upon with a degree of ironic forethought, but which nevertheless tells the sad tale of a super-successful pop star, watching a busker as he played on the street and yearning for those uncomplicated days.

Carole King had recently been hard at work rearranging "Up On the Roof," a joyful song that she and Gerry Goffin had written for the Drifters back in 1962, but twisting it into a sorrowful dirge. Taylor leaped on the new arrangement for his own shows, and then he took a grinning backseat as he introduced King to the audience, pulling her out from behind the piano where she'd been modestly hiding all set long, to reveal her as the writer of "The Locomotion."

"And you could see his fans going, 'She wrote that? No way!'" Kootch laughed.

The album continued to sell as Taylor toured. It was still small potatoes compared to the giants of the day: farewell platters from Simon and Garfunkel (*Bridge over Troubled Water*) and the Beatles (*Let It Be*), debuts from Paul McCartney and Crosby, Stills, Nash and Young. But the people whose job it was to watch the sales figures as Taylor toured, and to watch the charts as the numbers were juggled, could see *Sweet Baby James* growing sweeter by the minute.

It entered the chart at #90 on March 14, 1970, seven days after the Gaslight show and ten places above Tom Rush's latest, self-titled, LP—which itself reflected back on its predecessor by revisiting both Taylor and Jackson Browne's catalogs; the Flying Machine's "Rainy Day Man" and Browne's "These Days" were both on board. By May 23 it had risen to #42, and Taylor was moving into larger venues.

He opened for Laura Nyro at Princeton, in front of the first concert-size audience he had ever faced, and weeks later, on June 12, he was at Carnegie Hall, playing two concerts that left him as astounded by his surroundings as he was by the fee—$5,000 per show was the most he had ever earned. Two weeks after that, on June 27, 1970, Taylor opened for the Who at the Cleveland Music Hall, an absurd juxtaposition that even he confessed placed him in front of "an audience of about 10,000, not many of them facing the stage during my set."

The Who were at the peak of their live powers at that time, thundering through the set that would soon be immortalized on the *Live at Leeds* concert album (recorded just two months before the Cleveland show, and still regarded as among the greatest live records of all time). With or without his modest pianist, how could any one-man show hope to compete with that?

It was time to expand.

"It was only until we released *Sweet Baby James*, in that year after I came back from London, that I did any real time playing by myself," he told *Guitar World*. "After that I started to work with [a band]. It just started off being a matter of economics, because I couldn't keep a band going. After that I started to get some opening slots on shows. But as things progressed, we started being able to book concert halls, instead of clubs, with just me. I think the first time I ever played with a band was at the Troubadour. Then *Sweet Baby James* did real well."

"Touring was tremendously tiring," Kootch recalled. "But it was a real different experience. The first two or three years we toured, we all sat down, we all sat in chairs. I hated that! But James didn't want to rile up the audience and get them excited. He wanted to calm them down, which was always . . . it was not what I wanted. I wanted to fire them up and get them screaming and yelling.

"We were playing places like the Spectrum in Philadelphia, big places, and I thought audiences would be horribly bored. James was just so laid back. He played a tune and then he'd tune guitar for like a minute onstage and I thought, 'Oh no!' But nobody ever walked out, nobody ever wrote a review saying, 'This is the most boring shit ever'; they came, they flocked. Because James was right. It was his music, and it was meant to calm people down."

On July 26, 1970, Taylor was invited to perform at the Mariposa Folk Festival, in Ontario, Canada, sharing a bill with Joni Mitchell. Asher shrugged the invitation away by demanding a $20,000 performance fee; Estelle Klein, the festival's director, countered with an offer of the same fee that every other performer received, regardless of their status or fame—$78. Asher, utterly bamboozled by her stoic resistance, agreed and, for the second year in succession, watched, gratified, as Taylor seized one of North America's premier folk events by the throat and pulled the audience to his side.

He pulled the headlining Mitchell to his side, too. Taylor had seldom wanted for female company; even back on the Vineyard as a teen, he had been regarded as quite the catch by vacationing teenage girls. Two women were in his life now, Margaret Corey, whom he'd met back in London, and Toni Stern, a Laurel Canyon–ite who was numbered among Carole King's recent songwriting partners, and who accompanied him on his spring tour. So, there was (and there would be) no shortage of women in Taylor's life. Mitchell, however, was something else.

They had already met the previous year. Booked into the same Unicorn coffeehouse in Cambridge where Tom Rush had recorded his very first LP, Taylor found himself opening for Mitchell, and Graham Nash, Mitchell's boyfriend of the time, even took a photograph of the pair of them talking, the first time they ever met.

Mitchell and Nash had parted now, but the Canadian was instantly entranced with the lanky, brooding Bostonian. They became lovers; she knitted him a sweater vest that he wore constantly that summer; he wrote a new song, "You Can Close Your Eyes," for her.

13

The Cat Came Back
(They Thought They'd
Seen the Last of It)

Jackson Browne did not want to become a part of the Troubadour furniture. But he could not turn his back on the place, either. He was now sharing a house at 1020 Laguna Avenue, Echo Park, with J. D. Souther (Linda Ronstadt's boyfriend) and Glenn Frey (her guitarist); and late into the night, their conversations would revolve around the sights and sounds of their last evening in the club, images that, years later, Frey's next band, the Eagles, would include in their own tribute to the Troubadour, "The Sad Café."

"[The Troubadour] was and always will be full of tragic fucking characters," Frey mourned to journalist Cameron Crowe. "It is true that a lot of artists got their so-called big break at the Troubadour. But it's also infested with spiritual parasites who will rob you of your precious artistic energy."

Browne had no intention of being robbed.

One night in late summer 1969, Doug Weston pulled him aside and voiced the musings that had been bedeviling him for a few weeks now, as he marveled at the still teenage boy's songs and wondered what might happen if he did get that "big break."

It wasn't idle speculation. The previous year, in her groundbreaking *Rock Encyclopedia*, journalist Lillian Roxon happily predicted that "when [Browne] does happen, when he's good and ready, the wait will be worth it."

Weston agreed with her. In a decade-plus of promoting, he had long since learned to split the lucky one-timers from the lasting talents, and he was a long way to certain which camp Browne fell into.

It was not only the boy's open mike appearances that intrigued him. So many other people were calling Browne a star in waiting; through 1968 and into 1969, Browne only had to pick up his guitar for great swathes of the Troubadour family circle to fall silent in readiness for the performance.

But Browne simply didn't play ball. Monday nights notwithstanding, he rarely played out. There was one night back in March 1968 when he joined a virtual festival bill, a dozen or so acts lining up behind Danny Kotchmar's Clear Light at the Pasadena Music Hall; another in April when he popped up at the Ash Grove, opening for the folk duo Hearts and Flowers. Occasionally he would make his way out to small clubs in San Clemente, and he was still around the McCabe's Guitar Shop scene too, strumming the occasional guest performance there, and playing a full set at the store's first ever "official" concert.

But that's all he did, one-offs and surprises, pickup performances and zero-promotion hoots. It was time, Weston determined, to put an end to Jackson Browne's meanderings and, as he put together a week of shows by Linda Ronstadt for September 16–21, 1969, he may have had a moment or two when he questioned his decision, but he went ahead with it. Jackson Browne would be her support act.

The granddaughter of the man who invented the flexible ice-cube tray, Lloyd Groff Copeman, Tucson, Arizona–born Linda Ronstadt was just shy of eighteen when she moved to Los Angeles in 1964. A friend, Bob Kimmel, was already out there, writing and demoing songs with guitarist Kenny Edwards, and impromptu sing-alongs convinced the trio to form a band together. The Stone Poneys signed with Capitol in summer 1966 and over the next two years cut three albums together. They broke up before the release of the third . . . whose title, *Linda Ronstadt, Stone Poneys and Friends, Vol. III*, perhaps suggests one reason for the break.

Devastatingly beautiful but possessed of a voice that pushed her looks into the shade, Ronstadt was one of those rare performers who was a star before she had even been heard of. Andrew Gold, the local songwriter who would join her band in the early 1970s, recalled, "Nobody could believe Linda was so young, even during the Stone Poney days. Sometimes you hear a record and you just know the singer has lived every word of the song he or she is singing, and it's a one-off. Usually it's a one-off, because nobody can pour that much of themselves into every song they perform. Linda could.

It didn't matter who wrote the song in the first place, or who else had sung it; when Linda took a song, she made it her own."

Ronstadt herself discovered this one night at the Troubadour. She had recently taken possession of "Silver Threads and Golden Needles," the country ballad that made Mike Hurst and Dusty Springfield's Springfields into stateside superstars, and recorded it for her debut LP, *Hand Sewn, Home Grown*. Now she was on her way to the bathroom, midway through a performance by a band called Shiloh, when they suddenly kicked into that same song, strummed to her own rearrangement. She was, she later laughed, "flabbergasted."

Ronstadt adored the Troubadour. "We all used to sit in a corner . . . and dream. The Troubadour was like a café society. Everyone was in transition. No one was getting married, no one was having families, no one was having a particular connection, so our connection was the Troubadour. It was where everyone met, where everyone got to hear everyone else's act. It was where I made all my musical contacts and found people who were sympathetic to the musical styles I wanted to explore."

Ronstadt's week was a guaranteed sellout. *Hand Sewn, Home Grown*, already six months old, had not charted, but her two-year-old hit with the Stone Poneys, Monkee Mike Nesmith's "Different Drum," was still a radio favorite, and the album's eye for songwriters as far afield as Bob Dylan, Fred Neil, Chip Douglas, Randy Newman and, unsurprisingly, her old Stone Poneys mate Kenny Edwards, suggested an interpretative talent that any aspiring songwriter would want to keep an eye on.

Gold continued: "There were a lot of songwriters around at that time, myself included, and boy were we competitive. We'd meet up, people like Jackson, J. D. [Souther], Warren [Zevon], all of us, and the first thing out of our mouths every time would be, 'Well, so-and-so is interested in one of my songs,' or, 'I sang whatever to this or that person and they might record it.' And for all of us, Linda was the one we dreamed of, not because we'd make the most money or anything, but because if Linda sang one of your songs, you could not get a better storefront."

The audience for her Troubadour week may not have been wall-to-wall writers and musicians, but there were certainly enough of them there for Browne, at least, to see his future spooling out before him. When he came offstage after one night's performance, it was to find David Crosby waiting backstage, demanding to know whether the singer had a record deal yet, and offering to produce his first LP when he did.

They were not simply hollow words, either. Crosby had already cut his teeth as a producer, handling Joni Mitchell's *Songs for a Seagull* debut the previous year. Now he was boasting to all and sundry that Browne was as great a talent as Joni, even telling *Rolling Stone*'s Ben Fong-Torres, "that cat just sings rings around most people, and he's got songs that'll make your hair stand on end."

And Browne botched it again. Or he refused to be robbed. His friends were split on that score.

Doug Weston's policy for recruiting talent to the Troubadour at that time was simple. If an artist struck him as worth persevering with (which, as Browne discovered, usually did mean taking advantage of every bone thrown your way), he would offer him a contract, effectively guaranteeing him live work, whatever happened to his career. Which would be great if you were a slow mover, happy to simply inch up the ladder, but not so hot if you came out of the traps with your clothes on fire.

For an unknown at the outset of his career in 1969, Weston's guarantee of $1,000 a night was great money. But the wily old entrepreneur wasn't signing artists for a night at a time. He was signing them up for five years, at the same rate of pay throughout.

"He was smart," Andrew Gold laughed. "But nobody forced you to take the deal. Later you'd hear people complaining that Doug ripped them off, signing them up play for a grand when they could have earned ten times that amount playing some other place. But the way I looked at it was, it was the artist's way of thanking the Troubadour for giving him the break in the first place. Besides, playing a few nights in front of the greatest audience in the world was not exactly a punishment, was it?"

Nevertheless, Browne would not play the game.

"I did a week at the Troubadour and they passed on my option because I hadn't taken up any record offers that came in, so they thought I wasn't interested. Doug Weston, who'd been very helpful to me really, was disgusted and didn't hire me."

Neither was he interested in Browne's reasoning, the fact that he wasn't one of those people who could just be popped onto the rock conveyor belt, signing a deal on Monday, taping the album on Tuesday, and touring the country in support of it Wednesday. Browne didn't want to belabor terms like *sensitivity* and *artistry*, but he had not come as far as he had (however far that might have been, he'd add on darker nights) to just throw everything into the mangler and see what got spat out.

Even David Crosby's offer left him less than impressed. Yes, he agreed, there *was* talk about him being sent into the studio with some superstar overseer, but he turned his back on it. When it was time to make his record, he said, it would be his record and his alone. And it would stand or fall on his terms.

But some things did emerge from the Troubadour's exposure, and Browne wasn't so self-immolative that he was about to turn them all down. Criterion Music stepped in with a big vote of confidence, signing Browne to a songwriting contract and, over the next few months, dispatching him to the studio to turn out the string of demos that would show the world what he could do.

Some twenty-two songs made it onto acetate between fall 1969 and spring 1970, sparsely strummed out with voice and guitar alone, a remarkable coterie that included some of the finest songs of Browne's career so far, and some of his most lasting, as well. "Song for Adam," "Doctor My Eyes," "The Birds of St. Marks," "Mae Jean Goes to Hollywood," "From the Silver Lake," "Nightingale," and "Rock Me on the Water" all eased out of these sessions, with Linda Ronstadt declaring herself so impressed by the last that she had already earmarked it for herself. (It would appear on her self-titled third album, in 1972).

Yet just one song from this enviable clutch, "Jamaica Say You Will," was to prove to be the charm. In February 1970, Browne sat down to make a list of everything he needed to take a serious leap in the direction he needed to. He had never doubted that, at some point, somebody would come along, offer him the chance to make a record, and actually see it through with him. Now he began to understand that maybe, just maybe, he needed to let that person know he existed.

His friend Essra Mohawk, the Philadelphia born singer-songwriter whose *Primordial Lovers* album was the talk of the town, had recently had some business handled by David Geffen, and she reported back nothing but good things. If Browne really was serious about finding himself a manager, he should start at the top.

Browne nodded and set about getting a demo together.

David Geffen was twenty-eight years old, a graduate of the William Morris Agency, where he met and mentored his future business partner

Elliot Roberts. Geffen had originally hoped to work with movie stars but, having been assured that his youth was against him, he turned instead to rock management. Quitting the agency, he took singer-songwriter Laura Nyro as his first client, followed by Crosby, Stills and Nash; now, despite his relative youth, he was already a feared figure in the world of West Coast rock managers, as David Crosby affectionately mused.

Everybody knew that the music business was full of sharks, most of them out to rob an artist blind. Geffen, said Crosby, was the man you wanted on your side when that happened, and even the mere mention of his name was sufficient to get a recalcitrant promoter or record label back in line. "We'll send Dave Geffen over; he'll take your whole company and sell it while you're out at lunch."

Andrew Gold agreed. "We all knew Dave, and we all liked him, but there was always that feeling when you shook hands with him that you should count your fingers afterwards. Not because he was a thief, but because if he saw something and he knew he could do a better job with it than anybody else, he would do everything in his power to get it."

Geffen was handling one raft of artists that Browne knew his music could be aligned with. His partner Roberts managed another: Neil Young and Joni Mitchell were both in his stable. Together, they had all but sewn up the Laurel Canyon scene.

Rounding up J. D. Souther, Glenn Frey, David Jackson, and Ned Doheny, Browne laid down what, by his usual standards, was a passionate performance of "Jamaica Say You Will," which he promptly and publicly regretted having done. The whole song sounded wrong, he shivered. Back to front and upside down and all round terrible. But he was about to leave town for a few weeks in Colorado, and had neither the time nor the money to try again. So he packaged up the acetate with a newly taken photograph and dropped the lot in the mail.

"I am writing to you," Browne's carefully crafted letter began, "out of respect for the artists you represent." But Geffen took one look at the photograph that accompanied the note, and he didn't even play the acetate that had been packaged up with it. He just dropped the lot into the wastepaper bin.

From whence, goes the legend, his secretary Dodie Smith retrieved it while she was tidying the office, glanced at the picture, and liked what she saw. She salvaged the disc and played it at home. It was as good as the photo. The following morning she was back at work to tell her employer that he maybe shouldn't be so impulsive in the future. She sat while Geffen gave the acetate a spin, and at last Browne had a manager. Or he would, once he returned from vacation. Browne arrived home to find a mass of messages from Geffen, all urgently seeking to set up a meeting. But when they actually met face-to-face, Geffen had another surprise in store. He told Browne to simply relax and have some fun. Geffen would figure out what to do next.

And he would . . . eventually.

No matter how much Geffen seemed to believe in Jackson Browne, no matter how encouraging his words, or how enthusiastically he listened to all of the young man's dreams and plans, Geffen didn't believe Browne was ready to record. He had three albums' worth of songs in his catalog, and Criterion, his publishers, were already sitting on offers from Columbia and Vanguard Records. But Geffen swatted them aside as effortlessly as he batted away Browne's insistence that he should take them.

In fact, Columbia all but committed suicide as label head Clive Davis invited Browne and Geffen in to audition in his office, and then had the temerity to take a phone call in the midst of Browne's performance of "Doctor My Eyes." Seated beside his protégé, Geffen flipped. Incandescent with rage, he instructed Browne to stop playing and pack up his guitar. "We're leaving."

In truth, Geffen had no intention of signing Browne to Columbia. Laura Nyro was already there, and that was all Geffen required. He accepted Davis's offer to meet because it was good to appear polite, but he spurned the old man's apologies because he wanted to make a stand. Davis might have been the head of one of the biggest record labels in America. But that was all he was, a record company man.

Geffen was in the business of talent, and when Browne protested, Geffen waved his concerns aside. Instead, he handed him $300 and told him to go off and have a good summer. Management would be back in touch when it was time to begin managing.

≋

While Jackson Browne seethed and James Taylor soared, Cat Stevens celebrated. He too had a new label expressing an interest in him, and he wasn't going to be turning his back on it.

Island Records was launched by Chris Blackwell in 1962 as a UK outlet for its Jamaican-born owner's love of the island's ska and bluebeat sounds.

Britain's Caribbean population was booming, but if there was one thing that the newly arriving immigrants missed about home (apart from decent weather and familiar food), it was the music they had grown up with.

Licensing the hottest island sounds from their producers back in Kingston, and then selling them in the UK, Island moved through the first half of the 1960s as a niche concern but little more, at least in the eyes of the major labels of the day. But Blackwell had ambition. As manager of the Spencer Davis Group, he had already proved his dedication to homegrown rock sounds, and when vocalist Steve Winwood announced his intention to leave the band and form a new group, Traffic, Blackwell saw his chance.

Overnight, it seemed, Island was realigned from a minority concern pumping reggae into the inner cities, into a major player on the now-burgeoning British underground rock scene, as it surged from the last days of the psychedelic era and mutated into something more organic.

Bands like Mott the Hoople, King Crimson, and Spooky Tooth, with their rocking guitars against earthy atmospheres, or Quintessence, Traffic, and Fairport Convention, electrifying notions that they developed in the folk clubs, all were bonded beneath Blackwell's bright pink label to create a musical doorway that was as eclectic as it was wide open.

Cat Stevens himself may not have immediately seen how he could fit into this brittle community. But Chris Blackwell had no doubt, all the more so after he told Stevens that he agreed with the Cat's last pronouncement: All he needed was his guitar.

A contract slipped into place that was the absolute corollary of anything Deram had ever placed on the table.

How does it feel, asked the *Record Mirror*, to know you are expected only to deliver one album a year? Stevens's smile would have answered the question even before he spoke.

"I think that accounts for good quality. A load of people bring out two albums, one might be good and one might not be what they want, but they have to bring it out anyway, and that's terrible for music and for everybody."

In the past, Stevens insisted, his best performances were his demos, the homemade tapes he would take to Mike Hurst before they even got into a recording studio. "Those were the best," he averred, "with just me double-tracking, playing piano, guitar. I realized that was the way."

At almost precisely the same time as Peter Asher understood that what James Taylor required was less, not more; and just as Mike Hurst would realize after the fact; it was the little vocal embellishments that the producer would hear as orchestral opportunities, but which Stevens intended to be merely wordless lyrics, that gave those demos their initial flavoring. And that was what Stevens intended to concentrate upon.

In the end, Stevens would add a rudimentary rhythm section (a pure solo route, he shuddered, might have felt "too contrived"). But the mood remained the same, "shaving things down to the bare minimum." The songs were so important to him, he said, that he didn't want there to be anything that could detract from their meaning, cloud his lyrics with any other impressions. And, for the most part, his Spartan approach wasn't simply triumphant, it was only the beginning. He had recently spent some time in Spain, where he entertained the local children with his guitar and some impromptu children's songs. Now he talked of writing songs aimed specifically at children. In an age when so many rock bands (even those on Island) were becoming more flash and dramatic, Stevens was adamant that he was heading in the opposite direction entirely.

He relished the Island Records regime. At Deram, he complained, the only feedback he ever received from the record company hierarchy was the constant call for another song like "Matthew and Son." And it didn't matter how often an exasperated Stevens told them that there had already been one song like that, and that the world did not need another; the chorus remained incessant.

At Island, the demand was likely to be the complete opposite, and that suited him fine.

One thing that Stevens was determined about was that there would be no reprising his past; no attempt to grasp the audience that had followed him two or three years earlier, and drag them screaming into adulthood alongside him. He sought, he said, a whole new audience, a crowd that might have overlooked him completely in the past not because they didn't like his music, but because they didn't like what he was perceived as representing, the teenybop poster boys with their pictures in *Fabulous 208* every week.

That was another reason why he signed with Island. Because the label's name alone marked its artists out as serious business. When Island had hit singles (and they'd had a few, despite their almost dour devotion to long-playing discs), it was because the record *deserved* to be a hit, not because the promo men had greased the right palms at the prerelease stage.

But there was another motivation: the knowledge that the days when a slick producer and even slicker arranger would take the song and craft their own creation around it, dubbing on anything they thought would help it fly, were over, at least so far as Stevens was concerned. He was proud to have landed with a label that agreed with him.

"My only consideration was to write what I liked, and what I hoped my friends would like. Before I had an audience, I wrote for them. This is the age of sharing your thoughts, and that's what I am doing—that's the only way you become established. People who like good music share it with their friends, and your reputation spreads by word of mouth. It's a good, honest way for it to happen."

He wasn't interested, he said, in becoming a part of a larger scene. Again, he had done that when he glanced at Deram's marketing plans and saw himself being aimed at the same pubescent female crowd that lapped up Scott Walker and Engelbert Humperdinck. Walker too had rebelled, plunging his solo career into the baroque nightmare fantasies of the Belgian songwriter Jacques Brel; Stevens would not go there but, like Walker, he was fascinated with self-expression all the same.

"My aim," Stevens told writer Keith Altham, "is to communicate something very personal and to have working with me those people who are sympathetic enough to help me present those ideas in the best way."

That was why he was so thrilled to be working with producer Paul Samwell-Smith.

A former member of the rock band the Yardbirds, whom he left to pursue a career on the other side of the studio console, Samwell-Smith had done his best-known work so far with Renaissance, a group formed by fellow ex-Yardbirds vocalist Keith Relf and guitarist Jim McCarty, and which had since developed into a staggeringly original folk rock outfit.

Stevens admitted that recruiting Samwell-Smith was a gamble of sorts, one that was predicated solely on what he'd heard of Renaissance. But it was a gamble that paid off, because it was Samwell-Smith who passed on the names of the musicians who would wind up accompanying Stevens around the world for the next two years: guitarist Alun Davies, bassist John Ryan, percussionist Harvey Burns. Plus, for one afternoon only and strictly in the

James Taylor and Carole King at the BBC Studios, London, in 1970.
Gijsbert Hanekroot/Redferns/Getty Images

Laura Nyro and a kneeling David Geffen in New York in 1969.
Michael Ochs Archives/Getty Images

Two-Lane Blacktop: James Taylor on set with Warren Oates, Dennis Wilson, and Laurie Bird.
Universal Pictures/Photofest

Cat and an unknown passer-by contemplating the horses of insanity, at Island's Basing Street Studios in 1970.
Michael Putland/Hulton Archive/Getty Images

Creating a legend: Carole King and (left to right) Danny "Kootch" Kortchmar, Russ Kunkel, Charles Larkey, and Ralph Schuckett caught during the *Tapestry* sessions at A&M Records Recording Studio in January 1971.
Jim McCrary/Redferns/Getty Images

James Taylor and Joni Mitchell add their own weight to Carole King's *Tapestry*.
Jim McCrary/Redferns/Getty Images

James Taylor and Carly Simon at home in New York City, October 1971.
Michael Ochs Archives/Getty Images

Cat Stevens and Alun Davies on the set of BBC TV's *Into 1971* year-end television show.
Ron Howard/Redferns/Getty Images

Manager Elliot Roberts (left) and Jackson Browne (center) join Joni Mitchell onstage in Amsterdam in 1972.
Gijsbert Hanekroot/Redferns/Getty Images

Jackson Browne and Warren Zevon with comedian John Belushi at the Bottom Line.
Richard E. Aaron/Redferns/Getty Images

name of additional embellishment, a nervous young flautist named Peter Gabriel.

Samwell-Smith had recently recorded some demos with an aspiring young band named Genesis, who were coming down from a nonperforming LP on Decca and were yet to emerge as the prog rock supermen they would ultimately become.

"It was excellent. He really heard the music," Genesis front man Peter Gabriel enthused of the sessions once they were complete, and though Genesis's attempts to lure Samwell-Smith into working with them on further projects were always politely rebuffed, the producer was nevertheless captivated by the fresh-out-of-school band. With work on Cat Stevens's album already underway at Olympic Studios, Samwell-Smith invited Gabriel down to the sessions, to add flute to the song "Katmandu."

It was not Gabriel's finest moment. Samwell-Smith detailed, "[He] came into the studio, very young and very, very nervous. He almost couldn't play the flute because his lip was shaking, and his hands were shaking. I had to go out and tell him, 'Don't worry, it'll be all right.'" After the guest was gone, however, his very audible fear became something of a standing joke among the more experienced musicians in the studio—Gabriel's hard pants of breath were recorded and spliced into a track of their own, for the studio to laugh at later.

Gabriel would not be invited back. Guitarist Alun Davies, however, would not only serve alongside Stevens for the remainder of the 1970s, he was the first musician Cat contacted upon his return to action in 2005.

Welsh-born Davies was another of those youthful wannabes who launched their musical careers with ukuleles; he played along with the reinterpreted American folk of Lonnie Donegan and the rest of the mid-1950s British skiffle crew. From there he graduated to acoustic guitar, by which time he and a school friend, Michael Burchell, were already performing and writing songs together.

Burchell, who would soon adopt the name Jon Mark, was destined to become one of the 1960s' most in-demand and versatile guitarists; his work on Marianne Faithfull's early albums, for example, is exemplary. Before that, however, he had already secured a berth at Decca Records, as he and Davies were signed to cut an impossibly enjoyable folk album, 1963's *Relax Your Mind*.

Cut in one day with producer Shel Talmy, then best known for his work with the Irish singing group the Bachelors (and still a year or more from his groundbreaking work with the Kinks and the Who), *Relax Your Mind* could have set the pair up in the folk clubs of the land. Instead, they landed a job with Cunard, the shipping line, and were hired to provide entertainment on the company's transatlantic liners. They made eight trips across to the U.S. and back before returning to dry land and a career in session work.

Davies joined Mark in Marianne Faithfull's camp; he also became a house session musician at Fontana Records, before he and Mark reunited in a new band, Sweet Thursday. Completed by another session legend, pianist Nicky Hopkins, drummer Brian Odgers, and bassist Harvey Burns, the group signed with the American label Tetragrammaton, recorded an LP—and then saw both album and record company vanish when Tetragrammaton went bust on the day *Sweet Thursday* was released. The band split, and all concerned returned to session work, which is where Paul Samwell-Smith found both Davies and Sweet Thursday bandmate Burns.

"Paul has a very clear mind," Stevens enthused. "He can see things clear. He's very technical. Immensely so. I'm just 'anything as long as it feels good and sounds good.'"

He admitted there were flash points between the two modes of operation, but that none was more than a passing misunderstanding. One morning, early in the sessions, Stevens arrived at the studio to do a vocal take and found himself surrounded by ten microphones. Stevens knew instinctively it was wrong; and Samwell-Smith listened while he outlined the reasons why, even helping Stevens to express himself when his explanation foundered on the gut response that it just did not feel right. And that was why the team worked. They understood one another.

Samwell-Smith would remain the dynamic glue that held the gestating album together, his musical sensitivities allowing him to appreciate not only the artist's requirements, but also an audience's demands. But his own instincts would be firmly balanced throughout by Stevens's.

The artist's input did not end with the music, either. Intending *Mona Bone Jakon*, as the album would be titled, to be all his own work, Stevens seized upon Chris Blackwell's offer to allow his artists to design their own record sleeves, and handed in a striking portrait of a battered old garbage can, with one tear forcing its way out of the lid.

It was an enigmatic image to match an enigmatic title; following the record's release, purchasers around the country would fiercely debate the significance of title and sleeve design; and so inventive (not to mention obscene) were some of the solutions that it was a positive disappointment when Stevens admitted that the cover was originally designed while the album labored beneath an altogether more prosaic title: *The Dustbin Cried the Day the Dustman Died.*

"What we did . . . was deliberately not have a photograph on it, so that people wouldn't accuse me of going back and doing the [teenybopper] thing again. I didn't want that; I just wanted completely nonbiased appreciation if the album was due to get it. So we went straight for the music. I mean, the trash can on the front of *Mona* was the same thing. I was understating everything, the arrangements—the whole thing was done as subtly as possible. I didn't want people to think I was trying to hype them. Basically I just wanted the music to be heard, that's all, and the words."

Indeed, on every level where he had the opportunity, Stevens approached his second breath of musical fame with considerably more caution than before.

A hit single in the form of the lovely "Lady D'Arbanville" drew no more than the necessary minimum of promotional activities. Stevens refused to be drawn out by comparisons between his song and the Rolling Stones' "Lady Jane," or on the rumor that the lyric somehow espoused necrophilia. He rejoiced, however, in the reviews that discussed the song in more intellectual terms, which admired the words of soft tender sweetness, which acknowledged the care that had clearly been lavished on the backing track.

Yes, there were moments when it sounded as though the studio door had been left wide open, for anyone to wander in and add an instrument to the unfolding spectacle, but people said that about Ravel's "Bolero" too. It was a valid observation, and it was one to be proud of.

Other observations. "I Think I See the Light" highlighted the similarities between Stevens's "new" singing style and that of Jethro Tull's Ian Anderson; a comparison that was not only predicated upon both singers' penchant for harmonizing just a few sonic inches away from the expected melody. They shared tonality as well, and the way Samwell-Smith teased the guitars in the mix, rendering them sometimes quiet, sometimes jarring ("Katmandu"), only amplified the match.

Kevin Coyne, too, was invoked, albeit at a time before many people even knew who he was. But a pair of well-received LPs for disc jockey John Peel's Dandelion label had pushed the cornflake-tonsilled former nurse into the critical estimation, and when Stevens unleashed "Pop Star," a knowingly ironic mantra that mercilessly skewered the life he'd left behind, he did it in tones that were achingly familiar to anyone who had heard Coyne perform. The similarity would become even more pronounced a couple of years later, when Coyne released the song "Good Boy" on his masterpiece *Marjorie Razorblade*. Was there, he was asked in the early 1980s, any reason he should write such a familiar-sounding song?

"Whatever makes you think that?" Coyne responded, his face cracking wide with a mischievous grin.

Hopes that Stevens would tour in support of either the single or its parent album, too, were dashed by his refusal to throw himself back into that circus. If he toured, he said, it would be as a duo with guitarist Alun Davies alone, and the one UK show he did agree to, at the Plumpton Festival in August 1970, was to his mind quite enough. He'd worked with bands, he'd worked with orchestras, and neither had left him feeling at all satisfied. At last he had settled upon a format that succeeded.

Officially billed as the tenth National Jazz and Blues Festival, a forerunner to the Reading Festival of later years, the Plumpton Racecourse bash was very much overshadowed by the truly international events staged at Bath and the Isle of Wight that same summer. The festival spread over an unprecedented four days regardless, with performances from the likes of Jellybread, Family, the Groundhogs, Deep Purple, Peter Green, Black Sabbath, the Incredible String Band, Van Der Graaf Generator, and Wishbone Ash.

Stevens appeared to be in bizarre company, then, but the success of "Lady D'Arbanville," as it rose to #8 in the UK that summer of 1970, gratified him and painted a far warmer welcome-back to the fray than he had ever expected, or even hoped for. The festival show, too, was a success. The folk-tinged Saturday afternoon during which Stevens headlined over Sandy Denny's Fotheringay, Magna Carat, and the Strawbs was, declared the *New Musical Express*, the afternoon in which "the Cat Came Back . . . or, to be far more accurate, Cat Stevens made his most welcome return to public performing.

"With just guitarist Alun Davies for both musical and moral support, plus a happy if rather mysterious gentleman on tambourine, he sang his very own personal songs in his very own distinctive manner, then shyly announced, 'Here is the song that's made me a pop star again . . . "Lady D'Arbanville."' Next songs were 'Longer Boats' and 'Father and Son,' which went down so well that he just carried on with an extension of the song.

Without a doubt, Cat Stevens gave the best solo performance of the entire weekend."

Later in the month, Stevens appeared at the Bilzen Jazz Festival in Belgium, and Alun Davies had a choice to make. His old friend Jon Mark was forming a new band with John Almond, the very sensibly titled Mark-Almond. There was, of course, a place reserved for Davies if he wanted it. But Cat Stevens, too, was making an offer now, and his was even more exciting.

"By that time I was getting to know Steve quite well. One day he said: 'Why don't we go out on the road together?' At that time, Mark-Almond were forming, and as I'd known Jon for so long I had to toss up to decide. But I was getting a buzz off Steve's music, and I wanted to follow that path through."

He made his decision just in time. An American visit, at long last, was scheduled for November 1970. But one reason for Stevens's reluctance to launch into any time-consuming touring was his need to get another album out.

No matter that his contract demanded no more than one album a year. *Tea for the Tiller Man* would be released just five months after *Mona Bone Jakon*, its release hastened not only to let Stevens plow through the colossal backlog of songs he had accumulated in the nearly three years since *New Masters*, but also to confirm in the outside world's mind that, this time, he was back to stay. And that his new direction was one he intended to pursue.

A sneak preview of what the album might contain, in the form of Jimmy Cliff's version of Stevens's "Wild Child," appeared in the singles charts in September, rising up the Top 20 at the same time that "Lady D'Arbanville" commenced her graceful descent. While Island was introducing the new Cat Stevens to a modern rock audience, the label was also busy presenting reggae singer Jimmy Cliff to the same constituency; the marketing of Cliff served as a dry run for what they would later attempt and achieve with Bob Marley and the Wailers.

Jimmy Cliff was reggae music's first international superstar. Already a Jamaican chart veteran by the time the anthemic "Wonderful World, Beautiful People" gave him his first U.S. hit, in 1969, Cliff opened the door through which a host of his countrymen would pass over the next few years. Prior to Cliff, reggae artists spoke to reggae fans alone. The erstwhile James Chambers, however, appealed across the board.

Cliff was just twenty-one when he was thrust into the international spotlight, but he wrote and performed with the assurance of someone who already had seven years' worth of Jamaican success behind him. His first single, "Daisy Got Me Crazy," was released in 1962, and the decade also saw him performing as far afield as London, Paris, Brazil, and the 1964 New York World's Fair.

Further evidence of his abilities was revealed when Cliff won the 1968 International Song Festival with "Waterfall." But it was the next four years that truly established Cliff among the most significant artists of the age, as "Wonderful World, Beautiful People" was followed into the chart by "Vietnam," an antiwar number that Bob Dylan described as the best protest song he'd ever heard.

The success of "Vietnam" confirmed Cliff's arrival on the scene. It also evidenced his versatility. At a time when reggae was still regarded as a minor force on the world musical stage, songs like "Vietnam," "Come into My Life," and the sufferer's anthem "Hard Road to Travel" brought him to the thoughtful attention of the same fans that bought records by the other adult-oriented troubadours of the day.

Indeed, that same linkage was strengthened first when Cliff covered Cat Stevens' "Wild World" for his next hit single (Stevens himself produced the record); then when Paul Simon traveled to Kingston, Jamaica, to record with the same producer (Leslie Kong) and musicians, and in the same studio that Cliff had utilized on his earlier hits.

Released four months before its composer's version, "Wild World" returned Cliff to the upper reaches of the chart and confirmed what "Lady D'Arbanville" had already suggested (by echoing what "Matthew and Son" and "Here Comes My Baby" had achieved). The Cat *was* back.

Three decades after its release in fall 1970, *Mojo*'s Colin Irwin would seize upon Cat Stevens's fourth album, *Tea for the Tillerman*, as the consummate illustration of the singer's "search for a spiritual meaning from a mean material world . . . articulat[ing] the confusion felt by many people at that time with songs like 'Father and Son,' 'Where Do the Children Play,' 'Hard Headed Woman,' and 'Wild World.'"

So had he, Irwin asked, realized what a genre-defining album he was making at the time?

Stevens shook his head. "No. I was just following my heart, and the music was coming out and was being dressed absolutely appropriately with the musicians that I had, and kept very sparse and pure. It was a very purist period of songwriting and recording. I had a feeling there was something special, but I didn't know how people would take it."

Discussing his UK audience in that same interview, Stevens confessed, "Some people . . . weren't quite sure whether to believe what had happened when I came back. To me it was just as natural as growing the beard. I had simply matured. Other people were saying: 'What's going on?' I think that's the cynical side of the record business. They couldn't quite understand it."

Which, he explained, was why the United States was so important to him. "In America, where they had never really heard me before, they understood immediately. And it happened."

Stevens's newly acquired American representative, lawyer Nat Weiss, would be coordinating the tour, with the aid of Peter Asher, with whom he recently set up a management company. Named for the region of London that Asher still thought of as home, but stoically planted across the road from his Los Angeles abode, Marylebone Productions would now be handling both James Taylor and Cat Stevens's American activities.

Stevens arrived in the United States for the first time in early November 1970. His maiden tour was a short hop that introduced him immediately to the sheer enormity of the country; his U.S. stage debut on November 18, 1970, saw him ambling nervously onto the Fillmore East stage, ahead of the rock band Hammer and labelmates Traffic, to fill that first half hour or so while the audience were finding their seats.

It was a terrifying baptism, preserved for posterity in the words of *Rock* magazine's Bud Scoppa. "From the Fillmore East balcony, Cat Stevens and [Alun Davies] looked hopelessly tiny. Just two seated figures holding guitars; no banks of amps, no massed drums, no sparkle suits."

Scoppa portrayed the concert as a battle of wills; an audience impatient for the headliners, talking over the "funny little songs" that the little men on the big stage were strumming, but then pausing in midsentence as the singer started talking to them, speaking "between songs as if he were in someone's apartment for the first time—polite, friendly, warm. This kind of intimacy was practically unheard of at the Fillmore, with its reputation for toughness. The kid must be awfully naive. Forty minutes later, this unknown who called himself Cat Stevens had the audience on its feet."

The following night Stevens repeated the exercise at the Academy of Music in Philadelphia, and there would be other mismatches in New Orleans and Chicago before Stevens flew back to New York for what he, and history, would record as his true American debut, an intimate performance in a very intimate club.

Later to find lasting glory as the man who wrote "I Love Rock 'n' Roll" for Joan Jett, guitarist and songwriter Alan Merrill was already a teenage superstar in Japan when he returned to New York for a short break, just before Christmas, 1970. It was his cousin Laura Nyro who ensured he would be at Stevens's Gaslight performance; she wanted to introduce Merrill to her manager, David Geffen, who was also intending to be at the show.

"It was Cat Stevens's first ever New York gig," Merrill recalled. "It was winter 1970—my passport shows I visited NYC in late November that year—and there are probably photos of me sat in between Odetta and Laura in some archived audience shots from the show. Cat was very good, and I liked his material. 'Wild World' was a standout of course, a great song."

Backstage, Nyro, Geffen, and Merrill gathered to meet the star of the moment and Nyro, as she always did when her young cousin was around, promptly started looking around for a guitar so that he could throw in an impromptu audition. She seized upon Cat Stevens's own instrument, while instructing Merrill to perform "Knot Tier," a song he had recorded for his first solo album, and which she had helped him arrange.

"Cat generously allowed me to play the song on it for Geffen. There were quite a few people backstage who clapped when I finished the tune, and Laura sang the harmony on the chorus with me, which was intimidating since she was so amazing and had such a huge voice. Geffen was mildly impressed with my strumming and singing the song, but he didn't offer me a deal. And Cat shot off to talk to other people backstage. So he never even heard it."

Those were the stars that shone at Stevens's New York debut. On the other side of the country, however, a very different galaxy awaited him, but not necessarily because he was the cat. They were curious because he was an unknown Brit, and the last act of that description to walk into the Troubadour was now making a lot of people an awful lot of money. His name was Elton John

What was it about these Englishmen and their craze for funny names?

An underachiever both at home and abroad, by early 1970 Elton John had more or less been rejected by every reputable concert promoter in the

United States. His first album had picked up a smattering of encouraging reviews, and it was no secret at all that pianist John and his songwriting partner Bernie Taupin were influenced by Americana to the point of near obsession. There was no reason on earth why America shouldn't take such devoted disciples to its bosom. No reason beyond the recalcitrance of a network of head-in-their-ass concert promoters.

That is when John's UK agent, Vic Lewis, decided to take matters into his own hands and start making contacts of his own. He had recently seen the English folk band Pentangle make a successful appearance at the Troubadour, and he was convinced that Elton John could make a similar impression if he was only given the chance.

So, it transpired, was Doug Weston, who booked the solo pianist into the venue for one full week in August 1970, apparently on the strength of one promise: that if he took a chance on this English unknown, he would be guaranteed a club full of watching stars. And Vic Lewis followed through on the promise: Gordon Lightfoot, David Gates of Bread, and Beach Boy Mike Love were in attendance; Neil Diamond (who shared Elton's U.S. label, UNI) was on hand to introduce him.

The media flipped. Los Angeles *Times* correspondent Robert Hilburn headlined his review with the simple phrase "Elton John New Rock Talent," and his opening line was a simple "Rejoice." Within days of John's first Troubadour concert, the Los Angeles *Free Press*, the *Hollywood Reporter*, the *Chicago Sun Times*, and the *San Francisco Chronicle* had all made similar pronouncements; within two weeks, his hitherto unheralded *Elton John* album had sold more than 30,000 copies. Elton John was a superstar and, for the moment, his flare eclipsed that of everyone who attempted to follow him.

Including Cat Stevens, which was ironic, because just a few months earlier, Elton would gladly have swapped places with Stevens—he had, in fact, already done so. The pair had already met when Elton was hired to add piano to some demos Stevens was recording at Pye Studios in January 1970. And a few months later, Elton was moonlighting as a session man for Pickwick Records, a budget label whose raison d'être was a series of albums that featured anonymous musos playing the big hits of the day, and doing their best to sound like the originators.

In truth, Elton's efforts for the series rarely sounded like anybody other than Elton John, but such was his obscurity at the time that nobody paid attention to that. And so it was that in June 1970, Elton found himself singing and playing his own interpretation of "Lady D'Arbanville" for a cheapo LP's worth of soundalike hits.

Thanks to the Troubadour shows, it would also be one of the last jobs he ever did for Pickwick.

Stevens did not receive the same plaudits as Elton. "The receptions were more mild than wild," *Rolling Stone* continued, "but it's a strange time for troubadours like him. The audience at the Troubadour somehow reflects the whole pop scene of Los Angeles, and maybe Cat came in a little too soon after the city's collective orgasm over Elton John. That gave Cat a few friendly strokes and just one encore call, and the trade press, which doesn't come that often anyway, also held back."

It could have been that Vic Lewis's gamble had failed. But FM radio was less resistant, picking up on the best of *Tea for the Tillerman* and then, when that had been thoroughly absorbed into the medium's DNA, gratefully devouring the rest of it.

A&M, the label that handled Island's American releases, sprang into action. The marketing department struck a deal with *Rolling Stone* that offered a copy of the LP to every new subscriber; and by April 1971, Cat Stevens had no fewer than three albums on the U.S. charts: the Top 10 smash *Tea for the Tillerman*, the lesser-selling but still registering *Mona Bone Jakon*, and a hastily conceived (some might say mercenary) double pack of his two Deram albums. By comparison, *Mona Bone Jakon* had languished at #63 on the British chart and remained on the listings for just one month, while *Tea for the Tillerman* barely kissed the Top 20, although it did hang around for thirty-nine weeks.

April 1971 saw Stevens back in New York, back at the Gaslight, a venue which critic Nancy Ehrlich condemned as "brutally uncomfortable," only to then praise Stevens for making the pain "worth enduring." Stevens's music, she told *Billboard* readers, combined "unforgettable lines of melody . . . filled with wonderful interlocking chains of internal rhymes," and her words set the tone for the remainder of Stevens's next tour, a six-week scouring of the United States, the longest outing of his life so far, which Marylebone Productions rendered a true family affair by slotting James Taylor's sister Kate in as his support act.

He was rewarded on arrival with the news that *Tea for the Tillerman* had gone gold (it would eventually hit triple platinum), not merely completely outperforming its UK counterpart, but outstripping every bard this side of James Taylor.

14

Shaky Town

"Music is my living," James Taylor told British journalist Keith Altham in 1971. "I don't enjoy selling *myself*. Photographers and reporters are mostly after me. They want to know what I read and what I'm like and I don't really know myself, so how can I tell them?"

He would, he insisted, have been happy to see "a lot of this confusing rubbish go away and get back to [the] old times. If I could go back I would. I'm looking forward to being able to retire from being a public figure and being able to afford to be myself!" Even the media's growing penchant for labeling him the first in a new wave of players called the singer-songwriters dismayed him.

Where, he asked, was the dividing line between what he did and what Bob Dylan had been doing for eight years? He sang and he wrote songs. "We were just following on from . . . all those [other] players who wrote their own stuff," he reflected forty years later.

Taylor retreated from view. Even with *Sweet Baby James* still reasonably fresh on the racks, he eschewed a lot of the live work and touring with which he could have filled his time, opting instead to return to the studio and repay Carole King's friendship and support by guesting on *Writer*, her first solo album.

He ducked out of public appearances, and he ducked out of the media whirl as well. Requests for interviews with Taylor were invariably greeted with a polite "no, thank you," the apparent media blackout first bemusing and then bewildering the growing line of journalists who were hanging on his telephone. Because suddenly, without any more promotion than a gentle word of mouth, and a few obliging FM disc jockeys who swung *Sweet Baby James* into radio rotation, things were picking up.

"We really are not trying to be nasty to the press," Peter Asher pledged. "We are not saying, 'Fuck off, you nasty snotty plebby press,' because we really are grateful for the nice things that have been written here, but James just doesn't like interviews. It's not what he does [that matters], it's what he sings!"

So Taylor stepped as far from the limelight as he could, heading into the studio with Kootch and Carole King to craft the album that, perhaps more than any other, epitomizes what the media required of this new musical breed: "a hunger for the intimacy," said King. "The authenticity of someone telling their own story," agreed Jackson Browne.

Writer, said Kootch, "is phenomenal. I thought, 'Man, this is it. This is so fucking great. It's got to be the breakthrough. Lou [Adler] produced it; he knew exactly how to record her. It was like going to Harvard, man. Those sessions . . . anyone who had been on *Writer* learned how to play on records. Being on those sessions was such an education.'"

Writer remains superlative, from the opening blast of "Spaceship Races," the sound of Jo Mama in full-tilt boogie, through the plaintive "Child of Mine," the psych-flavored "Can't You Be Real," the countryish "To Love," and on to that rendition of "Up On the Roof" that Taylor had been previewing in concert, oozing with strings and piano.

The album's highlight, however, was "Goin' Back," a return to child-ish pleasures and innocence that King and Gerry Goffin wrote for Dusty Springfield back in 1966 and that had since been recorded by the Byrds, but which might easily have been written to order around Taylor's own growing nervousness as the outside world continued beating a path to his door. "Things started to get out of control when I began reading that I was a superstar," Taylor admonished writer Altham. "I'm not what a superstar should be—it's a box with a label on it."

And so Taylor was off again. The *Writer* sessions had barely wrapped when he found himself busy preparing for, and then filming, his first (and, as it transpired, only) motion picture role, in *Two-Lane Blacktop*.

"I'm not sure how he was convinced to go off and do that movie," Kootch reflected on the fortieth anniversary of its release. "It probably seemed a good idea at the time. [But] when I saw it, I thought it was the most boring thing . . . deadly boring."

Two-Lane Blacktop saw Taylor linking with director Monte Hellman, a former Roger Corman protégé, and Beach Boy Dennis Wilson, in what was never envisioned as anything more than a bog-standard rods- and bodsploitation flick, the kind of film that went straight to the drive-ins sandwiched between a couple of other movies with much the same plot and direction. Indeed, the story of two men (Taylor and Wilson) drag-racing their way down the Route 66 in a primer-gray 1955 Chevrolet, paying their way by staging races with every other racer they meet, was scarcely one that could hope to do battle in any arena other than that, and without the cachet of its leading men's names, it might well have been forgotten before the ink was even dry on the theater tickets.

Instead it became a cult classic.

The movie opens with the pair preparing to set out, but really only gets going once they arrive in New Mexico and encounter Warren Oates, the motormouth at the wheel of a 1970 Pontiac GTO. The inevitable flash point, whose car is better, arises, and while the cynical viewer will already have determined that it would probably have been easier for the pair just to beat the crap out of the obnoxious little show-off and wrap the movie there, they instead agree to race him to Washington D.C., winner take all.

Oates promptly gets the better of them when he drives off with the female hitchhiker that Taylor and Wilson have been sharing since they picked her up in Flagstaff, Arizona; winning back the girl soon becomes as much a motive for the pair as winning the GTO's pink slip, but with a fatal charm that surely borrowed some ideas from that other cross-country freakoid film, *Easy Rider*, we never discover who won the race. As the two cars battle down a deserted airstrip somewhere in eastern Tennessee, first the soundtrack drops away, then the film begins to judder, and as the cars pick up speed, the cellulose catches, discolors, and burns. The credits roll over the viewer's interpretation of precisely what happened next.

The movie's casting was as haphazard as its action. Hellman cast Taylor after seeing his face on a Sunset Strip billboard, advertising *Sweet Baby James*, and recruited Wilson just four days before principal photography got under way, in August 1970. Neither did he intend allowing such inexperienced actors any opportunity to feel their way into their roles. Not only did the director refuse to allow them to read the script ahead of filming, he also refused to allow them any other clue toward their characters' personalities. He even refused to give them names. In script and movie credits alike,

Taylor, as the driver, was simply called The Driver; Wilson, the mechanic, became The Mechanic. Oates, the rival driver, became GTO, and the girl was just The Girl.

So far, so grinding, and even fans of the film must be grateful that Hellman's original three-hour cut was ultimately slashed down to 105 minutes for release. Yet when *Two-Lane Blacktop* was released in April 1971, reviews were more than generous.

"What I liked about *Two-Lane Blacktop* was the sense of life that occasionally sneaked through," said Roger Ebert, as he lavished three out of four stars on the film.

Vincent Canby in the *New York Times* admitted it was a "far from perfect film (those metaphors keep blocking the road), but it has been directed, acted, photographed and scored (underscored, happily) with the restraint and control of an aware, mature filmmaker."

The *Village Voice* declared, "*Two-Lane Blacktop* is a movie of achingly eloquent landscapes and absurdly inert characters"; and *Esquire* went positively apeshit for it, reprinting the original script (including much, therefore, that was cut from the film) and declaring with a total absence of either irony or self-consciousness that *Two-Lane Blacktop* was "our nomination for movie of the year." There were eight months of the year still to come.

Six weeks of filming kept Taylor out of the limelight; he returned to Los Angeles, however, to discover the spotlight was now going supernova. First "Fire and Rain" slipped out as a single and, in a world that had been at least partially reshaped by the magnificent melancholia of Simon and Garfunkel's "Bridge over Troubled Water" single, followed that song's tone of maudlin tenderness toward the uppermost reaches of the Hot 100. Entering the chart at the beginning of September, "Fire and Rain" would ultimately rise to #3.

Sweet Baby James followed, and would soon eclipse every one of the single's achievements. It too peaked at #3, trapped behind such immovable logjams as Creedence Clearwater Revival's *Cosmo's Factory*; Led Zeppelin's third LP, *Led Zeppelin III*; and the soundtrack to the festival that Taylor never played, *Woodstock*. But it remained on the chart for close to two years, and U.S. sales were swift to march past a million, while the industry simply sat back in amazement. The new decade had its first superstar. And if Taylor thought the last six months had been crazy, he had no idea what the next six would bring.

In October 1970, Taylor and Joni Mitchell coheadlined a benefit concert for the protest group Greenpeace in Vancouver, at the event that history declares marked the very birth of the organization.

It was Mitchell who landed him the gig, although even she had not been organizer Irving Stowe's first choice. That was Joan Baez, but her schedule was already too crammed for her to fit the festival in. She sent her apologies, a $10,000 check, and a suggestion that Stowe contact Mitchell.

Stowe's daughter, Barbara, recalled, "Joni came on 100 percent.... [Then] she called us up one night at dinner and Dad put his hand over the mouthpiece and said, 'It's Joni! She wants to know if she can bring James Taylor, is that okay?' [And] we didn't know who James Taylor was. I actually thought he was a black blues singer, I had him confused with James Brown. My family was so out to lunch.

"But my dad said to Joni, 'Okay.' And then he hung up and said to us, 'Don't tell anyone. We don't know who this James Taylor is. If he's no good, it could ruin the concert.' Then my brother said, 'Hey, let's go down to Rohan's and find out [who he is].' And there it was, [the album] *Sweet Baby James* [laughs], which was on its way to platinum."

Greenpeace was unknown at the time. Indeed, it only became Greenpeace in the days before the concert. Prior to that, Stowe and his wife, Dorothy, had intended calling their Vancouver, B.C.-based group the Don't Make a Wave committee, and had just one aim, to protest and, if possible, prevent: the latest round of American hydrogen bomb tests on Amchitka, a small but, in terms of wildlife, densely populated island off the Alaskan coast. Staging a festival to raise funds and awareness was the most direct form of promotion they could think of. The ultimate goal, setting the stage for future decades of Greenpeace activism, was to send a ship to the luckless plot of land.

So Baez suggested Mitchell, Mitchell suggested Taylor. Greenwich Village stalwart Phil Ochs was there, and so were Chilliwack, a Canadian rock band that went onto enjoy some U.S. success much later in the decade, and whose invlovement might better be remembered today had they not been the only participants that evening who refused to allow their performance to be recorded. But sound engineer Dave Zeffertt of Kelly-Deyong Sound taped the remainder of the show and, forty years later, the Stowe family opened a fascinating window to the past with the release of *Amchitka: The Concert That Launched Greenpeace*.

The performers were not simply turning out to offer token support. "Greenpeace is beautiful, and you are beautiful because you are here tonight," Irving Stowe told the crowd as he gazed out a packed Pacific Coliseum. Though Taylor later admitted that he was distracted because his guitar was out of tune, he fully understood the importance of the event.

"People were very excited and very fired up. It was exciting, it was very contagious. [And] since then people have . . . become more aware of the urgency of the environmental issue. When I encountered the people at Greenpeace and saw the work they were doing, and the way they had engaged the problem, I felt a big sense of relief that people were working on it."

By modern standards, Barbara Stowe continued, the concert itself "was anarchy." Greenpeace itself provided the venue's security, volunteers drawn from its fledgling membership whose job, essentially, was to watch as the vast venue filled up, and hope there was no trouble. So the crowd spilled in and sat where it wanted; there were no aisles, no seating blocks, no brightly jacketed rent-a-thugs to quash the slightest sense of occasion. Placards waved, banners were unfurled, chants and war cries arose from the masses, and they were not only targeted at the United States' activities.

That very morning had seen the passage of Canada's War Measures Act, effectively outlawing any actions or behavior that could be seen as supporting the anti-Vietnam protests that were burning up Canada's next-door neighbor. Indeed, there were very real fears that the concert itself might fall afoul of the new regulations. It didn't, but Phil Ochs remained in a state of shock. So far as the majority of Americans were concerned, Canada was a peace-loving country miles removed from the political and militaristic belligerence then shaping the United States. Ochs had crossed the border to discover a land under what amounted to martial law.

He remained furious onstage. "Phil Ochs was so angry his whole set," Barbara Stowe said. "It permeated that, his anger, and that gave it a certain electricity and power. Then when Chilliwack came on, they had to sort of chill out the crowd. They were amazing. James Taylor chilled it out further, and then Joni came on and just let her lyrics speak: 'Bombs turning into butterflies,' you know?"

The festival raised a staggering $17,000, and maybe that was the night when Taylor realized precisely how astronomically high his profile had risen. "Fire and Rain" was marching up the chart, and when he introduced the song toward the end of the show, the audience began applauding after just two lines. It was a moment of recognition that, more than any other, confirmed Taylor's ascendancy and nothing else that happened that evening, not even the encore he shared with Joni Mitchell, performing Dylan's "Mr. Tambourine Man" and the Mitchell-penned title track to Tom Rush's *The Circle Game*, could compare.

Days later, on October 28, Taylor and Mitchell were sharing a stage again, this time at the Royal Albert Hall in London. Broadcast live on BBC radio, the performance caught the pair giggling and laughing through their between-song patter like high schoolers enjoying their prom.

Mitchell opened the show, peforming two of her own songs—"That Song About Midway" and "The Gallery"—solo before she turned the spotlight onto Taylor for a resonant "Rainy Day Man," and a jocular "Steamroller" ("the heaviest blues tune I know, ladies and gentlemen"). Mitchell followed through with "The Priest" (from that year's *Ladies of the Canyon*) and "Carey," a song destined for her next album, *Blue*. Taylor came back for "Carolina in My Mind," and then the pair joined forces for Mitchell's "California," laughing through its travelogue introduction.

They swung into "For Free," that staple of Taylor's own early live show. "The first time I ever heard this tune," Taylor told the crowd, "I was at Newport. Joni and I were both doing some workshop out in the middle of a field; it was raining, and the mike system was shorting on and off. It was kind of a weird day. But I'd never heard this tune before, and I've never played it with her either. . . ."

They duetted through an achingly sparse "The Circle Game" and closed with a beautiful "You Can Close Your Eyes." The recording of this song is perhaps the finest existing recording of the two lovers to have come to light in forty years. And every word they uttered, here and anyplace else they stepped out that year, seemed to be recorded for posterity by somebody or other.

He portrayed the grand sad loner, then, but James Taylor was decidedly not alone as he reeled from the sudden lightning strike. Suddenly it was as though his very family name had become a license to print (or at least hope to print) money. Seemingly sidestepping any kind of broad musical apprenticeship, brother Livingston already had an album out through Phil Walden's Capricorn label. Siblings Alec and Kate were both awaiting the release of their debut LPs, with Kate about to head out on tour with Cat Stevens. And though very few people ever expected all three to hit it as big as their famous brother had (Livingston's LP was sweetly melodic but hardly anything to write home about; Kate's was better, but scarcely more formed), still, *Rolling Stone* headlined Taylor's March 1971 cover story "The First Family of the New Rock," and there were few people who doubted that was true.

In the handful of interviews he did give, now and over the months to come, Taylor seized gratefully on the opportunity to speak about anything apart from himself. Carole King's emergence from the shadows of stage fright, for example, was a favorite topic.

In the run-up to Thanksgiving 1970, Taylor played a sold-out six day season at the Troubadour and convinced Carole King to be his opening act. She pulled it off, too, not even flapping when there was a bomb scare during her opening night set, phoned in by who knew which radical, entertaining who knew what grudge. And Taylor, too, remained unperturbed, sitting with Joni Mitchell and flicking instead through the good-luck telegrams that had flooded in.

"Best of luck on opening night to one hell of a swell guy," from his publisher; "I wish I was there, but you sold out," from musician John Stewart. "I knew someday you'd sell out."

"Carole was waiting to happen," he told writer Kerry O'Brien. "The singer-songwriter thing had sort of happened with Dylan, really with Woody Guthrie, from my point of view. But it was time for Carol to sort of step up to the plate and knock it out of the park." The first time King ventured out onto a public stage, "in the context of my set," was when he played a show on the roof of Queens College. Now, however, she had taken the Troubadour stage at last, billed as Taylor's support, and he proudly recalled, "It was—she was very tentative and—but, you know, the music takes over and those songs that she wrote are such vehicles, you just can't lose. Once you hook into it, it's sort of 'away we go.'"

King's *Writer* album did little. But her next record, *Tapestry*, cut in two weeks with everybody wondering how it could possibly succeed after *Writer* had failed, was destined to soar. By June 1971, the woman who once canceled a gig at the Troubadour because she was too nervous to go on stage was headlining two nights at Carnegie Hall.

Taylor, meanwhile, continued to feel vulnerable.

"It is very strange making a living out of being yourself," Taylor mused, and his bandmates sympathized with his dilemma. Kootch: "It was absolutely great. For me it wasn't just James breaking through, it was all of us, Peter, Russ, myself, all of us, we were all a part of the picture.

"It was a big deal. Here we were suddenly getting all this attention, and I loved it, I was having a ball. It was great, we made it, we can go on a big tour, we can go all over the country.

"But James was miserable, he was struggling, he was still on dope. He'd get through the gigs and everyone was having a great time but James."

Sweet Baby James was still selling like diapers. Reactivated, the Apple album was now marching up the chart and dragging "Carolina in My Mind" in its 45-rpm wake. Chip Taylor had even reached back into the vault and, at last, pulled together the afternoon's worth of Flying Machine material he had taped, and that was likewise gnawing at the Hot 100—much to its makers' disgust.

Kootch spoke for the entire band when he condemned, "When James hit, which had nothing to do with Al or Chip, along they come sticking this album out on the tails of James's success. [Chip] didn't ask us our permission, he didn't tell us it was happening, and he certainly didn't pay us, and we were furious. The guy blew more money at the gambling tables in five minutes than he spent on the goddamned album. It was a lowball, classless, jive-ass move."

But Chip was, and remains, unrepentant. A contract had been signed, and it needed to be honored. Allen Klein had refused to negotiate, and Apple was in any case in no fit state to fight. The only other option would have been to sue James Taylor himself, and Chip Taylor was adamant: "We didn't want to do that."

≈≈≈

In March 1971, James Taylor became the first self-professed heroin addict ever to appear on the cover of *Time* magazine, and one of a select band of pop performers, too. The Beatles and the Band were about as far out as the venerable weekly journal had journeyed, which meant that even Bob Dylan had still to appear. But *Time* was unequivocal in its support for Taylor.

"The man who best sums up the new sound of rock, as well as being its most radiantly successful practitioner, is a brooding, sensitive twenty-two-year-old rich man's son who sings, he says, 'because I don't know how to talk.'"

The article reflected how Taylor's first album, *James Taylor*, sold just 30,000 copies in its first year; while his second, *Sweet Baby James*, had topped a million and a half in the same amount of time. He was a favorite for five awards at the upcoming Grammys, and just a month earlier, he was a star turn at the predominantly classical Great Performers series at New York City's Lincoln Center. He was, quite simply, the first American superstar of the seventies, and he hated it. Years later, he would admit to *Stereo Review*, "I think that the early success and recognition really froze me up. The *Time* magazine thing was a big deal. Back then it was a big thing. I can't remember it that well."

He did not resent his success. "It was very gratifying to have a hit." But, he continued, "there were some things about it that I wasn't really ready for; perhaps there are some aspects of being a star that I'm not very strong in. Some people can really handle an awful lot of it. And other people just continue to do their work and continue to do it well and have a good attitude toward what they're doing and know how to enjoy themselves and disregard things that are gonna mess with their heads."

He was not one of them, and the *Time* magazine article dwelled upon that with what might have been seen as almost intrusive detail. "The press want something that'll sell copy," Taylor acknowledged to *Rolling Stone* in 1979. It was their job, or at least their duty, to pick up on subjects that their readership would be interested in, regardless of how prurient that interest might be.

So "they pick up on the mental hospital, family stuff, try to invent some category of rock that I belong to, or perhaps they pick up on my drug problem. [And] it gets to the point sooner or later when you start to think about your kids: 'What does your daddy do for a living?' 'He plays the guitar and he talks about his drug problems.' It's embarrassing to read the drivel that comes out of your mouth sometimes. . . ."

Embarrassing, too, to read some of the drivel that Taylor's detractors could come up with, as the long-established countercultural imagery of smack as a somehow acceptable artistic statement ran headlong into his own decidedly uncool public persona.

Images of course abound. Ray Charles standing on a South of France seafront, shivering in his overcoat on the warmest day of the year. Johnny Thunders pinprick-eyeballing an audience that has just spent three hours waiting in a run-down club while he sent back to New York for some merchandise.

Keith Richards *not* having his blood changed at a Swiss clinic every year, but rarely saying anything to send the rumor packing. Lou Reed writing two of the greatest love songs of his life about the drug, one about scoring it ("I'm Waiting for the Man"), one about using it ("Heroin"). Iggy Pop on stage in 1977, screaming to the bleachers, "Mama, I shot myself up!" And Sid Vicious's mama shooting him up herself, with enough high-grade smack to pack her Sex Pistol son off to the graveyard.

And what do they all have in common?

They're cool.

Which isn't to say heroin itself is cool. Its imagery, though, and its acolytes, flow through some of the most archetypal notions in rock 'n' roll—none of which have anything to do with a singer-songwriter strumming his guitar: "the only junkie," more than a handful of commentators have quipped, "whose audience nods out before he does."

Taylor was working now on his third LP, but he was doing so from beneath shadows that could never have imagined before: the weight of expectation from an apparent universe full of followers; the sibling rivalry induced by his familial contemporaries (sister Kate's *Sister Kate*, another Peter Asher production, was now bubbling under the chart); and, suddenly, the race among the other record labels to launch their own New James Taylor.

Taylor was dropped into the thick of this hubbub, in spring 1971, on a twenty-seven-date American tour packaging him, Carole King, and Kootch's Jo Mama onto one bill, the musicians slipping and sliding between their own spots and one another's in an outing that would later offer Bob Dylan a template for his Rolling Thunder Revue. It also left Taylor facing the most grueling schedule he had ever confronted.

From the outset, it was an ill-starred outing. Later, *Rolling Stone* would reflect on Taylor's live appearances and muse, "[His] last tour had not been an artistic success. He had become sluggish and more distant from his audience." But even before they hit the road, neither Taylor nor King was comfortable with the mind-numbing repetition of a full tour. But ticket demand was so vast that, had they stuck to the size of venues they preferred to play, the tour would have lasted twenty-seven weeks, not twenty-seven days.

There was further discontent when the ticket prices were announced—admission to the closing performance, at Madison Square Garden, topped out at a staggering $7.50, and Asher admitted that he was horrified at the cost.

They did their utmost to compensate audiences for the lack of intimacy. Video screens were brought in to project the onstage action as far as possible, and Asher at least took solace in the knowledge that a Taylor ticket at the Garden still cost 25 percent less than Tom Jones's fans had to fork out when their idol performed there. And, as Asher must have grown tired of reminding people, $7.50 was the *maximum* cost of attending the spectacle. There were a lot of cheaper seats as well, and all of them had an excellent view of the stage.

So the audience could see, but what were they watching? Even his supporters could tell there was something amiss, that Taylor was growing increasingly distant from the audience who came to worship at his feet. And watching from across the ocean, Cat Stevens made no secret of his opinions. "If you play Madison Square Garden as a soloist then you've had it," he told *Hit Parader*. "I suppose the trouble with America is that you're either a superstar or you're nothing and you're expected to play the large auditoriums. But it can easily get out of hand and become quite frightening."

"I don't go in for all that," he told writer Roy Carr. "They're only in it for the bread, it's definitely a bread thing. The only thing is that you do get heard by a lot more people, but then you don't, really, because you sacrifice the quality of your performance. They only see the event, that's all. Now that's what I call a drag. That's not what it's about."

Taylor, it seemed, agreed with every word.

It would be childish to blame stress for whatever happened next; childish, but also childlike. Accustomed to living his own life, but all too willing to turn to other crutches rather than try and fight through his problems alone, Taylor was getting high again.

He wasn't, he insisted, stoned throughout the entire tour. Occasionally he would pop an upper or two if he was feeling especially tired, or too weak to take the stage. But when the tour hit Chicago, Taylor hit rock bottom. He had a jones like none he had experienced in a long time.

"I got in touch with a doctor who was a friend of mine and he got me methadone somewhat illegally. He figured it was either he'd break a law or else I'd go down, so he straightened me out. I stayed on that methadone he gave me for almost a month."

The problem with addiction, however, "is that it's consistent. What the junkie is looking for when he picks up his syringe or goes out to cop is something that will be the same every time, and that will completely supersede all other goings-on. And smack does that. It's the circumstances around it that kill you. Heroin maintenance has worked well in England. But it's like being dead. It knocks out your sensitivities at the same time that it gets rid of the suppressed emotion that you can't stand anymore."

He found it very difficult to write when he was strung out.

If his personal capacity for self-indulgence had run dry, however, his mailbag bulged with fresh inspiration for song. Having established himself, as Al Aronowitz put it, as the voice of his generation, he had also maneuvered himself into place as its mouthpiece, and it seemed as though every sad-sack romantic who felt that life was beating him with the sharp end of the stick was putting pen to paper to tell Taylor all about it.

He could, his friends joked, have readily given the music business up, and set himself up instead as an agony aunt, catering to the miseries of American adolescence and answering his many fans' problems with a few lines of verse.

That the material he wrote for what became *Mud Slide Slim and the Blue Horizon* was, for the most part, as lasting as that which comprised its predecessor was no surprise. Even as Taylor looked for a possible escape from his life as a tortured soul (ironically by giving himself fresh fodder for the role), he also knew what his audience required and, by that token, what his paymasters demanded.

Onstage, he continued to play the down-home humble boy, even affecting the ghost of a Southern accent for the benefit of audiences who would see that as a mark of authenticity. Other people noticed how his revelations about drug abuse and mental illness offered him an almost tangible sense of vulnerability, one that kept his friends close and his enemies closer. To savage James Taylor in print, one writer of the time recalled, was to bring down a mailbox of merciless opprobrium, seething with that brand of self-righteous fury that only the truly liberated mind can bring to bear on a subject, accusing the author of hate crimes against addicts and lunatics, and any other disadvantaged group that could be shoehorned into the diatribe.

The intriguing aspect of such a firestorm was that Taylor himself did not need to be defended with such ire; was, in fact, as tired of his apparent sainthood as the critics who bemoaned its conferral in the first place.

There would be flashes, across the course of the album, of a new sense of personal distance from the problems he sang of, but there would also be a tired lament for the life that he was no longer allowed to live—his own.

"Hey Mister, That's Me Up On the Jukebox" was, and would remain, one of Taylor's greatest creations; Kootch told Taylor biographer Timothy White that "it was exactly how he felt. He knew he was spread thin, and needed some time alone to get better again." But more than that, the song was a plea for moderation, an acknowledgment of the fortune that had come his way, but also a request that the spotlight be turned off occasionally.

Taylor: "That song was actually as much as anything else to Peter Asher, who bore the brunt of my discomfort about the deadline aspect of *Mudslide Slim*. I wrote that song in the studio. The bridge, which was 'Do you believe I'll go back home / Hey, mister, can't you see that I'm dry as a bone?' is about having to write a song. It's an album cut about having to make an album cut. It's kind of a rip-off, except that it's a really nice tune."

He scrambled for material. No fewer than three of the songs he took into the studio with him dated back to that frenetic burst of songwriting energy that consumed Taylor the previous year. One was the slight "Long Ago and Far Away," but the other two rank among the best songs he had yet written—the ode to Joni, "You Can Close Your Eyes," and "Riding on a Railroad," voicing his frustrations over the moviemaking experience. He had expected a lot of things from his big-screen debut, and worried about a lot as well. But the total lack of creative control was one that he had never anticipated.

How telling, then, that neither song was to be presented in anything approaching its most flattering light here. Two years later, Peter Asher would utterly reinvent "You Can Close Your Eyes" for Linda Ronstadt, as a highlight of her breakthrough album, *Heart Like a Wheel*; while "Riding on a Railroad" had already been presented in definitive form, after Taylor sent Tom Rush a demo of it as he worked toward his next album, *Wrong End of the Rainbow*.

Not that Taylor necessarily agreed with Rush's treatment of it.

Rush: "James sent me the song on a tape, a piece of tape, wrapped around a stick, and at the start of the tape, after I'd wound it onto a reel, he's saying, 'Sorry, I didn't have a take-up reel, Tom,' and there was the sound of carpenters hammering in the background. So I did 'Riding on a Railroad' on the album and the next time I saw James, which was about a year later, he said, 'You know, next time you do one of my songs let me show you the chords.'"

Significant, too, was Taylor's own choice for the album's stand-out track—a song that spilled not from his pen but from Carole King's "You've Got a Friend."

It was King's idea for him to record it, and she remained adamant even after Taylor teased that her old Brill Building training was kicking in again, the notion that she had written a great song and now needed to find someone to record it. No, she assured him, she had already taped her own version and it was going to be on her own next record. She simply wanted to hear Taylor perform it as well.

King's version of the song would, in fact, greet the public first: *Tapestry* saw daylight in November 1970, almost half a year ahead of *Mud Slide Slim*, and it had long since commenced its skyward rise. But there is no doubting that Taylor's version played a major role in further popularizing King's, all the more so after it was released as the follow-up single to the distinctly underperforming "Country Road" single, which had come out earlier in the year. While the album rose to #2, "You've Got a Friend" was destined to climb all the way to the top, and the demand for Taylor to keep on doing what he did grew even louder.

"You've Got a Friend" is the single that established Taylor at the peak of his profession, though his supporters had been claiming for a year that he was already there. Even more impressively, however, it beat off competition not only from Tommy James, the Bee Gees, and Jean Knight, but also from itself. A cover of the song by Roberta Flack and Donny Hathaway had been released almost simultaneously by one of Warner Brothers' sister labels, Atlantic, and the ensuing battle was considered worthy enough to make the front page of *Billboard* magazine's May 29, 1971, issue.

"Several things are at stake," Atlantic's Jerry Wexler told the paper. "In addition to the natural desire to win, there is also the matter of responsibility to your artist." Atlantic would go "all out" to promote the cover version, although even there, there could have been little doubt that it would be Taylor who won out. And so it was; Taylor was #1, Flack and Hathaway got no higher than #29.

Taylor should have been celebrating. He just wasn't sure what, exactly, it was that he needed to be so happy about. Performing, he once said, "is terrifying. And it has to stay that way. Your really need that energy and that urgency, or else you'd get complacent. . . . You'd just lay back and nothing would happen."

That was what he wanted now, to lie back and allow nothing to happen. But he couldn't do that. All he could do was look forward to the little breaks that had been dropped into the itinerary, to give the players a little downtime. Like the one that allowed him to return to Los Angeles for a few days at the beginning of April 1971. He grabbed it, and grasped, too, the opportunity to check out the latest in the long line of singer-songwriters who were apparently coveting his crown.

Still warming up for that six-week American tour, Cat Stevens was back in Los Angeles . . . back at the Troubadour.

15

On the Road
to Find Out

Jackson Browne did not agree, and neither did the majority of his friends and supporters. But when David Geffen effectively mothballed his talents for close to a year, the wily young entrepreneur knew precisely what he was doing, and why.

The music industry was about to undergo a profound shift, and the ability to spot such moments is what raises an exemplary manager above his average contemporaries. That and sufficient chutzpah to quietly disregard the evidence of one's own eyes and listen instead to one's heart.

Right now, "singer-songwriter" was a genre that could apparently do no wrong and, from where the nearsighted bean counters in major-label land were seated, the goose might never stop laying the golden eggs. You needed several dozen hands and feet to even begin to list them all: James Taylor, Cat Stevens, Elton John, Randy Newman, Jim Croce, Warren Zevon, Laura Nyro, Janis Ian, Carole King, Joni Mitchell . . . not Judee Sill, if only because Geffen had her pegged as a talent equal to Browne, only for her impatience to finally push him beyond the point of no return.

But they were piling up against the doors of the Troubadour now, earnestly clutching their acoustic guitars and sheaths of spidery, handwritten lyrics, all torn from the depths of the darkest human misery, and all . . . The thought train slows there, pauses to ponder, what precisely *were* these people selling? Understanding, sympathy, a sense of togetherness; the notion that artist and audience were somehow linked by the shared experience of "not belonging."

But that was fine when there was only a few of them who felt that way. James Taylor could reach out to the million or so people who first bought *Sweet Baby James*, because he was the only one who was doing so. A year, eighteen months, later, and the percentages had been slashed.

Now you could not turn around without another lost troubadour panhandling his misery, stopping traffic with a placard that promised, "I'll make you weep for cash." Wearily, Cat Stevens spoke words that a lot of other people agreed with when he complained, "People don't dance now at many gigs because they are dancing in their heads. We are evolving toward a time of purely mental involvement. That s the way I see things going—so it gets to the stage where people might go to watch someone doing something as simple and personal as pouring out a cup of tea but sharing in the experience."

Geffen certainly understood Stevens's prediction, but he also knew that things would never be allowed to go that far. The public's taste would have shifted long before that, just as it always had and just as it always would. It was only three years before, after all, that the whole world was going psychedelic, and how long had that lasted? A year later, people were talking about a blues revival, and Ten Years After had cleaned up at Woodstock simply by living up to those predictions.

Nineteen-seventy was the year of the singer-songwriter, and 1971 would be as well, Geffen believed. But 1972 would see everything change, and as he eyed the stable of artists he was building around him, checking the progress of each of them like a mother hen looking over her brood of chicks, Geffen saw potential enough in all of them to grasp America by the ears. He just needed a hook to lure in listeners, and a little bit more time to ready his artists for the experience.

Deep into the night, Geffen argued with the pangs of conscience that arose when he thought about Jackson Browne's isolation, knowing he was right to be holding the boy back—and at the same time hoping he would recognize the right time to unleash him.

Neil Young, an artist whom Geffen held in such great regard that, years later, he'd sue him for not sounding like himself, shared Geffen's view. He was a year away from releasing *Harvest*, the album that would catapult him into the heart of singer-songwriter land, but he had no intention of remaining there; no intention, either, of wrestling Taylor (who, ironically, guests on the album) or Elton or Cat for their thrones. In fact he shivered at the thought and Geffen took fresh energy from Young's determination. Why *should* an artist be slotted into a ready-made box just because of the way he appears to the world? He could be creating his *own* box, and slotting the rest of the world into that?

Slowly, in the back of Geffen's mind, an idea began to ferment. And Jackson Browne, for so long the media's superstar-in-waiting, was its centerpiece.

Laurel Canyon had been its own little community for a couple of years now, and within the Los Angeles music industry it was as well-defined a package as any musical genre named by some journalist. Well defined, and coalesced. Ronstadt was up and running already; *Silk Purse*, her second solo album, had only just missed out on a Top 100 placing, probably on the strength of local sales alone.

Eagles (they were adamant about the lack of the definitive article) would soon be taking flight as the quartet of Glenn Frey, Don Henley, Randy Meisner, and Bernie Leadon gathered around the scene that Geffen was creating in his image. Neil Young and Joni Mitchell, Canadians transplanted into the thick of the action, were preaching the gospel even farther afield. And Jackson Browne would soon be ready to join them.

Browne bristled at the thought. "It's a real uncomfortable feeling to have people speculating on your fame, because you get the feeling that it has nothing to do with anything you're doing. That it's got nothing to do with reality. Pretty soon you can be believing that you're the person that everybody wants to know what kind of toilet paper you use. You can go on that trip and forget who you really are. I'm very impressed with people who make great music, and not too many of them are famous. There are lots of famous people I've never heard, and many I wish I'd never heard. As far as I'm concerned, you don't want to be too famous."

While Geffen grafted, then, Jackson jived.

Joe Cocker and Leon Russell's Mad Dogs and Englishmen traveling revue swept into town in March 1970, scooping up seemingly random handfuls of accompanying musicians and minstrels and then transporting them in almost vaudevillian fashion the length and breadth of the nation.

Pamela Polland, Browne's old girlfriend from his Gentle Soul days, was one of the ten choir singers recruited to the show, and she brought Browne along to spend time at the Los Angeles rehearsals. There, he hung with the likes of Leon Russell, Don Preston, Rita Coolidge, Carl Radle, Jim

Gordon, Bobby Keys, Jim Price, the vast and sprawling army of players who would be accompanying Cocker across the USA and whose antics would be served up the following year on both a smash hit (#2) live album, and a well-received concert film.

He might even have been hoping to be added to the revue, although that didn't happen. But the expatriate Irishman who had been producing Joe Cocker for the last three years, a thickly accented dodger and diver named Denny Cordell, did spot him, and although he could not have known straightaway who the young American was, he made it his business to find out.

"I don't even remember how I met Jackson," Cordell recalled a couple of years before his death in 1995. "It was in Los Angeles; he was with one of the girls, and he was probably just playing his guitar for some people, and singing a song that I happened to hear. There was a lot of that going on, people wandering in and effectively auditioning themselves during rehearsals and stuff, in the hope that someone would hear them and invite them on board."

However it transpired, Browne and Cordell clicked, all the more so, admitted Cordell, "after I discovered how well connected he was. David Geffen, that whole crowd." Cordell was scheming his own record label at the time, a tiny concern that he would call Shelter, and part of his personal Mad Dogs brief was to seek out some names that he could add to its roster. "I knew Jackson was out of the question; Geffen would make sure of that. But I also knew that he would need a producer, and I wanted to be that person."

He would, but not yet, and Browne continued killing time. Every night, he would return home to his latest base, a house that Geffen owned on Alto Cedro Drive, just a few blocks from the Mulholland Tennis Club. He spent the money Geffen gave him, buying the clothes that Geffen recommended, dressing like the star that he was being groomed to become. When friends visited, he would entertain them there, or else he'd head over to Geffen's mansion in Beverly Glen, to swim in his pool, lounge in his luxurious house, or play his guitar for Geffen's other guests.

Idleness can be so tiresome, sometimes.

In May 1970, Browne appeared at a benefit for the Foothill Free Clinic, organized by some CalTech friends out at the university's Baxter Hall in Pasadena. But that was it. There would be no more gigs, no more shows. And there would certainly be no more tapes. It would be the end of the year, Christmas 1970, before Geffen was finally ready to unleash his young protégé. With her third album, *Christmas and the Beads of Sweat* poised for release, Laura Nyro was about to head out for a handful of live shows around California, and then across to the East Coast. Jackson Browne would be her support act.

As with everything else that Geffen turned his attention toward, the package was a well crafted one. Nyro and Browne had recently begun stepping out as a couple, and Geffen knew that the presence of a girlfriend on the tour would help Browne cut through any nervousness he might have been feeling. Nyro's cousin Alan Merrill recalled, "Laura dated Jackson and had really nice things to say about him. Jackson gave her a Martin guitar and she kept a photo of him in the case under the guitar. She showed me the photo and said something like 'He's my honeydew.'"

The young man had never stepped out on stages as large as those to which Nyro would be introducing him. The opening Los Angeles shows, on December 12 and 13, placed him alone on a stage in front of 3,000 people a night, packing out the Dorothy Chandler Pavilion at the Los Angeles Music center. In San Diego five days later, they filled the Community Concourse; in Berkeley the following night, it was the Community Theatre's turn to be packed out. And in New York City, they headed to the Fillmore East, the imposing edifice from which promoter Bill Graham ruled the American rock scene in the early 1970s.

For three nights leading up to Christmas Eve, Browne held forth, a tiny figure on a stage carved by giants, and when it was all over, *New York Times* critic Mike Jahn reported, "It seems obvious that Jackson Browne has a promising career ahead of him . . ." even if all he did was "play . . . only slow ballads, sticking to a traditional format of songs."

Browne acknowledged that criticism (if criticism it was) when he spoke with British journalist Steve Turner six years later. There was no great secret to his style of writing, he insisted. "It's cathartic. I'm not exactly sure what I'm writing about until the song is written, and even then it might take me a while to figure it out. But there is a sense of having said something, and even if I don't understand it, there'll be some kind of recognition on a much more basic level."

At the same time, however, he acknowledged that, at least in his earlier writing days, he certainly considered the possibilities of "cultivat[ing] disappointment in order to write . . . you know, that perhaps things did go wrong intentionally in order to have something to write about. At some point it occurs to you that it might be easier to write a forlorn love song than to write something positive, but it has to be such a strong balance all the time. I can't write songs that are mindlessly happy. I'm just not like that, although there are a million things that I love. It's not in me to do that. I write about things that concern me and try to depict things the way I see them and I'm actually incapable of writing anything without instilling a certain optimism."

He warmed to the same subject in an interview with *Melody Maker*'s Colin Irwin. "I haven't had worse experiences than anybody else, I don't think. A lot of the songs may deal with that, but in writing them and singing them, it's a way out of it. You want to be able to tell someone, right? It's therapeutic to be able to tell somebody what you feel. If you mean, do I get depressed, no, I don't really get down very much. I've no time for *that*."

From New York, the Nyro/Browne package crossed the Atlantic for a single London show, a performance at London's Royal Festival Hall on February 6, 1971. The British press adored Nyro, and *Melody Maker* scribe Richard Williams spoke for everyone when he opined, "She symbolizes the breadth of pop music—the way it can embrace such widely disparate performers. Nyro is at one end of the spectrum, and she has it all sewn up."

Browne, on the other hand, was introduced to Williams's readers with the offhand observation that he "used to compose and play guitar for Nico." And while "his warm voice, rough but driving guitar and piano and sad songs made a strong impression before the interval," Williams shrugged, "the first glimpse of Miss Nyro drove all else out of everyone's head."

Browne had no time to be disappointed. Having parted company with Denny Cordell the previous summer, Browne had just one invitation on his mind. Cordell remembered, "I told him, 'If you're ever in London, look me up,' and he did."

Cordell was still working with various members of the Mad Dogs tour ensemble, most notably Leon Russell, and when Browne showed an interest in getting some recording done, Cordell quickly roped in a stellar backing band; Rolling Stones compadre Jim Keltner, guitarist Chris Stainton and pianist Russell, dropping by to pound distinctively through a drama-drenched "Jamaica Say You Will."

Albert Lee, guitarist with Heads Hands and Feet, stepped in on lead, and Cordell later recalled cutting "maybe half an album's worth of material. Good stuff too. But Geffen wasn't interested, or he wasn't interested enough, so I told Jackson that whatever he wanted to do, I'd support him, and he went with Geffen. Which is what I'd have done if I was him." The sessions were scrapped and Browne returned to Los Angeles.

Browne confessed, "Denny saw that either we would have to do the album real quick and it would be real bad, or he would have to put in a whole load of work on it, which he didn't have time to do. I wasn't even on his label and he had his hands full with Shelter, which was just opening, so we decided to pass."

Meanwhile, another label, Atlantic, had shown an interest in Browne, and this time, there was no hissy fit to pull the carpet out from beneath an astonished label head. Instead, Ahmet Ertegun listened to Browne's music and then listened to Geffen's pitch. Forget signing Jackson Browne. Sign David Geffen . . . sign his ears, sign his eyes, sign his nose for sniffing out talent. Geffen had had enough of managing artists for other labels to mess with. He wanted to control the label as well. And it is a sign of how impressive he was that Ertegun agreed. So long as Geffen could deliver the product, Atlantic would distribute it for him.

Now Geffen was trying to decide what to call the new enterprise. Onstage at Syracuse University, opening for Bonnie Raitt on March 27, 1971, Browne joked with the audience about Geffen's indecision. "We thought of so many names and the lawyers kept saying we couldn't use them—Apple, Capitol. . . . My manager's such a square, he's thinking of Integrity Records."

Geffen would eventually settle on Asylum because, record producer Bones Howe recalled, "he wanted musicians he thought were really creative people to be on the label, and feel as though they were protected. He wanted to develop a label that was about writers and artists and not about commercial success necessarily." He wanted to re-create Laurel Canyon in wax. One day, Howe laughed, Geffen told him he had signed the singer David Blue. Howe doubted that Blue would ever make a releasable record, but Geffen simply shrugged. It didn't matter, he said. "I just want to say he's on my label."

Jackson Browne would become the label's first signing (and the fledgling Eagles its first creation).

Not everybody took Geffen's announcement to heart. Writer Dave Marsh, who'd been following Browne's career since that long-ago *Crawdaddy* piece, simply shrugged "When David Geffen announced Asylum's formation, one of the first acts he proclaimed was Jackson, but I didn't take it very seriously. I mean, I didn't think there'd ever be a record, actually, and by that time, I didn't figure I'd like it much."

He proved to be wrong on both scores (Marsh would go on to describe Browne's self-titled debut as "when it is good, it's as good as Van Morrison when he's on"). But he, and all of Browne's other supporters, had long since earned the right to be pessimistic. "I didn't believe Jackson would ever make a record," Nico said.

She had recently signed with Reprise, another of the labels in the ever-growing Warners/Atlantic family, and Browne's was a name she frequently dropped when talking with her new employers. "They said he was yesterday's man," Nico smiled gently. "But David [Geffen] knew that he was really tomorrow's."

Flying directly home from the Syracuse show, Browne was back at the Troubadour on March 30, opening a week of shows by hippie sweetheart Melanie Safka. But another summer of inactivity loomed until finally, with contracts signed and arrangements made, and with Geffen having already sunk an estimated $100,000 into preparing Browne for stardom, the young man was sent into the studio to begin recording in September 1971. It had taken him four years of promises, hopes, and expectations, but Jackson Browne was finally about to cut his first record.

He wrapped up his debut album with a minimum of stress and a minimum of fighting. But there was one ferocious dispute with Geffen when, with an eye clearly on the checkbook, the label chief demanded that Browne call Carole King in to duet with him on one song or another.

Browne refused. He didn't know King, he'd never met King, and, while he appreciated the success that *Tapestry* had torn through, he really didn't think that having a big hit record was any good reason to invite a total stranger to sing on a record he'd been waiting his entire adult life to record. According to various watching sources, Browne and Geffen did not speak for several days after this, so furious was the disagreement.

He did, however, choose the cream of local talent to accompany him. James Taylor's rhythm section of Russell Kunkel and Leland Sklar would be the underpinning of the entire album, with pianist Craig Doerge also making an appearance. Albert Lee, in town with his own band Heads Hands and Feet, was recalled from the aborted Denny Cordell sessions to slash guitar through a couple of tracks. Jim Gordon, David Crosby, Leah Kunkel, Clarence White, David Jackson, Sneaky Pete, and Jesse Ed Davis all dropped by the studio. Afterwards, both Browne and Geffen could look back and wonder whether Carole King would even have made a difference.

Like Browne, Asylum's promotional department was slipping into gear weeks ahead of the album's completion, drafting the ad copy with which Geffen intended wallpapering the media once *Jackson Browne* was on the schedules: "If the name looks familiar, it should. It's a name you've read a lot on albums by . . . Tom Rush, the Byrds, Three Dog Night. . . . They've all recognized his songs because they were quick to recognize Jackson's great talent with words and music. Jackson Browne has finally recorded an album of his own. And it proves the time-tested adage, 'Nobody can sing a song like its composer.'"

In fact, Browne steered deliberately clear of what could be considered his best-known songs. The following year, he reflected upon his debut album having been constructed as "forty-five-minute experience, a little chrono-logical study from song one side one to the last track on side two."

But he purposefully eschewed recording "These Days," the song that his admirers argued was his greatest creation yet, and other expected songs were absent too. True, "Jamaica Say You Will" would have been familiar now from the Nitty Gritty Dirt Band's *All the Good Times* and the Byrds' *Byrd Maniax* releases of the previous year; while Johnny Rivers had already joined Linda Ronstadt in covering "Rock Me on the Water."

But you had to reach back to the 1968 Hedge and Donna album for another artist's vision of "From Silver Lake," and almost everything else on the record would have been unfamiliar to all but the most dedicated concert audiences.

Yet still *Jackson Browne* had an ace to play. "Doctor My Eyes," he told *Mojo* in 1997, had been around as a song for over a year. Now, with the LP complete, David Geffen asked Graham Nash if anything on the album struck him as a potential single. Nash did not even need to pick up the track listing. "Doctor My Eyes," he said.

Browne: "I was better known for long, rambling, introspective ballads, so it was quite ironic that it should be the hit. Jesse Ed Davis, who did the guitar solo, was a local guitar god in Los Angeles—guys would try to check his fingering, but he'd turn his back and dash off these impossible licks, looking over his shoulder like, 'Don't you wish you could do this?'

"Doctor My Eyes" would indeed become a hit, soaring into the Top 10 in May 1972, and then repeating the feat twelve months later in utterly unexpected hands. In February 1973, no less or more unlikely an entity than the Jackson Five scored a monster UK hit with "Doctor My Eyes," introducing their singing, songwriting namesake to a teenybop audience that, quite frankly, was left utterly baffled by the coincidence. The rest of the family had "Jackson" as their last name—what kind of peculiar American convention allowed the songwriter to have it as his first?

There was more! The Jackson clan's label, Motown, had recently signed a new performer, Browne's brother Severin. The pair weren't close; or, at least, they had not been. "Two different people who weren't together during the period when they did what they actually wanted to do for the first time," explained Jackson. "We were with different parents. We're good friends, though, and we're going to write a tune together and who knows what will happen?"

A name of a different kind was destined to confuse buyers of Jackson Browne's album. Officially, the LP was to be titled for its creator. But the sleeve design's replication of a canvas radiator cooling bag, including the "saturate before using" warning that appears on the real things, would quickly lead to the record being given an alternate title—one that its CD counterpart, some fifteen years later, would guilessly perpetuate.

Rolling Stone would have no time for confusion. Boxing Bud Scoppa's review away from the reviews of other releases on the page (new efforts by King Crimson, Gary Wright, and Asylum labelmate David Blue's *Stories*), the magazine proclaimed, "It's not often that a single album is sufficient to place a new performer among the first rank of recording artists," before going on to align *Jackson Browne* with, indeed, three of the most proficient LPs of recent memory—Neil Young's *After the Goldrush*, Van Morrison's *Astral Weeks*, and Rod Stewart's *Gasoline Alley*. Three albums, in other words, that allowed Browne and his reputation to spread their limbs throughout a musical world that paid only the vaguest obeisance to the conventions of the singer-songwriter genre.

In fact, Van Morrison was a name that was frequently being dropped by Browne's allies—mystifyingly, perhaps, for listeners who struggled haplessly to note any musical linkage between the two men, but gratifyingly for those who chose instead to search for more intellectual gifts. Indeed. *Phonograph Record's* Jeff Walker's "only criticism" of the album was: "On first hearing this record, watch yourself; you're likely to shrug it off as pseudo–Van Morrison or Elton John." But stop, he cautioned; "listen closer. Pretend that Jackson is an old friend and slowly he will emerge. Oddly enough, he probably influenced these artists more than they he, and what similarities there are, are mostly in presentation, not content."

For Browne himself, *Jackson Browne* simply reiterated the kind of set he might have performed at any club over the past couple of years, alone with his guitar, while the audience stood in half-respectful semisilence listening to the lyrics. But *Jackson Browne* so solidly distanced itself from any school of confessional writing that, even when the lyrics did turn to introspection, Browne delivered them for the everyman. Not simply for himself.

"Not so long ago," agreed *Washington Post* writer Alex Ward, "I was convinced that hearing just one more folkie-turned-soft-rocker would drive me right around the bend." *Jackson Browne* made it "a downright pleasure to swallow that assumption."

Had Jackson Browne had his own way, all of these kind words and more might have been stacking up like Christmas cards at the end of 1971. He even had a clutch of live shows lined up on the East Coast, half intended to help him break out of the routine of the studio by playing for an audience, but halfheartedly envisioned as advance promotion for the LP.

In Bryn Mawr, Pennsylvania, he opened a three-night stand with Bonnie Raitt at the Main Point, and dropped by nearby Philadelphia's WMMR to perform a quartet of songs for DJ Gene Shay. In Milwaukee, Wisconsin, on November 22, he was an unlikely ant on the stage of the Performing Arts Center, as Yes and the Beach Boys fought out their own peculiarly mismatched doubleheader. And back in Los Angeles, he imagined the pressing plants spitting copies of *Jackson Browne* out into their jackets, ready to deluge the record stores of the world.

He had set his heart on a December release date, had pushed the sessions as hard as he could to ensure that would be possible, only for sundry less impetuous business heads to suggest (which of course translated as "insist") he hold back a few weeks more, to miss the march of the musical giants who also regarded the holiday season as a prime time for new releases.

Sly and the Family Stone, Chicago, Three Dog Night, Santana, and Humble Pie all had new albums scheduled for the last weeks of the year. So did Van Morrison. And so did Cat Stevens, one of the artists with whom Geffen was adamant that Browne should never be compared, because he would be far too busy supplanting him.

16

Under the Falling Sky

I t turned out that [Cat Stevens] had an impeccable sense of timing," wrote journalist Bud Scoppa in May 1971. "At the time, everybody was too busy with Elton John and James Taylor to pay another new one any attention (at the time, I couldn't even talk my good friend the editor into letting me review *Tea for the Tillerman*, Cat's then brand-new album). Two months later, as the populace wearied of all that hyper-aggressive promotion, what should quietly float into the choked atmosphere but '. . . ooh, baby, baby, it's a wild world, and it's hard to get by just upon a smile,' words and melody so beautifully unprepossessing that hardly anyone could resist it."

"Honestly, I didn't expect things to happen in the States like they did," the object of Scoppa's devotion told *Hit Parader* in 1972. "But when I got there everything just felt right."

He was angry, he would admit, that *Mona Bone Jakon* didn't get off the ground either at home or in the U.S. (although it was a big hit in France), but he allowed his disappointment to fuel his dedication. "I was really upset about that, so when I went over I was really determined to make it on my first trip. I wasn't into like doing three trips and like they say earn money gradually. I earned money on the first tour. Even though it was only $250, it was enough to come out and say, 'I've done it.' You don't have to do loads of tours and like you don't have to go through all that hassle. Not if you really mean what you say."

While Chris Blackwell told all and sundry that *Tea for the Tillerman* was the best album Island had ever released, ears began to prick up. "America was like a sleeping beauty for me," Stevens continued. "I never thought it would ever get to this point. I've always wanted to get into America because so much influence has come from there and it's always a great challenge to make it in America. I thought I'd get to the same stage as perhaps I am in England but things have really gone so much wider than that because there's no pre-conception about who Cat Stevens is. They're really taking it on music value and whatever comes out on record."

It was not, after all, the concerts and the radio that pushed Stevens into the local consciousness. "They got onto the lyrics very strongly," Stevens pointed out, and he admitted that that might well have been his greatest point of pride. After all, he said, "they have James Taylor [who] is similar, except that I still get the feeling he's very insulated within himself, he hasn't opened up *that* much."

Stevens, on the other hand, "had no reason to hold back, no inhibitions on the record, and I think they see that and I think they like the hot and cold of it, too, the change of level."

James Taylor might not have had a competitive bone in his body. But he would still have sensed Stevens coming up on the inside, a new singer-songwriter (though he loathed that phrase as well), a new oddly introspective one-man band; and there was that personal connection too, through Peter Asher's Marylebone Productions.

Taylor was not strictly at the Troubadour to pet the Cat, however. Russ Kunkel, his drummer for the previous year, was taking advantage of the break in the tour schedule to appear alongside the evening's opening act, a young female singer named Carly Simon. She had specifically asked for his presence; almost made her performance contingent upon his availability, and Taylor wanted to cheer his old friend along.

The daughter of the president of the Simon and Schuster publishing company, Carly Simon had just seen her debut album released by Elektra. A familiar face on the coffeehouse circuit in early 1960s Massachusetts, where she performed with her sibling, Lucy, as the Simon Sisters, she had already scored a minor hit (the Sisters' "Winkin', Blinkin' and Nod" reached #73 in 1964) by the time she gravitated to the Greenwich Village solo rounds. There she was just another, admittedly distinctive, face in the crowd, until the evening one of her friends threw a party and arranged for a very special guest to attend.

Jerry Brandt, destined to become one of the lions of seventies rock management, was now best known as the proprietor of the Electric Circus, the venue that picked up Andy Warhol's old lease on the Dom. Before that, he was the Rolling Stones' go-to guy at the William Morris Agency (home, too, to the young David Geffen). He had just quit the club when, he explained, "I was invited to this party by a boy named Jacob Brachman. He was a song-writer with Carly, and it was all a setup, although I didn't know it.

"I heard this girl singing. I was playing pool and I heard this singing—I thought it was the radio, actually, because he had no furniture so it was great acoustics, so I said, 'What station is this?' And he said, 'It's Carly Simon, she's sitting on the floor behind you.' So I said, 'Come by my house tomorrow and do it again,' and that's how it started. The next day at my place she still sounded good, but a little flatter, because I had carpeting."

Carpeting or not, Brandt wasted no time. Tapes of Simon's songs had already circulated around the New York music industry, but they tended to rest unplayed, just one more unsolicited delivery from an unknown name. Brandt, however, had his foot in several doors and one of the first ones he pushed open was Jac Holzman's. Now her first album, *Carly Simon*, was fresh on the shelves; her first single, "That's the Way I've Always Heard It Should Be" (cowritten with Brachman) was knocking on the door, and she was also what the press would call Cat Stevens's girlfriend, although their relationship was scarcely any older than the tour that Stevens was undertaking.

In fact, brand-new in her repertoire was a song called "These Are the Good Old Days," written about her first date with Stevens, how he kept her waiting long after the appointed time, and she responded by grab-bing her guitar and writing a song on the spot. ("These Are the Good Old Days" would soon be renamed "Anticipation," and became the title track to Simon's second LP, recorded in London with Stevens at the sessions, and Paul Samwell-Smith producing.)

Her meeting with James Taylor at the Troubadour, on the other hand, was filed away more as a chance encounter with a ghost from her past. She too had grown up around Martha's Vineyard, gigging with her sister around the same circuit Taylor and Kootch used to play, and always making a point to catch their performances when she could. But she never plucked up the courage to do more than admire them from afar, which, it transpired, was the same thing that Taylor had been doing.

Taylor recalled, "She was professional at that point and I wasn't, so we never sang on the same show. I thought she was quite attractive, but she was, and still is, four years older than I was, so back then when she was eighteen and I was fourteen, she was a bit less approachable then she was when I was twenty-four. . . ."

More recently, Taylor told *Rolling Stone*, "we passed once in the parking lot of my house. Out in front of my mother's house were [Carly's brother] Peter Simon and Carly, going to talk to my brother Livingston about a job that she and Livingston were going to do together. I passed Peter and Carly and said, 'Hi,' and Peter said, 'Hi, this is my sister Carly,' and then I left. I guess I had one album out by then."

Simon's set was short, just half a dozen songs plus an encore of "That's the Way," and fraught with difficulty. Alone at her piano, she spent the set battling with a microphone that kept slipping out of position. But the audience had already been won over as they arrived at their tables to find each one decorated with a rose, and a note that read, "With love from Carly and Elektra."

Tonight, Simon and Taylor swapped telephone numbers, arranged to see each other again soon, and then got back to their own careers. Simon and Stevens would continue touring until June washed them up at Carnegie Hall; while for Taylor, the release of *Mud Slide Slim and the Blue Horizon* was imminent, and he was already bracing himself for the inevitable media backlash. He knew that the new record had been a struggle to complete; knew that every word in every song was going to be pored over and psychoanalyzed by literally millions of listeners worldwide, and that the full-page review that *Rolling Stone* accorded the LP was only the tip of the critical iceberg that this generally unassuming gaggle of songs would have to scale.

In the event, the faithful old *Stone* remained faithful. True, reviewer Ben Gerson admitted that "the first few times . . . it is dull listening," but then, he acknowledged, its "subtle tensions begin to appear." The album did offer "pleasant, absorbing listening," he celebrated. But still, "there is a terrible weariness to it which is part of its artistic statement"—and which, of course, was precisely what Taylor's audience demanded.

On May 8, 1971, *Mud Slide Slim* entered the *Billboard* chart at #22, the highest new entry on a listing that was dominated by such soundtracks as *Woodstock* and the chart-topping *Jesus Christ Superstar*, by TV fodder like the Partridge Family and the Jackson Five; by Black Sabbath, Grand Funk, and Emerson, Lake and Palmer; and, nestling a few places above, Elton John's *Tumbleweed Connection* (#16) and Cat Stevens's *Tea for the Tillerman* (#9).

Mud Slide Slim would eventually rise to #2, but, as so many other artists found that year, there was no passing Carole King's *Tapestry*, which hit #1 on June 19 (the same day as "It's Too Late" topped the singles listings) and remained there for the next fifteen weeks, the longest uninterrupted span at the top since the Beatles' *Sgt. Pepper* four years earlier.

There was no rivalry, though. The day before that impressive streak began, June 18, Taylor was alongside King when she played her solo head-lining show at Carnegie Hall, stepping out late in the set to accompany her first through a sweet rendition of "You've Got a Friend," and then through a trilogy of King's own greatest compositions, "Will You Love Me Tomorrow," "Some Kind of Wonderful," and "Up On the Roof."

And Cat Stevens remained unimpressed.

"I think music at the moment is going through a mediocre stage," he told *Sounds* that September. "I don't mean mediocre in the bad sense of the word, but simply that it is no longer confusing. It's now the complete expression of an artist that is becoming the medium, a period where Carole King emerges because she's beautiful but very plain and simple lyrically, where James Taylor becomes huge even though his voice isn't anything ultra-extraordinary, where Joni Mitchell and all these people can simply express themselves. So that instead of the music holding them up, *they* hold the music up."

Of course, he could have been accused of doing the precise same thing himself, but that was somehow excusable. "It's exactly the way I feel comfort-able," he said, and the insinuation that those other sensitive souls were doing things for less-than-pure motives was not hard to avoid. "It's the only way I can do it at the moment. I mean, there was a stage when I'd have loved to play sixty-four semi-demi quavers in one bar on a guitar. At the time when the main feat was to be as fast, slick, and technical as possible. But now I've found I can create the same feeling in a song on one chord."

He admitted, of course, that the breakthrough of King and Taylor had helped his own career along. "Because now you don't have to connive, you don't have to be a fantastic brain to be able to communicate." He told *Sounds* in May 1971, "You don't have to be clever in that respect. Whereas my great-est hang-up I think—and a lot of people's hang-ups—were that they always had this fear of intellectualism. A terrible fear that 'I can't really talk about that because I don't know too much about it.' So what we're doing now is we're getting back to the point where we accept we don't know that much about it, but what do you have to know? All you really have to know is about yourself. Know yourself and you can know other people too, then you can know about your environment and what you are and who you are."

Besides, Cat Stevens could sing a great song when he wanted to, even when the studio lights were out. On the one hand, he could wax poetic about his status in the firmament that was the singer-songwriter boom, confident in his audience's ability to hang on his every word as though it were a new heavenly Commandment; proud of his ability to express the softest sentiment and see it transformed into a mantra for the masses.

And on the other, he raged against the invasiveness of audiences who, because they identified with a few of his songs, felt that somehow they knew the songwriter. "One thing, Americans try to make too much of my songs. They're lust songs. I don't know why I write them. But they try and find all kinds of hidden meanings in my songs," when he almost teasingly pointed out that his own meanings were bizarre enough. "Longer Boats" (which was actually one of the lesser songs on *Tea for the Tillerman*) was written about the night he was lying in bed, gazing out of the window, when suddenly a flying saucer "[shot] across the sky and stop[ped] over me. And it sucked me up into it. When it put me down, I shot up in bed. I knew it wasn't a dream, It didn't feel like a dream. It was real, I know it was real."

Yet even as he railed against the cult of contemplation that autopsied his art with scalpel-sharp precision, he was not about to change. Work on Stevens's third Island album (and fifth overall), *Teaser and the Firecat*, was now under way, and it was as relaxed as its contents were, at least in hindsight, archetypal.

Once again, Paul Samwell-Smith took charge of the proceedings, and many of the musicians who appeared on the two earlier albums returned. But their approach to the business of getting the songs down on tape would alter, just as Stevens's approach to songwriting had shifted.

Mona Bone Jakon and *Tea for the Tillerman*, Stevens explained, were inward-looking. For *Teaser and the Firecat*, however, he reversed the polarity. "Now I'm thinking outward. . . . I feel like I want to help more, simply because people are helping me. I want to help others by my own experiences. I don't want to lay any heavy idea on anyone. No matter how much good advice I get, I still have to go through it myself.

"For me there are no shortcuts."

It was not easy. In the past, Stevens told *Hit Parader* in late 1971, the moment he had a song completed, "you want to put in drums. You want to put in bass. You think 'How am I going to . . .?'"

That didn't work anymore. "At least not for me. I like to be surprised. It has to fit perfectly. Not just drums, rhythm. It has to be much more than that. That's why sometimes I break in to the middle, completely, suddenly. You've got people. The moment it stops, it begins. It's like you don't have to play so loud. In fact, the quieter you play, the more people will listen."

Amidst this new musical discipline, there was room for a handful of new faces; string arranger Del Newman, bouzouki maestros Andreas Toumazis and Angelos Hatzipavli, and (though he would not be credited on the original LP) pianist Rick Wakeman, a member of the folk band the Strawbs.

Wakeman was introduced to the proceedings by Stevens's road manager, after he overheard Cat complaining about his own piano playing one day. Still several months from his emergence as the extravagant wizard who would soundtrack many of the prog band Yes's finest moments, Wakeman was nevertheless a modestly in-demand pianist at the time, who happily added organ and harmonium to the tapes as well.

But Stevens sought more esoteric instrumentation, too. "Obviously if you want a certain sound you have an idea in your head like the bouzouki. I couldn't play it that well so I found someone who was really good. In fact, the guy I picked . . . we never found out till afterwards . . . but my half brother used to play bouzouki about ten, fifteen years ago, and this was the guy who went around with him playing violin. It was a really strange coincidence. He's really good and he's going to play me a few songs, and if he's got enough good songs, I'm going to do an album with him."

Still, *Teaser and the Firecat* took shape, a generally louder and rockier record than its predecessors, which culminated in what would become Stevens's most commented-upon statement yet, the rousingly anthemic "Peace Train."

It was, he said, one of the hardest songs he had ever tried to record. Three separate attempts were made to drag the song into life, but it was not until producer Samwell-Smith suggested that the musicians abandon their tried and trusted method of playing the song "live," and piece it together instrument by instrument, that it came together and, "by some freak," said Stevens, "we got a live feel to it. It shouldn't have happened but somehow it did."

The flip side of that particular coin was the sweetly contemplative "Moon Shadow," an almost cripplingly simplistic but deliciously ironic song that looked back to Tim Hardin's "If I Had a Hammer" or "El Condor Pasa" (an old adaptation of a Peruvian folk song that Simon and Garfunkel included on their final album) to list all the things Stevens wouldn't have to do anymore if he lost his arms, legs, brain, and so on.

As a reflection of the dissection that his music routinely received, it was a remarkable piece of satire with which to introduce a new LP to the public. But it proved a fine follow-up to "Wild World" in America in June, and it finally reintroduced him to the British chart as well. "Moon Shadow" reached #22 in Britain that fall, more than a year after "Lady D'Arbanville" made the Top 10.

Yet the album's peak was neither of these, nor was it one of the album's other thoughtful glimpses inside the Stevens mind. Rather, that honor was reserved for a beautiful rendering of Welsh writer Eleanor Fareon's "Morning Has Broken," a Victorian-era hymn that writer Colin Irwin later described as being "stripped of its pomposity but not its dignity."

The song's inclusion on the album was a surprise, not least of all to Stevens. Not since "Portobello Road" saw him amend what was essentially a Kim Fowley composition had he attempted to write around somebody else's lyric, and he acknowledged, "I don't think I can. I tried that once and I think I can only write for myself basically. I'm very strange about that because, ever since I played guitar, I've never sung anybody else's songs." Back when he was first starting out, he said, he had tried. "But it never worked out because I didn't do it so well, so I thought, 'To hell with it, I'll write my own.' So I've never really sung anybody else's."

But browsing in a bookstore one day, he suddenly felt an inexplicable urge to walk upstairs to the religious section, where he came across a hymnal "and started to read the words. It took me about forty-five minutes to really understand them. Then it was all getting very heavy, so I left and learned the melody later, because I can't pick up a melody from looking at printed music."

Sadly, he never elaborated on precisely what it was about his chance discovery of this simplistic children's hymn that engendered that feeling of heaviness. But this "old Welsh melody" captivated him. "It's just beautiful. I just fell in love with the melody." If "Morning Has Broken" was to be regarded as his first cover version, it was one of which he could be immensely proud.

Teaser and the Firecat was a cosmopolitan album. "Moon Shadow," he explained, and "The Boy with the Moon and Star on his Head" were both written in Spain. "And I went to Sicily. I just thought I'd go to Sicily, and stayed in a place with dead dogs on the beach and flies in the room. I wasn't going to make friends with anyone, but I ended up making fantastic friends with people. A lady who had this love affair going with Mount Etna. I'm writing a song about her."

Elsewhere, too, he was in demand. He appeared on British television's *Old Grey Whistle Test* on October 5, while an appearance on the soundtrack to the movie *Deep End* reminded him of his own ambitions to step into the realm of moviemaking, as he told *Creem*.

"I'd . . . like to do a film of my own because it's hard to write for someone else. It's a strange thing, either you do the whole film yourself or you can't really have that much control over it—the vision's already there. But I just love the idea of visual and music because it brings a spark to it. You can have the most diabolically boring piece of film and the same kind of music and when you put them together you get something else—friction and a kind of movement, show and time and everything. It suddenly gives it more of a whole, you know, a roundness. Whereas just music on its own or just visual on its own doesn't work. It fits together so perfectly."

He had learned from past mistakes, however, from those nights when he would thrill passing journalists with the details of his latest musical notion, or projected protégé. "I've got ideas for my own film, but I'm going to think it over first before I say anything 'cause I'll most likely change my mind. That's one thing I must admit I do do. I change my mind an awful lot. I can be inspired about something and then I look really into it and I say, 'Well, no, that's wrong,' and I'll change my mind on that. . . .'"

Besides, he already had his hands full writing a score for another upcoming movie. And, of course, promoting an album that had advance orders of over half a million in the United States alone. A recent poll of America's top radio programmers, conducted by *Billboard* magazine, had established Stevens firmly in the upper echelons of their favorite performers (Stevens ranked sixth; James Taylor and Carole King tied for third). Now he was preparing for his third U.S. tour in less than a year, going out with the duo of Mimi Farina and singer Tom Jans as support, and when it did get under way, *Circus* magazine was swift to remind readers again just how impossibly intimate a Cat Stevens performance could be.

"Stevens always arrives hours ahead of time to rehearse. Since he is not the world's greatest guitarist, he takes great pains to be as good as he can possibly be. In his dressing room, he is surrounded by the people who make the tour click. Manager, booking agents, second guitarist Alun Davies, and bass guitarist Larry Steele. The concert was due to go on at eight, but when eight o'clock arrived, about twenty or thirty people were scattered through the first few rows listening to a private concert, while outside 3,000 waited in the cold wondering what the hell was going on. The few people who were inside watched with mixed feelings. The concert was being held up due to a faulty P.A. system. There was a sadness throughout the crowd because the quality was so poor. But there was joy too, because the worst sound system cannot kill a Cat Stevens performance."

Billboard, too, drooled. The Greek Theater in Los Angeles had recently hatched the idea of winter matinee shows, outdoor "picnic-in-the-park"-type events at which "the bearded, head-bobbing Stevens" and his "gently rhythmic repertoire" were the ideal guest.

It was that intimacy and immediacy that Stevens wanted to capture as he talked of his next album being a live set; a notion, he then shrugged, that was crushed when he discovered that one of the highest-selling bootleg albums of the age was an illicit recording of one of his own shows, the Trademark of Quality label's *Father and Son* recounting of a recent FM radio broadcast. Even his plan of including some otherwise unheard songs on the set (the newly written "Lord of the Trees" had recently entered his repertoire) could not overcome that disappointment for him.

His awareness of the importance of live performance had certainly sharpened. He told *Hit Parader*, "The secret is to keep away, well away, from the larger venues, because in these places it is so very easy to lose contact with your audience. I insist on playing halls that hold no more than five thousand people. Frankly, I'd rather do two shows a night in a smaller hall than one a night in a larger venue.

"Records are private things, personal things, and it doesn't always mean the same thing to everyone who is listening, yet it has to be heard. You see, in America a large proportion of the audience comes for the event instead of the artist. Elton John got caught up in this trap and he didn't know it at the time. I guess that's what festivals were really all about. It didn't matter who was on; it was a nice summer and you'd go along to dig it because you knew other people would be there."

Yet he could not completely avoid the larger venues and, on December 12, 1971, Stevens played the very same venue he used to pass every day on his way to and from school, the Theatre Royal in Drury Lane.

The event was a charitable affair, all proceeds to the drug rehab agency CURE, and the watching press themselves were feeling more than generous as Stevens took the stage. "The concert began in a most enthralling way," joked *Sunday Times* critic Philip Norman. "On time. Stevens hitched his guitar across his knees, and with the hollow bump it made the audience wanted, almost physically, his every word. He spoke little, except to say what he would sing: the audience, at such a phenomenon, gasped. He declined to give an encore and they, though renewing the demand out of politeness, seemed to acknowledge he was right. Pop is either starvation or surfeit. Only rarely is it satisfactory."

Stevens, the venerable Norman was saying, was satisfactory. More than satisfactory.

17

The Blues Is Just
a Bad Dream

Journalist Lester Bangs was writing about punk rock years before the rest of the world even knew what it might be, and long after it had all but forgotten. His first published article was a review of the MC5, one of the hottest of the rhetoric-heavy rockers that emerged from Detroit in the late 1960s, and his last, prior to his death in April 1982, lauded Oi!, an antisocial skinhead noise that rose from the streets of working-class England in the early years of the 1980s.

In between times, he praised the Sex Pistols, canonized Iggy Pop, and worshipped the Velvet Underground and several million other words, all hell-bent in the pursuit of rock 'n' roll excellence.

He believed in rock 'n' roll music as the ultimate cultural artifact, our one shot at scoring everlasting youth. We listen, he suggested, not to stay young, but to stay feeling young. Pete Townshend once said all anybody really needs is a record that does for them what their first few records did. They want that first fuck, and that was what kept Bangs going for as long as he did. He knew he would never get it again, but he kept on looking all the same.

Fellow writer Greil Marcus reckons it was Bangs who christened punk "punk" in the first place, and Bangs claimed his hermit crab Spud used to dance to old Lou Reed LPs. So, ten years after Bangs's final, fatal drug overdose, the world of rock 'n' roll journalism held a memorial read-in.

"It was disappointing," mourned Richard Hell, one of the evening's performers, and a man whose ass Bangs once publicly threatened to kick.

"I thought it was going to be people talking about Lester. Instead, they just got up and read passages from his book."

What did you do?

"I read the index."

Hell brandished a two-inch-thick hardback. It was called *Psychotic Reactions and Carburetor Dung* and, inasmuch as it was a collection of Bangs's best (and best-remembered) essays and reviews, it is probably the most acerbic and dedicated rock book anyone has ever published. It has the hippest index, too. The Clash receive more mentions than the Beatles, the Fugs appear more often than John Fogerty, and the only time you hear of James Taylor is when Bangs is plotting to kill him. "I hate to come on like a Nazi, but . . ."

The occasion, if such sentiments actually demanded an occasion, was the random happenstance of Bangs waking up one morning in late 1971 and wanting to write about the Troggs, the band from Andover, UK, who might have ground their way around the pubs of sixties England forever had they not had a remarkable piece of luck: the chance to be the first band in the world to record Chip Taylor's "Wild Thing." The same Chip Taylor who would then discover James Taylor.

Strangely, Bangs did not make that connection. He *did* delve into his personal and musical biography; he *did* deviate around a dozen different other topics; and, in tandem with fellow scribe Richard Meltzer (the same Richard Meltzer who had already discovered Jackson Browne), he transformed the December 1971 issue of *Who Put the Bomp* magazine into a two-man eulogy to the Troggs. Meltzer's article was called, simply, "Richard Meltzer on the Troggs." Bangs, with an eloquence and passion that even his most dedicated acolytes admit is a sometimes-acquired taste, called his "James Taylor Marked for Death."

Who Put the Bomp was not a major magazine. Indeed, in the scheme of the American music media, it was scarcely even a small one; a few dozen rudely typed and illustrated pages Xeroxed and then stapled together in the spirit of fanzines all over the world. It certainly wasn't available in the same way as the *Esquire* article that first served notice, six long years before, that rock 'n' roll could be taken in so many fresh directions that poetic vocabularies and a studied lack of volume were no longer cardinal sins; and it certainly didn't reach as many homes as the genuine giants of the printed music scene.

What marked it out was the quality of the writers that editor/publisher Greg Shaw attracted (Bangs, Meltzer, and another contributor to that issue, Lenny Kaye, were all regular *Rolling Stone* correspondents), and the passion for music that Shaw demanded they evince. With a print run that rarely exceeded a couple of hundred, not many people could have read each issue. But those who did paid attention, both to the words and writers that filled each issue, and to the pronouncements therein—even when those fantasies entailed disemboweling the crown prince of I-Rock (a phrase Bangs had just invented, he said, for any music that was "so involutedly egocentric that you . . . just want to take the poor bastard out and get him a drink, and then kick his ass, preferably off a high cliff . . .").

"It amused me because James Taylor would make mincemeat out of Lester Bangs in about three seconds," Kootch reflected in 2010. "People decide who's successful. Not Lester Bangs and not any other critic. At that time, critics had a lot more clout than they have now. Nobody remembers Lester Bangs, but they all remember James Taylor."

Yet (and only in hindsight is it possible to make this observation; it was not remarked upon at the time, nor would it become apparent for a year or so more) something did change at the end of 1971, as James Taylor retreated to Martha's Vineyard, to dread the demands of his *next* LP; as Cat Stevens basked in the success of *Teaser and the Firecat*, and wondered what he, too, could possibly do next; and as Jackson Browne nervously contemplated his promised role within the music industry following the imminent musical sea change his manager was predicting.

Something happened and something changed. Because the records that all three would produce during the next twelve months (and across the years and decades that have passed since then) would be those of artists who had each outgrown the expectations of their early-1970s followings, and were now truly reaching out to touch a destiny of their own.

Browne started slowly. Almost unwillingly following in the footsteps of the hit single, *Jackson Browne* choked at #58 on the *Billboard* chart, an uncertain performance that only appeared more diffident when matched against the promotion that the record received. The slavering devotion of the media was only the start; at Seattle's Paramount Theater on February 16, 1972, Browne took his bow as the opening act for Joni Mitchell's latest tour: a month of shows across the U.S. and Canada in February/March, followed by a return to the Europe in May for half a dozen shows around the UK, West Germany, the Netherlands, and France.

He appeared on the UK's top rock show, *Old Grey Whistle Test*, and recorded a spectacular solo concert performance for BBC TV's *In Concert*. But the London concert was a disaster. In the thirty or so minutes that he spent onstage, a malfunctioning microphone ensured he battled his way through no more than four heavily interrupted songs before finally conceding defeat; yet Mitchell, by all accounts, played one of the greatest shows of her career, circumventing the stage setup to play through the house system.

In June, Browne and Mitchell were in Hawaii; in July, they hit the Mariposa Folk Festival in Toronto, Ontario, behind homecoming king Neil Young, another artist who, as Browne thoughtfully mused, employed the events that shaped his own life as a means of communicating with others, but who did so—and this was the key to the entire debate and divide that was shaping the singer-songwriter "movement"—without paying lip service to the "overwhelming universality" that the less imaginative record labels seemed to think was the key to success.

It was originality that marked out an artist, Browne (like Taylor and Stevens, Mitchell and Young) believed, the need to keep pushing forward, regardless of the barriers that their audience's expectations erected. It didn't matter whether or not commercial success came knocking immediately; better for an artist to act out his own feelings and beliefs than to simply play blind, bland follow-the-leader.

Browne and Mitchell were lovers by now. Their tempestuous affair lasted little longer than the time they spent together on the road and, according to David Geffen biographer Tom King, "had an ugly ending"—from Mitchell's point of view, anyway.

It was Browne who ended the affair. He had met a new lover, Phyllis Major, falling for her one night at the Troubadour when quite by chance he tried to break up a fight between a woman and an unemployed actor. In fact, he failed, as he was felled by the actor, but Major thanked Browne for at least trying to stand up for her and, slowly, they grew to know one another.

She was born in California but grew up in Europe—following her parents' divorce, Phyllis and her mother lived on the Greek island of Hydra; she worked as a governess in Switzerland and a model in Paris. She had dated Keith Richards in France and Bobby Neuwirth in New York, and she cowrote a couple of songs with Al Kooper for the ex-Dylan organist's *New York City (You're a Woman)* LP. Now she was in Los Angeles and was an immediate muse to Browne. "Ready or Not," a song that would be gracing his gestating second album, was written for Major, around the same time as his career took another upward turn: He headed out on his next tour, this time with that newly formed Los Angeles aggregation, Eagles.

Swiftly graduating from being, simply, Linda Ronstadt's band (the core quartet of Frey, Leadon, Henley, and Meisner had accompanied her through the recording of her third, eponymous, solo album), Eagles were quick to cut their own first LP. *Eagles* was now out, earning reviews at least as ravenous as those that awaited Browne's, and aiding Browne's own star with the inclusion of "Take It Easy," a song he'd been tinkering with during his own first album sessions, and had even previewed on the Gene Shay WFFM radio broadcast back in November 1971.

Eagle Frey had been at the studio one day and could never understand why Browne so cavalierly placed the unfinished number to one side. So he called him up and asked if he could have a go at finishing the song. Browne gave his blessings and Frey completed the song in time for his own album sessions and Eagles' first hit single.

On the road, Browne was joined by fiddler David Lindley, that passing acquaintance from his Troubadour debut, but the nightly highs of the live show were counterbalanced by the darker shadows that were looming around Browne's much-anticipated second album—namely, the fact that he didn't have one.

Loath to dig back into his past for another round of songs, Browne set himself the task of creating a whole new LP's worth of music. Unfortunately, the speed with which his life was whirling around the release of *Jackson Browne*, the suggestions that he ought to write another radio-friendly "Doctor My Eyes"–type song, and the ups and downs of his personal life were all distractions he could never have imagined as he'd stockpiled songs in the past.

The record that finally emerged in October 1973 as *For Everyman* took him nine months to complete, as he fought with each song, intent upon perfecting it and then, once he had done so, perfecting it again. Songs deemed complete one day were adjudged in need of a new verse or a new guitar part the next. It wasn't quite a never-ending process because, at some point, the record needed to be complete. But while he had the freedom to tinker and toy, Browne took full advantage of it.

The result was a record that sounded exquisite, and readily confirmed all the promise of its predecessor. Yet life was not all strife and struggle. Phyllis became pregnant and they moved into Browne's grandfather's Abbey San Encino home to raise son Evan Browne. "I've always known I would live there someday," Browne reflected. "I have a real appreciation for the bare walls and plants . . . and now I'm going to be a father there, in the house where I was a child."

He cowrote a couple of songs for the next Eagles album, the western epic "Doolin' Dalton" and the fifties throwback "James Dean" (ultimately held over for the band's third LP), and that summer, he went out on tour with "Horse with No Name" hitmakers America—an August-long outing that was originally booked when he thought he'd have the new record completed in time for an early-fall release.

That date had long since been pushed back when the first show came around, one more consequence of the inordinate amount of time (by contemporary standards) he had taken on the album. But again, he knew he had been right to prevaricate—if that's what he was doing.

His principal problem was one that both James Taylor and Cat Stevens would recognize, and which both would swiftly be attempting to resolve in their own fashion: the perceived need to continue writing songs that were, in the parlance of the time, "heavy." No matter that Browne himself had long ceased to consider his songs in that light; his audience did, and they responded accordingly. And now he found himself trying to force out more of the same. "That's a bad connection," he admitted to Cameron Crowe. "I'm taking someone else's word for them. That's what fame does. It's a crusher."

Slowly, however, *For Everyman* came together. He included "Take It Easy," following Eagles' own blueprint for a song that was effectively his; and he finally tackled "These Days" too, but only after hearing what his old friend Gregg Allman did to it, when he included a version on his debut album, *Laid Back*. For five years, Browne had heard the song in the manner that he wrote it and the style that Nico (among so many others) had preserved it. Allman turned it around, abandoning the wistful, folky strum for a slow stroll and an impassioned vocal, reimagining a song that had once seemed set in stone. Gratefully, Browne reclaimed the greatest song of his youth and pointed it forward into his future.

He didn't disagree, either, when people assumed another song on the album, "Redneck Friend," was about his friendship with Allman. In fact, the song was about his penis, a theme that slotted nicely into "The Times You've Come," an almost juvenile ode to orgasm.

"Ready or Not" was his love song for Phyllis; "For Everyman" was originally written for David Crosby, who didn't record it himself but added harmonies to Browne's recording and then told *Rolling Stone*, "[Browne] stopped me cold in my tracks. He nailed a certain thing in me, that escapist thing, and he called on something . . . that I really believe in. . . . Human possibility."

A quarter century later, *Rolling Stone*'s Anthony DeCurtis took another look at the song. "The title track of Jackson Browne's second album, *For Everyman*, was a response to the escapist vision of Crosby, Stills and Nash's 'Wooden Ships.' As violence, fear, and paranoia overtook sixties utopianism, 'Wooden Ships'(written by Crosby and Stills, along with Paul Kantner of the Jefferson Airplane) imagined a kind of hipster exodus by sea from a straight world teetering on the edge of apocalypse.

"'We are leaving. / You don't need us,' the song declared.

"Browne wasn't giving up so easily."

As Jackson Browne carved that new face into the consciousness of the early 1970s, Cat Stevens seemed to have forgotten the very existence of his former self. Leaving his reputation in the confident hands of *Teaser and the Firecat*, he returned to the Fillmore at the end of June 1972; then toured Australia and New Zealand through August and early September. Back to the U.S. at the end of that outing, it was no surprise when he admitted, that his upcoming new album, *Catch Bull at Four*, was already six months old by the time it was released. Yet still he was shocked to discover the American media regarding his return to their shores as something akin to the second coming. Australia? What's that?

"Twelve-month silence," insisted *Circus* magazine. "Cat Stevens may be acting like an embryonic Beethoven in private, but in public he has seemed much more like the Invisible Man. For the better part of a year, the Cat remained fastidiously out of the public eye, safely away from the press and fans alike. No performances, no records, no interviews, no nothing."

Ah, so that was what had changed. Taking a leaf from a new book of management techniques that his old Deram label mate David Bowie's manager, Tony Defries, had just opened, that of withdrawing the star from circulation to allow a little mystique to build up, Stevens's manager Barry Krost insisted that they had always intended to duck out of the spotlight for a time. But what he really meant was, Stevens had asked for time in which to shift his musical priorities, because *Catch Bull at Four* was to emerge as almost brutal in comparison to its predecessors.

It was harder, it was more produced, it was more experimental. Guitars faded beneath the weight of keyboards. Songs became less about "me" and more about "us," the universal "us" that had been addressed in "Peace Train," but while *Sounds* writer Penny Valentine, one of Stevens's most vociferous UK press supporters, was swift to comment on the album's more up-tempo approach, Stevens insisted that he saw it simply as the end of "a four-album period." It's probably more noticeable, she responded, that he was really trying to break away from a format that he'd found himself trapped in on the previous three. A puppet of his own design.

Stevens conceded the point and even pinpointed its genesis, a review of *Teaser and the Firecat* that suggested that, just maybe, all of his songs were beginning to sound alike. That only three of the album's ten songs really stood out.

Stevens was incensed. At first. But then he began to think about it. He still disagreed, still believed that the other seven songs had been sorely mistreated by the reviewer's opinion. (Because that's all it was, an opinion.) But he could also see how people might think that way; people who listened to the radio or records with only half an ear, who didn't have the time or the inclination to become as emotionally involved in a song as its writer. The people, in other words, whose disposable income made the difference between an artist having a minor hit and a major smash.

Had he grown predictable? Had his pen become set on autopilot? Was he becoming indistinguishable from every other literally or figuratively bearded bard who sat on a stool and strummed his guitar? And had his vibe become so relaxed that he was in very real danger of actually sliding off that chair?

It was time to tighten up. He looked around at the musicians who would be working with him on this latest project—guitarist Alun Davies, who had worked alongside him since *Mona Bone Jakon*; drummer Gerry Conway, who came in for *Teaser and the Firecat*; pianist Jean Roussel and bassist Alan James—then called in photographer Homer Sykes to take their pictures. It would be the first time any face other than Cat's had appeared on one of his record sleeves, because it was the first time he had ever gone into the studio with a *group*. In the past, they had just been his musicians.

It was crucial to bond, both with the songs and with one another. Other artists would have booked a rehearsal room in a disused cinema somewhere and spent a couple of weeks getting drunk between songs. Adding producer Samwell-Smith to the ticket, Stevens flew the entire party out to Portugal for two weeks, not to learn the songs so much as to learn what one another could bring to them. The benign dictatorship with which Stevens had once overseen the treatment of his songs was gone. The band had to play the songs; the band should have some say in what they played.

Four months of sessions continued the party atmosphere, as the team bounced from Morgan Studios in the center of London, to the Manor in rural Oxfordshire, and then the Château d'Hérouville in the Parisian countryside, the honky hangout of Elton John fame. And everywhere, Stevens kept on reinforcing the mantra that would, ultimately, make his most magnificent LP yet. They were all in this thing together.

And once it was all complete, he panicked. Listening back to the ten songs they'd competed, hearing the synthesized tribalism of "Angelsea," the hard-nosed electric rock of "Can't Keep It In," the burbling baby boogie of "Freezing Steel," the Iberian drama of "Ocaritas," he wondered for the first time what he had done, what he'd been thinking. "*Catch Bull* was very paranoid," he told *Sounds* the following year. "I mean 'Ruins,' that last track? It said it all."

In the past, recording his songs, he had always seen them as sketches and possibilities, upgraded versions of the demos that he had so much fun producing. Not since the bad old days of *Matthew and Son* and *New Masters* had he subjected his music to anything more than the fringes and embellishments that a simple acoustic guitar and voice could not manifest. *Catch Bull at Four* reversed that policy completely, painted the songs into musical corners from which he knew they would never be allowed to escape. "Can't Keep It In" would always be a rocker now; "Sweet Scarlet" would always be a piano ballad; "18th Avenue" would always be a dramatic urban epic.

But was that a bad thing? *Catch Bull at Four* was a child of spontaneity, the meetings of half a dozen minds in the studio, and a witheringly honest reflection of that collision. Who was he to deny those things? Who was he to try and hide them? If Stevens's core audience recoiled from it, then let them. Besides, the old cat was still there, curled up within his lyrics; the first verse of the album's first song, "Sitting," admitted that, with its defiant declaration of "sitting on my own, not by myself." He may have been surrounded by bandmates and buddies, but the writing was still a solitary pursuit.

He had no cause to worry. *Catch Bull at Four* became the first Cat Stevens album to top the America chart, bumping Curtis Mayfield's *Superfly* soundtrack out of the way in the process; but, perhaps, even more rewardingly, it came close to repeating the feat in Britain. *Catch Bull at Four* peaked at #2 in his homeland, "Can't Keep It In" rocked to #13, and when Stevens announced a full-scale world tour, the self-styled "most unquotable person" in the world told journalist Michelle O'Driscoll, "I'm really looking forward to the whole world tour. For a while now, I've been taking it easy. I've been recording my new album and helping Alun [Davies] with his; so it will be stimulating to get back on stage, performing."

The Alun Davies album was, in fact, especially dear to his heart. Recorded with both Gerry Conway from Stevens's current band, and Harvey Burns, drummer on the three albums that preceded it, *Daydo* comprised seven of Davies's own compositions, a couple of covers (Buddy Holly and the Mad Hatter—"I'm Late," from Disney's *Alice in Wonderland*), plus a Cat Stevens oldie that Davies had loved ever since the night in Los Angeles when Stevens strummed it loosely out at the audience without either warning or rehearsal, "Portobello Road." "I really liked the scuffling guitar accompaniment," Davies told *Sounds*. "I always liked the European rhythms he used right from the early days." The album's overall title, meanwhile, immortalized the nickname Davies had borne since his schooldays.

The Australian and Japanese dates in August were the shows that launched the world tour; the United States and the UK followed in the weeks leading up to Christmas. But Stevens was already looking ahead. Making *Catch Bull at Four*, he said, felt like a new beginning; the birth of a whole new phase in his career, and in the same way that *Mona Bone Jakon* exorcised the memory of the two discs that had preceded it, so this latest album placed a period at the end of the pair that followed that.

Writing the latest album had been a chore, he admitted, because it required him to completely reevaluate the way in which he had always made music (or always wanted to, at least). Now that the reevaluation was over, it was time for him to determine what he wanted to do with his discoveries, and although the road was probably not the best environment in which to indulge in too much meaningful thought, still a notion was germinating that he could never even have given credence to a year or so before.

"I'd like to come out with something now that's freer and more natural and I think I will," Stevens told writer Penny Valentine, and if he had telegraphed that intent across the ocean to James Taylor, he would have found a compatriot whose own thoughts had spent the past twelve months pursuing exactly those same liberated notions.

Mud Slide Slim and the Blue Horizon was still fresh on the record racks when Taylor retreated to Martha's Vineyard, abandoning the semi-nomadic life he had led in Los Angeles in order to build his own home just off Lambert's Cove Road. It was there, he decreed, that he would begin work on his next album, echoing former mentor Paul McCartney's homespun philosophy as he and Asher demoed material on a portable tape recorder, branching out into different environments—A&R Studios in New York with producer Phil Ramone, and Clover in Los Angeles with Robert Appere—as material came together.

The result would be a sparse, stark collection that Taylor, again surely in a fit of post-McCartneyism, titled *One Man Dog* in honor of his sheepdog David; McCartney, famously, recorded "Martha My Dear" in tribute to his own representative of that noble, hairy breed.

The gestating album and the gestating house were exquisite echoes of one another. Cardboard boxes stood in for tables, but they also doubled as drums. Rocking chairs dotted the attic, but they were great for rhythmic creaking as well. Taylor himself was running on sheer inspiration. One song, "Little David," saw him augment the conventional instrumentation of an acoustic guitar with a chain saw and various workshop tools left lying around by the builders. One of the workmen, Mike Paletier, even "played" the crosscut saw.

It sounds idyllic, but it was not. "Unfortunately," Kootch recalled, "there was still dope involved, and James at that point was always either on dope or trying to get off it, using methadone or some other inferior technique." The result, he said, was that *One Man Dog* "is scattered all over the place."

Ideally, Taylor would have been left to his own devices, given time to clean up or at least find some level of equilibrium. Instead, Kootch explained, "he needed another album. There was a lot of pressure, and he was in no position to do it. He couldn't take two years off. You had to keep going, so here's another album, and we decided for James's comfort zone that we would start it on Martha's Vineyard at his barn. We moved a twenty-four-track machine in there and moved upstairs and recorded in this barn.

"But he wasn't in great shape. I thought the album, although it had some really great stuff on it, was a little disjointed and not really focused."

Ironically, however, it is that lack of focus that gives *One Man Dog* its flavor and ensured that, like Stevens's *Catch Bull at Four* (whose release preceded it by a month, and with which it was destined to joust at the top of the chart), its maker was able to slip the generic shackles of singer-songwriterdom a lot more effectively than either his audience or his contemporaries.

Whether out of necessity or not, the fact is, *One Man Dog* is an inherently funky album, a mood that is overtly conjured by "Fool for You" and "Woh, Don't You Know," but is percolating forever under the surface elsewhere.

Songs are fragmentary. Just two top three minutes in length; seven more stretch above two. On an album laden down with a mind-boggling eighteen tracks, many are more or less a minute long, vignettes and shreds that *seem* complete but are over before you realize it. The shortest, the gentle chant of "Mescalito," clocks in at just twenty-nine seconds.

Small wonder, then, that Taylor described the record as being comprised of "cooperative pieces." Nor is it surprising that the band—a core quartet of Kootch, Russ Kunkel, the magnificently bearded bassist Leland Sklar, and the schoolmasterly keyboard player Craig Doerge (henceforth to be known collectively as the Section)—that dictates the course of the music would become synonymous with the sound of Los Angeles rock for the next two or three years.

If only to keep its creator on an even keel, then, *One Man Dog* was a relaxed affair, with the literal open-door nature of the barn accentuated by a similar policy when the recording light was on. Dash Crofts (of Seal and Crofts) contributed mandolin; Randy and Michael Brecker added urban horns. Linda Ronstadt turned in a shimmering performance on "One Morning in May," a traditional English folk song that had moved into the American kit bag courtesy of two other Vineyard folkies, Bill Keith and Jim Rooney.

Carole King dropped by to add some characteristically sweet backing vocals, and so did Taylor's brother Alex and sister Kate. Carly Simon (whom

Taylor would wed on November 3, 1972) was constantly around; so was Kootch's wife, Abigail Haness.

Perhaps the most fascinating guest, however, was John McLaughlin, the thirty-year-old Englishman whose Mahavishnu Orchestra union with jazz rockers Jan Hammer and Billy Cobham would effectively rewrite the laws of jazz rock for the next decade. That, however, was still to transpire when Nat Weiss, Peter Asher's partner in Marylebone Productions, called Kootch and Russ Kunkel over one evening to hear an acetate of the Orchestra's then pending debut album, *The Inner Mounting Flame*.

Kootch: "John was being managed by Nat Weiss and he was James's attorney, he represented the Mahavishnu Orchestra, and he played Russ and [me] the acetate of the first Mahavishnu Orchestra album. We couldn't believe our ears—nobody had ever heard anything like that before. It was way ahead of its time. So that's how John came into the picture, and before you knew it, he and James had written a song together, 'Someone'; John had created some music—he might have written those lyrics, too—and there we are in the studio, James and me and John McLaughlin, sitting in a circle. I could not believe it.

"So there were some great things about the album. We started playing with some jazz guys, and I got to play with my all-time idol John McLaughlin."

Still, Taylor was in no doubt as to what *One Man Dog* could do to his career, one reason why he joked with the title *Farewell to Showbiz*. Carly Simon and Peter Asher put the mockers on that because, listened to completely dispassionately, there were moments when that is precisely what the finished tapes sounded like.

Taylor tried again. *Throw Yourself Away*. No, that one didn't fly either, and for much the same reason. Finally he hit on *One Man Dog*, and his exhausted advisors breathed a sigh of relief. It was still a loaded title if anybody cared to look for clues in its name, but the album's artwork—Carly Simon's brother Peter's snap of Taylor and doggy David boating on a pond outside Brattleboro, Vermont—at least justified it. Now to see what the rest of the world thought about it.

Early portents were good. There was no indication that Taylor would tour; indeed, he had barely been sighted in public for a year now, aside from a handful of campaign appearances for presidential candidate George

McGovern. But *Rolling Stone* found much to love in an album that "will hit you from behind because on the surface it all sounds so simple, and yet underneath the horns—so dazzlingly arranged—and the beautiful rhythm, the voice and the thoughts resonate long after the record is over. . . ."

Warner Brothers, too, made the best of it. Passing over what many people saw as the most obvious single on the record, the son of "Steamroller" that emerged as the rocking recipe "Chili Dog," and closing their eyes to the knowledge that absolutely nothing on the record leaped out with the same emergency as the previous three album's standouts, the label chose "Don't Let Me Be Lonely Tonight" as the first 45, and it slowly made its ascent to #14.

It was a disappointment, even if the Taylor household did have cause to celebrate as Carly's "You're So Vain," a song she wrote about David Geffen, was destined to hit the #1 slot. There would be a round of triumphs at the Grammys, too, as Simon scooped Best New Artist, Taylor won Best Pop Vocal Performance for "You've Got a Friend," and King rushed off with Song of the Year ("Friend" again), album of the year (*Tapestry*), Record of the Year ("It's Too Late"), and Best Female Vocal ("Tapestry").

But *One Man Dog*, too, was destined to move with the kind of creaking uncertainty that is always perceived to haunt an artist in decline—because it is only with the benefit of hindsight that he can instead be revealed to have been in transition.

Cat Stevens's latest, *Catch Bull at Four*, entered the *Billboard* chart on October 14, 1972, at a surprisingly lowly #135, then leaped to #42 and #21 before zeroing in on the top spot. *One Man Dog* jumped in at an equally disappointing #128 on November 25, and had only just breached the Top 10 at Christmas. The dog would ultimately come to rest at #4, with the Cat still breathing down its neck, the wife gazing down from the top of the chart (Simon's *No Secrets* LP topped the chart on January 13), and Carole King's latest, *Rhymes and Reasons*, one spot better off.

One Man Dog became the first James Taylor LP since his debut to not even sniff platinum status. And Taylor didn't care. It would be 1974 before he returned to the record racks, hiding behind the autopilot controls of the dismal *Walking Man* album, and another year before *Gorilla* even hinted at a musical life away from the solitude of his greatest years.

Things had changed; the mood had shifted. Lonely bards were no longer the flavor of the month, probably because there were simply too damned many of them, and few of them were any good. A new mood had emerged from the same milieu, though, one that was superficially indistinguishable from what went before, but vastly different regardless.

The mood of loosey-goosey funky fun was in, the sound of the Doobie Brothers, Eagles and Little Feat, Jackson Browne and Linda Ronstadt, Andrew Gold and Warren Zevon, all the West Coast sounds that would not have been possible without the sounds that went before, but could never have existed in tandem with them.

The mood in fact was one that *One Man Dog* both prophesied and personified, as Lester Bangs predicted when he reviewed *One Man Dog* for *Creem* in February 1973.

Gone was the vitriol of *James Taylor Marked for Death*—which was, in any case, merely a throwaway paragraph or so within a far longer dissertation on the meaning of rock 'n' roll. In its stead was an acknowledgment that "when ya get right down to it . . . James Taylor's a real punk. He just sits around and gets fucked up . . . just like most of us."

And, if he'd only "come on outta the closet . . . stop trying to be the J. D. Salinger of the count-out culture . . . [and] slouch on down . . . with the rest of the wetbacks," he would become an even greater inspiration than he was already.

Taylor, like Stevens, was not marked for death. Instead, he was being nudged toward a rebirth, one that would see him—again like Stevens—carve a whole new musical direction from the introspection and insularity with which he had first introduced himself to the world.

That it was a direction that Jackson Browne had already signposted should not detract from the accomplishment; nor should the rocky roads down which all three artists would occasionally bump over the decades that followed. Each had opened his soul and bared a heart filled with darkness to a watching, fascinated, world. And each, through careers that intersected as much as they spiraled alone, had ultimately set himself to resolve that darkness.

EPILOGUE

Where Are They Now?

APPLE RECORDS

The Apple dream did not last, although it survived for longer than a lot of people remember. The label was still issuing non-Beatle-related material into 1972, four years after its inception, and it is for the Beatles (individually and collectively) that it is remembered, both musically and commercially. Between them, the four band members were responsible for some of the most memorable 45s of the period, and one forgets how effortlessly their ideas dovetailed with one another, even in isolation.

It's one of Beatledom's favorite hobbies, compiling solo tracks into some approximation of a postsplit "Beatles" album . . . well, you can stop now. They did it themselves on single, long ago, while individual cuts like McCartney's "Another Day," Ringo Starr's "Back Off Boogaloo," Harrison's "My Sweet Lord," and the Lennons' "Happy Christmas" might even shade the best of the big band's output.

Such memories do it a disservice. Any catalog that could find room for David Peel, the Black Dyke Mills Band and the Radha Krishna Temple (not to mention Yoko Ono) certainly wasn't chasing platinum records. Not all the time, anyway.

The label's big wheels—actual (Badfinger, Billy Preston, Ravi Shankar) and proposed (Doris Troy, Ronnie Spector, James Taylor)—remain ear-catching today, but it's the minor-league attractions that raise the most temperatures, thanks to a major and much-anticipated reissue campaign in early 2011 that restored much of Apple's catalogs to the shelves for the first time in decades.

Lon and Derrek Van Eaton's low-fi Spectorisms have a lilting appeal that is as thrilling now as it was out to lunch back then, while the signing of Chris Hodge suggests that Apple knew the way the winds were blowing in Britain, long before the Brits themselves had figured it out; "Contact Love" is the best early T. Rex single that Elton John never made. Plus, five years before the world and its mother were raving about Hot Chocolate's smooth blending of pop, funk, and politics, John Lennon was encouraging them to reggae-fy "Give Peace a Chance" and change his own sainted lyrics as well!

PETER ASHER

It may or may not be considered a compliment, but Mike Myers once claimed to have modeled Austin Powers on Peter Asher's mid-1960s appearance. More lasting, however, is the track record that attends Asher's musical career, as the producer who learned on the job through the first James Taylor LP became one of the primary sculptors of the West Coast sound that swept America in the early to midseventies' post-Taylor fallout.

His work with Linda Ronstadt, beginning with the landmark *Heart Like a Wheel* album in 1973, and further recordings with J. D. Souther, Andrew Gold, and Bonnie Raitt stand among the genre's most timeless creations. Asher also helped rebrand Hollywood itself, when he teamed with Lou Adler, David Geffen, Elliot Roberts, and Elmer Valentine to open the Troubadour's first viable rival in a decade, the Roxy.

Other Asher productions include albums by 10,000 Maniacs, Cher, Neil Diamond, and Randy Newman, while he continued to work on and off with Taylor through the 1970s and early 1980s, before reuniting with him in 2007 for the *Live at the Troubadour* album. He has also enjoyed several stints in the boardroom, as senior vice president at Sony Music Entertainment between 1995 and 2002, president of Sanctuary Artist Management until 2006, and, subsequently, one half of Strategic Artist Management.

Asher also reformed Peter and Gordon with bandmate Gordon Waller, conducting several well-received tours before Waller's death in 2009.

ASYLUM RECORDS

To the fan and collector of early 1970s West Coast rock, Asylum Records represents the mother lode. From Jackson Browne and Linda Ronstadt to Eagles and Andrew Gold, Asylum dominated the genre, both sonically and via the type of quality control that few other labels of the era could dream of matching.

Browne was the first artist signed to Asylum; he was followed by J. D. Souther, Judee Sill (her debut LP was Asylum's first release—SD 5050), David Blue, and Eagles. Jo Jo Gunne, featuring ex-Spirit member Jay Ferguson, brought Asylum its first major hit 45 that summer, when "Run Run Run" reached #27. Before the end of 1972, Jackson Browne's "Doctor My Eyes" and "Rock Me on the Water," and Eagles' "Take It Easy" and "Witchy Woman" had all marched into the Top 100, and the label was printing LPs like other institutions print banknotes.

The arrival of Linda Ronstadt (from Capitol) and Joni Mitchell (from Reprise) added further weight to Asylum's already hefty cachet, with Mitchell's *For the Roses* and Ronstadt's *Don't Cry Now* opening their label accounts with major hits. Contrarily, albums by Batdorf and Rodney and Mick Jagger's brother, Chris, were seldom seen even at the time, but rewarded the dutiful sleuth.

In late 1973, with Asylum's success still speeding ahead, Geffen sold Asylum to Warners, although he would remain head of the company. At the same time, Elektra Records head Jac Holzman was keen to step down from the day-to-day running of that company, whose own distribution was through Warners. In a surprising but nevertheless logical move (stylistically there were numerous similarities between the two catalogs), the labels were merged under Geffen's control, consolidating their catalogs.

Immediately, the union hit headlines, with the arrival of Bob Dylan from Columbia. Unhappy with the label he'd spent the past decade with, and infuriated by the its clumsy efforts (including raiding the outtakes bin for the *Dylan* album) to blackmail him into renewing his contract, Dylan joined Asylum in 1973, linking with the Band to cut 1974's *Planet Waves* and *Before the Flood* live album. Point made, he then returned to Columbia in 1975.

Asylum and Elektra retained their label identities (and therefore their own artists and A&R departments) within the merger. Asylum releases continued from both established and new artists—aside from Dylan, these latter included Jack the Lad, a spin-off from the successful British act Lindisfarne, Tim Moore, Traffic, Essra Mohawk, Orleans, Albert Brooks, and John Fogerty.

As the late 1970s progressed, however, Asylum releases became scarcer within the catalog, all the more so following David Geffen's departure in 1980 to launch his own Geffen label. Of almost 300 LPs released on Elektra-Asylum between 1977 and 1981, fewer than sixty bore the Asylum identity. The label is still issuing today, but remains a mere shadow of its former self.

KATHY DORRITIE

. . . is better known today as Cherry Vanilla. Having starred in the off-Broadway theatrical production *Island* and the London presentation of *Andy Warhol's Pork*, she moved into PR, working for David Bowie's MainMan management company until 1974. Briefly relaunching herself as a published poet and a rock 'n' roll star, she cut two albums for RCA in the late 1970s, but she has spent much of the time since then working for keyboard wizard Vangelis.

She never forgot James Taylor, however, and with their respective careers allowing a few more meetings over the years that followed, a nodding acquaintance developed. In the mid-1980s, however, the pair reconnected at Thea Korek's aerobic studio up over the Fairway Market at Seventy-Fourth and Broadway. "It's not a big story," Vanilla smiled. "But I finally got a kiss from him. Not a big romantic one . . . more like a sister-brother one, but on the lips.

"We saw each other almost every day there. He was the only male taking those classes . . . smart guy. He always took his place at the back of the room, and all of the girls in their little workout outfits were all in his view. And we all knew that when we bent over, our bums were right in his line of vision. We all loved it, and him, of course. He was so friendly, spent time talking with all of us almost every day. . . ."

ELEKTRA RECORDS

The Doors' "Light My Fire" gave Elektra its first chart-topping single; fresh signings in its aftermath included Tim Buckley, Ars Nova, David Ackles, and Eclection, while the sale of the label to Warner Brothers in 1967 (with Jac Holzman remaining on board, of course) only amplified Elektra's visibility.

At the same time, however, the label's traditional penchant for the extraordinary and the eccentric continued to bear strange fruit. The UK's

Incredible String Band, Nico, the Holy Modal Rounders, and David Peel were as bizarre as any Elektra-watcher could hope for, while the arrival of Detroit hard rock bands the MC5 and the Stooges saw Elektra pursue its vision to the extremes of rock iconography.

But if Elektra ended the 1960s as a haven for some of the most unique freak shows in the American mainstream, it entered the 1970s as a repository for another musical force entirely.

The mature ruminations of David Gates's Bread debuted on the label in 1969 with the single "Any Way You Want Me" and a self-titled album; by 1971, when singer-songwriters Harry Chapin and Carly Simon were added to the roster, Bread ranked among Elektra's biggest-selling acts ever. Carly Simon would swiftly join them, and by the time Holzman retired in 1973 and the label merged with Asylum, Elektra was poised to dominate the middle of the soft-rock road.

Of course, the label's historical love for the oddball continued to shine through. Queen, the British hard rock band whose appeal embraces everyone from dyed-in-the-wool headbangers to students of absurdly tongue-in-cheek satire, are rightly ranked among the most popular bands in the world, more than twenty years after front man Freddie Mercury's death.

Sparks, a California band whose career probably touches more record labels than Link Wray's, issued one album through Elektra, 1979's massively influential 1 in Heaven; and Boston New Wave band the Cars opened their Elektra career in 1978 with the quirky "Just What I Needed"; they closed it a decade later as one of the entire genre's most reliable novelty hit machines, at least in America.

In 1982, Elektra founded its own jazz-rock-oriented subsidiary, Elektra Musician, while maintaining its presence in the rock mainstream as skillfully as before. Artists recruited during the 1980s and beyond include the Cure and Depeche Mode (via licensing deals with the British Fiction and Mute labels, respectively), the Sugarcubes, and, following their demise, Björk, Metallica, Third Eye Blind, and rap star Ol' Dirty Bastard.

Elektra folded in 2004 when parent Warner Brothers merged it with Atlantic records. A five-CD boxed set of hits, classics, and rarities, *Forever Changing: The Golden Age of Elektra Records 1963–1973* appeared in 2006; the Elektra label itself resurfaced in 2009.

DAVID GEFFEN

Departing Asylum in 1980, David Geffen founded Geffen Records with $25 million from Warner Brothers, and found immediate success with the arrival of Donna Summer and John Lennon, whose debut for the label, *Double Fantasy*, was still fresh in the stores when the former Beatle was murdered.

The label would go on to release hits by artists as disparate as Olivia Newton-John, Asia, XTC, Peter Gabriel, Guns N' Roses, Sonic Youth, and Elton John, while courting controversy with Geffen's well-publicized decision to sue Neil Young. Signed for $1 million per record and guaranteed complete creative freedom, Young took his contract at face value and released some of the most challenging music of his career so far. Geffen responded by suing Young, in November 1983, for $3.3 million, for deliberately making records that were "not commercial" and "uncharacteristic of Young's previous recordings." Young countersued for $21 million, before the two cases were dropped in 1985.

Young remained at Geffen until 1988; Geffen remained there until 1995 (having already sold the company to MCA in 1990), when he absorbed his decade-old Geffen Film Company into the DreamWorks SKG studio, founded with Steven Spielberg and Jeffrey Katzenberg. Geffen left DreamWorks in 2008.

MIKE HURST

Cat Stevens was only the start. The late 1960s also saw Hurst produce the likes of the Cymbaline, the Alan Bown, Nirvana, and Manfred Mann (the megasmash "Mighty Quinn"), together with a clutch of classics for Andrew Oldham's Immediate label. Over the next decade, then, Mike Hurst would emerge as the architect behind some of the most distinctive sounds and hit makers in UK rock history.

Early 1970s work with Mickie Most's RAK label saw him notch up a string of lightweight hits with the folky trio New World, while 1974 saw him create a major U.S. hit with Fancy's supersexed re-creation of Chip Taylor's "Wild Thing." (The band's vocalist, Helen Caunt, was a former Penthouse pet.)

But it was Hurst's abiding passion for 1950s rock 'n' roll that paid dividends, with the discoveries first of Showaddywaddy (1974), whom he kept

at the top of the UK chart for the remainder of the decade; and then Shakin'
Stevens, who likewise dominated the first half of the 1980s. During this
same period, he also produced Summer Wine, the Four Tops, Cilla Black,
Hello, and more.

In 1979, Hurst oversaw the original recording of "Video Killed the Radio
Star" by Bruce Woolley and the Camera Club (Woolley's cowriters Trevor
Horn and Geoff Downes, aka Buggles, scored the hit version); and in 1984,
he headed up Lamborghini Records and foisted the singing talents of model
Samantha Fox upon the world.

Still active today as the operator of a theater group (a passion he
inherited from his mother), Hurst is currently preparing for a revival of
the Springfields, timed to coincide with the fiftieth anniversary of "Silver
Threads and Golden Needles" in 1962. Much of his output as a producer,
meanwhile, is available across three volumes of the *Producers Archives* CDs
(Angel Air).

CAROLE KING

King's *Tapestry* album would remain America's all-time biggest-selling album
by a solo artist for the next decade, until it was finally displaced by Michael
Jackson's *Thriller*; it would also be one half of a remarkable double act
through 1972, as King's next studio LP, *Carole King: Music*, joined it in the
Top 10 at the end of the year, and itself proceeded to the top.

Subsequent albums *Rhymes and Reasons* (1972), *Fantasy* (1973), *Wrap
Around Joy* (1974), and the soundtrack to the TV production of Maurice
Sendak's *Really Rosie* (1975) were less successful, but only by the standards
of King's preceding albums; all were sizeable hits. Her final gold disc arrived
with 1977's *Simple Things*, written with her new husband, Rick Evers. tragi-
cally, it was to be their only full LP together; Evers died from a heroin
overdose a year after their marriage.

Later King albums were sporadic and patchy: *Welcome Home* (1978), *Touch
the Sky* (1979), *One to One* (1982), and *Speeding Time* (1983) did little, while
an attempt to update her 1960s catalog via 1980's *Pearls—The Songs of Goffin and King* scarcely bothered the chart either, although it did unleash a
hit single, "One Fine Day." King continued writing and contributing to
soundtracks through the 1980s, and also moved into acting, starring in

1988's off-Broadway production if *A Minor Incident*. The following year she teamed up with the likes of Eric Clapton and Branford Marsalis for a new album, *City Streets*, and she was nominated for a Grammy in 1992 for "Now and Forever," featured in the movie *A League of Their Own*. A new album, *Color of Your Dreams*, followed in 1993, while 1997 saw her score a massive worldwide hit when she wrote "The Reason" for Celine Dion.

Launching her own Rockingale label in 2001, King released her first new album in almost a decade, *Love Makes the World*, and in 2004 she undertook her first tour in even longer, the so-called Living Room tour, which spun off a Top 20 live album of the same name in 2005.

Two years later, King was back with James Taylor, and back at the Troubadour, too, as part of the club's fiftieth-anniversary celebrations. In 2010 this spawned a world tour, together with a live album (*Live at the Troubadour*) and an acclaimed PBS documentary, *Troubadours*.

DANNY KORTCHMAR

Three successive James Taylor chart busters (*Sweet Baby James, Mudslide Slim* and *One Man Dog*, plus the pre-fame *Original Flying Machine*), three more by Carole King (*Writer, Tapestry*, and *Rhymes and Reasons*), and another album (*Now That Everything's Been Said*) with pre-stardom combo the City had established Danny Kortchmar among the elite of American sidemen, while his membership in the Fugs and the fondly remembered Jo Mama confirmed both his versatility and his abilities.

But even those works could not prepare people for the tastefully raw R&B that hollers from the grooves of *Kootch*—an album that even *Rolling Stone*, which had done more than most to push Kortchmar's other employees in the public eye, ignored. But Kortchmar laughed (and still laughs) the album's failure away. He made it because he was asked if he wanted to, and he had a lot of fun while he did so. So what if hardly anyone heard it? He'd never even expected to make it in the first place.

Kootch was not its maker's first flight outside of the Taylor/King orbit, however. The previous year the band that he, Russ Kunkel, Lee Sklar, and Craig Doerge formed to accompany Taylor on tour had cut its own debut album, the eponymous *The Section*; and so highly rated was the band that two further LPs would appear over the years, *Forward Motion* (1973) and *Fork It Over* (1977).

November 1973 saw Kootch join Cat Stevens's band for *Moon and Star*, the ABC network's televised premiere of the Englishman's most ambitious album yet, *The Foreigner* (Linda Ronstadt and Dr. John also appeared), while the following year his new band, Attitudes, signed with George Harrison's Dark Horse label and cut two albums, *Attitudes* (1975) and *Good News* (1977). Kootch's second solo album, *Innuendo*, was released in 1980.

Throughout the 1970s, Kootch ranked among the most in-demand session guitarists on the Los Angeles scene, recording with Bill Wyman, Keith Moon, Crosby and Nash, Jackson Browne, and Linda Ronstadt, among others. Moving into production at the end of the decade, he oversaw the first album by Carole King's daughter Louise Goffin, before becoming Don Henley's coproducer and cowriter through the Eagles drummer's 1980s solo career. He has also produced Neil Young, Bon Jovi, and Billy Joel; played alongside Bob Dylan; and cowritten some of Jackson Browne's best-loved 1980s compositions, including "Shaky Town" (1977), "Somebody's Baby," "Tender Is the Night," and "Knock On Any Door" (all 1982). The pair also toured Europe together in 1982.

The 1990s and beyond saw Kootch remain an in-demand producer (Venice, Freedy Johnston, Spin Doctors, Dada). He reignited his own career as a musician with the bands Slo Leak and the Midnight Eleven. Occasional reunions with James Taylor, meanwhile, saw him produce one song on Taylor's most recent hits collection and, of course, rejoin him and King for the Troubadours tour in 2010.

NICO

Nico continued recording and gigging, albeit sporadically, until the end of her life. Rarely less than controversial (her mid-1970s label Island dropped her for perceived racist comments about labelmate Bob Marley), she followed *Chelsea Girl*, her Jackson Browne–fired debut, with a succession of never-less-than fascinating and ferociously independent solo LPs: *Marble Index* (1968), *Desert Shore* (1971), *The End* (1974), *Drama of Exile* (1981), and *Camera Obscura* (1985), the hiatus between each release indicating just how far removed from the commercial norm she was then considered.

It was only toward the end of her life that Nico was seen as any kind of musical pioneer, as she toured relentlessly (a string of semi-official live albums dates from this period).

Nico died in Spain on July 18, 1988.

STEVE NOONAN

Jackson Browne's closest teenage friend effectively retired from performance following the debacle of his Elektra debut album. A band he formed in the early 1970s made pioneering use of a Moog synthesizer, opened for Emmylou Harris, and came close to signing to Columbia; according to Noonan, the deal fell through when he admitted that he had no songs that sounded like Boz Scaggs, and that if that was what the label wanted, they'd be better off asking Scaggs to provide them.

He finally returned in 2008 with the acclaimed *Bringin' It Back Home*

PAUL ROTHCHILD

While Jac Holzman was indisputably the heart of Elektra Records, Paul A. Rothchild was its musical soul, the producer of many of the label's best-loved albums. The Doors remain his best-known work, with Rothchild a constant presence in the Oliver Stone's notorious biopic, but it can also be said that if a mid- to late-1960s Elektra album sounded good, Rothchild was probably behind the board.

He also stepped outside the company to work with the likes of Joni Mitchell (1969's *Clouds*), Janis Joplin (1970's *Pearl*), the Everly Brothers (1972's *Stories We Could Tell*), the Outlaws, Elliott Murphy, and many more.

Rothchild died in 1995, at fifty-nine, from lung cancer.

TOM RUSH

With *The Circle Game* having been completely rediscovered in the wake of James Taylor's and Joni Mitchell's breakthroughs, Tom Rush signed with Columbia in early 1970 and promptly turned in two new albums, *Tom Rush* and *Wrong End of the Rainbow*. Both featured further Taylor compositions, including those spellbinding takes on "Sweet Baby James" and "Riding on a Railroad," and over the next four years, Rush would maintain the relationships fired by *The Circle Game* via two further albums, *Merrimack County* (1972) and *Ladies Love Outlaws* (1974).

Disillusioned with the music industry, however, and frustrated in his attempts to break from Columbia and find a new home, Rush retired from recording in 1975, a year before the reformed Walker Brothers scored a massive hit with *The Circle Game*'s "No Regrets."

He worked in promotions and management for a time, before relaunching himself as a performer in 1981, with a sold-out show at the Boston Symphony Hall. (The gig was recorded for 1982's *New Year* live album). He returned to that venue in 1982 to play a Club 47 date. The show was so popular that it became an annual event, recapturing the spirit of the old Cambridge folk club through a combination of established (Bonnie Raitt, Emmylou Harris) and (at the time) unknown artists (Alison Krauss, Mark O'Connor). Club 47 has since toured the U.S. and been featured on a number of PBS and NPR specials.

Nineteen eighty-four brought a new album in the form of a collection of songs recorded for NPR, *Late Night Radio*, but it would be the end of the century before Rush recorded and released a new song, when "River Song" (featuring Marc Cohn and Shawn Colvin) was included as a bonus track on the compilation *The Very Best of Tom Rush: No Regrets*.

Four years later another live album, *Trolling for Owls*, again captured the magnificence of his live show, and in 2009, Rush traveled to Nashville with one of his old Club 47–era friends, Jim Rooney, to record his first studio album in thirty-five years, *What I Know*.

PAUL SAMWELL-SMITH

Cat Stevens's producer is probably still best remembered for his membership in the Yardbirds earlier in the 1960s. But he was also the overseer of all of Stevens's key albums, including 1974's *Buddha and the Chocolate Box* and 1978's *Back to Earth*. In addition, he followed up Carly Simon's 1971 *Anticipation* with a string of albums beginning with *Spoiled Girl* (1983) and continuing on to 1995's *Letters Never Sent*. Other Samwell-Smith productions include albums by Illusion, Chris de Burgh, All About Eve, and Jethro Tull.

JUDEE SILL

Although she hailed from the same West Coast stable of talent that gave the world the likes of Jackson Browne, Andrew Gold, Karla Bonoff, Eagles, and more, Judee Sill has been more or less ignored by modern musical history—a brutal oversight that belies the fact that, of them all, she was probably the most gifted songwriter.

Certainly labelmate J. D. Souther thought as much, while UK fans flocked to Sill's side long before they picked up on any of her colleagues. Yet two albums for Asylum in the early 1970s mark the sum of her output—by 1974, less than a year after the release of the second, her career was at an end. Five years later, she was dead. Maybe it was something she said?

Well, yes, it apparently was. Infuriated by David Geffen's refusal to promote her in the same manner that he pushed his other artists (a state of affairs brought on by Sill's crippling drug dependency), she is reputed to have camped out on his front lawn for a period of time to try and remind him of her existence. He remembered and dropped her from the label.

But J. D. Souther told author Barney Hoskyns, "She was light-years ahead of most of us. I thought Jackson Browne was the furthest along at having learnt songwriting, but then I met Judee and thought, 'Fuck, man, she's school for all of us.'"

CHIP TAYLOR

Chip Taylor never stopped writing songs. He did, however, stop having hits with any new ones following his retirement from the music industry in the mid-1970s to become, in his own words, a professional gambler.

It was the early 1990s before he resolved to return, self-financing an album's worth of material that became his *The Hit Man* album in 1996. Since that time, Taylor has maintained an almost annual CD output, embracing the Americana that was his first musical love, back in White Plains, New York.

DISCOGRAPHY

The following is a chronological and, as far as can be ascertained, complete guide to all known studio and concert recordings made (whether for official release or otherwise) by the artists during the period discussed in this book. Where appropriate, release data and chart data is provided for all LPs and 45s released in the U.S. and UK; additionally, information is provided for a number of unofficial "bootleg" releases. Also included are key radio and television performances and significant demo or recording sessions. LPs that include full track listings are those by any of the three primary artists this book focuses on or by artists who play a major part in the story. For LPs that contain a small contribution from one of the three primary artists, full track listings are not provided. Finally, a broad selection of cover versions by other artists has also been included.

1963—JON AND ALUN

LP: *Relax Your Mind*

Original UK release: Decca LK 4547

Tracks: "Relax Your Mind" / "Walk to the Gallows" / "I'm My Own Grandpa" / "The Poor Fool's Blues" / "Black Is the Colour" / "Easy Rambler" / "I Never Will Marry" / "Alberta" / "John B" / "The Song of the Salvation Army" / "Lone Green Valley" / "The Way of Life" / "Sinking of the Reuben James"

Notes: Future Cat collaborator Alun Davies and Michael "Jon Mark" Burchell were just a couple of years out of school when they delivered this fine collection of folk-themed originals and rearranged traditional airs.

1964—THE FABULOUS CORSAIRS

45: "You're Gonna Have to Change Your Ways" b/w "Cha Cha Blues" (demo)

Notes: James and Alex Taylor's debut recording, a demo cut at local producer Jimmy Katz's two-track studio in Raleigh, North Carolina. Alex composed the A side, James the B side.

1965—CAT STEVENS

Recording: Demo session

Notes: Anxious to get some of his songs down on tape, Stevens hired a small Denmark Street studio, Regent Sound, in London, and cut at least one song, "Back to the Good Old Times," which was unreleased until its inclusion on the 2001 *Cat Stevens* boxed set.

Released to coincide with what was then regarded as Cat Stevens's reemergence as a media-friendly (if not musically popular) personality, *Cat Stevens* also coincided with an altogether unexpected rejuvenation of interest in his back catalog. Between 1971 and 1975, after all, Stevens ranked among the most sainted singer-songwriters in that entire genre, and was so popular that, by the time the decade reached its midpoint, his downfall wasn't simply inevitable, it was imperative.

The bard behind a stream of cocktail-party confessionals, the sensitive soul who uncorked the very wellspring of human consciousness, Stevens was so intrinsically bound up within the peculiar zeitgeist that defined early-seventies America that neither death nor retirement could have liberated him. In terms of prolonging his career, his conversion to Islam probably wasn't up there with his best ideas. But in terms of personal survival, it was the smartest thing he ever did.

The boxed set does not address such weighty issues, of course. Just one disc, the fourth, traces Stevens's activities from 1975 on; only two songs postdate his disappearance, a live "Father and Son," recorded at a UNICEF concert in 1979, and a single track from 1997's *Raihan—Syukar* album. And, should you choose to play the boxed set backwards, little therein prepares the listener for all that came before. Even by the most generous criteria, late-1970s albums like *Numbers* and *Izitso* were overwrought turkeys, every last ounce of soul and passion squeezed out by Stevens's relentless pursuit of the honesty for which he was renowned. Again, if he hadn't disappeared, he'd have vanished anyway.

Go back to the beginning, though, and listen in awe. The collection opens with Stevens's first recording, a flimsy demo from 1965; it kicks into gear with his first 45 and the slew of minor classics he unleashed between 1966 and 1968. Hits "I Love My Dog," "I'm Gonna Get Me a Gun," "Matthew and Son," and "The First Cut Is the Deepest" punctuate selections from two late-1960s albums, together with a generous helping of B sides and even a few choice unreleased tracks, including "Honey Man," a union with the then-unknown Elton John, which, though nobody could have guessed it at the time, would essentially dictate the course of popular music through the next five years.

His former gift for familial whimsy had been utterly replaced by a new thoughtfulness. Cut through the still-effervescent pop melodies that he was spinning, and Stevens's best compositions possess a seriousness that defied the expectations of his early audience, at the same time that it defined his future crowd. So it was that even the trite philosophy of "Moon Shadow" took on the weightiest of meanings; so it was that a radio-lite version of the hymn "Morning Has Broken" took on the magnitude of the Sermon on the Mount. And so it goes on until we reach 1973's *Foreigner*, with its horribly misjudged, side-long title suite, and the conscientious lyric reader is left wondering which is going to collapse beneath the portentousness first, singer or song. In fact, both give way simultaneously, and the Cat would never purr so contentedly again.

None of which is to detract from the beauty, fragility, and, yes, occasionally, majesty of Stevens's finest recordings—which in turn represent at least three-quarters of this box. With between four and five tracks apiece culled from his most crucial albums, the seamless sequence that voyaged from *Mona Bone Jakon* to *Catch Bull at Four* and then briefly resurfaced for *Buddha and the Chocolate Box*, the box is unquestionably a magnificent edifice, while the booklet's inclusion of Stevens's own recollections about songs and sessions offers an irresistible glimpse into the inner workings of those records.

The bare simplicity of "Lady D'Arbanville," the muted nostalgia of "Where Do the Children Play," the exuberant punch of "Oh Very Young," the sweet sparseness of "I Want to Live in a Wigwam"; even at his most gauchely naive, Stevens tapped emotions that few pop stars even dreamed of approaching, and the fact that he remained (for want of a better term) a pop star throughout only testifies to the universality of those emotions.

1965-66—THE KING BEES

45: "What She Does to Me" b/w "That Ain't Love"

45: "Rhythm and Blues" b/w "On Your Way Down the Drain"

45: "Lost in the Shuffle" b/w "Hardly Part 3"

Original U.S. releases: RCA 8688, RCA 8787, and RCA 8979, respectively

Notes: Danny Kortchmar, Joel Bishop, bassist Dicky, and singer/organist John John McDuffy recorded a triptych of soulful 45s for RCA during their time in New York City, released in the order listed above. "Lost in the Shuffle" was also recorded by Blues Project, the band that McDuffy would join following the King Bees' breakup.

SEPTEMBER 1966—CAT STEVENS

45: "I Love My Dog" b/w "Portobello Road"

Original UK release: Deram DM 102

UK chart peak: #28 (7 weeks, total)

Notes: A putative Mike Hurst solo single, the Mike D'Abo–composed "Going Going Gone" was recorded at the same session as Steve's debut single. Unreleased at the time, it finally debuted on the CD compilation *Mike Hurst: Producers Archives Volume 3* in 2009.

OCTOBER 1966—JACKSON BROWNE

LP: *The Columbia Demo*

Notes: See January 1967, *The Nina Demo*.

DECEMBER 1966—CAT STEVENS

45: "Matthew and Son" b/w "Granny"

Original UK release: Deram DM 110

UK chart peak: #2 (10 weeks)

JANUARY 1967—JACKSON BROWNE

LP: *The Nina Demo*

Tracks: "Holding" / "Somewhere There's a Feather" / "I've Been Out Walking" / "Funny You Should Ask" / "Love Me, Lovely" / "You've Forgotten" /

"Someday Morning" / "Cast Off All My Fears" / "In My Time" / "Melissa" / "It's Been Raining Here in Long Beach" / "You'll Get It in the Mail Today" / "Shadow Dream Song" / "The Light from Your Smile" / "Gotta See a Man About a Daydream" / "Time Travel Fantasy" / "The Fairest of the Seasons" / "Sing My Songs to Me" / "Lavender Windows" / "The Painter" / "Fourth and Main" / "Bound for Colorado" / "We Can Be" / "And I See" / "Ah, But Sometimes" / "Marianne" / "Tumble Down" / "You Didn't Need a Cloud" / "Lavender Bassman" / "She's a Flying Thing"

Notes: Two-LP demonstration disc produced by Nina Music. Largely recorded at Jaycino Studios, New York, on January 7, 1967, but also incorporating an earlier session for Columbia on October 5, 1966.

JANUARY 1967—THE TREMELOES

45: "Here Comes My Baby" b/w "Gentlemen of Pleasure"
Original UK release: CBS 202519
UK chart peak: #4 (11 weeks)
Notes: Originally known as Brian Poole and the Tremeloes, in which form they ranked among the early British Invaders, the group lost vocalist Poole in late 1966 and seemed doomed to obscurity after their next two singles ("Blessed" and "Good Day Sunshine") sank without trace. Instead, Stevens's "Here Comes My Baby" became the first in a run of hits that would carry the band into 1971 and include the UK chart topper "Silence Is Golden" alongside further smashes "Even the Bad Times Are Good," "Call Me Number One" (which got to #2), and "Me and My Life."

FEBRUARY 1967—PAUL AND BARRY RYAN

45: "Keep It Out of Sight" b/w "Who Told You?"
Original UK release: Decca F12567
UK chart peak: #30 (6 weeks)
Notes: Brothers Paul and Barry Ryan were nearing the end of their chart career when they covered this Cat Stevens number. A Mike Hurst production, it rewarded them with a return to the Top 30 for the first time in almost a year. Too little too late, however; one single later the pair went their separate musical ways, although Barry would bounce back the following year with a bombastically brilliant English-language rendition of Claude François's French hit "Eloise."

"Keep It Out of Sight" is most readily available on the compilation CD *Mike Hurst: Producers Archives Volume 3*

MARCH 1967—THE NITTY GRITTY DIRT BAND

LP: *The Nitty Gritty Dirt Band*

Original U.S. release: Liberty 7501

U.S. chart peak: #151 (8 weeks)

Notes: Contrary to the oft-quoted insistence that Nico was first to record a Jackson Browne song, the honor actually rests with his old bandmates in the Nitty Gritty crew. Their debut album includes versions of Browne's "Holding" and "Melissa," together with the Steve Noonan/Greg Copeland composition "Buy for Me the Rain" (a #45 U.S. hit single).

MARCH 1967—CAT STEVENS

LP: *Matthew and Son*

Original U.S. release: Deram 18005

Original UK release: Deram DML/SML 1004

UK chart peak: #7 (16 weeks)

Tracks: "Matthew and Son" / "I Love My Dog" / "Here Comes My Baby" / "Bring Another Bottle Baby" / "Portobello Road" / "I've Found a Love" / "I See a Road" / "Baby Get Your Head Screwed On" / "Granny" / "When I Speak to the Flowers" / "The Tramp" / "Come On and Dance" / "Hummingbird" / Lady"

Notes: A CD version released later included the bonus tracks "School Is Out" and "I'm Gonna Get Me a Gun."

MARCH 1967—CAT STEVENS

45: "I'm Gonna Get Me a Gun" b/w "School Is Out"

Original UK release: Deram DM 118

UK chart peak: #6 (10 weeks)

APRIL 1967—P. P. ARNOLD

45: "The First Cut Is the Deepest" b/w "Speak to Me"

Original UK release: Immediate 047

UK chart peak: #18 (10 weeks)

Notes: P. P. Arnold arrived in the UK in 1966 as a member of Ike and Tina Turner's Ikettes. "Discovered" there by Mick Jagger, she remained in the UK as a solo artist, signed to Stones manager Andrew Loog Oldham's Immediate label. It was Mike Hurst, another early supporter, who suggested she record Stevens's "The First Cut Is the Deepest," and his production was certainly a large part of the ensuing performance's immortal beauty.

APRIL 1967—NICO

Recording: Rehearsal

Original bootleg release: The Velvet Underground: *Ultra Rare Tracks Volume 4* (3D-Reality Classics)

Notes: No recordings are known to be in existence of Nico performing at the Dom, with or without Jackson Browne. However, bootlegs do exist capturing an hour or so of Nico and Reed practicing songs together, around the same time. The quality is rough and it doesn't bear much repeated listening. But the duo hacking, chatting, giggling, and squabbling through an effervescent clutch of songs drawn from both *Chelsea Girl* and the Lou Reed songbook does have a compulsive appeal, whether one is listening to Nico previewing a verse of "Secret Side," six years before she finally recorded the song, or Lou stumbling through a line of "All Tomorrow's Parties," before Nico dissolves into a disbelieving "Oh my God!" You also get to hear just how much David Bowie stole from "These Days" for his first album-era opus "When I'm Five."

More importantly than any of that, however, you get a sense of how Nico must have sounded in 1967, playing the Dom, with just a guitarist. Tim Buckley for a while, or Sterling Morrison, Lou Reed or Jackson Browne, singing her lovely little songs in a gentle, gorgeous croon, pausing between songs, or sometimes midway through, a little uncertain, a little aloof . . . Properly remastered, neatly spliced and edited (where, oh where, is the Nico boxed set?), this would actually be an essential document.

Another ghost of this era emerges on a tape recorded at the Whisky A Go Go on June 5, 1979. It was Danny Fields who first suggested Tim Hardin and Nico get together to play in 1967; Tim Hardin preceded Jackson Browne as her regular accompanist and went onto gift one song to *Chelsea Girl*, "Eulogy to Lenny Bruce."

A decade later, the pair reunited in L.A., as Nico toured the U.S. on the eve of her early-1980s comeback. The opening two numbers are dominated by Nico's harmonium; you hear Hardin for the first time tuning up for "Henry Hudson" before coming to the fore with "Femme Fatale" and, most notably, John Cale's "A Child's Christmas in Wales," a song that is usually ascribed to a mythical Nico-Cale reunion. Hardin himself then performs a couple of songs, before Nico and her harmonium return for a spectral "Valley of the Kings" and, finally, "The End."

MAY 1967—DAVID GARRICK

45: "I've Found a Love" b/w "(You Can't Hide) a Broken Heart"
Original UK release: Piccadilly 7N 35371
Notes: Proof that not everything Cat Stevens touched could turn to gold, as Garrick followed up two minor hits (the Stones' "Lady Jane" and "Dear Mrs. Applebee") with a resounding flop.

JULY 1967—CAT STEVENS

45: "A Bad Night" b/w "The Laughing Apple"
Original UK release: Deram DM 140
UK chart peak: #20 (8 weeks)

JULY 1967—CAT STEVENS

Recording: Soundtrack session for *Twinkie*
Original UK release: *Mike Hurst: Producers Archives Volume 3* (Angel Air SJPCD 302)—2009
Notes: Archived for almost forty years, this is Stevens's abandoned contribution to a proposed Lindsay Anderson movie.

JULY 1967—THE FLYING MACHINE

Recording: LP recording sessions subsequently released as *James Taylor and the Original Flying Machine* (1971)
Tracks: "Rainy Day Man" / "Knocking Round the Zoo" (multiple takes) / "Something's Wrong" (instrumental) / "Night Owl" (multiple takes) / "Brighten Your Night with My Day" (multiple takes) "Kootch's Song"

SEPTEMBER 1967—THE FLYING MACHINE

45: "Night Owl" b/w "Brighten Your Night with My Day"
Original U.S. release: Rainy Day 8001
Original Canadian release: Barry 3477

OCTOBER 1967—NICO

LP: *Chelsea Girl*
Original U.S. release: Verve V5032/V6 5032
Notes: Includes versions of Jackson Browne's "Fairest of Seasons," "Somewhere There's a Feather," and "These Days." Yet when pressed to name his own favorite Nico performance, Browne eschewed this LP altogether and selected a song from her sophomore set, produced by Frazier Mohawk and John Haeny.

"Frozen Warnings," the penultimate cut on 1968's *The Marble Index*, emerges one of her iciest performances, with Browne singling it out as "an exceptional melody and an atmospheric ballad." The recurrent vision of the "frozen borderline" is genuinely haunting, heaving into view in the a cappella opening verses, then growing closer as the instrumentation slides in behind her.

OCTOBER 1967—THE NITTY GRITTY DIRT BAND

LP: *Ricochet*
Original U.S. release: Liberty LRP 3516
Notes: Includes versions of Jackson Browne's "It's Been Raining Here in Long Beach" and "Shadow Dream Song."

DECEMBER 1967—CAT STEVENS

45: "Kitty" b/w "Blackness of the Night"
Original UK release: Deram DM 156
UK chart peak: #47 (1 week)

DECEMBER 1967—CAT STEVENS

LP: *New Masters*

Original U.S. release: Deram 18010

Original UK release: Deram DML/SML 1018

Tracks: "Kitty / "I'm So Sleepy" / "Northern Wind" / "The Laughing Apple" / "Smash Your Heart" / "Moonstone" / "The First Cut Is the Deepest" / "I'm Gonna Be King" / "Ceylon City" / "Blackness of the Night" / "Come On Baby" / "I Love Them All"

Notes: When the album was released on CD, the following bonus tracks were included: "Image of Hell" / "Lovely City" / "Here Comes My Wife" / "The View from the Top" / "It's a Supa Dupa Life" / "Where Are You" / "A Bad Night."

FEBRUARY 1968—CAT STEVENS

45: "Lovely City" b/w "Image of Hell"

Original UK release: Deram DM 178

MARCH 1968—THE HOUR GLASS

LP: *Power of Love*

Original U.S. release: Liberty LRP 3555/SRP 7555

Notes: The Hour Glass formed from the wreckage of two Southern rock bands, Duane and Gregg Allman's Florida-based Allman Joys, and the Alabama-rooted Men-Its, featuring Pete Carr, Johnny Sandlin, and Paul Hornsby. Gigging in St. Louis, they were discovered by Nitty Gritty Dirt Band manager Bill McEuen; he landed the band a deal with Liberty and oversaw their relocation to Los Angeles. He also introduced them to Jackson Browne, whose "Cast Off All Your Fears" would be included on the band's debut album.

MARCH 1968—THE FUGS

LP: *Tenderness Junction*

Original U.S. release: Reprise 6280

Tracks: "Turn On-Tune In-Drop Out" / "Knock Knock" / "The Garden Is Open" / "Wet Dream" / "Hare Krishna" / "Exorcising the Evil Spirits from the Pentagon, October 21, 1967" / "War Song" / "Dover Beach" / "Fingers of the Sun" / "Aphrodite Mass (Litany of the Street Grope-Genuflection at the

Temple of Squack-Petals in the Sea-Sappho's Hymn to Aphrodite-Homage to Throb Thrills) "

Notes: Danny Kortchmar and Charlie Larkey weren't quite taking a musical vacation for the months that they were Fugs, but both admit that they had faced more challenging propositions. Nevertheless, *Tenderness Junction* is a scintillating listen, a combination of period agitprop politics and poetry, shot through with the kind of "far out" dialogue so beloved of the era. The exorcism of the Pentagon, included here as a far-too-short live excerpt from the actual event, would swiftly inspire British underground rockers the Edgar Broughton Band to pen their own anthem "Out Demons Out."

MARCH 1968—TOM RUSH

LP: *The Circle Game*

Original U.S. release: Elektra EKS 74018

U.S. chart peak: #68 (14 weeks)

Notes: Includes versions of Jackson Browne's "Shadow Dream Song" and James Taylor's "Something in the Way She Moves" and "Sunshine Sunshine." The album was prefaced by a single in late 1966, Joni Mitchell's "Urge for Going" b/w "Sugar Babe."

MAY 1968—STEVE NOONAN

LP: *Steve Noonan*

Original U.S. release: Elektra EKS 74017

Notes: "Filled," said *Billboard*'s review, "with all the promise of a folk spotlight . . . [Noonan's] debut will offer a persuasive array of folk music to buffs." Includes versions of Jackson Browne's "The Painter," "Trusting Is a Hard Thing," "Tumble Down," "She's a Flying Thing," and "Shadow Dream Song."

JULY 1968—THE NITTY GRITTY DIRT BAND

LP: *Rare Junk*

Original U.S. release: Liberty 7540

Notes: Includes a version of Jackson Browne's "These Days," a cut that was also released as a single.

SUMMER 1968—JAMES TAYLOR

Recording: The London sessions and demos for Taylor's *Apple* LP

Notes: These recordings provided two of the bonus tracks featured on the 2011 remaster of *James Taylor*, "Sunshine Sunshine" and "Carolina in My Mind."

SEPTEMBER 1968—HEDGE AND DONNA

LP: *Hedge and Donna 2*

Original U.S. release: Capitol ST 107

Notes: Doug Weston once described the mixed-race Hedge Capers and Donna Carson as "literally the best act" to emerge from the Troubadour's Monday open mike sessions all year, although it makes sense he would have said that; he was their manager. The duo signed to Capitol in late 1967; this, their second LP includes a version of Jackson Browne's "From Silver Lake."

OCTOBER 1968—CAT STEVENS

45: "Here Comes My Wife" b/w "It's a Supa Dupa Life"

Original UK release: Deram DM 211.

Notes: A demo from this period, "If Only Mother Could See Me Now," recorded at East London Recording Studios, was included on the 2001 *Cat Stevens* boxed set.

LATE 1968—CLEAR LIGHT

Recording: Tracks for an unfinished, unreleased Clear Light album

Notes: Work on a second Clear Light LP, the first to feature Kootch, got under way and at least two tracks, "Darkness of Day" and "What a Difference Love Makes," were recorded before the band broke up. Ralph Schuckett and Michael Ney would swiftly resurface, playing on the Carole King–composed "Porpise Song," a highlight of the Monkees' *Head* movie. Schuckett would then reunite with Kootch in Jo Mama.

DECEMBER 1968—JAMES TAYLOR

LP: *James Taylor*

Original U.S. release: Apple 3352

Original UK release: Apple SAPCOR 3

U.S. chart peak: #62 (28 weeks)

Tracks: "Don't Talk Now" / "Something's Wrong" / "Knocking Round the Zoo" / "Sunshine Sunshine" / "Taking It In" / "Something in the Way She Moves" / "Carolina in My Mind" / "Brighten Your Night with My Day" / "Night Owl" / "Rainy Day Man" / "Circle Round the Sun" / "The Blues Is Just a Bad Dream"

Notes: When the album was released on CD, bonus tracks included "Sunny Skies" and "Let Me Ride," both of which were recorded at Crystal Sound Studios, Los Angeles, in 1969; and "Sunshine Sunshine" and "Carolina in My Mind," which were demos recorded in London in the summer of 1968.

JANUARY 1969—THE CITY

LP: *Now That Everything's Been Said*

Original U.S. release: Ode 244012

Tracks: "Snow Queen" / "I Wasn't Born to Follow" / "Now That Everything's Been Said" / "Paradise Alley" / "Man Without a Dream" / "Victim of Circumstance" / "Why Are You Leaving" / "Lady" / "My Sweet Home" / "I Don't Believe It" / "That Old Sweet Roll (Hi-De-Ho)" /" All My Time"

Notes: Carole King's first step toward a solo career aligned her with Charlie Larkey, Jim Gordon, and Kootch for a Lou Adler–produced LP that the guitarist describes as "an excellent album, one of those period albums that went completely under the radar, one of those undiscovered gems. This was way before anybody was aware of Carole's abilities as a performer, including Carole. She'd never been on the stage before, she was strictly behind the scenes."

Led out by a single coupling the insistent "Paradise Alley" with "Snow Queen" (Ode 113), *Now That Everything's Been Said* offered a dry run for everything that King would go on to accomplish over the next three years. The band already plays with the clunky garage feel that so exquisitely hallmarks 1970's *Writer*, although the only ears that seem to have been open at this time were the Byrds'. By fall, their definitive version of the album's "I Wasn't Born to Follow" was pursuing "The Ballad of Easy Rider" up the U.S. chart.

A second City single, "That Old Sweet Roll" b/w "Why Are You Leaving," would be released in May 1969.

SPRING 1969—JAMES TAYLOR

Recording: Demos

Notes: Attempts to get Taylor's second Apple album under way saw two songs cut at Crystal Sound Studios in Los Angeles, "Sunny Skies" and "Let Me Ride." Unreleased at the time, they were finally issued as bonus tracks on the 2011 remaster of *James Taylor*.

MARCH 1969—JAMES TAYLOR

45: "Carolina in My Mind" b/w "Taking It In"

Original U.S. release: Apple 1805 (withdrawn)

Notes: The rarest of all Taylor's "official" releases, released to radio and the media and then withdrawn to be repressed with a different B side.

MARCH 1969—JAMES TAYLOR

45: "Carolina in My Mind" b/w "Something's Wrong"

Original U.S. release: Apple 1805

U.S. chart peak: #118 (1 week)

Original UK release: Apple 1805

Notes: The single would not break the Top 100, but it prompted two very swift covers, by country singer George Hamilton IV and the Everly Brothers. Melanie (LP: *Candles in the Rain*, April 1970), John Denver (LP: *Take Me to Tomorrow*, April 1970), Scottish popsters Marmalade (LP: *Reflections of the Marmalade*, June 1970) and Tony Orlando and Dawn (LP: *Candida*, November 1970) would also record the song, but the most successful version was by the Philadelphia band Crystal Mansion, who scored a #73 hit with the song in November 1970.

The Tony Orlando connection was not a fluke. A successful performer early in the 1960s, Orlando saw his recording career grind to a halt, and by 1963, he was working in music publishing, first at Robbins, Feist and Miller, than at April-Blackwood, where he handled the same James Taylor catalog that Chip Taylor acquired back in 1967.

And there he might have remained had producers Hank Medress and Dave Appell not called him in to replace the lead vocalist in a Detroit-based trio they were leading through a song called "Candida." Without ever meeting his bandmates, whose parts were recorded in California, Orlando laid down his vocals, convinced that the song would never be heard of again. Instead, it became the biggest hit of his career so far, and within two months, Orlando had quit his music-publishing job and joined Dawn full-time.

Like Orlando, the remainder of the Dawn team had impressive careers as undeserving underachievement behind them. Telma Louise Hopkins and Joyce Vincent Wilson were ex-Motown backing vocalists (their credits included Marvin Gaye's "I Heard It Through the Grapevine," Freda Payne's "Band of Gold," and Isaac Hayes's "Theme from *Shaft*"), and producers Appell and Medress (a former member of "The Lion Sleeps Tonight" hit makers the Tokens) were simply that, producers. But naming the band after Bell Records boss Wes Farrell's daughter, Dawn, and picking "Candida" for their first release was more than just a good idea. It was a decision that would redraw the boundaries of pop through the 1970s.

"Candida" entered the charts in August 1970; by September, it had sold over a million records. And while it would only reach #3, the next four years would see Tony Orlando and Dawn run up three #1 hits of such magnitude that today one of them, "Tie a Yellow Ribbon Round the Old Oak Tree," remains an integral part of America's popular culture. An album followed and, loyal to his erstwhile employers, Orlando selected two Taylor songs from the April-Blackwood file, "Carolina in My Mind" and "Rainy Day Man."

MID-1969—SWEET THURSDAY

LP: *Sweet Thursday*

Original UK release: Polydor 2310 051

Original U.S. release: Tetragrammaton T12

Tracks: "Dealer" / "Jenny" / "Laughed at Him" / "Cobwebs" / "Rescue Me" / "Molly" / "Sweet Francesca" / "Side of the Road" / "Gilbert Street"

Notes: Future Cat Stevens sidemen Alun Davies and Harvey Burns join Nicky Hopkins, Jon Mark, and Brian Odgers on a fine slice of late-1960s UK folk. Barely noticed at the time it came out (and lost altogether in the U.S., when the band's label went bust on the day of release), *Sweet Thursday* would be reissued in 1973.

JUNE 1969—CAT STEVENS

45: "Where Are You" b/w "The View from the Top"
Original UK release: Deram DM 260

JULY 1969—VARIOUS ARTISTS

EP: *Walls Ice Cream*
Original UK release: Apple CT 1
Notes: A promotional four-track extended-play (EP) record that featured James Taylor's "Something's Wrong" alongside cuts by labelmates Mary Hopkin, Jackie Lomax, and the Iveys.

AUGUST 1969—ASHES FEATURING PAT TAYLOR

LP: *Ashes Featuring Pat Taylor*
Original U.S. release: Vault 125
Notes: Soft rock obscurity includes version of Jackson Browne's "Gone to Sorrow."

SEPTEMBER 1969—HEDGE AND DONNA

LP: *All the Friendly Colors*
Original U.S. release: Capitol ST 279
Notes: The duo's third LP includes a version of Jackson Browne's "There Came a Question."

SEPTEMBER 1969—EVIE SANDS

LP: *Any Way That You Want Me*
Original U.S. release: A&M 1090
Notes: Chip Taylor never lost faith in James Taylor's songwriting, as evidenced by the inclusion of "Carolina in My Mind" on the latest LP by the King Bees' old friend Evie Sands.

JANUARY 1970—CAT STEVENS

Recording: Demos
Original bootleg release: Elton John, *Rarities Collection 1969–1972* (no label, 1 CD)

Notes: Looking for a new record label, Stevens cut a number of demos in early 1970. One of these, the wonderfully clunky "Honey Man," cut at Pye Studios on January 30, subsequently appeared on the *Cat Stevens* boxed set. The unknown Elton John provides piano, thus paving the way for "Honey Man," to first surface aboard this disc.

This is one of the most comprehensive gatherings of genuine Elton rarities to have resurfaced, although one should take the title's *"1969–1972"* billing with at least a little pinch of salt—"Billy and the Kids," after all, is best known as a mid-1980s B side; "Go It Alone" and "I Fall Apart" hail from the *Leather Jackets* era, and that's just the first three songs. Later, "Cry to Heaven" was on *Ice on Fire*; "Sweetheart on Parade" is from Elton's Gary Osborne days; "Chameleon" was on *Blue Moves*; and "Whatever Gets You Through the Night" . . . Yeah, well, you get the picture.

When it sticks to its brief, however, the boot is great. True, the sound quality is thin enough to slide under doors, but a demo for *Empty Sky's* "Lady What's Tomorrow" kicks off a sequence that also includes "Sixty Years On," "Son of Your Father," "I Need You to Turn To," and "Indian Summer," together with such acetate-only jewels as "Sara's Coming Back," "There Is Still a Little Love," and "There's Still Time for Me." "Honey Man" was definitely worth the price of admission.

MARCH 1970—JAMES TAYLOR

LP: *Sweet Baby James*

Original U.S. release: Warners 1843

Original UK release: Warners K46043

U.S. chart peak: #3 (102 weeks)

UK chart peak: #7 (59 weeks)

Tracks: "Sweet Baby James" / "Lo and Behold" / "Sunny Skies" / "Steamroller" / "Country Road" / "Oh Susanna" / "Fire and Rain" / "Blossom" / "Anywhere Like Heaven" / "Oh Baby, Don't You Loose Your Lip on Me" / "Suite for 20G"

Notes: Considering its sacred place in the pantheon of singer-songwriters in general and Taylor's oeuvre in particular, *Sweet Baby James* is a surprisingly unambitious album, its stone-cold classics (the title track, "Fire and Rain") very much outnumbered by the songs that could be considered little more than lighthearted muso rock. The mood makes a mockery of the record's reputation for introspection and self-absorption. True, it never becomes a barrel of laughs. But the Flying Machine–era "Steamroller," the disingenuous "Suite for 20G," and a throwaway cover of "Oh Susanna" grin a lot wider than the maudlin man on the cover looks like he ought to.

MARCH 1970—CAROLE KING

45: "Up On the Roof" b/w "Eventually"
Original U.S. release: Ode 66006
Notes: A trailer for King's upcoming solo debut LP, reprising the old Drifters hit.

MARCH 1970—TOM RUSH

LP: *Tom Rush*
Original U.S. release: Columbia 9972
U.S. chart peak: #76 (16 weeks)
Notes: Includes Jackson Browne's "Colors of the Sun" and "These Days."

APRIL 1970—JACKSON BROWNE

LP: *The Criterion Demo*
Tracks: "Last Time I Was Home" / "Jamaica Say You Will" / "Song for Adam" / "Doctor My Eyes" / "Low Road" / "Door into the Morning" / "Another Place" / "The Birds of St. Marks" / "Mae Jean Goes to Hollywood" / "Gone to Sorrow" / "Hot Like Today" / "A Child in These Hills" / "The Top" / "My Opening Farewell" / "The Times You've Come" / "From Silver Lake" / "Some Kind of Friend" / "There Came a Question" / "Have I Seen Her? " / "Colors of the Sun" / "Dancing Sam" / "Taking So Long"
Notes: The fruits of a handful of sessions dating back to the previous fall, recorded for Browne's new publishers, Criterion.

SPRING 1970—VARIOUS ARTISTS

LP: *Bumpers*
Original UK release: Island IDP 1
Notes: A bountiful double-album package showcasing the cream of the Island label's early 1970 output, highlighting recent releases and anticipating

forthcoming ones and following a tradition launched by the earlier *You Can All Join In* and *Nice Enough to Eat*.

Of all the labels operating in the UK as the decade turned, Island was unquestionably the most adventurous, at the same time maintaining a stable whose internal logic now seems impeccable. Leaning toward the folkier side of hard rock and the bluesier edge of prog, Island rounded up the stars of the British underground, and these periodic compilations showcased the label at its best, maintaining a cohesion and sense of musical purpose that few (if any) samplers can match.

Cat Stevens's contribution was the still-unreleased *Mona Bone Jakon*'s gorgeous "Maybe You're Right."

MAY 1970—JOHNNY DARRELL

LP: *California Stop-Over*
Original U.S. release: United Artists UAS 6752
Notes: Includes version of Jackson Browne's "Mae Jean Goes to Hollywood" and "These Days."

MAY 1970—CAROLE KING

LP: *Writer*
Original U.S. release: Ode 77006
Original UK release: A&M AMLS 996
Tracks: "Spaceship Races" / "No Easy Way Down" / "Child of Mine" / "Goin' Back" / "To Love" / "What Have You Got to Lose" / "Eventually" / "Raspberry Jam" / "Can't You Be Real" / "I Can't Hear You No More" / "Sweet Sweetheart" / "Up On the Roof"

JUNE 1970—CAT STEVENS

45: "Lady D'Arbanville" b/w "Time/Fill My Eyes"
Original UK release: Island WIP 6086
UK chart peak: #8 (13 weeks)

JUNE 1970—CAT STEVENS

LP: *Mona Bone Jakon*
Original U.S. release: A&M 4260

275

Original UK release: Island ILPS 9118

U.S. chart peak: #164 (16 weeks from March 1970)

UK chart peak: #63 (4 weeks)

Notes: An outtake from the album, the B side "Time/Fill My Eyes," was featured on the *Cat Stevens* boxed set.

JULY 1970—JAMES TAYLOR

45: "Sweet Baby James" b/w "Suite for Zog"

Original U.S. release: Warners 7387

Notes: Taylor appeared on TV's *Mike Douglas Show* in the run-up to this release (June 11) to perform "Sweet Baby James" and "Blossom."

JULY 1970: JIMMY CLIFF

45: "Wild World" b/w "Be Aware"

Original UK release: Island WIP 6087

UK chart peak: #8 (12 weeks)

Notes: The studio band that accompanied Cliff on the single would also work with Cat Stevens as he began demoing material for his next album. One track from this process, "The Joke" (recorded at Island Studios on September 17), would appear on the *Cat Stevens* boxed set.

JULY 1970—LIVINGSTON TAYLOR

LP: *Livingston Taylor*

Original U.S. release: Capricorn SD 33-334

Tracks: "Sit On Back" / "Doctor Man" / "Six Days on the Road" / "Packet of Good Times" / "Hush a Bye" / "Carolina Day" / "Can't Get Back Home" / "In My Reply" / "Lost in the Love of You" / "Good Friends" / "Thank You Song"

Notes: One single was culled from Liv's debut album, "Carolina Day" b/w "Sit On Back."

AUGUST 1970—JOHN STEWART

LP: *Willard*

Original U.S. release: Capitol ST 540

Notes: Best known for writing the Monkees' "Daydream Believer," folkie Stewart put out a second album that was a veritable family affair, as producer Peter Asher recruited James Taylor, Carole King, Joel Bishop, Russ Kunkel, Abigail Haness, and Danny Kortchmar to the proceedings. Taylor contributed guitar and/or vocals to four songs: "Big Joe," "Clack Clack," "All American Girl" and "Oldest Living Son"—none of which was singled out as "especially noteworthy" by *Billboard*'s review.

FALL 1970—VARIOUS ARTISTS

LP: *El Pea*

Original UK release: Island IDLP 1

Notes: Following on from *Bumpers, El Pea* features crucial cuts from across the label's then-forthcoming release schedule; each assuredly drew an entire new audience into Island's grasp, in an age when the label was simply pumping out new product.

The punningly titled (and sleeved) *El Pea* highlights much of what 1970 had in store for the label, with selections ranging from cuts from much-anticipated new albums by superstars Traffic and Free to those by cult demigods Mott the Hoople and Quintessence, and a handful of names that might well have been new to the average browser: Mike Heron slipping out of the Incredible String Band with his *Smiling Men with Bad Reputations* debut, Nick Drake still laboring away in absolute obscurity, and so on.

And so it goes on—from Jethro Tull to Blodwyn Pig, from Fairport Convention to Sandy Denny, twenty-one tracks spread across four sides of vinyl, with Cat Stevens nestling on side three with his version of Jimmy Cliff's signature hit "Wild World."

SEPTEMBER 1970—JAMES TAYLOR

45: "Fire and Rain" b/w "Anywhere like Heaven" (U.S. B side) or "Sunny Skies"(UK B side)

Original U.S. release: Warners 7423

Original UK release: Warners 6104

U.S. chart peak: #3 (16 weeks)

UK chart peak: #42 (3 weeks)

Notes: Taylor's breakthrough hit, at least in the USA, "Fire and Rain" is also his most oft-covered composition. Immediate versions by Anne Murray, Johnny Rivers, R. B. Greaves, R. Dean Taylor, and Blood Sweat and Tears were followed in 1971 by versions from John Denver, Andy Williams, Richie Havens, the Isley Brothers, Skeeter Davis, Bobby Womack, Gladys Knight and the Pips, Cher, and more. Today, more than fifty different artists have released their own interpretations of the song.

OCTOBER 1970—JAMES TAYLOR

45: "Carolina in My Mind" b/w "Something's Wrong"
Original U.S. release: Apple 1805 (1969)
U.S. chart peak: #67 (7 weeks)
Notes: A timely reissue for Taylor's first Apple 45, successfully riding the coattails of the hit.

OCTOBER 1970—JAMES TAYLOR

LP: *Amchitka: The 1970 Concert That Launched Greenpeace* (recorded live October 16, 1970)
Tracks: Introduction / Introduction of Phil Ochs / "The Bells" / "Rhythms of Revolution" / "Chords of Fame" / "I Ain't Marching Anymore" / "Joe Hill" / "Changes" / "I'm Gonna Say It Now" / "No More Songs" (all Phil Ochs) / Introduction of James Taylor / "Something in the Way She Moves" / "Fire and Rain" / "Carolina in My Mind" / "Blossom" / "Riding on a Railroad" / "Sweet Baby James" / "You Can Close Your Eyes" (all James Taylor) / Introduction of Joni Mitchell / "Big Yellow Taxi" / "Bony Maroney / "Cactus Tree / "The Gallery" / "Hunter" / "My Old Man" / "For Free" / "Woodstock" (all Joni Mitchell) / "Carey" / "Mr. Tambourine Man" (Joni Mitchell and James Taylor) / "A Case of You" (Mitchell) / "The Circle Game" (Joni Mitchell and James Taylor)
Notes: The album was originally released by Greenpeace in November 2009.

OCTOBER 1970—JAMES TAYLOR AND JONI MITCHELL

LP: *In Perfect Harmony*
Original bootleg release: Escargot records (no catalog number)

Tracks: "That Song About Midway" / "The Gallery" (Joni Mitchell) / "Rainy Day Man" / "Steamroller" (James Taylor) / "The Priest Song" / "Carey (Joni Mitchell) / "Carolina in My Mind" (James Taylor) / "California" / "For Free" / "The Circle Game" (Joni Mitchell) / "You Can Close Your Eyes" (Joni Mitchell + James Taylor)

Notes: The album was recorded live at the London Royal Albert Hall, October 29, 1970. Both Joni and James would also make solo appearances on BBC TV's *In Concert* series during this visit, Mitchell opening the first series on October 9; Taylor following on November 16.

LATE 1970—JAMES TAYLOR

LP: *Roses for Carole*

Original bootleg release: Main Street

Tracks: "For Free" / "Carolina in My Mind" / "Okie from Muskogee" / "Sweet Baby James" / "Circle 'Round the Sun" / "Greensleeves" / "Blossom" / "Up On the Roof" (Carole King vocal) / "Country Road" / "Night Owl" / "Brighten Your Night with My Day" / "Long Ago and Far Away" / "Riding on a Railroad" / "Highway Song" / "Fire and Rain" / "You Can Close Your Eyes"

Notes: Recorded at the Berkeley Community Center in California, 1970.

NOVEMBER 1970—CAT STEVENS

LP: *Tea for the Tillerman*

Original U.S. release: A&M 4280

Original UK release: Island ILPS 9135

UK chart peak: #20 (39 weeks)

U.S. chart peak: #8 (79 weeks)

Tracks: "Where Do the Children Play" / "Hard Headed Woman" / "Wild World" / "Sad Lisa" / "Miles from Nowhere" / "But I Might Die Tonight" / "Longer Boats" / "Into White" / "On the Road to Find Out" / "Father and Son" / "Tea for the Tillerman"

Notes: An outtake from the album, "Love Lives in the Sky," was featured on the *Cat Stevens* boxed set.

NOVEMBER 1970—CAT STEVENS

LP: *The World of Cat Stevens*

Original UK release: Decca SPA93

Notes: A budget-priced compilation of material from Stevens's two Deram LPs.

NOVEMBER 1970—CAT STEVENS

Recording: French TV bootleg video

Tracks: "Lady D'Arbanville" / "Wild World" / "Katmandu" / "Maybe You're Right"

NOVEMBER 1970—CAROLE KING

LP: *Tapestry*

Original U.S. release: Ode 77009

Original UK release: A&M AMLS 2025

U.S. chart peak: #1 (302 weeks)

UK chart peak: #4 (90 weeks)

Tracks: "I Feel the Earth Move" / "So Far Away" / "It's Too Late" / "Home Again" / "Beautiful" / "Way Over Yonder" / "You've Got a Friend" / "Where You Lead" / "Will You Love Me Tomorrow" / "Smackwater Jack" / "Tapestry" / "A Natural Woman"

Notes: Even if you have never heard *Tapestry*, its contents are a part of your musical furniture. From the reprise of "Will You Love Me Tomorrow," a hit in 1961, to "Where You Lead"'s rebirth as the theme to television's *Gilmore Girls* in the late 1990s, and on to the sheer ubiquity of "I Feel the Earth Move," "It's Too Late," and "A Natural Woman," *Tapestry* is the soundtrack of the baby boom generation and beyond. And for that, if nothing else, the album deserves every plaudit that has ever been showered upon it.

Tapestry was reissued within Sony's Legacy series in April 2008, accompanied by a second disc re-creating the album in live form, drawn from concerts recorded in 1973 and 1976.

NOVEMBER 1970—TOM RUSH

LP: *Wrong End of the Rainbow*

Original U.S. release: Columbia 30402

U.S. chart peak: #110 (9 weeks)

Notes: Includes a version of James Taylor's "Riding on a Railroad."

NOVEMBER 1970—GATOR CREEK

LP: *Gator Creek*

Original U.S. release: Mercury SR 61311

Notes: Gator Creek was a sprawling eight-piece band made up of some of L.A.'s most in-demand session players: husband-and-wife duo Kathy and Mike Deasy, saxophonist Allen Beutler, keyboard players Mike O'Martin and Dee Barton, bassist Ray Neapolitan, drummer Gene Pello, and a Messina-less singer/guitarist named Kenny Loggins. Their first and only LP includes a version of Jackson Browne's "These Days."

DECEMBER 1970—JO MAMA

LP: *Jo Mama*

Original U.S. release: Atlantic SD 8269

Tracks: "Machine Gun Kelly" / "Midnight Rider" / "Searching High, Searching Low" / "Lighten Up, Tighten Up" / "Venga Venga" / "Sailing" / "Great Balls of Fire" / "The Sky Is Falling" / "The Word Is Goodbye" / "Check Out This Gorilla" / "Cotton Eyed Joe" / "Love'll Get You High"

Notes: Peter Asher perhaps inevitably produced the debut album by Kootch's Jo Mama, a high-octane funky rock band completed by Abigail Haness, Joel Bishop, Charlie Larkey, and former Clear Light organist Ralph Schuckett.

The album is loose and boogiesome, packed with slinky originals, and one of the sexiest "Great Balls of Fire" ever waxed. With Haness an irresistible force that peaks with the sensuous "The Word Is Goodbye," and the folk hoedown "Cotton Eye Joe" transformed into a blue-eyed soul, *Jo Mama* slithers out of the speakers like a swamp snake, yet its direct lineage to *Writer*, *Tapestry*, and *Sweet Baby James* is unmistakable.

EARLY 1971—MARIANNE FAITHFULL

LP: *Rich Kid Blues*

Original UK release: Demon DIAB 861

Notes: Anybody searching for the finest ever cover of a Cat Stevens song should halt here, with Marianne Faithfull's version of "Sad Lisa."

Faithfull was at the end of her tether when she got together with producer Mike Leander to record the sessions that what would, after almost three decades in the archive, become her *Rich Kid Blues* LP. She was living rough on a Soho bomb site in early 1971; Leander agreed to help her back onto her feet, finding her an apartment, encouraging her to go into detox (she lasted a day and a half before she persuaded someone to bring her some smack), and arranging for publishers Gem Music to finance the making of a new album. Then, with Faithfull sporting the dental damage wreaked by a male nurse at the detox clinic, a broad gap where her front teeth had once been, Leander took her into the studio.

It was a peculiar situation. "People, even people I was working with every day on the record, persisted in seeing me as this glittering, wealthy, high-living chick, when it was perfectly obvious that I wasn't anything like that anymore. I'd moved on. I wasn't living in Chelsea, I was hanging out on a bomb site in Soho. I was missing my two front teeth."

Her teeth weren't the only thing she'd lost. Her voice had completely abandoned its original richness; had shed even the husk that had rattled through her last single, "Sister Morphine." Even there, she had at least been recognizable. Now, she was reduced to speaking in a pained whisper, shot through with gaping holes from which her very soul hung out to dry, and Faithfull herself admits, "My voice is so weak . . . I can't bear to listen to it. It's the sound of somebody incredibly high, probably on the edge of death. There's no energy. Anybody who heard that record would have just said, 'Well, that's that. We'll never hear from her again.' "

Although the sessions unquestionably feed out of the same basic mindset that inspired Faithfull's original recording of "Sister Morphine," back then, she had only been wondering what it might feel like to be so close to death. Now she knew, and her choice of songs echoed that knowledge: sparse, stark interpretations of Tim Hardin's "Southern Butterfly," Sandy Denny's "Crazy Lady Blues," Phil Ochs's "Chords of Fame," and, of three Dylan covers, a positively spine-chilling "Visions of Johanna."

But it is "Sad Lisa" that truly haunts, a rendering that wrings so much meaning from Stevens's lyric that it could almost be a different song. But it isn't.

FEBRUARY 1971—CAT STEVENS

45: "Wild World" b/w "Miles from Nowhere"
Original U.S. release: A&M 1231
U.S. chart peak: #11 (13 weeks)

FEBRUARY 1971—JAMES TAYLOR

45: "Country Road" b/w "Sunny Skies"
Original U.S. release: Warners 7460
U.S. chart peak: #37 (8 weeks)
Notes: A surprisingly underperforming follow-up to one of the signature hits of the previous year, but with so much Taylor on the market now, who can blame anyone if they decided to just keep listening to the songs at 33 rpm?

FEBRUARY 1971—CAT STEVENS

Recording: Soundtrack session
Notes: Recording for the *Harold and Maude* movie soundtrack took place on February 15 at the Paramount Studios in Los Angeles. "Don't Be Shy" and "If You Want to Sing Out, Sing Out" were featured on the *Cat Stevens* boxed set.

FEBRUARY 1971—THE FLYING MACHINE

LP: *James Taylor and the Original Flying Machine*
Original U.S. release: Euphoria 2 (recorded 1967)
U.S. chart peak: #74 (8 weeks)
Tracks: "Rainy Day Man" / "Knocking Round the Zoo" / "Something's Wrong" (instrumental) / "Night Owl" / "Brighten Your Night with My Day" / "Kootch's Song" / "Knocking Round the Zoo" (Danny Kortchmar vocal)
CD bonus tracks: "Knocking Round the Zoo" intro / "Brighten Your Night with My Day" intro / "Knocking Round the Zoo" (alternate version) / "Night Owl" (alternate version)
Notes: An opportunistic first release for the long-archived recordings made the afternoon that Taylor, Kootch and Co. spent in the studio with Chip Taylor. The album was accompanied by a single, "Brighten Your Night with My Day" b/w "Knocking Round the Zoo."

FEBRUARY 1971—JAMES TAYLOR

Notes: Taylor appeared on television's *Johnny Cash Show* on February 17, performing four songs: "Fire and Rain," "Country Road," and "Sweet Baby James," plus a duet of "Oh Susanna" with the host. It was after this broadcast that he and fellow guest Linda Ronstadt were spirited away by Neil Young to contribute to Young's gestating *Harvest* LP (see below).

MARCH 1971—CAT STEVENS

LP: *Matthew and Son / New Masters*
Original U.S. release: Deram 18005/10
U.S. chart peak: #173 (12 weeks)
Notes: A two-LP set pairing Stevens's first two Deram albums.

MARCH 1971—ALEX TAYLOR

LP: *Alex Taylor with Friends and Neighbors*
Original U.S. release: Capricorn SD 860
U.S. chart peak: #190 (2 weeks)
Tracks: "Highway Song" / "Southern Kids" / "All in Line" / "Night Owl" / "C Song" / "It's All Over Now" / "Baby Ruth" / "Take Out Some Insurance" / "Southbound"

MARCH 1971—KATE TAYLOR

LP: *Sister Kate*
Original U.S. release: Cotillion SD 9045
U.S. chart peak: #88 (8 weeks)
Tracks: "Home Again" / "Ballad of a Well Known Gun" / "Be That Way" / "Handbags and Gladrags" / "You Can Close Your Eyes" / "Look at Granny Run, Run" / "Where You Lead" / "White Lightning" / "Country Comfort" / "Lo and Behold" / "Jesus Is Just All Right" / "Do I Still Figure in Your Life" / "Sweet Honesty"
Notes: It would be seven years before Kate followed up *Sister Kate*, with a self-titled album coproduced by brother James.

MARCH 1971—TOM RUSH

LP: *Classic Rush*

Original U.S. release: Elektra 74062

U.S. chart peak: #198 (1 week)

Notes: Compilation including "Shadow Dream Song" (Browne) and "Something in the Way She Moves" (Taylor) from *The Circle Game.*

MARCH 1971—JACKSON BROWNE

LP: *Syracuse University*

Tracks: "Under the Falling Sky" / "World to Gain" / "Together Again" / "Mae Jean Goes to Hollywood" / "Last Time I Was Home" / "Jesus in 3-4 Time" / My Opening Farewell from Silverlake" / "Rock Me on the Water" / "Jamaica Say You Will" / "Holiday Inn (aka "Together Again")" / "Take It Underground" / "When You Lose Your Money" / "Our Lady of the Well" / "These Days" / "Someday Morning" / "Shadow Dream Song" / "Song for Adam" / "Looking into You"

Notes: An oft-circulated recording of Browne's March 27 show includes four songs that are not known from any other source: "Holiday Inn," "Take It Underground," "When You Lose Your Money," and "World to Gain."

MARCH 1971—JAMES TAYLOR

LP: *Live at the Anaheim Convention Center*

Original bootleg release: CBM (no cat number)

Tracks: "Sweet Baby James" / "I Feel Fine" / "Hey Mister, That's Me Up On the Jukebox" / "Sunny Skies" / "Chili Dog" / "Steamroller" / "Riding on a Railroad" / "Conversation" / "Places in My Past" / "You Can Close Your Eyes" / "Soldiers" / "Carolina in My Mind" / "Long Ago and Far Away" / "Country Roads" / "Fire and Rain" / "Sixteen Candles" / "Love Has Brought Me / "Oh Don't You Know" / "Come On Brother Get Up and Help me Find the Screw" / "The Promised Land" / "Isn't It Nice to Be Home Again"

Notes: The most ubiquitous of early James Taylor bootlegs, this album, which was recorded live on March 21, 1971, features cuts that have also appeared on the discs *In Disneyland, Isn't It Nice to Be Home Again,* A *King and Two James,* and *Tailor Made.*

MARCH 1971—JONI MITCHELL

LP: *Blue*

Original U.S. release: Reprise 2038

Original UK release: Reprise K44128

U.S. chart peak: #15 (28 weeks)

UK chart peak: #3 (18 weeks)

Notes: With a voice that could accelerate from foxy to foghorn without pausing for breath, Mitchell was always the auditory joker in the singer-songwriter pack, a point that she would prove with her later embrace of jazz and even avant-garde possibilities. For now, however, she was happy to have found a home, and *Blue*, the album that history rates as her best, is her most devout concession to the form. James Taylor appears on "California."

APRIL 1971—CAT STEVENS

Recording: An audience recording of Stevens's return to the Gaslight, a Greenwich Village club

Tracks: "Moon Shadow" / "On the Road to Find Out" / "Wild World" / "Longer Boats" / "Maybe You're Right" / "Sad Lisa" / "Miles from Nowhere" / "Hard Headed Woman" / "Peace Train" / "Father and Son" / "Charges IV"

APRIL 1971—CAROLE KING

45: "It's Too Late" b/w "I Feel the Earth Move"

Original U.S. release: Ode 66015

Original UK release: A&M 849

U.S. chart peak: #1 (17 weeks)

UK chart peak: #6 (12 weeks)

Notes: The most successful of singles culled from *Tapestry* but by no means the sole smash. "So Far Away" b/w "Smackwater Jack" would make #14 later in the year, while UK buyers were tempted with a Top 20 reactivation of King's first solo hit, 1962's "It Might as Well Rain Until September."

MAY 1971—CAROLE KING

LP: *California Concept*

Original bootleg release: Carnaby Records (no cat number)

Tracks: "I Feel the Earth Move" / "Whispering Wind" / "Child of Mine" / "Beautiful" / "It's Too Late" / "Smackwater Jack" / "So Far "/ "Will You Love Me Tomorrow" / "Up On the Roof" / "You've Got a Friend" / "Natural Woman"

Notes: Recorded at the Troubadour, May 1971.

MAY 1971—JAMES TAYLOR

Notes: Taylor made his second appearance on the top BBC TV series *In Concert* on May 3, 1971.

MAY 1971—JAMES TAYLOR

LP: *Mud Slide Slim and the Blue Horizon*

Tracks: "Love Has Brought Me Around" / "You've Got a Friend" / "Places in My Past" / "Riding on a Railroad" / "Soldiers" / "Mud Slide Slim" / "Hey Mister, That's Me up on the Jukebox" / "You Can Close Your Eyes" / "Machine Gun Kelly" / "Long Ago and Far Away" / "Let Me Ride" / "Highway Song" / "Isn't It Nice to Be Home Again"

Original U.S. release: Warner 2561

Original UK release: K46085

U.S. chart peak: #2 (45 weeks)

UK chart peak: #4 (42 weeks)

JUNE 1971—CAT STEVENS

45: "Moon Shadow" b/w "Father and Son"

Original U.S. release: A&M 1265

Original UK release: Island WIP 6092

U.S. chart peak: #30 (11 weeks)

UK chart peak: #22 (11 weeks)

JUNE 1971—CAT STEVENS

LP: *Father and Son*

Original bootleg release: Trademark of Quality TMOQ 71036

Tracks: "Moon Shadow" / "On the Road to Find Out" / "Wild World" / "Longer Boats" / "Father and Son" / "Hard Headed Woman"

Notes: These tracks were taken from the PBS (KCET Los Angeles): *Full Circle* TV performance broadcast on June 8, 1971. The LP was completed with the following cuts from a Chicago performance the following year: "Where Do The Children Play" / "Miles from Nowhere" / "Maybe You're Right" / "Peace Train" / "Sad Lisa" / "Changes IV" / "Into White."

JUNE 1971—CAT STEVENS

LP: *Chapter 4*

Original bootleg release: CBM 681

Tracks: "Moon Shadow" / "Where Do the Children Play" / "Wild World" / "How Can I Tell You" / "On the Road to Find Out" / "Miles from Nowhere" / "Lisa Lisa" / "Longer Boats" / "Peace Train" / "Hard Headed Woman" / "Father and Son" / "Changes IV"

Notes: Taken from a performance recorded live June 21, 1971. A number of shows on this tour were recorded and subsequently bootlegged, including Berkeley (June 30, 1971) and Santa Monica (July 1, 1971—the show that featured the off-the-cuff rendition of "Portobello Road" that prompted Alun Davies to include the song on his solo LP).

JUNE 1971—CAROLE KING

LP: *Carnegie Hall Concert, June 18, 1971*

Original U.S. release: Sony 485104 (released 1996)

Tracks: "I Feel the Earth Move" / "Home Again" / "After All This Time" / "Child of Mine" / "Carry Your Load" / "No Easy Way Down" / "Song of Long Ago" / "Snow Queen" / "Smackwater Jack" / "So Far Away" / "It's Too Late" / "Eventually" / "Way Over Yonder" / "Beautiful" / "You've Got a Friend" / "Will You Love Me Tomorrow" / "Some Kind of Wonderful" / "Up On the Roof" / "Natural Woman"

Notes: Having already informed the audience that "Song of Long Ago" was written under the influence of James Taylor, King surprised positively nobody by stepping out for the end of the show with Taylor in tow, to duet through a remarkable "You've Got a Friend," an imploring "Will You Love Me Tomorrow," and a heartbreaking "Up On the Roof." It's a magnificent performance, your ears almost urging King's fragile, sometimes even childlike voice not to give out or give in, even though you know it won't. Unconscionably archived for a quarter of a century before finally being released, *Carnegie Hall Concert* is King at her undisputed peak.

JUNE 1971—THE BYRDS

LP: *Byrd Maniax*
Original U.S. release: Columbia 30640
U.S. chart peak: #46 (10 weeks)
Notes: Includes version of Jackson Browne's "Jamaica Say You Will."

AUGUST 1971—JOHNNY RIVERS

LP: *Home Grown*
Original U.S. release: United Artists UAS 5532
U.S. chart peak: #148 (4 weeks)
Notes: Includes versions of James Taylor's "Fire and Rain" and Jackson Browne's "Our Lady of the Well" and "Rock Me on the Water."

AUGUST 1971—JAMES TAYLOR

45: "You've Got a Friend" b/w "You Can Close Your Eyes"
Original U.S. release: Warner Brothers 7498
Original UK release: Warner Brothers K16085
U.S. chart peak: #1 (14 weeks)
UK chart peak: #4 (15 weeks)

SEPTEMBER 1971—CAT STEVENS

45: "Tuesday's Dead" b/w "Miles from Nowhere"
Original UK release: Island WIP 6102
Notes: An unexpected miss.

SEPTEMBER 1971—CAT STEVENS

45: "Peace Train" b/w "Where Do the Children Play"
Original U.S. release: A&M 1291

U.S. chart peak: #7 (12 weeks)

Notes: Two of Stevens's best-known, most successful and most loved tracks, astonishingly never released as singles in his homeland.

SEPTEMBER 1971—CAT STEVENS

LP: *Teaser and the Firecat*
Original U.S. release: A&M 4313
Original UK release: Island ILPS 9154
U.S. chart peak: #2 (67 weeks)
UK chart peak: #3 (93 weeks)
Tracks: "The Wind" / "Ruby Love" / "If I Laugh" / "Changes IV" / "How Can I Tell You" / "Tuesday's Dead" / "Morning Has Broken" / "Bitterblue" / "Moon Shadow" / "Peace Train"
Notes: An outtake from the album, "The Day They Make Me Tsar" (from the two-year-old *Revolussia* stage play), was featured in the *Cat Stevens* boxed set.

SEPTEMBER 1971—JAMES TAYLOR

45: "Long Ago and Far Away" b/w "Let Me Ride"
Original U.S. release: Warner Brothers 7521
U.S. chart peak: #31 (8 weeks)

SEPTEMBER 1971—JO MAMA

LP: *J Is for Jump*
Original U.S. release: Atlantic SD 8288
Tracks: "Keep on Truckin'" / "Back on the Street Again" / "Smackwater Jack" / "If I Had a Billion Dollars" / "My Long Time" / "When the Lights Are Way Down Low" / "Love Is Blind" / "3 A.M. in L.A. " / "Sweet and Slow" / "Have You Ever Been to Pittsburgh" / "Sho 'Bout to Drive Me Wild"
Notes: Kootch and Co.'s second (and final) album was a considerably slicker, more laid-back beast than its incendiary predecessor, slinky still but dipping deep into a blue-eyed soul vein that American rock would not truly be mining for another couple of years. A cover of Carole King's "Smackwater Jack" is a highlight, however, and "Have You Ever Been to Pittsburgh" travels on an almost mantric hook line. "Back on the Street Again," would receive a major boost when James Taylor covered it on his next album, *One Man Dog*.

Following the band's breakup, Abigail Haness, like the rest of the members, moved into a long career in sessions, but she may be best remembered as the singing voice of Janet Weiss (Susan Sarandon) in *The Rocky Horror Picture Show*.

OCTOBER 1971—CAROLE KING

Notes: King took a very pink-clad bow on BBC TV's *In Concert* series on October 2, 1971, with James Taylor as her special guest guitarist ("So Far Away").

NOVEMBER 1971—JAMES TAYLOR

Notes: Having already guested on Carole King's *In Concert* BBC TV broadcast on October 2, Taylor returned for his own performance, broadcast on November 13.

NOVEMBER 1971—CAT STEVENS

Recording: Bootleg video/DVD
Tracks: "Moon Shadow" / "Tuesday's Dead" / "Wild World" / "How Can I Tell You" / "Maybe You're Right" / "I Love My Dog" / "Bitterblue" / "Changes IV" / "Into White" / "Father and Son"
Notes: Unreleased officially, but oft-circulated, the video is of Stevens's *BBC In Concert* TV performance broadcast November 27, 1971.

NOVEMBER 1971—THE NITTY GRITTY DIRT BAND

LP: *All the Good Times*
Original U.S. release: United Artists 5553
U.S. chart peak: #162 (10 weeks)
Notes: Includes a version of Jackson Browne's "Jamaica Say You Will."

NOVEMBER 1971—LINDA RONSTADT

LP: *Linda Ronstadt*
Original U.S. release: Capitol ST 635
U.S. chart peak: #163 (10 weeks)

Notes: Includes a version of Jackson Browne's "Rock Me on the Water."

DECEMBER 1971—CAT STEVENS

45: "Morning Has Broken" b/w "I Want to Live in a Wigwam"
Original U.S. release: A&M 1335
Original UK release: Island WIP 6121
U.S. chart peak: #6 (14 weeks)
UK chart peak: #9 (13 weeks)
Notes: B side "I Want to Live in a Wigwam" was a *Teaser and the Firecat* leftover that would remain unavailable on LP until its inclusion on 1985's *Footsteps in the Dark—Greatest Hits Volume Two* LP (Island ILPS/ICT 3736). It has since been collected in the *Cat Stevens* boxed set.

DECEMBER 1971—CAROLE KING

LP: *Music*
Original U.S. release: Ode 77013
Original UK release: A&M AMLH 67013
U.S. chart peak: #1 (44 weeks)
UK chart peak: #18 (10 weeks)
Tracks: "Brother Brother" / "Song of Long Ago" / "Brighter" / "Surely" / "Some Kind of Wonderful" / "It's Going to Take Some Time" / "Music" / "Sweet Seasons" / "Carry Your Load" / "Growing Away from Me" / "Too Much Rain" / "Back to California"
Notes: It is oh-so-fashionable to describe *Music* as *Tapestry Part Two*: same band, same studios, same producer—it's an easy course to take. But it is not the correct one, for one thing had changed. *Tapestry* was recorded with King still a commercial and, so far as the mainstream was concerned, critical unknown, following up two utterly overlooked LPs with what everybody involved assumed would be another. Instead, she found herself not simply with the biggest hit of the year, but one of the biggest hits of all time, and the fact that a woman who had never set foot on a stage before was now expected to write and record a suitable follow-up while also pounding the boards of the land placed an unimaginable burden on both singer and songs.

Despite spinning off the Top 10 hit "Sweet Seasons" b/w "Pocket" (Ode 66022), *Music* is archetypal King, but it is not remarkable King. "Some Kind of Wonderful," the now-obligatory golden oldie, is the album's peak; "It's Going to Take Some Time" is its indisputable classic (even if it took Chicago's "If You Leave Me Now" to make us realize that), and "Song of Long Ago" is a warmly wonderful duet with James Taylor.

Her own dislocation shows through in the number of songs that refer to being on the road and separation, which might have been okay if she'd not already said all there was to say on the subject in "So Far Away." The album was still an enormous hit. But if *Writer* and *Tapestry* were the sound of a young woman not particularly looking for her place in this world, *Music* is the sound of her finding it regardless. And maybe not being bowled over by the discovery.

DECEMBER 1971—LIVINGSTON TAYLOR

LP: *Liv*

Original U.S. release: Capricorn SD 863

Tracks: "Get Out of Bed" / "May I Stay" / "Open Up Your Eyes" / "Gentlemen" / "Easy Prey" / "Be That Way" / "Truck Driving Man" / "Mom, Dad" / "On Broadway" / "Caroline" / "I Just Can't Be Lonesome No More"

Notes: One single, "Get Out of Bed," was culled from Liv's sophomore album, but did not progress beyond promotional copies.

DECEMBER 1971—CARLY SIMON

LP: *Anticipation*

Original U.S. release: Elektra 75016

Original UK release: Elektra K42101

U.S. chart peak: #30 (31 weeks)

Notes: Recorded in London with Cat Stevens in attendance and his producer Paul Samwell-Smith overseeing the sessions, *Anticipation* was titled for the song Simon wrote about her first date with Cat, itself a hit single (#13) in early 1972.

JANUARY 1972—CAT STEVENS

LP: *Very Young and Early Songs*

Original U.S. release: Deram 18061

U.S. chart peak: #94 (10 weeks)

Notes: Compilation of Deram-era material, largely focusing on non-LP tracks and hits.

FEBRUARY 1972—JACKSON BROWNE

LP: *Jackson Browne* aka *Saturate Before Using*

Original U.S. release: Asylum 5051

Original UK release: Asylum SYL 9002

U.S. chart peak: #53 (23 weeks)

Tracks: "Jamaica Say You Will" / "A Child in These Hills" / "Song for Adam" / "Doctor My Eyes" / "From Silver Lake" / "Something Fine" / "Under the Falling Sky" / "Looking into You" / "Rock Me on the Water" / "My Opening Farewell"

FEBRUARY 1972—ALEX TAYLOR

LP: *Dinner Time*

Original U.S. release: Capricorn CP 0101

Tracks: "Change Your Sexy Ways" / "Let's Burn Down the Cornfield" / "Comin' Back to You" / "Four Days Gone" / "Payday" / "Who's Been Talkin'" / "Who Will the Next Fool Be" / "From a Buick Six"

Notes: Alex would cut further albums, including *Third for Music* (Dunhill 50151—1974), *Dancing with the Devil* (Ichiban—1981) and *Voodoo in Me* (King Snake CD 15). He died in 1993.

FEBRUARY 1972—NEIL YOUNG

LP: *Harvest*

Original U.S. release: Reprise 2277-2

Notes: In Nashville in February 1971 to record at the city's Quadrafonic Sound Studios, Neil Young was booked for a February 17 appearance on the *Johnny Cash* TV show, alongside James Taylor and Linda Ronstadt. Following the broadcast, the trio returned to the studio, where they recorded Young's newly written "Heart of Gold." Taylor and Ronstadt handle backing vocals; Taylor also played banjo on the song "Old Man."

MARCH 1972—JACKSON BROWNE

45: "Doctor My Eyes" b/w "I'm Looking into You"
Original U.S. release: Asylum 11004
Original UK release: Asylum K13403
U.S. chart peak: #8 (12 weeks)

MARCH 1972—TOM RUSH

LP: *Merrimac County*
Original U.S. release: Columbia 301306
U.S. chart peak: #128 (10 weeks)
Notes: Includes a version of Jackson Browne's "Jamaica Say You Will."

MARCH 1972—JENNIFER WARNES

LP: *Jennifer*
Original U.S. release: Reprise MS 2065
Notes: Produced by John Cale, one of Jackson Browne's colleagues on Nico's *Chelsea Girl* LP in 1967, *Jennifer* includes a stunning reprise of that album's "These Days."

MAY 1972—JACKSON FIVE

LP: *Lookin' Through the Windows*
Original U.S. release: Motown 750
Original UK release: Tamla Motown STML 11214
U.S. chart peak: #7 (33 weeks)
UK chart peak: #16 (8 weeks from Nov. 1972)
Notes: Includes UK Top 10 hit version of Jackson Browne's "Doctor My Eyes."

AUGUST 1972—JACKSON BROWNE

45: "Rock Me on the Water" b/w "Something Fine"
Original U.S. release: Asylum 11006
Original UK release: Asylum AYM 506
U.S. chart peak: #48 (9 weeks)

SEPTEMBER 1972—CAT STEVENS

LP: *Catch Bull at Four*

Original U.S. release: A&M 4365

Original UK release: Island ILPS 9206

U.S. chart peak: #2 (27 weeks)

UK chart peak: #1 (48 weeks)

Tracks: "Sitting" / "The Boy with the Moon and Star on His Head" / "Angel Sea" / "Silent Sunlight" / "Can't Keep It In" / "18th Avenue" / "Freezing Steel" / "O Caritas" / "Sweet Scarlet" / "Ruins"

SEPTEMBER 1972—ALUN DAVIES

LP: *Daydo*

Original UK release: CBS 65108

Tracks: "Market Place" / "Old Bourbon" / "Portobello Road" / "Poor Street" / "Abram Brown Continued" / "Waste of Time" / "I'm Gonna Love You Too" / "Vale of Tears" / "I'm Late" / "Young Warrior"

Notes: A solid if occasionally workmanlike solo album from Cat Stevens's longtime collaborator, largely recorded with Stevens's regular band and with Cat and Paul Samwell-Smith in the producers' chairs. The *Melody Maker* review points out that "there are plenty of good, interesting songs, and from working with Cat he has a full understanding and appreciation for writing good, strong melodies, so when in places his lyrics tend to fall down a little, there is still a tune to keep interest going." Which about sums it up.

SEPTEMBER 1972—JACKSON BROWNE

LP: *The Return of the Common Man*

Original bootleg release: The Amazing Kornyfone Record Label TAKRL 1993

Tracks: "Take It Easy" / "A Song for Adam" / "My Opening Farewell" / "For Everyman" / "Redneck Friend"

Notes: Jackson Browne's first bootleg was released in 1976. Side one dates from September 1975; side two (above) was recorded in New York City precisely three years earlier.

SEPTEMBER 1972—BONNIE KOLOC

LP: *Hold onto Me*

Original U.S. release: Ovation OVOD 14-26 208

Notes: Includes a version of Jackson Browne's "Jamaica Say You Will."

OCTOBER 1972—EAGLES

LP: *Eagles*

Original U.S. release: Asylum 5054

Original UK release: Asylum AYM 508

U.S. chart peak: #22 (49 weeks)

Notes: Includes versions of Jackson Browne's "Nightingale" and "Take It Easy," the latter a U.S. hit single (#12) that same summer.

OCTOBER 1972—BONNIE RAITT

LP: *Give It Up*

Original U.S. release: Warner Brothers BS 2643

U.S. chart peak: #138 (15 weeks)

Notes: Having played a number of shows with Jackson Browne opening for her, Burbank, California–born Raitt included Browne's "Give It Up or Let Me Go"—a song that would also be featured on the B side of her latest 45, "Stayed Too Long at the Fair"—on her second album.

OCTOBER 1972—CAT STEVENS

LP: *Catnip*

Original bootleg release: CBM (no catalog number)

Tracks: "Moon Shadow" / "On the Road" / "Where Do the Children Play" / "Longer Boats" / "Maybe You're Right" / "Miles from Nowhere" / "Strange Sound" / "Hard Headed Woman" / "I Know I Have to Go" / "Sad Lisa" / "Let's All Start Living" / "Into White"

Notes: A number of dates on Cat's 1972 U.S. fall tour were recorded and subsequently distributed as bootlegs, including Columbus, Ohio (October 21), Tampa (October 25), Cleveland (October 30) and Toronto (November 12).

NOVEMBER 1972—CAT STEVENS

45: "Sitting" b/w "Crab Dance"
Original U.S. release: A&M 1396
U.S. chart peak: #16 (11 weeks)

NOVEMBER 1972—CAT STEVENS

45: "Can't Keep It In" b/w "Crab Dance"
Original UK release: Island WIP 6152
UK chart peak: #13 (12 weeks)

NOVEMBER 1972—JAMES TAYLOR

LP: *November 1972 Volumes 1 and 2*
Original bootleg release: Sweet Records 4033/Country Records 4022
Tracks: "Sweet Baby James" / "Making Whoopee" / "Long Ago and Far Away" / "Lo and Behold" / "Anywhere like Heaven" / "Brighten Your Night with My Day" / "Something in the Way She Moves" / "Highway Song" / "Sunny Skies" / "Carolina in My Mind" / "To Cry" / instrumental / "Hymn" / "Fanfare" / "Nobody but You" / "You've Got a Friend" / "Chili Dog" / "New Tune" / "Back on the Street Again" / "Don't Let Me Be Lonely Tonight" / "Country Song" / "One Man Parade" / "Steamroller" / "Fire and Rain" / "You Can Close Your Eyes"
Notes: Recorded live at Radio City Music Hall, New York, November 4, 1972.

NOVEMBER 1972—DIANNE DAVIDSON

LP: *Mountain Mama*
Original U.S. release: Janus JLS 3048
Notes: The third album by singer-songwriter and multi-instrumentalist Davidson includes versions of Jackson Browne's "Something Fine" and "Song for Adam."

NOVEMBER 1972—CARLY SIMON

45: "You're So Vain" b/w "His Friends Are More Than Fond of Robin"
Original U.S. release: Elektra 45824

Original UK release: Elektra K42127

U.S. chart peak: #1 (17 weeks)

UK chart peak: #3 (15 weeks)

Notes: The erstwhile Mrs. James Taylor later revealed that "You're So Vain" was written about David Geffen, but only after almost forty years of rumor had allied its subject matter with actor Warren Beatty, singer Mick Jagger, husband J.T., and even former lover Cat Stevens. Stevens was swift to deny the rumor. The single was still on the chart when he remarked, "If 'You're So Vain' is dedicated to me, it's only as much as Carly Simon is a Cancer and so am I. She might in fact be writing about herself. In that song, I think she mentions 'Mirror.'"

Released alongside the single, the attendant album *No Secrets* (Elektra 75049) would also top the charts in 1973. Taylor sings backup on one song, "Waited So Long," while Simon also covers his Flying Machine–era "Night Owl."

NOVEMBER 1972—JAMES TAYLOR

LP: *One Man Dog*

Original U.S. release: Warner Brothers BS 2660

Original UK release: Warner Brothers K46185

U.S. chart peak: #4 (25 weeks)

UK chart peak: #27 (5 weeks)

Tracks: "One Man Parade" / "Nobody but You" / "Chili Dog" / "Fool for You" / "Instrumental I" / "New Tune" / "Back on the Street Again" / "Don't Let Me Be Lonely Tonight" / "Woh, Don't You Know" / "One Morning in May" / "Instrumental II" / "Someone / Hymn" / "Fanfare" / "Little David" / "Mescalito" / "Dance" / "Jig"

NOVEMBER 1972—THE SECTION

LP: *The Section*

Original U.S. release: Warner Brothers BS 2661

Tracks: "Second Degree" / "Same Old Same Old" / "Sporadic Vacuums of Thought" / "Sitting on the Dock of the Bay" / "Holy Frijoles" / "Doing the Meatball" / "Swan Song" / "The Thing What Is" / "Mah-Hoo-Dah-Vay" / "Zippo Dippo"

Notes: Released simultaneously with the latest James Taylor album, *The Section* finds his regular band of Danny Kortchmar, Leland Sklar, Craig Doerge, and Russ Kunkel stepping out on their own with a fine slice of rootsy R&B. Jo Mama revisited!

NOVEMBER 1972—JAMES TAYLOR

45: "Don't Let Me Be Lonely Tonight" b/w "Who, Don't You Know"
Original U.S. release: Warner Brothers 7655
Original UK release: Warner Brothers K46185
U.S. chart peak: #14 (11 weeks)

Notes: One further hit single would spiral from *One Man Dog*, as "One Man Parade" b/w "Nobody but You" limped to #67 in spring 1973. It would be Taylor's final solo hit for two years (a duet with Carly Simon, "Mockingbird," reached #5 in 1974).

ACKNOWLEDGMENTS

My thanks as always, and as usual, to all the friends and family who sat and tapped polite feet while the music seeped into their lives: Amy Hanson; Jo-Ann Greene; Karen and Todd; Linda and Larry; Deb and Roger; Mike Sharman; Dave Makin; Gaye and Tim; Oliver, Toby, Trevor and the Button; Jen; and the Bat clan.

Also, to my editor Mike Edison, and everyone else at Backbeat Books.

And to everybody who sat down, off and on the record, to discuss the lives and times that were absorbed into this story, including Jerry Brandt, Denny Cordell, Mo Foster, Roger Glover, Andrew Gold, Mike Hurst, Allen Klein, Danny Kortchmar, Richard Meltzer, Nico, Andrew Loog Oldham, Noel Redding, Paul Rothchild, Tom Rush, Greg Shaw, Shel Talmy, Chip Taylor, Cherry Vanilla, Mickey Waller, Kevin Welk, Doug Weston, Bill Wyman.

NOTES

Interview material used throughout this book is taken from the author's own original interviews and conversations, unless noted in the text or below.

PROLOGUE: BUT SATISFACTION BROUGHT HIM BACK

ix "I realized it was all going . . ." Colin Irwin, "Time to Make a Change," *Mojo*, June 2000.

xi "My next LP . . ." Robert Windeler, *Stereo Review*, October 1972.

xi "I don't want to go on . . ." Steve Gaines, "Cat Puts an End to the Cat Stevens Sound," *Circus*, September 1973.

xi "I wasn't really enjoying . . ." Gaines, "Cat Puts an End to the Cat Stevens Sound."

xi "I want the next album to really . . ." From an untitled, uncredited article in *Star*, month n.a., 1973. (From the author's collection.)

xiii "In no way could I have made . . ." Roy Carr, "Cat Under a Hot Tin Roof," *New Musical Express*, March 1973.

xiii "Those first three albums I did for Island . . ." Carr, "Cat Under a Hot Tin Roof.

xiii "Some people think it's . . ." Irwin, "Time to Make a Change."

xiii "I had hoped the States . . ." Gaines, "Cat Puts an End to the Cat Stevens Sound."

xiii "You see, I think just lately . . ." James Johnson, "Cat Stevens and a Revolution in Athens," *Melody Maker*, June 23, 1973.

xiii "I wanted an immediate feel . . ." Paul Gambaccini, "A Happier Cat Stevens Explains *Foreigner*," *Rolling Stone*, September 13, 1973.

xiv "Completely subconsciously . . ." Genevieve Hall, "I Can't Explain," *Record Mirror*, April 6, 1974.

xiv "This is the age of personal revolution . . ." Johnson, "Cat Stevens and a Revolution in Athens."

xiv "I'm glad it happened in that . . ." Gambaccini, "A Happier Cat Stevens Explains *Foreigner*."

xiv "Having a constant sound . . ." Charlesworth, Chris, "Cat on the Prowl," *Melody Maker*, March 23, 1974.

1. WHERE THE CHILDREN PLAY

4   "Most folk songs today are written in Tin Pan Alley . . ." From an undated recording of Bob Dylan in concert, venue and city n.a. (From the author's collection.)

8   "The first music that I heard that I really went crazy for was Bob Dylan's . . ." Anthony DeCurtis, "Jackson Browne," *Rolling Stone*, October 15, 1992.

9   "I would get the [new] Bob Dylan album . . ." DeCurtis, "Jackson Browne."

9   "to speak to people as Richard Farina had spoken to me . . ." Colin Irwin, "These Days," *Melody Maker*, December 1976.

2. SWEET BABY JAMES

17   "I . . . heard Tom Rush . . . and instantly became a big fan . . ." David Rensin, "Tom Rush's Circle," *Rolling Stone*, January 2, 1975.

23   "This was not to be an album of 'copies . . .'" Al Kooper, liner notes to Tom Rush, *Take a Little Walk with Me* (Elektra, 1965).

3. BEFORE THE DELUGE

27   "We didn't have that jive nothingness . . ." "James Taylor: One Man's Family of Rock," *Time*, March 1, 1971.

36   "All these heavy songs . . ." From an undated recording of James Taylor in concert, venue and city n.a. (From the author's collection.)

36   "I [just] wanted a sandwich . . ." James Taylor, *Troubadours: The Rise of the Singer-Songwriter* DVD (Hear Music, 2010).

4. FIRE AND RAIN

42   "nose-dive[d] into dark depressions . . ." Untitled article, *Star*, month n.a., 1973.

47   "bearded [men] in jeans [who] would bash out three chords on an acoustic guitar . . ." Karl Dallas, Dave Laing, Robin Denselow, and Robert Shelton, *The Electric Muse: The Story of Folk into Rock* (Methuen Paperbacks, 1975).

50   "Sandy Denny . . . nursing Cat Stevens . . ." Neville Judd, *Al Stewart: The True Life Adventures of a Folk Rock Troubadour* (Helter Skelter Publishing, 2005).

5. WILD WORLD

59   "There were two hundred black and Chicano kids . . ." Joe Smith, *Off the Record: An Oral History of Popular Music*, ed. Mitchell Fink (Warner Books, 1988).

60   "'Zeeks!' gasped one teenybopper. 'You can't even . . .'" "The New Troubadours," *Time*, October 28, 1966.

61   "Most people [never stop] living the first twelve, or maybe fifteen . . ." Mitchell Cohen, "Jackson Browne: Winning," *Phonograph Record*, November 1976.

66   "I had a gigantic crush on Nico . . ." Cameron Crowe, "A Child's Garden of Jackson Browne," *Rolling Stone*, May 23, 1974.

68   "I got a call, would I like to be her guitar player . . ." Crowe, "A Child's Garden of Jackson Browne."

68   "This famous publicist . . . and New York scene maker. . ." Richard Meltzer, "Young Jackson Browne's Old Days," *Rolling Stone*, June 22, 1972.

68   "I mean, I really didn't know what was going on . . ." Crowe, "A Child's Garden of Jackson Browne."

69   "tried to explain that this male person . . ." Meltzer, "Young Jackson Browne's Old Days."

69   "I went to see Nico with Leonard . . ." Ritchie Unterburg, liner notes to Steve Noonan, *Steve Noonan* CD reissue (Collectors Choice, 2006).

69   "This guy was a kid . . ." Barbara Charone, "The Road and the Sky," *Sounds*, December 11, 1976.

70   "I was stunned . . ." Richard Witts, *Nico: The Life and Lies of an Icon* (Virgin Books, 1993).

6. PLACES IN MY PAST

82   "My memory is pretty spotty about this stuff . . ." Timothy White, "James Taylor: A Portrait of an Artist," *Billboard*, December 5, 1998.

71   "When I first met Cat in July 1966 it took me . . ." Mike Hurst, liner notes to Cat Stevens, *Matthew and Son* (Deram, 1967).

71   "I was impressed by people who had been in the business . . ." Penny Valentine, "Talk In," *Sounds*, May 22, 1971.

72   "Cat likes to write songs . . ." Rodrigo Fresan, *Kensington Gardens* (Farrar Strauss and Giroux, 2005).

72   "Frightened of drying up as far as music is concerned . . ." Mike Ledgerwood, "Cat Stevens Talks . . ." *Disc and Music Echo*, October 29, 1966.

75   "The old boy who operated it . . ." Mo Foster, *Play Like Elvis! How British Musicians Bought the American Dream* (MPG Books, 2000).

73   "It's funny because, although I was lonely . . ." Penny Valentine, "Cat Stevens," *Disc and Music Echo*, January 21, 1967.

74   "I rather like that Cat Stevens thing . . ." Georgie Fame, "Interview with Georgie Fame," *Disc and Music Echo*, October 29, 1966.

76 "I've written about forty songs in all . . ." Philip Palmer, "Cat Stevens," *Record Mirror*, January 14, 1967.

76 "He walked along Carnaby Street . . ." Dawn James, "Cat Stevens," *Rave*, March 2, 1967.

77 "I like clothes very much . . ." "Cat's Story," *Mirabelle*, March 11, 1967.

78 "I felt terribly hurt after *Juke Box Jury* . . ." Jeremy Pascal, "*Juke Box* Bitchy Comment Hurt," *New Musical Express*, April 22, 1967.

78 "I really want to write a musical . . ." Derek Boltwood, "Mexico Mad Cat and His First Musical," *Record Mirror*, August 19, 1967.

79 "Up to a certain point, anyway . . ." Boltwood, "Mexico Mad Cat and his First Musical."

7. NOTHING BUT TIME

87 "People write sleeve notes for various reasons . . ." Hurst, liner notes to *Matthew and Son*.

88 "I used to dread recording sessions . . ." Danny Goldberg and Salli Stevenson, "Cosmic Superstar," *Circus*, July 1971.

89 "I think it's a great scene . . ." Boltwood, "Mexico Mad Cat and His First Musical."

91 "I'm at the crossroads now . . ." Norrie Drummond, "Sad Cat," *New Musical Express*, August 19, 1967.

91 "Everything happened at once for us . . ." Drummond, "Sad Cat."

92 "Because I had music and ideas which hadn't been heard yet . . ." Valentine, "Talk In."

8. ANOTHER SATURDAY NIGHT

98 "at the moment, my songs are in great demand . . ." Pascal, "*Juke Box* Bitchy Comment Hurt."

101 "It still doesn't seem to me that . . ." Rick Mitz, "A Talk with James Taylor," *Stereo Review*, January 1978.

104 "We've got this thing called Apple . . ." John Lennon speaking on *The Tonight Show*, May 14, 1968.

104 "Big companies are so big . . ." Paul McCartney speaking on *The Tonight Show*, May 14, 1968.

105 "I would arrive at a fairly normal time . . ." Russell Hall, "Peter Asher Talks 60s, Beatles and Apple Records," Gibson.com, accessed November 21, 2011, http://www.gibson.com/en-us/Lifestyle/Features/peter-asher-1119/.

106 "I was at home in my flat . . ." Peter Asher, liner notes to *James Taylor* CD reissue (Apple, 2011).

107 "We had A&R meetings once a week . . ." Smith, *Off the Record* . . .

107 "I brought [James] to the A&R meeting . . ." DeYoung, Bill, "Weighing In with Peter Asher," Billdeyoung.com, accessed November 21, 2011, http://www.billdeyoung. com/peteash.htm.

108 "Apple was open pickings for a long time there . . ." Stuart Werbin, "James Taylor and Carly Simon," *Rolling Stone*, January 4, 1973.

108 "I found James Taylor and I really believed in him . . ." Gary James, "Peter Asher of Peter and Gordon," Classicbands.com, accessed November 21, 2011, http://www. classicbands.com/PeterAsherInterview.html.

110 "drinking Romilar . . ." Timothy White, "James Taylor," *Rolling Stone*, June 11, 1981.

110 "I didn't want to be rude . . ." Chris O'Dell with Katherine Ketcham, *Miss O'Dell: Hard Days and Long Nights with the Beatles, the Stones, Bob Dylan and Eric Clapton* (Touchstone Books, 2009).

110 "I think of that early time in London . . ." White, "James Taylor."

111 "It was great. It was *unbelievable* . . ." Paul Zollo, "The Bluerailroad Interview," Bluerailroad.com, accessed November 21, 2011, http://bluerailroad.wordpress.com/ james-taylor-the-bluerailroad-interview/.

111 "I was really anxious with this record to impress people . . ." Noel Murray, "Peter Asher," *A.V. Club*, accessed November 21, 2011, http://www.avclub.com/articles/ peter-asher,48429/.

112 "I started to take a lot of codeine . . ." Werbin, "James Taylor and Carly Simon."

113 "They're not equipped to deal with junkies . . ." Werbin, "James Taylor and Carly Simon."

9. YOU LOVE THE THUNDER

119 "I've written a few good songs . . ." Tom Nolan, "Jackson Browne," *Cheetah*, January 1968.

120 "I thought he might be leaving some nice ideas behind . . ." Unterburg, liner notes to *Steve Noonan*.

121 "They were great musicians . . ." Smith, *Off the Record* . . .

122 "You'd meet all sorts of great people at Barry's house . . ." Jac Holzman and Gavan Daws, *Follow the Music* (First Media Books, 1998).

123 "He proposed a music ranch . . ." Holzman and Daws, *Follow the Music.*

124 "I don't know quite what happened . . ." Mick Houghton, *Becoming Elektra: The True Story of Jac Holzman's Visionary Record Label* (Jawbone Press, 2010).

124 "I've never been able to collaborate . . ." Smith, *Off the Record* . . .

125 "was badly played and badly realized . . ." Chris Charlesworth, "Jackson's Song for Everyman," *Melody Maker*, November 17, 1973.

10. HEY MISTER, THAT'S ME!

128 "In the hospital I was really bored . . ." Danny Goldberg and Salli Stevenson, "Cosmic Superstar," *Circus*, July 1971.

129 "Back in the hospital . . ." Bob Dawbarn, "Cat Treads Softly on His Return," *Melody Maker*, September 28, 1968.

129 "it was just what I needed . . ." Goldberg and Stevenson, "Cosmic Superstar."

130 "It's funny . . . because a review . . ." Derek Boltwood, "Cat's Back," *Record Mirror*, October 12, 1968.

131 "As far as songwriting was concerned . . ." Valentine, "Talk In."

131 "I think I've become more myself . . ." Boltwood, "Cat's Back."

132 "There were these clockwork players . . ." Fong-Torres, Ben, "Cat Out of the Bag," *Rolling Stone*, April 1,1971.

133 "This is one of my favorite songs . . ." From a 1971 recording of Cat Stevens in concert at London Coliseum. (From the author's collection.)

134 "some people think that I was taking the son's side . . ." Gambaccini, "A Happier Cat Stevens Explains *Foreigner*."

134 "I'm considered to be a bit underground . . ." Boltwood, "Cat's Back."

11. SILENT SUNLIGHT

140 "I knew, as a disc jockey . . ." Stan Cornyn with Paul Scanlon, *Exploding: The Highs, Hits, Hype, Heroes and Hustlers of the Warner Music Group* (Harper Entertainment, 2002).

142 "I think the Beatles have discovered . . ." Jerry Hopkins, "James Taylor on Apple," *Rolling Stone*, August 23, 1969.

142 "Everybody's been fired or quit . . ." Hopkins, "James Taylor on Apple."

143 "He's a wonderful kid . . ." Allen Klein, "I Cured All Their Problems," *Rolling Stone*, November 29, 1969.

143 "[is] in charge of my money now . . ." Hopkins, "James Taylor on Apple."

144 "I didn't negotiate anything . . ." DeYoung, "Weighing In with Peter Asher."

144 "Apple *made* James Taylor . . ." Craig Vetter, "Playboy Interview: Allen Klein," *Playboy*, November 1971.

144 "The rumor is . . ." DeYoung, "Weighing In with Peter Asher."

148 "botched it up. . ." Colin Irwin, "These Days," *Melody Maker*, December 1976.

148 "one of the few places . . ." Taylor, *Troubadours*.

148 "I'd go on sixth . . ." Charlesworth, "Jackson's Song for Everyman."

150 "We loved that James Taylor record . . ." Barney Hoskyns, *Hotel California: The True-Life Adventures of Crosby, Stills, Nash, Young, Mitchell, Taylor, Browne, Ronstadt, Geffen, the Eagles, and Their Many Friends* (John Wiley and Sons, 2006).

12. NIGHT OWL

154 "One of the promo men told me . . ." From a 1971 recording of James Taylor, venue and city n.a. (From the author's collection.)

158 "I never thought for a second . . ." Zollo, "The Bluerailroad Interview."

160 "when I was in New York . . ." James Taylor speaking to interviewer Kerry O'Brien on "James Taylor Reflects," a TV show airing on Australia Broadcasting Corporation TV, March 31, 2010.

161 "But my friends . . ." Taylor to O'Brien, "James Taylor Reflects."

161 "The second verse . . ." Taylor to O'Brien, "James Taylor Reflects."

161 "it has to be . . ." Hopkins, "James Taylor on Apple."

162 "What caused glam rock . . ." Kim Fowley, "Vampire from Outer Space" (unpublished memoir), n.d.

162 "I want to take all the new singers . . ." John Lennon, bootlegged session recording, 1973. (From the author's collection.)

162 "It was the atmosphere of [the] record . . ." Bob Harris, *Bob Harris: The Whispering Years* (BBC Books, 2001).

166 "It was only until we released . . ." Dan Forte, "The Instrumental Side of James Taylor," *Guitar World*, May 1984.

13. THE CAT CAME BACK (THEY THOUGHT THEY'D SEEN THE LAST OF IT)

169 "was and always will be . . ." Cameron Crowe, "Eagles," *Rolling Stone*, September 25, 1975.

171 "We all used to sit in a corner . . ." Linda Ronstadt, "Linda Ronstadt in Her Own Words," SuperSeventies.com, accessed November 21, 2011, http://www.superseventies.com/sslindaronstadt.html.

172 "that cat just sings rings around most people . . ." Ben Fong-Torres, "The *Rolling Stone* Interview," *Rolling Stone*, July 23, 1970.

172 "I did a week at the Troubadour . . ." Charlesworth, "Jackson's Song for Everyman."

174 "We'll send Dave Geffen over . . ." Fong-Torres, "The *Rolling Stone* Interview."

176 "I think that accounts for good quality . . ." Genevieve Hall, "I Can't Explain," *Record Mirror*, April 6, 1974.

176 "Those were the best . . ." Valentine, "Talk In."

178 "My only consideration . . ." Keith Altham, "The Honest Way," *Record Mirror*, June 5, 1971.

178 "My aim is to communicate . . ." Altham, "The Honest Way."

179 "[He] came into the studio, very young . . ." quoted in Dave Thompson, *Turn It On Again: Peter Gabriel, Phil Collins and Genesis* (Backbeat Books, 2005).

180 "Paul has a very clear mind . . ." Goldberg and Stevenson, "Cosmic Superstar."

183 "By that time I was getting to know . . ." "Player of the Month," *Beat Instrumental*, August 1972.

181 "What we did . . ." Penny Valentine, "Talk In."

183 "No. I was just following my heart . . ." Irwin, "Time to Make a Change."

184 "some people . . ." Irwin, "Time to Make a Change."

184 "In America, where they had never . . ." Irwin, "Time to Make a Change."

14. SHAKY TOWN

189 "Music is my living . . ." Keith Altham, "James Taylor," *Petticoat*, October 23, 1971.

190 "We really are not trying to be nasty to the press . . ." Keith, "James Taylor."

190 "a hunger for the intimacy . . ." Carole King, *Troubadours*.

190 "the authenticity of someone telling their own story . . ." Jackson Browne, *Troubadours*.

190 "Things started to get out of control . . ." Altham, "James Taylor."

196 "Carole was waiting to happen . . ." Taylor to O'Brien, "James Taylor Reflects."

193 "Joni came on 100 percent . . ." John Mackie, "Barbara Stowe on the Concert That Launched Greenpeace," *Vancouver Sun*, November 9, 2009.

194 "People were very excited . . ." James Taylor interview, Amchitka-concert.com, accessed 2010, http://www.amchitka-concert.com.

194 "Phil Ochs was so angry . . ." Mackie, "Barbara Stowe on the Concert That Launched Greenpeace."

196 "It is very strange making a living out of being yourself . . ." Jules Siegel, "Midnight in Babylon," *Rolling Stone*, February 18, 1971.

198 "I think that the early success . . ." Mitz, "A Talk with James Taylor."

198 "The press want something . . ." Peter Herbest, "The *Rolling Stone* Interview," *Rolling Stone*, September 6, 1979.

200 "I got in touch with a doctor . . ." Werbin, "James Taylor and Carly Simon."

201 "is that it's consistent . . ." Werbin, "James Taylor and Carly Simon."

202 "it was exactly how he felt . . ." Timothy White, *Long Ago and Far Away: James Taylor, His Life and Music* (Omnibus Press, 2005).

202 "That song was actually . . ." Werbin, "James Taylor and Carly Simon."

200 "If you play Madison Square Garden as a soloist . . ." Roy Carr, "Moving from Inward to Outward," *Hit Parader*, March 1972.

200 "I don't go in for all that . . ." Carr, "Moving from Inward to Outward."

203 "Several things are at stake . . ." Jerry Wexler, *Billboard*, May 29, 1971.

204 "it's terrifying . . ." Mitz, "A Talk with James Taylor."

15. ON THE ROAD TO FIND OUT

207 "It's a real uncomfortable feeling . . ." David Rensin, "Jackson Browne: Such a Clever Innocence," *Crawdaddy*, January 1974.

209 "It's cathartic . . ." Steve Turner, "Jackson Browne," unpublished article for *NME*, online at Rocksbackpages.com, accessed November 21, 2011, http://www.rocks-backpages.com/article.html?ArticleID=2093.

209 "cultivat[ing] disappointment in order to write . . ." Turner, "Jackson Browne."

210 "I haven't had worse experiences . . ." Irwin, "These Days."

211 "Denny saw that . . ." Charlesworth, "Jackson's Song for Everyman."

213 "I was better known . . ." Andy Gill, "Jackson Browne," *Mojo*, November 1997.

214 "Two different people . . ." Rensin, "Jackson Browne: Such a Clever Innocence."

16. UNDER THE FALLING SKY

217 "Honestly, I didn't expect things to happen . . ." Carr, "Moving from Inward to Outward."

217 "I was really upset about that . . ." Carr, "Moving from Inward to Outward."

217 "America was like a sleeping beauty . . ." Valentine, "Talk In."

218 "They got onto the lyrics very strongly . . ." Valentine, "Talk In."

219 "she was professional at that point . . ." Werbin, "James Taylor and Carly Simon."

221 "I think music at the moment . . ." "A Word from Cat Stevens," *Rock Magazine*, November 8, 1971.

221 "It's exactly the way I feel comfortable . . ." Penny Valentine, "Teaser and the White Hot Cat," *Sounds*, September 25, 1971.

221 "Because now you don't have to connive . . ." Valentine, "Talk In."

222 "One thing, Americans try . . ." Untitled article, *Star*, month n.a., 1973.

222 "[shot] across the sky . . ." Untitled article, *Star*, month n.a., 1973.

222 "Now I'm thinking outward . . ." Carr, "Moving from Inward to Outward."

223 "you want to put in drums . . ." Larry Leblanc, "Superstar?" *Hit Parader*, December 1971.

223 "He knew the Strawbs . . ." Valentine, "Talk In."

223 "Obviously if you want a certain sound . . ." Valentine, "Talk In."

223 "by some freak . . ." Carr, "Moving From Inward to Outward."

224 "I don't think I can . . ." Michelle Straubing, "But Does He Still Love His Dog?" *Creem*, September 1971.

224 "and started to read the words . . ." Gambaccini, "A Happier Cat Stevens Explains *Foreigner*."

225 "And I went to Sicily . . ." Philip Norman, "Top Cat," *Sunday Times*, March 5, 1972.

225 "I'd . . . like to do a film of my own . . ." Straubing, "But Does he Still Love His Dog?"

225 "I've got ideas for my own film . . ." Straubing, "But Does he Still Love His Dog?"

226 "The secret is to keep away . . ." Carr, "Moving From Inward to Outward."

17. THE BLUES IS JUST A BAD DREAM

231 "It amused me because . . ." Danny Kortchmar, *Troubadours*.

234 "I've always known I would live . . ." Lynn Van Matre, "Jackson Browne," *Chicago Tribune*, month and day n.a., 1973.

234 "That's a bad connection . . ." Crowe, "A Child's Garden of Jackson Browne."

235 "stopped me cold in my tracks . . ." Fong-Torres, Ben, "The Eagle Meets the Dove: The Reunion of Crosby, Stills, Nash and Young" *Rolling Stone*, August 29, 1974.

238 "I'm really looking forward . . . " Michelle O'Driscoll, "Tea with the Tillerman," *Disc*, July 24, 1972.

238 "I really liked the scuffling guitar . . ." O'Driscoll, "Tea With the Tillerman."

239 "I'd like to come out with something now that's freer . . ." Penny Valentine, "A Cat Breaks Free," *Sounds*, December 9, 1972.

237 "*Catch Bull* was very paranoid . . ." Penny Valentine, *Sounds*, July 14, 1973.

BIBLIOGRAPHY

FURTHER READING

Anson, Robert Sam. *Gone Crazy and Back Again: The Rise and Fall of the Rolling Stone Generation*. New York: Doubleday, 1981.

Auslander, Philip. *Performing Glam Rock: Gender and Theatricality in Popular Music*. Ann Arbor: University of Michigan Press, 2006.

Bangs, Lester. *Psychotic Reactions and Carburetor Dung*. London: Heinemann, 1988.

Bego, Mark. *Jackson Browne: His Life and Music*. New York: Citadel Press, 2005.

Biskind, Peter. *Easy Riders, Raging Bulls: How the Sex, Drugs and Rock and Roll Generation Saved Hollywood*. New York: Simon and Schuster, 1998.

Brend, Mark. *American Troubadours: Groundbreaking Singer-Songwriters of the '60s*. San Francisco: Backbeat Books, 2001.

Brown, George: *Cat Stevens: The Complete Illustrated Biography and Discography*. UK: printed by author, 2006.

Browne, David. *Fire and Rain: The Beatles, Simon and Garfunkel, James Taylor, CSN&Y and the Lost Story of 1970*. Cambridge, MA: Da Capo, 2011.

Charlesworth, Chris. *Cat Stevens*. London: Proteus, 1985.

Cohen, Ronald D. *Rainbow Quest: The Folk Music Revival and American Society 1940–1970*. Amherst: University of Massachusetts Press, 2002.

Cohn, Nik. *Awopbopaloobop Alopbamboom*. London: Weidenfeld and Nicolson, 1969.

Collins, Judy. *Trust Your Heart: An Autobiography*. Boston: Houghton Mifflin, 1987.

Cornyn, Stan, with Paul Scanlon. *Exploding: The Highs, Hits, Hype, Heroes and Hustlers of the Warner Music Group*. New York: Rolling Stone Press/Harper Entertainment, 2002.

Crosby, David, with Carl Gottleib. *Long Time Gone: The Autobiography of David Crosby*. New York: Doubleday, 1988.

Danne, Frederic. *Hit Men: Power Brokers and Fast Money Inside the Music Business*. New York: Times Books, 1990.

DiMartino, Dave. *Singer-Songwriters: Pop Music's Performer-Composers, from A to Zevon.* New York, Billboard Books: 1994

Doggett, Peter. *Are You Ready for the Country?* London: Viking, 2000.

Downing, David. *Future Rock.* St. Albans, UK: Panther, 1976.

Emerson, Eric. *Always Magic in the Air: The Bomp and Brilliance of the Brill Building Era.* New York: Penguin, 2005

Farren, Mick. *The Black Leather Jacket.* London: Plexus, 1985.

Fawcett, Anthony and Henry Diltz. *California Rock, California Sound: The Music of Los Angeles and Southern California.* Los Angeles: Reed Books, 1978.

Foster, Mo. *Play Like Elvis! How British Musicians Bought the American Dream.* Bodmin, UK: MPG Books, 2000.

Frame, Pete. *The Complete Family Trees.* London: Omnibus Press, 1993.

Goodman, Fred. *The Mansion on the Hill: Dylan, Young, Geffen, Springsteen and the Head-on Collision of Rock and Commerce.* New York: Times Books, 1997.

Green, Jonathon. *Days in the Life: Voices from the English Underground, 1961–1971.* London: Heinemann, 1989.

Guinness World Records. *The Guinness Book of British Hit Albums.* Various editions. London: Guinness, 2002.

Guinness World Records. *The Guinness Book of British Hit Singles.* Various editions. London: Guinness, 2002.

Hajdu, David. *Positively 4th Street: The Lives and Times of Joan Baez, Bob Dylan, Mimi Baez Farina and Richard Farina.* New York: Farrar, Straus and Giroux, 2001.

Halperin, Ian. *Fire and Rain: The James Taylor Story.* New York: Citadel Press, 2003.

Holzman, Jac and Gavan Daws. *Follow the Music: The Life and High Times of Elektra Records in the Great Years of American Pop Culture.* Santa Monica, CA: FirstMedia Books, 1998.

Hoskyns, Barney. *Hotel California: The True-Life Adventures of Crosby, Stills, Nash, Young, Mitchell, Taylor, Browne, Ronstadt, Geffen, the Eagles, and Their Many Friends.* Hoboken, NJ: John Wiley and Sons, 2006.

Hoskyns, Barney. *Waiting for the Sun: A Rock 'n' Roll History of Los Angeles.* London: Viking, 1996.

Houghton, Mick. *Becoming Elektra: The True Story of Jac Holzman's Visionary Record Label.* London: Jawbone Press, 2010.

Kort, Michelle. *Soul Picnic: The Music and Passion of Laura Nyro.* New York: Thomas Dunne Books, 2002.

Laing, Dave, Robin Denselow, Karl Dallas, and Robert Shelton. *The Electric Muse: The Story of Folk Into Rock.* London: Eyre Methuen, 1975.

Lewisohn, Mark. *The Beatles Recording Sessions: The Official Abbey Road Studio Session Notes 1962–1970.* New York: Harmony Books, 1988.

Luftig, Stacey, ed. *The Joni Mitchell Companion: Four Decades of Commentary.* New York: Schirmer Books, 2000.

Matheu, Robert, and Brian J. Bowe, eds. *Creem: America's Only Rock 'n' Roll Magazine.* New York: Collins, 2007.

McDonough, Jimmy. *Shakey: Neil Young's Biography.* London: Jonathan Cape, 2002.

Melly, George. *Revolt into Style: The Pop Arts in Britain.* London: Penguin, 1970.

Murray, Charles Shaar. *Shots from the Hip.* London: Penguin, 1991.

O'Brien, Karen. *Shadows and Light: Joni Mitchell.* London: Virgin Books, 2001.

O'Dell, Chris, with Katharine Ketcham. *Miss O'Dell: Hard Days and Long Nights with the Beatles, the Stones, Bob Dylan and Eric Clapton.* New York: Touchstone Books, 2009.

Olsen, Eric, with Paul Verna and Carlo Wolff, eds. *The Encyclopedia of Record Producers.* New York: Billboard Books, 1999.

Perrone, James E. *Carole King: A Biblio-Biography.* Westport, CT: Greenwood, 1999.

Risberg, Joel. *The James Taylor Encyclopedia.* Lulu.com, 2005.

Rock, Mick. *Blood and Glitter.* London: Vision On, 2001.

Rolling Stone. *Rolling Stone Cover to Cover: The First 40 Years.* New York: Bondi Digital Publishing, 2007.

Sander, Ellen. *Trips: Rock Life in the Sixties.* New York: Charles Scribner's Sons, 1973.

Shapiro, Mark. *The Long Run: The Story of the Eagles.* London: Omnibus, 1995.

Sinclair, John. *Guitar Army: Street Writing /Prison Writings.* New York: Douglas Book Corp., 1972.

Smith, Joe, with Mitchell Fink. *Off the Record: An Oral History of Popular Music.* London: Sidgwick and Jackson, 1989.

Spizer, Bruce. *The Beatles on Apple Records: The Stories Behind the Entire Beatles Catalog on Apple Records.* New Orleans: 498 Productions, 2003.

Tobler, John, and Stuart Grundy. *The Record Producers.* London: BBC Books, 1982.

Van Ronk, Dave, with Elijah Wald. *The Mayor of MacDougal Street: A Memoir.* Cambridge, MA: Da Capo Press, 2005.

Vanilla, Cherry. *Lick Me: How I Became Cherry Vanilla.* Chicago: Chicago Review Press, 2010.

Von Schmidt, Eric, and Jim Rooney. *Baby Let Me Follow You Down: The Illustrated Story of the Cambridge Folk Years.* Amherst: University of Massachusetts Press, 1993.

Walker, Michael. *Laurel Canyon: The Inside Story of Rock and Roll's Legendary Neighborhood.* New York: Faber and Faber, 2006.

Watts, Derek. *Country Boy: A Biography of Albert Lee.* Jefferson, NC. McFarland and Co., 2008

Weller, Sheila. *Girls Like Us: Carole King, Joni Mitchell, Carly Simon and the Journey of a Generation.* New York: Washington Square Press, 2008.

Whitburn, Joel. *Top Pop Albums.* Various editions. Menomonee Falls, WI: Record Research, 2002.

Whitburn, Joel. *Top Pop Singles.* Various editions. Menomonee Falls, WI: Record Research, 1997.

White, Timothy. *James Taylor: Long Ago and Far Away.* London: Omnibus Press, 2002.

Williams, Paul, ed. *The Crawdaddy Book: Writings (and Images) from the Magazine of Rock.* Milwaukee: Hal Leonard, 2002.

Wiseman, Rich. *Jackson Browne: The Story of a Hold-Out.* New York: Doubleday, 1982.

Witts, Richard. *Nico: The Life and Lies of an Icon.* London: Virgin, 1993.

Young, James. *Nico: The End.* New York: Overlook, 1993.

Zevon, Crystal. *I'll Sleep When I'm Dead: The Dirty Life and Times of Warren Zevon.* New York: Harper Collins, 2007.

INDEX